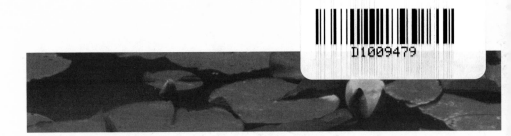

Southern
Women's
Writing

Edited by
Mary Louise Weaks and Carolyn Perry

University Press of Florida

Gainesville ✦ Tallahassee ✦ Tampa ✦ Boca Raton ✦ Pensacola ✦ Orlando ✦ Miami ✦ Jacksonville

Southern Women's Writing

Colonial to Contemporary

Copyright 1995 by the Board of Regents of the State of Florida
Printed in the United States of America on acid-free paper ∞
All rights reserved

00 99 98 97 96   6 5 4 3 2

Library of Congress Cataloging-in-Publication Data
Southern women's writing: colonial to contemporary/edited by Mary Louise Weaks and
    Carolyn Perry.
p.   cm.
Includes bibliographical references and index.
ISBN 0-8130-1410-7 (alk. paper).—ISBN 0-8130-1411-5 (pbk.: alk. paper)
1. American literature—Southern States.   2. Women—Southern States—Literary collec-
    tions.   3. Southern States—Literary collections.   4. American literature—Women
    authors.   5. Southern States—Civilization.   I. Weaks, Mary Louise.   II. Perry, Car-
    olyn.
PS551.S63   1995
810.8′09287′0975—dc20   95-33285

The University Press of Florida is the scholarly publishing agency for the State University
System of Florida, comprised of Florida A & M University, Florida Atlantic University,
Florida International University, Florida State University, University of Central Florida,
University of Florida, University of North Florida, University of South Florida, and Uni-
versity of West Florida.

University Press of Florida
15 Northwest 15th Street
Gainesville, FL 32611

For our mothers,
Elizabeth Wright Weaks
and
Mary McGregor Null

Contents

The Contemporary South (1961 to the Present)   293

In Caroline Gordon's novel *The Strange Children* (1951), the young Lucy Lewis describes *Life at Benfolly,* a portrait of the Lewis family and their home painted by a visiting friend. The painting was not an exceptionally good one (someone had to explain to Lucy that she was, indeed, in the picture), but Lucy knew that the form was a quilt, with her mother at the center. Revolving around the quilt, which had been pieced together from the fabric of her family's past, were pictures of life at Benfolly: "Daddy, in his big straw hat, mowing the lawn; Lucy and Bourke [the dachshund] running ahead of him; Electra, the cook they had had before Jenny, standing in a blue dress before the block, rolling out biscuits; a young poet swimming in the river, which, in the picture, was blue and not muddy, the way it was this time of year; her hens, Red Lily and Leaf Flower, with the red rooster Mammy had given her; some visitor going down the brick walk with his wife; and she herself and the four MacDonough children crouched beside one of the columns of the gallery" (50–51). The fictional painting portrays not only family relationships but also communities: the southern town comprising blacks and whites, tenant farmers and landowners; the literary community that brings northern visitors to the Lewis home. Neatly framed, the painting suggests an ideal of southern living in the 1930s.

But the poet swims in water painted blue; Lucy points out this illusion of tranquility when she notes that the river should be *muddy* this time of year. The community presented in the painting, likewise, is muddied by gender, racial, and class disparities. Lucy's mother, the unnamed figure sprawled across the quilt, appears exhausted by the flurry of activity, the many labors required of women by the code of southern hospitality. Furthermore, the single African-American depicted is hard at work baking. And it is the children of the poor tenant farmer who play with Lucy, much as slave children would have played with the master's children in the antebellum South. Although in her writing Gordon did not actively campaign for equality, the painting reflects tensions in Tennessee life during the 1930s that no southern writer could avoid.

Like Gordon's fictional painting, the selections included in this anthology can be appreciated as individual portraits patched together: as a whole, they present a rich body of literature produced by women writing in the South. But at the same time, collecting these works in one volume exposes conflicts long existent in the South, conflicts that have spawned divisions among women. Although they share a gender, the limitations placed upon them because of that gender, and concerns rooted in family, women have often been and are often still separated by racism, class conflict, and sexual politics.

All the writers included in *Southern Women's Writing* share the label "southern woman," but many are boundary testers for our term. Fanny Kemble, a British actress who moved to the Georgia plantation that her Philadelphia-born husband inherited, stretches the boundaries the furthest. Moreover, the youngest writer included, Leigh Allison Wilson, was born and raised in the South but typically writes about New York state in a time when the existence of a contemporary "southern literature" is being debated. After wrestling with the question of what makes works by southern women distinctive, we decided to include women who lived long enough in the South that a substantial portion of their writing focused on or otherwise refracted their experiences there. Their works, then, comprise those qualities and themes that make the South distinct from other American regions.

In ordering the selections for the anthology, we first attempted to present the works chronologically, based on the birthdate of each writer. As we separated writers into the major sections of the book, this principle worked well, for most writers fell neatly within the major periods of southern writing. However, exceptions to this rule convinced us to loosen our structure considerably. For example, "The Civil War South" contains only those writers of that generation whose selections focus on the war itself; therefore, even though Susan King Petigru Bowen and Frances E.W. Harper fit in this section chronologically, they were placed in "The Antebellum South" because their works deal with prewar concerns. Also, birthdates would place Flannery O'Connor in "The Contemporary South" and Margaret Walker in "The Modern South." But we found the opposite placement to be a more accurate reflection of their writing lives: O'Connor did all her writing at an early age, solidly within the range of the modern period, while Walker continues to write today. Finally, within the major sections, selections are often ordered not by birthdates but by chronology of the subject matter. Thus by studying the selections in "The Antebellum South" as we have ordered them, readers gain a greater sense of historical progression and a better understanding of the works as a whole.

The plantation system and southern agriculture, slavery and the Civil War and their pervasive repercussions, southern dialects and storytelling traditions, southern ladies and gentlemen bound together in patriarchal families: these elements typically identified with southern literature permeate the works of southern women in gender-specific ways. From the metaphors they used to describe the conflict of the Civil War to their personal accounts of the fight for racial and sexual equality, women offer a point of view that has not been fully explored in previous anthologies of southern literature.

The major texts for the study of southern literature—*The Literature of the South* (1952, 1968), *Southern Writing, 1585–1920* (1970), and *The Literary South* (1979)—all give a slim overview of the women's tradition in the South. The larger body of specialized anthologies of southern literature tend to be period or genre studies, such as Mary Ellis Gibson's *New Stories by Southern Women* (1989). The primary critical sources for students of southern literature by women are Anne Goodwyn Jones's *Tomorrow Is Another Day: The Woman Writer in the South, 1859–1936* (1981) and Carol Manning's *The Female Tradition in Southern Literature* (1993), both of which examine the development of the woman writer in the South. *Southern Women's Writing* serves as a companion to these critical studies and is the only text available that surveys women's literature in the South from the early settlement period to the present. The publication of our book thus comes at an exciting time for historians, literary scholars, students, and general readers of literature by southern women. On the one hand, we may be appalled by the lack of recognition that this body of literature has received, but we also focus on the pleasures of discovering new voices and of opening new literary fields for exploration.

We hope that our anthology of women's literature in the South will add to the larger endeavor of retrieving the "lost voices" of the southern past and will enlarge the context for studying southern literature. Perhaps our greatest challenge as anthologers lay not just in reshaping the southern literary canon but in making sense of the impassioned voices of women who have struggled with and against each other because of class divisions and gender or racial inequality. In bringing these works together, then, we have sought to capture the evolution of southern women's voices, and in doing so we believe we have uncovered a rich and vital collection seldom found in literary anthologies.

For help in preparing this book for publication, we would like to thank the following persons: Judith Murphy, Brande Martin, Karen Reinhold, Connie Reece, Kathleen Smith, and Dena Mattausch-Hicks for keyboarding the manuscript and researching footnotes; Tonya Maddox, Anne Zimmermann, Tonya Smith, Tim Goggin, Kristin Cope, Teena Clifford, Kristy Bowen, Chris Sumner, Jean Sokolowski, Donna Pitts, Lana Paris, Rex Rebstock, and Tracy Arnold for their help with proofreading; the Faculty Development Committee of Rockford College, for generous financial support; Susan Whealler, for encouraging Mary to teach a course in southern women's literature, and those

Rockford College students enrolled in that spring 1989 course, for their lively discussions; Westminster College, particularly members of the English Department and Liz Hauer of Reeves Library; Deborah Bayer, for her enthusiasm and her thorough reading of the manuscript; Doug Hunt, who proved himself indispensable as our anthology consultant; and finally our families, Tom, Elizabeth, and Becky Weaks, and Greg and Jessica Perry, for their encouragement, patience, and constant support.

The

Antebellum

South

(*to* 1861)

> efore the arrival of yesterday's ship [at Jamestown] there had been
> in this natural Eden (leaving the savages out of the reckoning)
> several thousand Adams, and but some threescore Eves. And
> for the most part, the Eves were either portly and bustling or withered
> and shrewish housewives, of age and experience to defy the serpent.
> These were different. Ninety slender figures decked in all the bravery
> they could assume; ninety comely faces, pink and white, or clear brown
> with the rich blood showing through; ninety pair of eyes, laughing and
> alluring, or downcast with long fringes sweeping rounded cheeks;
> ninety pair of ripe red lips.
>
> (Johnston 13)

Describing the arrival of the first European women to the South, Mary
Johnston tells of the summer of 1621 (it was actually 1619) when the
London Company sent a boatload of women as a "gift" to the men of the
Jamestown colony. In *To Have and To Hold* (1899), Johnston depicts
these "Eves" with a romanticism typical of the Victorian period. "Fair
and chaste, but meanly born," the women might not have been the
daughters of royalty, yet as one of Johnston's characters explains to Captain Ralph Percy, "those who come after us [will not] look too curiously
into the lineage of those to whom a nation owes its birth" (5). The novel
suggests the importance of the Jamestown men choosing mates so that
they can settle down to raise families, for it is family that will loosen their
ties to England and "bind [them] to this land in which [they] have cast
[their] lot" (6). After reading some Shakespeare and daydreaming of
home—and of his mother—Ralph decides that he must "put out,
posthaste, for matrimony" along with the other "free and able-bodied of
the plantations" (10).

Approaching the dock where the ship is unloading, Ralph sees men,
"panting, seize hand or arm and strive to pull toward them some reluctant fair; others snatched kisses, or fell on their knees and began
speeches out of Euphues" (13–14). Ralph, however, first sees his future
bride in church, where she introduces herself as Patience Worth. Within
minutes after the service has ended, he has saved her from the clutches
of a fellow soldier, an English lawyer "of whom [Ralph] knew no good"
(22). Ralph decides that this is the woman he must have for his wife.
Somehow, she seems different from the other women. She is, according
to Johnston, "a rose amongst blowzed poppies and peonies, a pearl
amidst glass beads, a Perdita in a ring of rustics, a nonparella of all grace
and beauty!" (18). That Ralph must first pay the shipmaster 120 pounds

contour, which suggests the idea of a slumbering smile." She was "a fair, delicate, and lovely young girl." And although she was gentle, modest and sensible, with a voice that sounded of "the sweetest music," Eoline was like the "fair-haired maid of Inis-huna, who, when the chiefs of Selma slept, went forth alone into the midnight, to warn the hero of the danger of Erin, and to urge him to deeds of renown" (22–23).

Matrons were often described as possessing a maturity that was a ripening of these same qualities. In her autobiographical novel, *Recollections of a Southern Matron,* Gilman describes Mamma as possessing "more than 'whole *acres* of charms.'" And although she was "not brilliant, she was good-tempered and sensible" and had a "demure look and reserved manner [that] concealed a close habit of observation" (24). Mamma's right and natural place was the home, especially the kitchen, where she fashioned her culinary creations: "her clabber was turned at that precise moment when a slight acidity tempers the insipidity of milk; her wafers bore the prettiest devices, or were rolled in the thinnest possible consistency; her shrimps, pickled or fresh, were most carefully prepared; her preserved watermelons were carved with the taste of a sculptor" (25). Despite Mamma's seeming ease both in the kitchen and the parlor, later in the book Gilman suggests that it is difficult for women to live up to the ideal of southern womanhood: "To repress a harsh answer, to confess a fault, and to stop (right or wrong) in the midst of self-defence, in gentle submission, sometimes requires a struggle like life and death; but these *three* efforts are the golden threads with which domestic happiness is woven; once begin the fabric with this woof, and trials shall not break or sorrow tarnish it." And because men, according to Gilman, do not understand "the moral and physical structure" of the feminine gender, a "good wife" has no choice but to "smile amid a thousand perplexities, and clear her voice to tones of cheerfulness when her frame is drooping with disease, or else languish alone" (256–57). With her eyes cast upon the ideal of the southern woman always before her, however, the matron would prevail.

Modern readers' assumptions about the domestic and social roles of southern women have been clouded by such mythologizing of the Old South, particularly as a land of belles and beaus and happy slaves. In reality, the lives of colonial and antebellum women were much more complicated than what these women novelists suggest. Furthermore, as Elizabeth Fox-Genovese explains in *Within the Plantation Household,* any study of southern women's history must take into account not only gender but race and social class as well. In the South, clear distinctions were made between a white woman whose husband owned hundreds of slaves and one whose husband owned only a dozen, between a woman

of leaf tobacco for this woman's hand in marriage seems quite nat
the story; that Patience has carried money with her to pay her ow
however, comes as quite a surprise, particularly to her husband
Ralph soon discovers that his bride has come to the New World
an assumed name: Patience, the heroine of Johnston's novel, is
Jocelyn Leigh, a woman of considerable means.

Johnston's book suggests the power of our national and sou
myths in the Victorian South. These young white women who lan
Jamestown were to be "mothers" of the new colony of Virginia, "c
cratic mothers" of the new nation's leading men. Yet they were
young Eves who were born into the masses—not into wealth. D
their modest beginnings, Johnston praises these women for qu;
typically associated with the woman of means: the grace with whicl
wear their clothing, their "eyes, laughing and alluring," and their
complexions and lips. The ambivalence of Johnston's position is em
sized, as well, when she honors these soon-to-be "democratic motl
but creates a heroine who possesses a wealth that raises her in st
and in beauty; Johnston does indeed look "curiously into the lineag
her heroine. Yet, though Jocelyn possesses an inner strength that n
come with money, she is also both vulnerable and in need of a n
care. Thus Johnston, writing from her postbellum perspective,
shaped her heroine with qualities of the southern belle: beauty
stature, virtue and dependence, and breeding notably linked to a ce
economic standing. Johnston's *To Have and To Hold* suggests that
myth of the southern lady finds its roots in the earliest years of se
ment, and before that in the patriarchal system of England, which
transported over the seas by these immigrants to the New World.

Women writers of the antebellum period shared Johnston's vie
the southern woman, whose portrayal changed very little through
years. Both Caroline Whiting Hentz's *Eoline* (1852) and Caroline H
ard Gilman's *Recollections of a Southern Matron* (1838) are part
popular genre of the pre–Civil War years, the domestic novel,
depicts women in relation to their traditional locale, the home.
Eoline, Hentz describes her heroine as a typical southern beauty:
skin has "the fairness of the magnolia blended with the blush of
rose," and her hair "reminded one of the ripples of a sunlit lake by
soft waves, giving beautiful alternations of light and shade, as it flov
back from her face into the silver comb that confined its luxurianc
With eyes "blue, soft and intense as the noonday sky in June," Eoline
"a kind of beseeching loving expression,—an expression that appea
for sympathy, protection, love,—and her mouth had that winn

whose husband owned some slaves and one whose husband owned none. Even sharper lines were draw between the races. White women did not suffer under the same restrictions and the same chauvinism of the southern patriarchy as black women, who were brought to America bound by slavery and considered chattel and breeders. Although some white women like Sarah and Angelina Grimké stepped forward to speak against slavery, most white women did not. They instead kept their expressions of fear, pity, hatred—perhaps even indifference—locked in diaries. Attempting to understand these responses, scholars have concluded that many white women did not react to the injustices of slavery because they enjoyed their status in society and that others merely reacted out of habit, seeing little reason for challenging the status quo.

White women of the antebellum United States felt pressured by family members and their social circles to conform to what was often referred to as the Cult of True Womanhood. Such women also put much pressure on themselves to follow the Cult, which stressed domestic skill, submissiveness, piety, and moral rectitude. Without these qualities, a woman was considered unfeminine and deemed unacceptable in both upper- and middle-class society. Popular magazines and books upheld this ideal. Thomas R. Dew explains in his 1835 essay "The Characteristic Differences between the Sexes, and on the Position and Influence of Woman in Society" that "[g]race, modesty and loveliness" are "the charms which constitute [a woman's] power" (qtd. in Carby 26). In a similar statement on feminine powers, George Fitzhugh wrote,

> So long as [a woman] is nervous, fickle, capricious, delicate, diffident and dependent, man will worship and adore her. Her weakness is her strength, and her true art is to cultivate and improve that weakness. Woman naturally shrinks from public gaze, and from the struggle and competition of life. . . . In truth, woman, like children, has but one right and that is the right to protection. The right to protection involves the obligation to obey. A husband, a lord and master, whom she should love, honor and obey, nature designed for every woman. . . . If she be obedient, she is in little danger of maltreatment. (214–15)

The ideal wife was a lady of charm and delicacy, an ornament not to be blemished with work like slaves in the fields or women on the frontier. Her primary roles were mother and wife, and her realm was the home.

A wife free from labors, a woman settled firmly on a pedestal (and the higher the better) was a sign of her husband's wealth. And it was slavery that allowed white women this freedom. In his 1852 essay "Professor Dew on Slavery," Thomas Dew argues that the white woman "has been in a most peculiar and eminent degree indebted to slavery, for that very elevation in society which first raised her to an equality with man" (341). Because of slavery, "we find her at once elevated, clothed with all her charms, mingling with and directing the society to which she belongs, no longer the slave" (339). Though this position brought her a certain degree of power, at least over her servants, it also isolated her from the world outside the plantation. Understandably, the cultivation of the myth of the southern lady allowed the patriarchy to keep the status quo and retain its power over white women and slaves: the strongest proponents of slavery were the strongest advocates of keeping white women "in their place." So as a delicate figurine encased in a sphere of glass represents both beauty and artifice, the very notion of the ideal southern woman suggests perfection but also entrapment, and even illusion.

Recent scholarship on southern women has increasingly questioned the white woman's role on the plantation. Pointing out the ambivalent nature of this role, Catherine Clinton tells of a gentleman who visited an antebellum plantation and was charmed by his hostess: she was a woman of grace, good looks, and gentility, seeming to live the life that he expected of a plantation mistress. One day, however, as he walked the grounds, he came across his hostess with her arms deep inside a salting barrel, her hoop removed, and her appearance dishevelled. The guest was in a bind. Should he speak to his hostess? Or should he walk on and avoid embarrassing her for being caught "behind the scenes"? He decided not to speak to her, preferring to leave the illusion of the southern lady unshattered (16–17). Similarly, privileged girls were often raised to believe that their lives would be leisurely ones, so they were frequently ill-equipped to manage large households and to care for both their children and their slaves. Anne Firor Scott quotes one Virginian who said her mother "often told us of her distress on realising for the first time the responsibilities devolving upon the mistress of a large plantation, and the nights of sorrow and tears these thoughts had given her" (1970, 27). Some white women even saw themselves as "slaves of slaves," subjected to a feminine ideal they had no means of sustaining.

This model of the southern lady makes even less sense, however, in light of the many women whose families owned few, if any, slaves, and who far outnumbered those women living on plantations. Although the ideal excluded frontier women, black women, and the majority of white women, it became an integral part of the antebellum southern culture. That ideal provided ideological support for both gender and racial inequities and thus helped to stabilize the antebellum social structure.

Historians frequently suggest that the model of the southern lady is a variation on the northeastern image of the "democratic mother," whose patriotic duty was to give birth to future leaders of the country, to populate the frontier, and to present her husband with heirs. As Catherine Clinton explains in *The Plantation Mistress,* southern women were bound by a similar sense of duty and could expect rebuke if they deviated from it. As an example of the exception, not the rule, Clinton cites a childless woman's response to her sister's prodding: "You say you think it is time I was doing something for my country, but I think it is time enough to enter such business as I am not so very fond of domestic affairs and brawling affairs of children" (8). Men were also eager that women's roles be limited to the private realm, and their development of a market economy allowed for sharper distinctions between the private realm of the home and the public realm of the marketplace (7–8).

Although the myth of southern womanhood was a common element of antebellum novels by white women, journals and letters that survive from the period perhaps give us the clearest understanding of the reality of women's lives. Yet these writings were most often published because of the unusual circumstances of the author's life, circumstances that moved her beyond the traditional realm of her gender. In general, antebellum women were not allowed to hold property, and if a woman was unmarried or was widowed, she was cared for by family members. Thus the independence of a woman like Eliza Lucas Pinckney was unusual. Pinckney was given full control of her father's six-hundred-acre plantation, Wappoo, when she was only fifteen years old, and she managed it for the next five years. When she was seventeen, Pinckney began the experiments with indigo for which she is still known. During those years, her father was serving as the colonial governor of Antigua because of the rebellion there, and her younger brothers were studying in England, living with their father's business agent in London. When George Lucas moved his ailing wife and two daughters to Wappoo, he had little choice but to leave the plantation to the care of one of his female heirs. Like many fathers and husbands who sent home instructions and suggestions during the Civil War years, George Lucas often corresponded with Eliza concerning business matters. Perhaps in an attempt to enjoy further her role as planter, Eliza asked her father not to think of her marrying until she was older; George Lucas seems to have respected her wishes. Today we have a personal record of her life at Wappoo because, as was typical for male planters and businessmen, Eliza Lucas Pinckney copied her correspondence into a letterbook. Her letters tell of daily happenings on the plantation, her reading, and her social engagements with friends from Charleston.

War and exploration, elements characteristic of male-written texts, prompted the composition of many works by Eliza Wilkinson and Anne Newport Royall. The Revolutionary War was the stimulus for Wilkinson's eyewitness accounts of the British invasion of South

Carolina when women, children, and slaves were often left alone on plantations. From her perspective on the homefront, she describes how war affects those removed from the battlefield. In the 1820s, when Anne Newport Royall was widowed and lost most of her inheritance from her husband, she began her travels in and writings about the South. Royall initially began traveling to collect material for her *Letters from Alabama* (1830). Nearly fifty years old, she left Cabell County Courthouse, Virginia (now West Virginia), in 1817; from there she rode to Mount Sterling, Kentucky, then to Bowling Green, Kentucky, to Nashville, and then on into Alabama. Her travels were unusual for the time because women rarely traveled, spending their entire lives in plantation or small farming communities. Also, travelers typically journeyed along waterways; Royall took the more rigorous inland route. Perhaps her courage and drive came from her early life's experiences: she was said to have been kidnapped by Indians as a young girl and raised among them.

The anthologized selections by these three women share a literary form, the letter, that played an important role in the South's early years. Letterbooks were used primarily by men to keep second copies of business and social correspondence; those that survive are now important historical documents that tell us about the business and social worlds of the period. The tasks of everyday living, even for those on plantations, were often so taxing that little time was left for fiction and poetry writing by either gender. But these three women made letter writing a part of their everyday lives, and in doing so they not only recorded historical events but also revealed the tensions and disparities between women's private and public lives.

Yet in colonial Virginia only one of three white women could sign her name, and the number of those who could read was far below the number of literate men. Even though literacy became more and more common among women in the nineteenth century, the education that most young girls received perpetuated the myths of the southern lady and of southern gentility. Privileged white girls who attended the boarding schools popular in the nineteenth century often studied lessons that emphasized modesty and piety. In wealthier houses, if a young white girl did not attend a boarding school, she was most likely taught at home, but only those skills such as needlepoint, the classics, and a foreign language—usually French—that made her a lady. Although novels became increasingly popular in the antebellum period, they were not deemed to be appropriate reading material for young ladies.

In spite of this model of what the southern lady was to be, fiction writing became one of the few occupations open to southern women in the nineteenth century. The very genre they were prohibited from reading, then, was the genre they began writing, oftentimes out of financial necessity. Writing, while bringing women in some contact with the world outside of the home, was still an occupation that women pursued within its confines. By 1855 novel writing had become so popular among women in the United States that Nathaniel Hawthorne, concerned that his own work was not selling well, complained to his publisher that "America is now wholly given over to a damned mob of scribbling women."

In keeping with their education, many of these "scribbling women" suggested that the virtues of domestic life were the stronghold of southern society. In her domestic novels, Caroline Howard Gilman asserts her belief that, through the shared tradition of domesticity in the North and South, the two regions might be bound together and in doing so might prevent war. Caroline Whiting Hentz presents a similar binding of North and South in matrimonial bliss in *The Planter's Northern Bride* (1854). The symbolic marriage in the novel is unique as the northern girl becomes the "southern belle" by a marriage that binds the couple in the southern tradition. This tradition, however, cannot be divorced from slavery. Many southern women novelists were dedicated to maintaining the tradition of the Old South, and, in doing so, they created images of slave women to fit that tradition. Novelists such as Hentz and Gilman frequently represented black women as domestically inclined mammies or as gentle, obedient chambermaids. On the other hand, if black women were not placed in the cloistered domestic realm, they were typically viewed as sexual creatures who lured white men from their wives and families. Often white men and white women alike placed the blame for the abuse and rape of black women onto the victims themselves. The white woman who was loyal to the image of the southern lady could not allow herself to believe the atrocities taking place in her own slave quarters. Viewing black women as seducers, then, allowed her to take on the pious role of showing the white man the way to godliness and salvation.

The laws of slavery and the living conditions forced upon slaves allowed the black woman little choice as to how her life might be led. Slave women were prohibited by law from marrying, as well as from learning to read and write. Those aspects of African culture that did survive the deculturalization of slavery—religious customs, celebrations, and folklore—probably did so because of the strength of an oral tradition within the black community. Slave women led lives controlled by white planters, both male and female. Their lives were most often filled with hard labor, violence, and sexual exploitation by white men. One male visitor to a plantation confirmed the sexual oppression of black women by white male planters: "The enjoyment of a negro or mulatto woman is spoken of as quite a common thing: no reluctance, delicacy or shame is made about the matter. It is far from being uncommon to see a gentleman at dinner, and his reputed offspring a slave to the master of the table. . . . The fathers neither of them blushed or seemed disconcerted. They were called men of worth, politeness and humanity" (qtd. in Carby 30).

Because the largest number of slaves by far worked in the fields rather than in the "Big House," masters made little distinction between gender roles for their slaves. A slave woman might have woken early in the morning to help her mistress with household chores before she was sent to the fields to plow, hoe tobacco, pick cotton, or thresh wheat. As Jacqueline Jones explains in *Labor of Love, Labor of Sorrow,* for work in the fields the slave woman was generally dressed in a coarse osnaburg gown, with her skirts "reefed up with a cord drawn tightly around the body, a little above the hips" (qtd. on 15). In addition, West African women brought with them a knowledge of weaving, spinning, and planting, skills that slavemasters were quick to take advantage of (39). Yet if a woman disobeyed her master, her mistress, or the overseer of the plantation, she was often whipped as harshly as slave men were. Jones tells, for example, of pregnant and nursing mothers who were whipped "so that blood and milk flew mingled from their breasts" (qtd. on 20). Slaves were not only forced into hard labor but were also robbed of their childhoods, as mistresses found more willing and congenial house servants among the slave children. Because slavery frequently separated women from their lovers, husbands, and children, slaves saw the family as a way to fight against racial oppression. In defining their own family structures—and, in effect, by regaining the roles of wife and mother— slaves attained some degree of control over their own lives.

Southern white society regarded the black woman as incapable of filling the role of true womanhood because she lacked the white woman's outward sign of purity: her white flesh. Hazel Carby points out that even in a northern novel such as *Uncle Tom's Cabin* (1852), Harriet Beecher Stowe was reluctant to endow any of her black female characters with the traits of the southern white woman; in fact, she attributed them more consistently to her male protagonist, Uncle Tom (34). In domestic novels, such as Hentz's *Eoline,* black women "repeatedly failed the test of true womanhood" because the sexual abuses they suffered under slavery did not allow them induction into the Cult. Black women, in effect, were only included in these texts to emphasize the womanly qualities of their white mistresses (33).

In light of the many stereotypes surrounding the slave woman, the importance of slave narratives cannot be overemphasized. Many were written and published in the North in the years preceding and during the war to gain support for the northern cause. In order to write and publish their narratives, southern slave women would have had to flee northward to freedom. Of the more than six thousand slave narratives written or orally transmitted by blacks, no more than thirty were written by black women and published as books during their lifetimes (Gwin, "Green-Eyed Monster" 41). In her narrative, the African-American woman typically recounted her life story from birth in slavery to freedom in the North. She attempted to establish a voice and a sense of selfhood, generally through straightforward prose that was often either melodramatic or moralistic, and thus typical of women's writing of the period. Audiences for slave narratives were most often white and female, and the money raised from their sale may have gone to the abolitionist cause and the support of the writer and her family. Because of the assistance African-Americans received from abolitionists, however, the authenticity of slave narratives is frequently questioned today. Scholars suspect that if white abolitionists helped in the writing, they may have felt justified in editing or embellishing the accounts because they believed such actions would aid the abolitionist cause. Regardless, these narratives offer a distinct point of view vital to our understanding of southern history.

Melvin Dixon explains in *Ride Out of the Wilderness* that the roots of African-American literary tradition are in slave songs, songs that tell of a "search for freedom," and slave narratives, or "arguments against slavery" (11). Dixon suggests that the "initial recognition of wretchedness voiced in [slave] songs" provides a structural device for the slave's own personal story in the slave narrative. He points to the following song as an example of the common themes of the slave song:

O wretched man that I am
O wretched man that I am
O wretched man that I am
Who will deliver poor me?

I am bowed down with a burden of woe
I am bowed down with a burden of woe
I am bowed down with a burden of woe
Who will deliver poor me?

Dixon says that this song suggests the same structure as Harriet Jacobs's story of her birth into and life in slavery, described in the first chapter of

Incidents in the Life of a Slave Girl (1861): "I was born a slave; but I never knew it till six years of happy childhood had passed away. . . . When I was six years old, my mother died; and then, for the first time, I learned, by the talk around me, that I was a slave" (5, 6). The same themes are at the forefront of both the song and the narrative: the wretched living conditions of the slave, the slave's call for freedom, and the question of who will act as deliverer.

Jacobs's *Incidents* and Frances E. W. Harper's poems, which read much like a slave narrative in poetic form, describe the tortured lives of black women in the antebellum South. The primary intent of both of these writers was to call white women to political action; in order to do so, both Jacobs and Harper appealed to the white woman's sense of the goodness and sanctity of womanhood and motherhood. Jacobs states in her narrative that "slavery is terrible for men; but it is far more terrible for women," "far more terrible" because black women were forced to suffer sexual abuses from white males and were reduced to serving as breeders. The subtitle of Jacobs's text, *Written by Herself,* serves as a means of authenticating the text's composition by an African-American author and of pronouncing the author's selfhood. Thus the text itself can be described as one black woman's struggle to attain and develop a "voice." Although numerous slave narratives were published in the nineteenth century, only four novels by African-Americans were published before the Civil War (B. Bell 37). The first of these novels published in the United States, *Our Nig* (1859), was by a northern woman, Harriet E. Wilson.

The achievement of voice for women of both races—whether it was a literary or a political one—was thus an integral part of woman's struggle in the prewar South. In 1838 Angelina Grimké became the first woman to speak before a legislative body of the United States as she addressed the Massachusetts legislature in support of the antislavery movement. Long before the battles of war raged, Grimké described herself as one "exiled from the land of [her] birth, by the sound of the lash, and the piteous cry of the slave" (312). To find and then use her voice she was forced to leave her home, her family, and the South.

Yet an equally powerful voice came from a woman born into slavery in New York state. At birth she was given the name Isabella, but after she fled her master she renamed herself Sojourner Truth. Believing she was an instrument of God, Truth became an important speaker against slavery and for women's rights. Described as a tall, gaunt woman, Truth spoke in a heavy Dutch accent and often used gospel songs to add passion to her talks. Speaking to a group of northern white middle-class women gathered to discuss women's rights, Truth explained the black woman's disenfranchisement in this, her most often quoted statement:

> Dat man ober dar say dat woman need to be lifted ober ditches, and to have de best place every whar. Nobody eber helped me into carriages, or ober mud puddles, or gives me any best place and ar'n't I a woman? Look at me! Look at my arm! I have plowed, and planted, and gathered into barns, and no man could head me—and ar'n't I a woman? I could work as much and eat as much as a man (when I could get it), and bear de lash as well—and ar'n't I a woman? I have borne thirteen chilern and seen em mos' all sold off into slavery, and when I cried out with a mother's grief, none but Jesus heard—and ar'n't I a woman? (qtd. in Fox-Genovese 50)

How fitting her question is for black women of the South, who were defined by others in light of cultural expectations for their gender, social class, and race: "Ar'n't I a woman?" In the years to come, battles for racial and gender equality, for black women as well as white, would offer answers to Truth's question.

(1722?–1793)

Eliza Lucas Pinckney was born in the West Indies, the eldest of four children. Her father, Lieutenant Colonel George Lucas of the British Army and later lieutenant governor of Antigua, educated his children in England until 1738 and then settled his family on a plantation on Wappoo Creek near Charleston, South Carolina. When Lucas was called back to Antigua in 1739, the responsibility of running this plantation, as well as Lucas's two others, fell to his daughter Eliza, then seventeen years old.

In addition to managing her father's property, Eliza also tutored her sisters and two slave girls she intended to be "school mistres's for the rest of the Negroe children." At the same time, she began experimenting with diversified crops, particularly indigo. Her love for agriculture is expressed in her letters and journals: she was "very early fond of the vegitable world." In fact, her work with indigo was substantial, for with the help of Nicholas Cromwell, an indigo expert sent to South Carolina by her father, she had established indigo as an important export crop for the colony by 1744. This work, in turn, established her as a legendary agricultural figure. Although she did not receive an education comparable to that of her brothers or sons, Eliza's letters suggest not only her ability to understand the management and economics of property but also her advanced ideas about marriage and slavery. Her discussion of books and her descriptions of her daily activities indicate that she, like other members of her social rank, was well-read and cultured.

Through their correspondence, Eliza's father advised her about plantation management for the next several years. But her letters during these years were also directed to Mary Bartlett, who provided Eliza with friendship and intellectual company, as did Mary's aunt and uncle Pinckney. Charles Pinckney's wife died in January of 1744, and in May of that year he and Eliza married. Her journal entries end with their marriage, but Pinckney resumed her letters in 1753 when she and her husband, then a colonial agent for South Carolina, were living in England with their three children. Five years later, when war with France broke out, the couple returned to South Carolina with their daughter, leaving their sons in England to receive an education. Several months after the

Pinckneys returned home, Charles died of malaria, leaving Eliza responsible for the support of their children and for the management of their seven separate properties. Pinckney spent the final years of her life living with her widowed daughter and her grandchildren. Her sons, Charles and Thomas Pinckney, became two of the most prominent men in South Carolina history; Thomas was elected governor in 1787, and Charles was an aide to George Washington and twice a Federalist candidate for president of the United States.

At Pinckney's death in 1793, George Washington, who once called her a model of "republican motherhood," asked to serve as a pallbearer. Although portions of her writings were published during her lifetime in *Journal and Letters of Eliza Lucas* (1850), two additional collections have been published: *Eliza Lucas Pinckney to C. C. Pinckney* (1916) and *The Letterbook of Eliza Lucas Pinckney, 1739–1762* (1972).

In the following selections, we have attempted to approximate the original organization of Pinckney's letterbook. We have silently replaced most abbreviations used in early editions of the letterbook with the entire word.

Eliza

Lucas

Pinckney

&

15

From *The Letterbook of Eliza Lucas Pinckney, 1739–1762*

[1740]
[To Colonel Lucas]
Hond. Sir

Your letter by way of Philadelphia which I duly received was an additional proof of that paternal tenderness which I have always Experienced from the most Indulgent of Parents from my Cradle to this time, and the subject of it is of the utmost importance to my peace and happiness.

As you propose Mr. L. to me I am sorry I can't have Sentiments favourable enough of him to take time to think on the Subject, as your Indulgence to me will ever add weight to the duty that obliges me to consult what best pleases you, for so much Generosity on your part claims all my Obedience, but as I know tis my happiness you consult [I] must beg the favour of you to pay my thanks to the old Gentleman for his Generosity and favourable sentiments of me and let him know my thoughts on the affair in such civil terms as you know much better than any I can dictate; and beg leave to say to you that the riches of Peru and Chili if he had them put together could not purchase a sufficient Esteem for him to make him my husband.

As to the other Gentleman you mention, Mr. Walsh, you know, Sir, I have so slight a knowledge of him I can form no judgement of him, and a Case of such consiquence requires the Nicest distinction of humours and Sentiments. But give me leave to assure you, my dear Sir, that a single life is my only Choice and if it were not as I am yet but Eighteen, hope you will [put] aside the thoughts of my marrying yet these 2 or 3 years at least.

You are so good to say you have too great an Opinion of my prudence to think I would entertain an indiscreet passion for any one, and I hope heaven will always direct me that I may never disappoint you; and what indeed could induce me to make a secret of my Inclination to my best friend, as I am well aware you would not disapprove it to make me a Sacrifice to Wealth, and I am as certain I would indulge no passion that had not your aprobation, as I truly am

> Dr. Sir, Your most dutiful and affecte. Daughter
> E. Lucas

May the 2ᵈ [1740]
To my good friend Mrs. Boddicott
Dear Madam,

I flatter myself it will be a satisfaction to you to hear I like this part of the world, as my lott has fallen here—which I really do. I prefer England to it, 'tis true, but think Carolina greatly preferable to the West Indias, and was my Papa here I should be very happy.

We have a very good acquaintance from whom we have received much friendship and Civility. Charles Town, the principal one in this province, is a polite, agreeable place. The people live very Gentile and very much in the English taste. The Country is in General fertile and abounds with Venison and wild fowl; the Venison is much higher flavoured than in England but 'tis seldom fatt.

My Papa and Mama's great indulgence to me leaves it to me to chose our place of residence either in town or Country, but I think it more prudent as well as most agreeable to my Mama and self to be in the Country during my Father's absence. We are 17 mile by land and 6 by water from Charles Town—where we have about 6 agreeable families around us with whom we live in great harmony.

I have a little library well furnishd (for my papa has left me most of his books) in which I spend part of my time. My Musick and the Garden, which I am very fond of, take up the rest of my time that is not imployed in business, of which my father has left me a pretty good share—and indeed, 'twas inavoidable as my Mama's bad state of health prevents her going through any fatigue.

I have the business of 3 plantations to transact, which requires much writing and more business and fatigue of other sorts than you can imagine. But least you should imagine it too burthensom to a girl at my early time of life, give me leave to answer you: I assure you I think myself happy that I can be useful to so good a father, and by rising very early I find I can go through much business. But least you should think I shall be quite moaped with this way of life I am to inform you there is two worthy Ladies in Charles Town, Mrs. Pinckney and Mrs. Cleland, who are partial enough to me to be always pleased to have me with them, and insist upon my making their houses my home when in town and press me to relax a little much oftener than 'tis in my honor to accept of their obliging intreaties. But I some times am with one or the other for 3 weeks or a month at a time, and then enjoy all the pleasures Charles Town affords, but nothing gives me more than subscribing my self

Dear Madam,
Yr. most affectionet and
    most obliged humble Servt.
Eliza. Lucas

Pray remember me in the best manner to my worthy friend Mr. Boddicott.

[1742]
[To Miss Bartlett]
Dr. Miss B

I was much concerned to hear by our man Togo Mrs. Pinckney was unwell, but as you did not mention it in your letter I am hopeful it was but a slight indisposition.

Why, my dear Miss B, will you so often repeat your desire to know how I triffle away my time in our retirement in my fathers absence. Could it afford you advantage or pleasure I should not have hesitated, but as you can expect neither from it I would have been excused; however, to show you my readiness in obeying your commands, here it is.

In general then I rise at five o'Clock in the morning, read till Seven, then take a walk in the garden or field, see that the Servants are at their respective business, then to breakfast. The first hour after breakfast is spent at my musick, the next is constantly employed in recolecting something I have learned least for want of practise it should be quite lost, such as French and short hand. After that I devote the rest of the time till I dress for dinner to our little Polly and two black girls who I teach to read, and if I have my papa's approbation (my Mamas I have got) I intend [them] for school mistres's for the rest of the Negroe children— another scheme you see. But to proceed, the first hour after dinner as the first after breakfast at musick, the rest of the afternoon in Needle work till candle light, and from that time to bed time read or write. 'Tis the fashion here to carry our work abroad with us so that having company, without they are great strangers, is no interruption to that affair; but I have particular matters for particular days, which is an interruption to mine. Mondays my musick Master is here. Tuesdays my friend Mrs. Chardon (about 3 mile distant) and I are constantly engaged to each other, she at our house one Tuesday—I at hers the next and this is one of the happiest days I spend at Woppoe. Thursday the whole day except what the necessary affairs of the family take up is spent in writing, either on the business of the plantations, or letters to my friends. Every other Fryday, if no company, we go a vizeting so that I go abroad once a week and no oftener.

Now you may form some judgement what time I can have to work my lappets. I own I never go to them with a quite easey conscience as I know my father has an aversion to my employing my time in that poreing work, but they are begun and must be finished. I hate to undertake any thing and not go thro' with it; but by way of relaxation from the other I have begun a peice of work of a quicker sort which requires nither Eyes nor genius—at least not very good ones. Would you ever guess is to be a shrimp nett? For so it is.

O! I had like to forgot the last thing I have done a great while. I have planted a large figg orchard with design to dry and export them. I have reckoned my expence and the prophets to arise from these figgs, but was I to tell you how great an Estate I am to make this way, and how 'tis to be laid out you would think me far gone in romance. Your good Uncle I know has long thought I have a fertile brain at schemeing. I only confirm him in his opinion; but I own I love the vegitable world extremly. I think it an innocent and useful amusement. Pray tell him, if he laughs much at my project, I never intend to have my hand in a silver mine and he will understand as well as you what I mean.

Our best respects wait on him and Mrs. Pinckney. If my Eyes dont deceive me you in your last [letter] talk of coming very soon by water to see how my oaks grow. Is it really so, or only one of your unripe schemes. While 'tis in your head put it speedily into execution and you will give great pleasure to

> Yr most obedient servt
> E. Lucas

[1742]
[To Miss Bartlett]
Dr. Miss B
    I have got no further than the first volume of Virgil but was most

agreeably disapointed to find my self instructed in agriculture as well as entertained by his charming penn; for I am pursuaded tho' he wrote in and for Italy, it will in many instances suit Carolina. I had never perused those books before and imagined I should imediately enter upon battles, storms and tempest that puts one in a maze and makes one shudder while one reads. But the calm and pleasing diction of pastoral and gardening agreeably presented themselves, not unsuitably to this charming season of the year, with which I am so much delighted that had I the fine soft language of our poet to paint it properly, I should give you but little respite till you came into the country and attended to the beauties of pure nature unassisted by art. The majestick pine imperceptably puts on a fresher green; the young mirtle joyning its fragrance to that of the Jesamin of golden hue perfumes all the woods and regales the rural wander[er] with its sweets; the daiseys, the honysuckles and a thousand nameless beauties of the woods invite you to partake the pleasures the country affords.

You may wonder how I could in this gay season think of planting a Cedar grove, which rather reflects an Autumnal gloom and solemnity than the freshness and gayty of spring. But so it is. I have begun it last week and intend to make it an Emblem not of a lady, but of a compliment which your good Aunt was pleased to make to the person her partiality has made happy by giving her a place in her esteem and friendship. I intend then to connect in my grove the solemnity (not the solidity) of summer or autumn with the cheerfulness and pleasures of spring, for it shall be filled with all kind of flowers, as well wild as Garden flowers, with seats of Camomoil and here and there a fruit tree—oranges, nectrons, Plumbs, &c., &c.

We are much concerned to hear of Mrs. Pinckneys illness. I have lately found benefit for the pain in my head by keeping my feet a little while every night before I go into bed in hott water. I dare say it would give her present ease if not cure her, but whether it may be hurtful for the spleen or not I can't say. I wish she would mention it to Dr. C.

Pray make our compliments and conclude me
    Yr. m. o. St.
    E. Lucas

[1742]
[To Miss Bartlett]
Dr. Miss B.

The contents of your last concerns us much as it informs us of the accident to Col. Pinckney. I hope Mrs. Pinckney dont apprehend any further danger from the fall than its spoiling him for a horsman. If it only prevents him riding that dancing beauty Chickasaw for the future, I think 'tis not much to be lamented, for he has as many tricks and airs as a dancing bear.

Wont you laugh at me if I tell you I am so busey in providing for Posterity I hardly allow my self time to Eat or sleep and can but just snatch a minnet to write to you and a friend or two now. I am making a large plantation of Oaks which I look upon as my own property, whether my father gives me the land or not; and therefore I design many years hence when oaks are more valueable than they are now—which you know they will be when we come to build fleets. I intend, I say, 2 thirds of the produce of my oaks for a charity (I'll let you know my scheme another time) and the other 3rd for those that shall have the trouble of putting my design in Execution. I sopose according to custom you will show this to your Uncle and Aunt. "She is [a] good girl," says Mrs. Pinckney. "She is never Idle and always means well." "Tell the little Visionary," says your Uncle, "come to town and partake of some of the amusements suitable to her time of life." Pray tell him I think these so, and what he may now think whims and projects may turn out well by and by. Out of many surely one may hitt.

I promised to tell you when the mocking bird began to sing. The little warbler has done wonders; the first time he opened his soft pipe this spring, he inspired me with the spirit of Rymeing, and [I] produced the 3 following lines while I was laceing my stays:

Sing on thou charming mimick of the feathered kind
and let the rational a lesson learn from thee,
to Mimick (not defects) but harmony.

If you let any mortal besides your self see this exquisite piece of poetry, you shall never have a line more than this specimen; and how great will be your loss you who have seen the above may jud[g]e as well as

Yr. m. obedt. Servt.
Eliza. Lucas

Wappo. May the 2ᵈ [1742]
To Miss Bartlett
Dr. Miss Bartlett

I send by the bearer my compliments to Mrs. Pinckney and the last volume of Pamela. She is a good girl and as such I love her dearly, but I must think her very defective and even blush for her while she allows her self that disgusting liberty of praising her self, or what is very like it, repeating all the fine speeches made to her by others when a person distinguished for modesty in every other respect should have chose rather to conceal them or at least to let them come from some other hand; especially as she might have considered those high compliments might have proceeded from the partiallity of her friends or with a view to encourage her and make her aspire after those qualifications which were ascribed to her, which I know experimently to be often the case. But then you answer she was a young Country Girl, had seen nothing of life and it was natural for her to be pleased with praise and she had not art enough to conceal it. True, before she was Mrs. B. it be excuseable when only wrote to her father and mother, but after she had the advantage of Mr. B.'s conversation and others of sence and distinction I must be of a nother oppinion.

But here arises a dificulty; we are to be made acquainted by the Authour of all particulars, how then is it to be done. I think by Miss Darnford or some other lady very intimate with Mrs. B. Here you smile at my presumption for instructing one so farr above my own level as the Authour of Pamella (whom I esteem much for the regard he pays to virtue and religion throughout his whole piece) but my Dear Miss Bartlett, contract your smile into a mortified look, for I acquit the Authour. He designed to paint no more than a woman, and he certainly designed it as a reflection upon the vanity of our sex that a character so compleat in every other instance should be so greatly defective in this; defective indeed, for when she mentions that poor Creature Mr. H. applusees it puts me in mind of the observation in Done Quixott How grateful is praise though it be from a madman. I have run thus farr before I was aware for I have nither capacity or inclination for Chritisism tho' Pamela sets me the example by critisizeing Mr. Lock and has taken the liberty to disent from that admirable Author.

One word more and I have done, and that is I think the Authour has kept up to nature (one of the greatest beauties in the whole piece) for had his Heroin no defect the character must be unnatural, as it would be in me to forget my respects to your worthy Uncle and Aunt Pinckney and that I am

    Yrs. &c.
    E. Lucas

2. Eliza Wilkinson

(1757–?)

Little is known about Eliza Yonge Wilkinson. She was born into a prominent planter family and grew up on Yonge's Island in the Stono River district of South Carolina. Her first husband, Joseph Wilkinson, died in 1775, scarcely a year after their marriage. In 1786 she married Peter Porcher, and the couple had one child.

Wilkinson's letters are of interest both for their historical and literary value. Many of them were addressed to no one in particular, as if she were using the letter form to write her view of history. Others were addressed to Mary Porcher, her sister-in-law; describing the invasion of South Carolina and the taking of Charleston in 1779, these letters were written with such care that together they resemble an epistolary novel. Wilkinson wrote of the British occupation of Charleston during the Revolutionary War, and she was quite outspoken in her criticism of the British Army. In the first entry of *Letters,* she writes that she "could not believe that a nation [England] so famed for humanity, and many other virtues, should, in so short a time, divest themselves of even the least trace of what they once were." The next several letters, including Letter VI, tell of British "visit[s] of plunder and insult" to the Yonge plantation, ways in which slaves aided the American fight for freedom, and the hardships experienced by fugitive women and children.

Wilkinson's major concerns were those of a plantation woman: the managing of the home and family, as well as the dependence of women on men despite their intelligence and capacity for self-sufficiency. She asserted that women were capable of formulating their own political views and had every right to hold those views; however, she did not go so far as to challenge the typical female role in the southern society. Also, though she was eager to protest the South's subjugation to the British, she apparently had no qualms about the subjugation of slaves to white southerners.

Wilkinson's letters were first published by Caroline Howard Gilman in her magazine, *Rose-Bud,* and then edited and collected in book form as *Letters of Eliza Wilkinson, During the Invasion and Possession of Charleston, S.C., by the British in the Revolutionary War* in 1839. In the introduction to the collected letters, Gilman notes that when Wilkinson wrote her letters, she was "a young and beautiful widow" and that "her handwriting . . . [was] clear and feminine." More important, Gilman emphasizes the significance of the letters by claiming that they "cannot fail to excite public interest at a period, when such anxiety is abroad to gather every relic of our past history before it floats away down the stream of time." As accounts of her life rely primarily on her letters, little is known about Wilkinson's later life, and the place and date of her death are unknown.

From *Letters of Eliza Wilkinson, During the Invasion and Possession of Charleston, S.C., by the British in the Revolutionary War*

Letter I

Yonge's Island, 1782.
To Miss M—— P——.

As I mean never to forget the *loving-kindness and tender mercies* of the renowned Britons while among us, in the ever-memorable year 1779, I shall transmit you a brief account of their *polite* behavior to my Father and family, where you will find me sufficiently punished for being something of an unbeliever heretofore. You know we had always heard most terrible accounts of the actions of the British troops at the northward; but, (fool that I was,) I thought they must be exaggerated, for I could not believe that a nation so famed for humanity, and many other virtues, should, in so short a time, divest themselves of even the least trace of what they once were.

Surely, said I, they can't, in so short a time, have commenced savages, and lost those virtues which have distinguished them from other nations. Yet, sometimes, when I heard fresh accounts of their cruelty to our Northern brethren when in their power, I could not repress my indignation against the barbarous, hard-hearted Britons, (how changed their character!) and believed, or almost believed, what I had heard of them. I say *almost,* for I was so infatuated with what I had formerly heard and read of Englishmen, that I thought humanity, and every manly sentiment, were their inherent qualities;—though I cannot but say that, much as I had admired the former lustre of the British character, my soul shrunk from the thought of having any communication with a people who had left their homes with a direct intention to imbrue their hands in the blood of my beloved countrymen, or deprive them of their birthright, Liberty and property. The thought alarmed me, shocked me. I began to look on the Britons in earnest as enemies.

At length I heard they had got possession of the Georgia State, and used the inhabitants cruelly, paying no respect to age or sex; but then, again, I heard to the contrary, that their behavior to the ladies was unexceptionable. I did not know what to think, much less what to do, should they invade our State, which was daily expected.

Thousands would I have given to have been in any part of the globe where I might not see them, or to have been secure from the impending evils, which were ready to burst over our heads.

I was in Charlestown when we heard that a large party of them had landed somewhere near Beaufort. I saw several detachments of our Southern troops leave town to oppose the invaders of their country. They marched with the greatest alacrity imaginable, not regarding the weather, though the rain poured down incessantly upon them. I cannot describe my feelings upon this sight—gratitude, affection, and pity for my countrymen filled my heart and my eyes, which pursued them until out of sight, and then every good wish attended them. However, it was not long before our little band of patriots returned to their homes in triumph, excepting a few, who had sealed the cause with their blood. Peace to their ashes, and everlasting happiness to their immortal part.

"Well have they perished—for in fight they fell." I think old Priam says this of his sons, who fell at the siege of Troy. But who can forbear the tear of sympathy for the distressed families, who are left behind to mourn the fall of those they highly valued, and from whom they derived their support? Pitiable reflection! "How seldom do the rich feel the distresses of the poor, and in the midst of conquest and acclamation, who regardeth the tears and afflictions of those who have lost their friends in the public?"

Now, the time drew near when this State was to have her day of suffering in sympathy with her sister States. Oh, how I dreaded the approaching enemy! I had thoughts (with my other friends,) to go higher up the country to avoid them; but as my Father, with many others of my relations, had not conveniences ready to carry off their effects with them, and as the enemy approached rapidly, they agreed to stay. It was a melancholy sight to see such crowds of helpless, distressed women, weeping for husbands, brothers, or other near relations and friends, who were they knew not where, whether dead or alive. When the enemy were at Ashepoo, or somewhere thereabouts, my sister and sister-in-law were then at my Father's, when one Sunday morning a negro wench, who had been out visiting, came running home in a violent hurry, informing us that a party of British horse were then at Mr. W.'s, not above five or six miles from us.

A boy on the road had informed our servant of the approach of the enemy. This created such confusion and distress among us all as I cannot describe. A boat was immediately pushed off. My sister Yonge, my sister Smilie, and myself, were desirous of putting the evil day afar off; so we went over the river to Mr. Smilie's. Father and Mother ventured to stay at home. Melancholy were the adieus on both sides. We had got but a small distance from the house when we met another lady, who, upon receiving the like information, had walked about two miles, (if not more,) to Father's. She joined us and away we went, often looking back, with watery eyes, to our Father's dwelling, thinking, at the same time, that in all probability, even while we were looking, he might be suffering all the insults and cruelties that a remorseless gang of barbarians could inflict. These thoughts drew sighs and tears from us; however, we made the best of it, and endeavored to console one another the best we could; but poor was that consolation, you may think.

We had but just got over, when a scene presented itself to us, enough to move the hardest heart in the British army could they have seen it. This was a large boat-load of women and children on their way to Charlestown, as that place promised more safety than any other. They called at Mr. Smilie's, and staid a day or two. I pitied them all greatly, (though we were much in the same situation;) one lady especially, who had seven children, and one of them but a fortnight old; thus, in her weakly situation, to venture her life and that of her babe, rather than fall into the hands of an enemy, whose steps have been marked with cruelty and oppression. Surely, if the British knew the misery they occasion, they would abate their rigor, and blush to think that the name of Englishman, (once so famous among the Fair,) should now produce terror and dismay in every female breast. I'll now lay by my pen—Farewell.

I will proceed by and bye with my narrative, for the various scenes I've been witness to are so much in my head, that I shall not want subjects to employ my pen for some time.

Once more adieu.

Eliza W.

Letter VI

After various discourses, the conversation took a turn on the subject of the present war. I was proud to hear my friends express themselves in a manner not unworthy of their country. Maj. Moore made a comparison, which, as I perfectly remember, I will give you. Your opinion is also required of the same.

"Suppose," said he, "I had a field of wheat, upon these conditions, that out of that field I was to give so much to a certain person yearly; well, I think nothing of it, I give it cheerfully, and am very punctual; it goes on thus for some years; at length the person sends me word I must let him have so much more, for he wants it; still I comply with cheerfulness. The next year he requires a still larger supply, and tells me he cannot do without it. This startles me! I find him encroaching, by little and little, on my property. I make some difficulty in complying; however, as he says 'he cannot do without it,' I let him have it, though I see it hurts me; but it puts me on my guard. Well, things go on so for some time; at length he begins again, and at last seems to have a design of taking my whole field. Then what am I to do?—Why, if I give it up, I am ruined, I must lie at his mercy. Is not this slavery? For my part," continued he, "I would rather explore unknown regions, blessed with liberty, than remain in my native country if to be cursed with slavery."

The land of Liberty! how sweet the sound! enough to inspire cowardice itself with a resolution to confirm the glorious title, "the land of Liberty." Let me again repeat it—how enchanting! It carries every idea of happiness in it, and raises a generous warmth in every bosom capable of discerning its blessings. O! Americans—Americans! strive to retain the glorious privilege which your virtuous ancestors left you; "it is the price of blood;" and let not the blood of your brave countrymen, who have so lately (in all the States) died to defend it, be spilt in vain. Pardon this digression, my dear Mary—my pen is inspired with sympathetic ardor, and has run away with my thoughts before I was aware. I do not love to meddle with political matters; the men say we have no business with them, it is not in our sphere! and Homer (did you ever read Homer, child?) gives us two or three broad hints to mind our domestic concerns, spinning, weaving, &c. and leave affairs of higher nature to the men; but I must beg his pardon—I won't have it thought, that because we are the weaker sex as to *bodily* strength, my dear, we are capable of nothing more than minding the dairy, visiting the poultry-house, and all such domestic concerns; our thoughts can soar aloft, we can form conceptions of things of higher nature; and have as just a sense of honor, glory, and great actions, as these "Lords of the Creation." What contemptible *earth worms* these authors make us! They won't even allow us the liberty of thought, and that is all I want. I would not wish that we should meddle in what is unbecoming female delicacy, but surely we may have sense enough to give our opinions to commend or discommend such actions as we may approve or disapprove; without being reminded of our spinning and household affairs as the only matters we are capable of thinking or speaking of with justness or propriety. I won't allow it, positively won't. Homer has a deal of morality in his works, which is worthy of imitation; his Odyssey abounds with it. But I will leave Homer to better judges, and proceed in my narration.

While the officers were there discoursing, word was brought that a party of the enemy were at a neighboring plantation, not above two miles off, carrying provisions away. In an instant the men were under arms, formed and marched away to the place. We were dreadfully alarmed at the first information, but, upon seeing with what eagerness our friends marched off, and what high spirits they were in, we were more composed, but again relapsed into our fears when we heard the discharge of fire-arms; they did not stay out long; but returned with seven prisoners, four whites and three blacks. When they came to the door, we looked out, and saw two of M'Girth's men with them, who had used us so ill; my heart relented at the sight of them, and I could not forbear looking at them with an eye of pity. Ah! thought I, how fickle is fortune! but two days ago these poor wretches were riding about as if they had nothing to fear, and terrifying the weak and helpless by their appearance; now, what a humbled appearance do *they* make! But, basely as they have acted in taking up arms against their country, they have still some small sense left that they were once Americans, but now no longer so, for all who act as they do, forfeit that name; and by adopting the vices of those they join, become one with them; but these poor creatures seem to have yet remaining some token of what they once were—else why did they, last Thursday, behave so much better to us than the Britons did, when we were equally as much in their power as we were in the others'? I will let them see I have not forgot it. I arose, and went out to them. "I am sorry, my friends, (I could not help calling them *friends* when they were in our power,) to see you in this situation, you treated us with respect; and I cannot but be sorry to see you in distress." "It is the fortune of war, Madam, and soldiers must expect it." "Well, you need not make yourselves uneasy; I hope Americans won't treat their prisoners ill. Do, my friends, (to the soldiers) use these men well—they were friendly to us." "Yes, Madam," said they; "they shall be used well if it was only for that." I asked if they would have any thing to drink. Yes, they would be glad of some water. I had some got, and as their hands were tied, I held the glass to their mouths; they bowed, and were very thankful for it. I was so busy, I did not observe the officers in the house; several of them were at the door and window, smiling at me, which, when I perceived, I went in and told them how it was. They promised that the men should be favored for their behavior to us. "Madam," said one, "you would make a bad soldier; however, if I was of the other party, and taken prisoner, I should like to fall into your hands." I smiled a reply, and the conversation took another turn.

In the meanwhile Miss Samuells was very busy about a wounded officer who was brought to the house (one of M'Girth's;) he had a ball through his arm; we could find no rag to dress his wounds, every thing in the house being thrown into such confusion by the plunderers; but (see the native tenderness of an American!) Miss Samuells took from her neck the only remaining handkerchief the Britons had left her, and with it bound up his arm! Blush, O Britons, and be confounded! your delight is cruelty and oppression; divested of all humanity, you imitate savages; neither age nor sex can move compassion; even the smiling babe suffers by your hands, and innocently smiles at its oppressor. The Americans are obliged to commit unavoidable acts of cruelty; the defence of their country requires it; you seek their lives and liberties, and they must either kill or be killed; yet, (imitating the all-merciful Creator,) "In the midst of anger, they remember mercy."

> "And will Omnipotence neglect to save
> The suffering virtues of the wise and brave?"

No; I cannot think we shall be overcome while we act with justice and mercy—those are the attributes of heaven. If our cause is just, as it certainly appears to be, we need not doubt success; an Almighty arm has visibly supported us; or a raw, undisciplined people, with so many disadvantages too on their side, could never have withstood, for so long a time, an army which has repeatedly fought and conquered, and who are famed for, or rather *were* famed, for their valor and determined bravery; but now their glory is fallen, and, thank heaven, we are their equals, if not their superiors in the field. I have somewhere read that "vice was the greatest coward in the world, when it knows it will be resolutely opposed;" and what have good men, engaged in a right cause, to fear? When they embarked for America, they were sure of success; for they expected no opposition from a people so little skilled in arms, and who had no experience in the art of war; but to their cost they found, that those who have a true sense of their rights and liberties, will "conquer difficulties by daring to oppose them."

> "Heaven's blessings always wait on virtuous deeds,
> And though a late—a sure reward succeeds."

Let me read what I have written—my pen is quite unmanageable this morning. I had determined not to make a digression or observation, and before I am aware, it flies from matters of fact or plain narration, and introduces my poor opinion on the stage. What will the men say if they should see this? I am really out of *my sphere* now, and must fly to Homer for direction and instruction on household matters. Begone, pen; I must throw you by until I can keep you in proper order. In good time have I discarded it; for I am this moment called to breakfast. Adieu—another message! Coming—coming.—"Surely, you would not have me break my neck down stairs for a breakfast."

Well, I obeyed the summons to breakfast, worked with my needle, visited; and now again take up my pen; for in the mornings, that is, from sunrise until 8 o'clock, I indulge myself in reading and writing. After that hour I meddle with neither. But let me see! where did I leave off? O! I left at Miss Samuells' parting with her only handkerchief—don't you think her a good girl?

After dinner our friends began to move towards camp; my brother persuaded us not to stay an hour longer, for the enemy, upon hearing what had been done, might come out, and use us worse than they had done already. Father had the same thoughts, and sent for us; but having not a horse left, he only sent umbrellas to shelter us from the sun, which was exceedingly warm. My sister packed up a few things, and gave the Negroes to carry, and then we went off. Hard case to us, who had never been used to walking, to walk three long miles in a hot summer's day; and in such danger too, for as a party of the enemy had just been routed, we did not know but some of them might be lurking about the woods, and the road we were obliged to go was very much frequented by them, so that we walked along with heavy hearts. If we had let the officers know we were going, we should have done very well; but we had not concluded on it until they were gone. Two of Father's Negro men attended us, armed with great clubs; one walked on before, the other behind, placing us in the centre.

It was not long before our guard had some use for their clubs; we were crossing a place they call the Sands, when one of the enemy's Negroes came out of the woods. He passed our advance guard with nothing but the loss of his smart Jocky cap, which was snatched from his head. He turned round, and muttering something, then proceeded on; when, attempting to pass our rear guard, he was immediately levelled to the earth; he arose, and attempted to run off, when he received another blow, which again brought him down. I could not bear the sight of the poor wretch's blood, which washed his face and neck; it affected me sensibly. "Enough, Joe! enough," cried I; "don't use the creature ill, take him at once, I wont have him beaten so." "Let me alone, Mistress, I'll not lay a hand on him till I have stunned him; how do I know but he has a knife, or some such thing under his clothes, and when I go up to him, he may stab me. No, no,—I know Negroes' ways too well." With that he fetched him another blow. I was out of all patience; I could not help shedding tears. I called out again; "Inhuman wretch, take the Negro at once, he cannot hurt you now if he would; you shall not—I declare you shall not beat him so." With that he took him, tied his hands behind him, and gave him to the fellow who went before; he himself stayed behind with us; but the poor wretch was sadly frightened. The fellow who had him in custody, walked on very fast, but he kept looking back on us. At last he said to me, "Do, Mistress, let me walk by you." "Don't be afraid," said I, "they shan't hurt you again, I wont let them." But he looked on me so pitifully—his head continually turning round towards me, with such terror in his countenance, that I felt for the poor creature, and, to make him easy, walked, or rather ran, close behind him; for, to keep up with them I was obliged to go in a half run, the fellow who had hold of him walking at a great rate, for fear of being overtaken by the enemy.

I was ready to faint; the exercise and extreme heat of the sun overcame me; but I would not quit the unhappy wretch as he claimed my protection, and my presence seemed some alleviation to his misery; so on I went, scarce able to support myself. I had got on a great way ahead of my sister and Miss Samuells, when I heard a confused noise, which, echoing in the woods, sounded like lamentations; my heart was at my mouth. "I'm afraid we are pursued," cried I; "I think I hear my sister and Miss Samuells crying!" The noise increased; I made a stop, and was ready to sink to the earth: the Negro, who had the prisoner in custody, heard what I said, and hearing the noise also, took it for granted that we were pursued, quitted his charge, and was making off. I was then some distance behind, for not a step could I take after the stop I made; when looking, I saw the prisoner standing alone in the path, watching the road very sharply, as if expecting a speedy deliverance. I then found my tongue; for, thought I, if the enemy should find the Negro in such a bloody condition, they would use us very ill. I called out as loud as I was able to the absconding fellow—"Stop, this moment, and take that Negro; make all the haste you can with him home, and keep him out of the way; remember, your life may be concerned in this matter, so take care." The mention of his life was enough; he grasped the prisoner's arm, and off he ran at such a rate, that they were both out of sight in a minute or two. In the mean time I stood trembling in the road, thinking it useless to attempt getting out of the way, for, so weak was I with the long walk (or rather run), that I could not have gone any distance in the wood if I had ever such an inclination so to do. So, thought I, I may as well die here as anywhere else; but, upon my sister's coming up to me, I found the noise proceeded from the Negroes with the baggage, who were quarrelling about carrying it.

When they heard, and indeed saw how I was frightened, (for they told me I looked as pale as death,) said Joe, "Do you think if it was so, I'd hab staid behind so long? Not I! Soon as ever I found how it was, I'd hab come out before, and that Negro should never hab told what *hurted* him. I'd have finished him, and got him out of the way; better for him to die, than all of us die for him." We pursued our way, and got safe to my Father's, but were greatly indisposed for some days after, at the end of which we were put in another little flury, (no end to them, I think,) by three or four horsemen riding up to the house very fast; but we were relieved from our fears by hearing one of them call out to us, "Do not be frightened;" and we found it was Major Moore, with three of his men. He staid and dined with us, spent a part of the afternoon, and returned to camp.

He had not been gone long, when a boat-load of *Red Coats* passed; with them an officer, who stood up all the way, pointing his hand this way and that, as if asking whose and whose settlements those were on the river. In a short time they re-passed, their bayonets fixed, as if apprehensive of danger. Conscience told them they deserved something for what they had been about; I suppose it was no good.

I see I shall not finish my narrative in this letter; so I will conclude, and am, as usual, your own

    Eliza

3. Anne Newport Royall

(1769–1854)

Considered the first American newspaperwoman, Anne Newport Royall was an author and traveler throughout her life. She was born near Baltimore, Maryland, the elder of two daughters. Before the Revolution, however, Royall's father felt compelled to leave for the Pennsylvanian frontier; his loyalty to the King made him an outcast among the colonists. Though an excellent provider and educator of his children, Newport died not long after moving his family west, leaving his family to survive on their own. According to legend, the young Anne Newport was stolen by Native Americans while in the wilderness and lived sixteen years with them. After her mother's second husband died, Anne accompanied her family to Virginia in search of financial assistance. After a long and dangerous journey the women located in Sweet Springs (now located in West Virginia) where Anne's mother became a servant for Captain William Royall, a wealthy gentleman and friend of George Washington. He became very interested in Anne and her education; in 1797 they were married.

When her husband died in 1812, Royall left for Alabama and soon found herself impoverished once again when, in 1823, her husband's relatives voided his will, claiming she was an adulteress. She eventually received some veteran compensation from Washington in 1848, but her husband's family took half the money, and her debts depleted the rest. Her financial hardships drove Royall to write in order to survive. She began by traveling throughout the country, recording her impressions of what she observed.

Royall's memoirs filled ten volumes and were considered a valuable source for understanding contemporary life of the 1820s; they include *Sketches of History, Life, and Manners in the United States* (1826), *The Black Book; or, A Continuation of Travels in the United States* (1828–29), and *Mrs. Royall's Southern Tour* (1830–31). *Letters from Alabama on Various Subjects* (1830), ostensibly addressed to a young lawyer friend from Virginia named "Matt," has been reprinted as *Letters from Alabama, 1817–1822* (1969); the letters anthologized here are from the latter volume. Some record regional dialects that give her audience a fuller sense of the language and culture of the people she describes. She characterizes the Tennesseans as "a very plain people" who live in houses "void of ostentation: The North Carolinians next; the South Carolians and Georgians, next; and the Virginians the most ostentatious of any." Other letters tell of women's religious lives, and of the lives of Native Americans and slaves. Like Mary Chesnut, Royall laments, "Oh, slavery, slavery! nothing can soften thee!" Yet, after observing Cherokee women caring for their children, she writes, "It is very probable that the most effectual means [for civilizing them] have been resorted to by our government. . . . I mean our rifles." Despite her objections to slavery, Royall seems to have believed in a social hierarchy based on racial prejudices.

After completing her travels, Royall moved to Washington, D.C., and began printing pamphlets and books and eventually a newspaper, which was first called *Paul Pry* and then *The Huntress*. She was very well known because of her bitter and sometimes malicious attitudes—both spoken and written—and was soon labeled the "terror of Washington." In fact, she is said to have been indicted by the grand jury as a "scold" and nearly sentenced to a ducking in the Potomac River. At the same time, however, Royall was greatly admired by those who approved of her spirit and her assertive nature; John Quincy Adams, for example, was one of her closest friends. Royall died in 1854, a pauper.

From *Letters from Alabama, 1817–1822*

Melton's Bluff, January 20th, 1818
Dear Matt,

      . . .

Hearing eleven boats had arrived about two miles from hence, and had haulted up the river, we set off, as I said before, in a little canoe, to see the Indians, which are on their way to their destination beyond the Mississippi. Government, agreeably to their contract, having completed the boats, the news of the arrival of the Indians had been received with much interest; but being unable to proceed by water, we quit the canoe, and proceeded by land in our wet shoes and hose.

We arrived at the Indian camps about eleven o'clock. There were several encampments at the distance of three hundred yards from each other, containing three hundred Indians. The camps were nothing but some forks of wood driven into the ground, and a stick laid across them, on which hung a pot in which they were boiling meat; I took it to be venison. Around these fires were seated, some on the ground, some on logs, and some on chairs, females of all ages; and all employed, except the old women. There were some very old gray-haired women, and several children at each camp. The children were very pretty; but the grown females were not. I saw but few men. I asked the interpreter where they were: he said they had gone to hunt; some of them had returned, and were skinning and others preparing their game for their journey. But none of them were near the women's department; they kept at a very respectful distance.

I have heard much of the elegant figures of the Indians; true, some nations of Indians are elegantly formed, but such is not the case with the Cherokees. They are low in stature, and there is nothing majestic or dignified about them. They have no expression of countenance. They have a dead eye; but their feet and hands are exceedingly small and beautiful. This is all the beauty I could distinguish about them. No lady that ever I saw has a hand so small or so well turned as these Indian women; and the same may be said of their feet. But, after all, they are ugly lumps of things. They are thick and short. Their hair is jet black, and very coarse. It parts from the crown of the head to its termination on the forhead, as the Dutch women wear theirs, and clubbed up behind with a blue or red ferret. Their colour is that of dark mulattos. They were all well dressed; at least as well as most white women are, when engaged in their ordinary employment. Some were engaged in sewing, some in cooking, and some in nursing their babies, which were the prettiest little creatures I ever beheld.

Their manner of nursing is singular. They do not hold their infants in their arms, or on their laps, as our women do; but on their backs, confined in such a manner that they are in no danger of falling, or moving in any direction. This is done by means of a blanket, or a part of one, drawn tight round the infant, leaving its head and arms out. This blanket is fastened round the waist of the mother, and the top I do not know exactly how; but the utmost confidence seems to be reposed in its tenacity, as the mother never touches the child with her hands, or is at any more trouble with it whatever. The little things clasp their arms round the necks of their mothers, which they never move: no crying, nor fretting, nor any apprehension of danger disturbed the serenity of these little philosophers, on our approaching them. I have been told that the mothers suckle them, where they are, by raising the breast up to the child's mouth, which is very probable.

The Indian women appear to sustain no inconvenience from the incumbrance of their children. They went through the different vocations of pounding their corn into meal, carrying wood and water, with the same apparent ease as those that had no children. Seeing several little girls of from ten to twelve years old, I asked the women why they did not make those little girls nurse their little ones. They answered no other way than by shaking their heads, and smiling at my ignorance, no doubt. I went up to one of them, who was pounding corn, took the pestle out of her hand and helped her to pound: she laughed at my awkwardness, and took it out of my hand. She had, sitting by her on a washing-tub, a large tray full of parched corn. This it was that she was pounding into meal; and as she finished each portion, she emptied it into another tray. Every thing about her was neat and clean. The Indian corn was parched to a nice light brown, and looked "very interesting." The meal manufactured from this corn is not fine, nor do they make it into bread at all, but mix it with common water and drink it. 'Tis rarely that they drink water in any other way. No one, who has never tasted it, would believe what a delicious drink it is.

Having walked about and made a number of inquiries, I sat myself down and made signs to an old Indian woman that I wanted to smoke: she very courteously handed me her pipe. The seat I had chosen was near one of those women, whom I had observed for some time, sedulously engaged with her needle. She was engaged making a family dress, in which she discovered all the skill and industry necessary to accomplish it. Their dresses were made like our ladies, and were put on. They had fine cotton shawls on their shoulders, and many of them had men's hats on their heads; but no bonnets were seen amongst them. They all had good shoes or mockasins on their feet, and some hundreds of beads round their necks; but their broad faces and coarse hair (as coarse as a horses mane) were quite disgusting. There is one elegance, however, which they possess in a superior degree to any civilized people that I am acquainted with; and this is not their beautiful hands and feet, already mentioned, but their walk. No lady, however skilled in the art of dancing, can walk with so much grace and dignity as these Indians, both men and women: and this, I am told, is peculiar to almost all Indians.

Although there were such a number of them, so near together as to be seen from one camp to the other, yet there was the greatest arder imaginable: not the least noise to be heard. How would so many whites have managed to maintain the good order evinced by these Indians? Even their dogs were not permitted to bark at us. The poor dogs! I felt for them: they were nothing but skin and bone! The same word that we use to encourage our dogs to seize on any thing, or to bark, the Indians use to control theirs, which is *hiss*! One of our party told me that it was *hiska*! which means "be still." The dress of the men was equally as decent and fashionable as that of the women. Many of them had on very neat half-boots, broad cloth coats, and good hats; though some prefer tying their heads up with a handkerchief, as being more convenient to hunt in.

By all that I have said in regard to these Cherokees, you may perceive they are far advanced in civilized arts and manners. This great work was accomplished by the indefatigable labors of the Reverend Gideon Blackburn! And yet, what an aversion they manifest toward our language! I was told that nearly all those that I saw, both understood and could talk good English; but not one word could I get out of them, of any sort. Their inter-communications were carried on by signs. I saw many of the half-breed, as they are called, here; the off-spring of a white and an Indian—but they were as unsociable as the others. I was thinking that this would be a good plan to promote their civilization, but the result proves that any plan would not succeed. It is very probable, that the most effectual means have been resorted to by our government to overcome their prejudices. I mean our rifles.

Please to give my best respects to Mrs. Wilson and Mrs. Dryden.

Yours, &c.

Moulton, April 30th, 1821.

Dear Matt,

You say you are pleased with the countryman in my last. Here is a score of them. Perhaps this may bring another reply. I am much pleased, in the meantime, to hear your health is restored, and hope to wish you much joy, on a certain occasion, ere long.

I strolled out with a friend to see a neighbor yesterday, who lives on the skirts of the town, merely for the sake of amusement. If you wish to ascertain the dialect of a country, you must seek for it amongst the common, or in other words, the lower order of the people, as all well bred people speak alike. But the children of both classes are good specimens of dialect, as the better sort, in this country, particularly, consign their children to the care of negroes. You see I am for another dish of philosophy. But to go on. Those who have black nurses, and those who have illiterate white nurses to attend children, are at much pains and cost for teachers to unlearn them what they need never have learned, had they kept illiterate people from them at first. This is not the case with the poorer class of people, as their children are nursed by themselves, and speak *their* language.

While we were chatting with our neighbor, a number of people rode up to the door, and we went out to see what was the matter. It appeared they were on their return from a barbacue, and had heard a stump speech. Some of these were mere children, and some were grown persons. Our neighbor, who was aware of their business, asked "What news from the barbacue?" "Oh there was a proper sight of people— Oh, my! but there was—You never seed the like! And a heap of 'em had on ruffled shirts, and shoeboots, and was so proud, stepin about; and there was some monstrous purty gals there, and some dinged ugly ones, too; and such a powerful chance of apples and cyder, and ginger cakes. I tell ye what, they were prime; and they made such a fuss, and *covaulted,* and was going to fight; you never saw the like in all the days of your life. Then these fellows that lives on Flint, had liked to abin whipped, steppin about. I tell you what, them fellows is monstrous proud; and old F——, was there, too, and got the maddest, he fairly snorted. Oh, he was rearin. And them fellows from Elum's Mill, turned in with old F——, and snorted and covaulted, and dared them ruffle-shirt fellows to turn out. Oh, they got the maddest! And Mr. E—— made a stump speech. He said if we voted for that there 'tother man, I forgot his name, that government would come and take away our land, and we would have to pay taxes and all that." These were mostly Tennesseeans and North Carolinians.

I saw a piece in the papers not long since, which went to satirize the Tennessee dialect. I would advise such people to look at home. Those who live in glass houses, ought not to throw stones. Let us compare this with the dialect of Virginia. You remember the bear hunting party from Bedford. I will stake them against the whole United States. One of them called at our house on his return, and entertained us with the following account of his adventures: "You know da is heap of baw (bear) on da Kenhawa; so I and Bill Prout, Jess Passin, and Zack Miller, are all goin to Kenhawa to hunt baw—Kenhawa mighty far—so we walk—we walk—last we come to da Kenhawa—Kenhawa b—i—g river, for true—Tell you what, it skears me—well, I goes out into de woods—I hear noise—I look up tree, and see a baw!—I went to da root o' da tree—I bark like any dog—presently da baw come husslin down—Ah, boy!—I took to my keels, and did hook it."—Now for the Pennsylvania dialect: "Jim, where are you and Sam; why but ye's pit (put) you cow in the pester, (pasture;) 'am sure a towled ye's the mornin.—Ye's cruel bad children—and there a fine job ye's done to leave you gears out by." The Yankee: "Flora, you want (ought) to wash them clothes right away. You hadn't ought to left 'em so." "What say?"

Covault is of Tennessee birth, and not unaptly applied in the sense they use it. It signifies an unruly or ungovernable man; also an untame horse, or any thing that cannot be controuled. It is quite a classical word, and I hope to see it admitted into the English language. It appears to be a compound of co and vault, which are both very significant. For the rest I find the Tennesseeans are a very plain people, and have a very high sense of honor. Their houses and equipage are void of ostentation: The North Carolinians next; the South Carolinians and Georgians, next; and the Virginians the most ostentatious of any. But the preaching; you must hear that. This country is run mad after preaching.—Here is a new sect called Cumberland presbyterians; and between these, the baptists, and methodists, the woods resound. As they have no churches they preach out of doors mostly. I have just returned from preaching, where I remained about two hours, and the parson, when I left him appeared to be only about midway through his sermon. He ought to have a patent-right, for he certainly has the strongest voice in the state.

I have met with several excellent orators since I have been in the country; the best I ever heard. Parson Burress, formerly of Virginia, is, doubtless, the finest public speaker in the Union. I have seen no parallel for him. The Reverend Mr. Butler and McMahon, the latter of Nashville, Tennessee, are, also, men of handsome delivery. These are methodists. I was truly astonished at this, as I never saw one of the sect, before, hardly worth hearing. The baptists, and the Cumberland presbyterians, are continually preaching and *covaulting.* Mr. Porter, a most amiable man; also a Mr. Madden, preached in Mr. B.'s house since I was here, and that busybody, Mr. *They say,* reported Mr. B. was to preach here to day, that is, out at the stand in the woods. I observed, "I will go and hear Mr. Porter." "Oh," said a bystander, "it is another preacher than Mr. Porter that preaches today—there is not such another preacher in the known world—he's a monstrous fine preacher." As I had heard some fine preaching, for the oratory I went to hear this none such. But never was I so disappointed. I placed myself in front of the preacher, (a great rough looking man,) and the congregation sat some on fallen timber, some on benches carried there for the purpose—some sat flat on the ground, and many stood up—about 500 in all. His text was, "He that hath ears to hear, let him hear." The people must have been deaf indeed that could not have heard him. He neither made division nor subdivision. He is one of the Cumberland presbyterians. They are Calvinists, it is said, but do not deem education a necessary qualification to preach the Gospel. But to the sermon: He began low but soon bawled to deafening. He spit in his hands, rubbed them against each other, and then would smite them together, till he made the woods ring. The people now began to covault, and dance, and shout, till they fairly drowned the speaker. Many of the people, however, burst out into a laugh. Seeing this, the preacher cried out, pointing to them with his finger, "Now look at them sinners there— You'll see how they will come tumbling down presently—I'll bring them down." He now redoubled his strength; spit in his hands and smote them together, till he made the forest resound, and took a fresh start; and sure enough the sinners came tumbling down. The scene that succeeded baffles description. Principally confined to women and children, the young women had carefully taken out their combs, from their hair, and laid them and their bonnets in a place of safety, as though they were going to set in for a fight; and it was much like a battle. After tumbling on the ground, and kicking sometime, the old women were employed in keeping their clothes civil, and the young men (never saw an old man go near them) would help them up, and taking them by each hand, by *their* assistance, and their own agility, they would spring nearly a yard from the ground at every jump, one jump after another, crying out, glory, glory, as loud as their strength would admit; others would be singing a lively tune to which they kept time—hundreds might be seen and heard going on in this manner at once. Others, again, exhausted by this jumping, would fall down, and here they lay cross and pile, heads and points, yelling and screaming like wild beasts of the forest, rolling on the ground, like hogs in a mire,—very much like they do at camp meetings in our country, but more shameless; their clothes were the color of the dirt; and like those who attend the camp meetings, they were all of the lower class of the people. I saw no genteel person among them. Are not people of education answerable for this degradation of society? It appears to me, since I have had opportunities of mixing with the world, that there are a certain class of citizens, whose interest it is to keep their fellow men in ignorance. I am very sure, half a dozen words of common sense, well applied, would convince those infatuated young women that they were acting like fools. In fact a fool is more rational. Not one of those but would think it a crying sin to dance.

The noise of the preacher was effectually drowned at length, and a universal uproar succeeded louder than ever.—Whilst this was going on, I observed an old woman near me, snivelling and turning up the whites of her eyes, (she was a widow—all the widows, old and young, covaulted,) and often applying her handkerchief to her eyes, and throwing herself into contortions, but it would not do, she could not raise the steam.

I pointed to one young woman, with a red scarf, who had tired down several young men, and was still covaulting, and seeing she jumped higher than the rest, I asked "who she might be?" One of the gentlemen, a Mr. Gallagher, who was standing near, gave such an account of her (men know these things) as would shock a modest ear. "D——n her, she gets converted every meeting she goes to." How much better had she been at a ball, (if they must dance,) where they would be obliged to behave decent, and where vile characters dare not appear.

Shortly after they began to rear and covault, a daughter of Mr. B's began too. He walked up to her, and led her off some distance, and sat her down at the root of a tree. When he returned, I inquired "if she was sick?" "No," he answered, "but she was beginning to go on as the rest, and I told her if she wished to worship God, to do it there, and not to expose herself before faces."

The preacher having spent all his ammunition, made a pause, and then called upon all the sinners to approach and be prayed for. Numbers went forward, all women and children, (children of ten years old get religion!) and the priest began to pray; when a decent looking man approached the stand, and took a female by the arm, and led her away. As he walked along, the preacher pointed to him, and said, "God, strike that sinner down!" The man turned around and in an angry tone said, "God has more sense than to mind such a d——d fool as you are!" and resumed his course. He was one of the brave Tennesseeans; and the lady was his wife.

Being tired of such an abominable scene, I proposed returning home, and, taking a near cut through a slip of woodland, we surprized the red scarf lady in a manner that gave us no favorable opinion of her piety.

Meeting has broke up, and several are coming to our house to dine. I wish to have some conversation with them, and shall finish my letter afterwards.

I took my seat at the table, by a stout, jolly looking lady, who, in replying to some of the party, observed "a great many had got religion that day." Now was my time—"And pray, Madam," said I, "what religion did they get?" "Why that is a queer question—there is but one religion, every body knows." "There you are a little mistaken, Madam; there are various religions. There is the Christian religion; the Jewish religion; the Mahometan religion, &c. &c; which of those religions was it you spoke of?" "I never heard of them before;" and stared at me in astonishment. "And what religion are you of?" said the lady. I told her my religion was piety. "Never heard of it before;" and doubtless she told the truth. And what sort of a religion is piety? "Why, Madam, it is simply to love God and my neighbor." "It is a queer name, and it's the first I ever heard of it. Is there many of the pieties where you come from?" "Not many." Mr. G. and several at the table could scarcely suppress a laugh. "And pray, Madam, since we have made up our acquaintance, may I take the liberty of asking which of these religions you profess?" "Ne're one," said the lady; "I'm a Cumberland presbyterian." The company could no longer retain themselves; they roared; whilst the subject of it had not the least idea of the cause.

Now, this woman, take her on any other subject, was a reasonable and intelligent woman. Thoroughly acquainted with the ordinary business of life. She was from the interior of Kentucky; and had attended preaching for twenty years! and yet is ignorant, not only of the duties, but of the very name of a christian! Whose fault is this? The fault of the priest! So they can draw the women (they do not seem partial to men) after them, they care for nothing else. If there is a hell, there will be more priests in it than any other description of people.

Yours, &c.

Anne

Newport

Royall

&

41

4. Caroline Howard Gilman

(1794–1888)

Born in Boston, Massachusetts, Caroline Howard Gilman began writing poetry at a very young age, shortly after her mother's death in 1804. Although an early poem, "Jephthah's Rash Vow," was published in a local newspaper, Gilman did not enjoy this recognition but rather felt embarassed to see her work in print. However, with the publication of "Jarius's Daughter" in the *North American Review* in 1817, Gilman began feeling more confident about her creativity, and by the 1830s she had settled into a successful writing career. In December of 1819 the young Caroline Howard married Samuel Gilman, a graduate of Harvard College and Divinity School. They moved to Charleston, South Carolina, where Samuel became a Unitarian minister, and eventually the couple had seven children.

Though Gilman grew to love the South shortly after moving there, she also remained loyal to her New England heritage; the tension between the differing cultures seems to have precipitated her literary career. The element that joined the northerner and southerner in Gilman was her depiction of domestic life, and she presented the home as the moral center of both societies. Her children's magazine, *Rose-Bud, or Youth's Gazette,* begun in 1832 and continued as the family magazine *Southern Rose* in 1835, demonstrates her concern for the education of all members of a family. These magazines were quite popular in their time, attracting such writers as Nathaniel Hawthorne, who requested that Gilman publish his story "The Lily's Quest."

Other important works by Gilman that portray both northern and southern domestic life are *Recollections of a Housekeeper* (1834), which, written under the pseudonym Clarissa Packard, depicts life in New England, and *Recollections of a Southern Matron* (1838), which tells of a girl growing up on a plantation. These works are of particular interest to feminist scholars, for they complement well the typical nineteenth-century sentimental, domestic novels; though domestic peace is actually a national goal for Gilman, and so she advises women to be submissive at all times, she openly admits to her frustration in enduring the "thousand perplexities" of being a woman in submission to men.

The anthologized work, "Mary Anna Gibbes," is an initiation story from *The Poetry of Travelling in the United States* (1838). In the poem, Gilman depicts Mary Anna breaking away from roles traditionally assigned to young women; yet Mary Anna still acts primarily out of her feminine instincts. She rescues a boy from a war-torn house after convincing soldiers along her route that she is indeed capable; nevertheless, she is motivated not by "masculine courage" but by her innate maternalism. She ascends the stairs of the house with "such a flight as the young eagle takes / To gain its nest."

Gilman published numerous volumes of poems, a collection of tales and ballads, and a woman's almanac. She is noted for her editions of the letters of Eliza Lucas Pinckney and Eliza Wilkinson, two invaluable collections for the study of southern literature and history. Gilman's works were extremely popular before the Civil War, but as her literary output declined after the 1850s, so did her popularity. By the end of the war she had ceased writing altogether. Throughout the Civil War, Gilman was a committed southerner; in 1862, after her home was destroyed, she moved to Greenville, South Carolina, and became active in the Ladies' Association in Aid of the Volunteers of the Confederate Army. She spent the final years of her life with her daughter in Washington, D.C., and died at age ninety-four.

Mary Anna Gibbes, the Young Heroine of Stono, S.C.[1]

    Stono, on thy still banks
The roar of war is heard; its thunders swell
And shake yon mansion, where domestic love
Till now breathed simple kindness to the heart;
Where white-arm'd childhood twined the neck of age,
Where hospitable cares lit up the hearth,
Cheering the lonely traveller on his way.
    A foe inhabits there,—and they depart,
The infirm old man, and his fair household charge,
Seeking another home.—Home! who can tell
The touching power of that most sacred word,
Save he, who feels and weeps that he has none?
    Among that group of midnight exiles, fled
Young Mary Anna, on whose youthful cheek
But thirteen years had kindled up the rose.
A laughing creature, breathing heart and love,
Yet timid as the fawn in southern wilds.

E'en the night-reptile on the dewy grass
Startled the maiden, and the silent stars,
Looking so still from out their cloudy home,
Troubled her mind. No time was there for gauds
And toilette art, in this quick flight of fear;
Her glossy hair, damp'd by the midnight winds,
Lay on her neck dishevelled; gathered round
Her form in hurried folds clung her few garments;
Now a quick thrilling sob, half grief, half dread,
Came bursting from her heart,—and now her eyes
Glar'd forth, as peal'd the cannon; then beneath
Their drooping lids, sad tears redundant flowed.
    But sudden mid the group a cry arose,
"Fenwick! where is he?" None returned reply,
But a sharp piercing glance went out, around,
Keen as a mother's towards her infant child
When sudden danger lowers, and then a shriek
From one, from all burst forth— "He is not here!"
    Poor boy, he slept! nor crash of hurrying guns,
Nor impious curses, nor the warrior's shout,
Awoke his balmy rest! He dreamt such dreams
As float round childhood's couch, of angel faces
Peering through clouds;—of sunny rivulets,
Where the fresh stream flows rippling on, to waft
A tiny sail;—and of his rabbits white,
With eyes of ruby, and his tender fawn's
Long delicate limbs, light tread, and graceful neck.
He slept unconscious.—Who shall wake that sleep?
All shrink, for now th' artillery louder roars;—
The frightened slaves crouch at their master's side,
And he, infirm and feeble, scarce sustains
His sinking weight.
                There was a pause, a hush
So deep, that one could hear the forest leaves
Flutter and drop between the war-gun's peal.
Then forward stood that girl, young Mary Anna,
The tear dried up upon her cheek, the sob
Crushed down, and in that high and lofty tone
Which sometimes breathes of woman in the child,
She said, "He shall not die,"—and turned *alone.*
    Alone? O gentle girlhood, not alone

Art thou, if ONE watching above will guard
Thee on thy way.
            Clouds shrouded up the stars;—
On—on she sped, the gun's broad glare her beacon!
The wolf-growl sounded near,—on—onward still;
The forest trees like warning spirits moaned,—
She pressed her hands against her throbbing heart,
But faltered not. The whizzing shot went by,
Scarce heeded went.—Pass'd is a weary mile
With the light step a master-spirit gives
On duty's road, and she has reached her home.
Her home—is this her home, at whose fair gate
Stern foes in silence stand to bar her way?
That gate, which from her infant childhood leap'd
On its wide hinges, glad at her return?
Before the sentinels she trembling stood,
And with a voice, whose low and tender tones
Rose like the ring-dove's in midsummer storms,
She said,
    "Please let me pass, and seek a child,
Who in my father's mansion has been left
Sleeping, unconscious of the danger near."
  While thus she spake, a smile incredulous
Stole o'er the face of one,—the other cursed
And barr'd her from the way.
                "O, sirs," she cried,
While from her upraised eyes the tears stream'd down,
And her small hands were clasp'd in agony,
"Drive me not hence, I pray. Until to-night
I dared not stray beyond my nurse's side
In the dim twilight; yet I now have come
Alone, unguarded, this far dreary mile,
By darkness unappall'd;—a simple worm
Would often fright my heart, and bid it flutter,
But now I've heard the wild wolf's hungry howl
With soul undaunted—till to-night, I've shrunk
From men;—and soldiers! scarcely dared I look
Upon their glittering arms;—but here I come
And say to *you,* men, warriors;—drive me not
Away. He whom I seek is yet a child,
A prattling boy,—and must he, must he die?

Caroline

Howard

Gilman

&

45

O, if you love *your* children, let me pass.—
You will not? Then my strength and hope are gone,
And I shall perish, ere I reach my friends."
     And then she press'd her brow, as if those hands,
So soft and small, could still its throbbing pulse.
The sentinels looked calmly on, like men
Whose blades had toyed with sorrow, and made sport
Of woe. One step the maiden backward took,
Lingering in thought, then hope like a soft flush
Of struggling twilight kindled in her eyes.
She knelt before them and re-urged her plea.
     "Perchance you have a sister, sir, or you,
A poor young thing like me; if she were here
Kneeling like me before *my* countrymen,
They would not spurn her thus!"
          "Go, girl—pass on"—
The soften'd voice of one replied, nor was
She check'd, nor waited she to hear repulse,
But darted through the avenue, attained
The hall, and springing up the well known stairs,
With such a flight as the young eagle takes
To gain its nest, she reached the quiet couch,
Where in bright dreams th' unconscious sleeper lay.
Slight covering o'er the rescued boy she threw,
And caught him in her arms. He knew that cheek,
Kiss'd it half-waking, then around her neck
His hands entwined, and dropp'd to sleep again.
     She bore him onward, dreading now for him
The shot that whizz'd along, and tore the earth
In fragments by her side. She reached the guards,
Who silent oped the gate,—then hurried on,
But as she pass'd them, from her heart burst forth—
"God bless you, gentlemen!" then urged her way;
Those arms, whose heaviest load and task had been
To poise her doll, and wield her childhood's toys,
Bearing the boy along the dangerous road.
Voices at length she hears—her friends are near,
They meet, and yielding up her precious charge,
She sinks upon her father's breast, in doubt
'Twixt smiles and tears.

Note

1. Gilman added the following note to her Revolutionary War poem: "This authentic anecdote is related by Major Garden. It is poetry in itself, without the aid of measured language, but it is hoped its present form may extend the knowledge of this Carolina maiden among her countrymen. 'The gallant Lieutenant—Colonel Fenwich, so much distinguished for his services in the war of 1812, was the person saved.'"

5. Fanny Kemble

(1809–1893)

Although Fanny Kemble has often been labeled a southerner because of her well-known account of the plantation South, *Journal of a Residence on a Georgian Plantation,* she was actually born in London, grew up in a successful theatrical family, and was educated in Paris. When she was fifteen, Kemble returned to London and began her acting career as Juliet in her father's production of Shakespeare's *Romeo and Juliet.* Although Kemble preferred writing and music to acting, she was such an immediate success that many critics compared her ability to that of her aunt, Sarah Kemble Siddons, who was then considered the greatest Shakespearean actress of all time. When financial troubles forced Kemble's father to take the family on an American tour in 1832, Kemble became the first truly great actress that America had ever seen, gaining considerable popularity through her role as Julia in *The Hunchback.* Walt Whitman and Henry Wadsworth Longfellow were among her fondest admirers.

Just two years later, however, Kemble suddenly left the stage and married Pierce Butler, a Philadelphian who was heir to one of the largest plantations in Georgia. The couple moved to Georgia, where Kemble witnessed plantation life firsthand. Owing in part to her harsh criticism of America and to her demands for equality in marriage, Kemble's life with Butler was not an easy one. The publication of her *Journal of a Residence in America* (1835), which included her first criticism of slavery, increased the tension between the couple, as by this time her husband managed several Georgia plantations and hundreds of slaves. In 1846 Kemble left Butler and their two daughters to return to England, where she began writing poetry and acting again, but she lived most of her remaining years in the United States, giving public readings of Shakespeare and writing. Her most stunning work, *Journal of a Residence on a Georgian Plantation, 1838–1839* (1863), was published during this time; the journal was originally written for her close friend Elizabeth Sedgwick. The journal selection included here focuses on the brutal treatment of the slaves and gives an especially detailed description of the lives of slave women, forced not only to endure hard labor in the fields but also continually to bear children for both their husbands and masters.

Although shocking in its realistic portrayal of plantation life, the book sold very well, particularly in England, and is credited with encouraging the British to side with the North during the Civil War.

An extremely versatile writer, Kemble wrote five plays, including *Francis the First* (1832) and *The Star of Seville* (1837), before producing several volumes of poetry, which were generally well received. In her later life, when most of her time was spent with her daughters in the United States, she also published *Notes upon Some of Shakespeare's Plays* (1882). Kemble returned to London in the 1880s, enjoying herself mostly by traveling through Switzerland and visiting her sister in Italy. Just four years before her death, Kemble published her first novel, *Far Away and Long Ago* (1889), a work highly praised by Henry James. She died in London at age eighty-four.

Women in Slavery

Dear E——.

I cannot give way to the bitter impatience I feel at my present position, and come back to the north without leaving my babies; and though I suppose their stay will not in any case be much prolonged in these regions of swamp and slavery, I must, for their sakes, remain where they are, and learn this dreary lesson of human suffering to the end. The record, it seems to me, must be utterly wearisome to you, as the instances themselves I suppose in a given time (thanks to that dreadful reconciler to all that is evil—habit) would become to me.

This morning I had a visit from two of the women, Charlotte and Judy, who came to me for help and advice for a complaint, which it really seems to me every other woman on the estate is cursed with, and which is a direct result of the conditions of their existence; the practice of sending women to labour in the fields in the third week after their confinement is a specific for causing this infirmity, and I know no specific for curing it under these circumstances. As soon as these poor things had departed with such comfort as I could give them, and the bandages they especially begged for, three other sable graces introduced themselves, Edie, Louisa, and Diana; the former told me she had had a family of seven children, but had lost them all through "ill luck," as she denominated the ignorance and ill treatment which were answerable for the loss of these, as of so many other poor little creatures their fellows. Having dismissed her and Diana with the sugar and rice they came to beg, I detained Louisa, whom I had never seen but in the presence of her old grandmother, whose version of the poor child's escape to, and hiding in the woods, I had a desire to compare with the heroine's own story. She told it very simply, and it was most pathetic. She had not finished her task one day, when she said she felt ill, and unable to do so, and had been severely flogged by Driver Bran, in whose "gang" she then was. The next day, in spite of this encouragement to labour, she had again been unable to complete her appointed work; and Bran having told her that he'd tie her up and flog her if she did not get it done, she had left the field and run into the swamp. "Tie you up, Louisa!" said I, "what is that?" She then described to me that they were fastened up by their wrists to a beam or a branch of a tree, their feet barely touching the ground, so as to allow them no purchase for resistance or evasion of the lash, their clothes turned over their heads, and their backs scored with a leather thong, either by the driver himself, or if he pleases to inflict their punishment by deputy, any of the men he may choose to summon to the office; it might be father, brother, husband, or lover, if the overseer so ordered it. I turned sick, and my blood curdled listening to these details from the slender young slip of a lassie, with her poor piteous face and murmuring pleading voice. "Oh," said I, "Louisa; but the rattlesnakes, the dreadful rattlesnakes in the swamps; were you not afraid of those horrible creatures?" "Oh, missis," said the poor child, "me no tink of dem, me forget all 'bout dem for de fretting." "Why did you come home at last?" "Oh, missis, me starve with hunger, me most dead with hunger before me come back." "And were you flogged, Louisa?" said I, with a shudder at what the answer might be. "No, missus, me go to hospital; me almost dead and sick so long, 'spec Driver Bran him forgot 'bout de flogging." I am getting perfectly savage over all these doings, E——, and really think I should consider my own throat and those of my children well cut, if some night the people were to take it into their heads to clear off scores in that fashion.

The Calibanish wonderment of all my visitors and the exceedingly coarse and simple furniture and rustic means of comfort of my abode is very droll. I have never inhabited any apartment so perfectly devoid of what we should consider the common decencies of life; but to them my rude chintz-covered sofa and common pine-wood table, with its green baize cloth, seem the adornings of a palace; and often in the evening, when my bairns are asleep, and M—— up-stairs keeping watch over them, and I sit writing this daily history for your edification,—the door of the great barn-like room is opened stealthily, and one after another, men and women come trooping silently in, their naked feet falling all but inaudibly on the bare boards as they betake themselves to the hearth, where they squat down on their hams in a circle,—the bright blaze from the huge pine logs, which is the only light of this half of the room, shining on their sooty limbs and faces, and making them look like a ring of ebony idols surrounding my domestic hearth. I have had as many as fourteen at a time squatting silently there for nearly half an hour, watching me writing at the other end of the room. The candles on my table give only light enough for my own occupation, the fire light illuminates the rest of the apartment; and you cannot imagine anything stranger than the effect of all these glassy whites of eyes and grinning white teeth turned towards me, and shining in the flickering light. I very often take no notice of them at all, and they seem perfectly absorbed in contemplating me. My evening dress probably excites their wonder and admiration no less than my rapid and continuous writing, for which they have sometimes expressed compassion, as if they thought it must be more laborious than hoeing; sometimes at the end of my day's journal I look up and say suddenly, "Well, what do you want?" when each black figure springs up at once, as if moved by machinery, they all answer, "Me come say ha do (how d'ye do), missis;" and then they troop out as noiselessly as they entered, like a procession of sable dreams, and I go off in search, if possible, of whiter ones.

Two days ago I had a visit of great interest to me from several lads from twelve to sixteen years old, who had come to beg me to give them work. To make you understand this you must know, that wishing very much to cut some walks and drives through the very picturesque patches of woodland not far from the house, I announced, through Jack, my desire to give employment in the wood-cutting line, to as many lads as chose, when their unpaid task was done, to come and do some work for me, for which I engaged to pay them. At the risk of producing a most dangerous process of reflection and calculation in their brains, I have persisted in paying what I considered wages to every slave that has been my servant; and these my labourers must, of course, be free to work or no, as they like, and if they work for me must be paid by me. The proposition met with unmingled approbation from my "gang;" but I think it might be considered dangerously suggestive of the rightful relation between work and wages; in short, very involuntarily no doubt, but, nevertheless, very effectually I am disseminating ideas among Mr. ——'s dependents, the like of which have certainly never before visited their wool-thatched brains.

Friday, March 1.—Last night after writing so much to you I felt weary, and went out into the air to refresh my spirit. The scene just beyond the house was beautiful, the moonlight slept on the broad river which here is almost the sea, and on the masses of foliage of the great southern oaks; the golden stars of German poetry shone in the purple curtains of the night, and the measured rush of the Atlantic unfurling its huge skirts upon the white sands of the beach (the sweetest and most awful lullaby in nature) resounded through the silent air.

I have not felt well, and have been much depressed for some days past. I think I should die if I had to live here. This morning, in order not to die yet, I thought I had better take a ride, and accordingly mounted the horse which I told you was one of the equestrian alternatives offered me here; but no sooner did he feel my weight, which, after all, is mere levity and frivolity to him, than he thought proper to rebel, and find the grasshopper a burthen, and rear and otherwise demonstrate his disgust. I have not ridden for a long time now, but Montreal's opposition very presently aroused the Amazon which is both natural and acquired in me, and I made him comprehend that, though I object to slaves, I expect obediant servants; which views of mine being imparted by a due administration of both spur and whip, attended with a judicious combination of coaxing pats on his great crested neck, and endearing commendations of his beauty, produced the desired effect. Montreal accepted me as inevitable, and carried me very wisely and well up the island to another of the slave settlements on the plantation, called Jones's Creek.

On my way I passed some magnificent evergreen oaks, and some thickets of exquisite evergreen shrubs, and one or two beautiful sites for a residence, which made me gnash my teeth when I thought of the one we have chosen. To be sure, these charming spots, instead of being conveniently in the middle of the plantation, are at an out of the way end of it, and so hardly eligible for the one quality desired for the overseer's abode, viz. being central.

All the slaves' huts on St. Simon's are far less solid, comfortable, and habitable than those at the rice-island. I do not know whether the labourer's habitation bespeaks the alteration in the present relative importance of the crops, but certainly the cultivators of the once far-famed long staple sea-island cotton of St. Simon's are far more miserably housed than the rice-raisers of the other plantation. These ruinous shielings, that hardly keep out wind or weather, are deplorable homes for young or aged people, and poor shelters for the hard-working men and women who cultivate the fields in which they stand. Riding home I passed some beautiful woodland with charming pink and white blossoming peach and plum trees, which seemed to belong to some orchard that had been attempted, and afterwards delivered over to wildness. On enquiry I found that no fruit worth eating was ever gathered from them. What a pity it seems! for in this warm delicious winter climate any and every species of fruit might be cultivated with little pains and to great perfection. As I was cantering along the side of one of the cotton fields I suddenly heard some inarticulate vehement cries, and saw what seemed to be a heap of black limbs tumbling and leaping towards me, renewing the screams at intervals as it approached. I stopped my horse, and the black ball bounded almost into the road before me, and suddenly straightening itself up into a haggard hag of a half-naked negress, exclaimed, with panting eager breathlessness, "Oh missis, missis! you no hear me cry, you no hear me call. Oh missis! me call, me cry, and me run; make me a gown like dat. Do, for massy's sake, only make me a gown like dat." This modest request for a riding habit in which to hoe the cotton fields served for an introduction to sundry other petitions for rice and sugar and flannel, all which I promised the petitioner, but not the "gown like dat;" whereupon I rode off, and she flung herself down in the middle of the road to get her wind and rest.

The passion for dress is curiously strong in these people, and seems as though it might be made an instrument in converting them, outwardly at any rate, to something like civilisation; for though their own native taste is decidedly both barbarous and ludicrous, it is astonishing how very soon they mitigate it in imitation of their white models. The fine figures of the mulatto women in Charleston and Savannah are frequently as elegantly and tastefully dressed as those of any of their female superiors; and here on St. Simon's, owing, I suppose, to the influence of the resident lady proprietors of the various plantations, and the propensity to imitation in their black dependents, the people that I see all seem to me much tidier, cleaner, and less fantastically dressed than those on the rice plantation, where no such influences reach them.

On my return from my ride I had a visit from Captain F——, the manager of a neighbouring plantation, with whom I had a long conversation about the present and past condition of the estate, the species of feudal magnificence in which its original owner, Major——, lived, the iron rule of old overseer K—— which succeeded to it, and the subsequent sovereignty of his son, Mr. R—— K——, the man for whom Mr.—— entertains such a cordial esteem, and of whom every account I receive from the negroes seems to me to indicate a merciless sternness of disposition that may be a virtue in a slave-driver, but is hardly a Christian grace. Captain F—— was one of our earliest visitors at the rice plantation on our arrival, and I think I told you of his mentioning, in speaking to me of the orange trees which formerly grew all round the dykes there, that he had taken Basil Hall there once in their blossoming season, and that he had said the sight was as well worth crossing the Atlantic for as Niagara. Today he referred to that again. He has resided for a great many years on a plantation here, and is connected with our neighbour, old Mr. C——, whose daughter, I believe, he married. He interested me extremely by his description of the house Major —— had many years ago on a part of the island called St. Clair. As far as I can understand there must have been an indefinite number of "master's" residences on this estate in the old Major's time; for what with the one we are building, and the ruined remains of those not quite improved off the face of the earth, and the tradition of those that have ceased to exist, even as ruins, I make out no fewer than seven. How gladly would I exchange all that remain and all that do not, for the smallest tenement in your blessed Yankee mountain village!

Captain F—— told me that at St. Clair General Oglethorpe, the good and brave English governor of the State of Georgia in its colonial days, had his residence, and that among the magnificent live oaks which surround the site of the former settlement, there was one especially venerable and picturesque, which in his recollection always went by the name of General Oglethorpe's Oak. If you remember the history of the colony under his benevolent rule, you must recollect how absolutely he and his friend and counsellor, Wesley,[1] opposed the introduction of slavery in the colony. How wrathfully the old soldier's spirit ought to haunt these cotton fields and rice swamps of his old domain, with their population of wretched slaves! I will ride to St. Clair and see his oak; if I should see him, he cannot have much to say to me on the subject that I should not cry amen to.

Note
1. John Wesley (1703–1791) founded the Methodist Church.

6. Susan Petigru King Bowen

(1824–1875)

Born in Charleston, Susan Petigru King Bowen has been described as South Carolina's best antebellum novelist. Her father was a famous antebellum lawyer who passed on to his daughter his quick wit and ease of speaking and writing; one of her literary admirers was William Thackeray. The fashionable social life of Charleston found the young Susan Petigru at its center and in turn gave her considerable material for her writing. In 1843, at the age of nineteen, she married Captain Henry C. King of Charleston, son of her father's law partner, and began her writing career shortly after.

Bowen's work is set in both the city and on the plantation. Her subjects often focus on love affairs and all their complications, and though they tend toward the romantic and sentimental, Bowen is noted for her psychological realism, which often resembles that of Henry James. She demonstrated considerable mastery of technique, for she consistently produced sharp and witty dialogue and vivid portrayals of characters. The 1850s were Bowen's most productive years; she published *Busy Moments of an Idle Woman* (1854), her somewhat autobiographical novel *Lily* (1855), and a collection of two short stories and a novella, *Sylvia's World; and, Crimes Which the Law Does Not Reach* (1859). "A Marriage of Persuasion" is included in the latter volume, but it was originally published in *Russell's Magazine* in 1857, a six-volume periodical for which Bowen wrote most of the fiction. This story, representing the realism that Bowen shares with James and Twain, studies conflicting motivations for marriage in a situation that forces a young woman into a loveless relationship. At the end of the story, the narrative voice takes on a decidedly didactic tone and asks us to consider what has become of a young, vibrant woman who now seems a "grand automaton."

Henry King was killed during the Civil War in the Battle of Secessionville. In 1873 Susan married Christopher Columbus Bowen, a U.S. representative from South Carolina from 1868 to 1874. Though many historians consider him a dishonest villain, Susan apparently worked with her husband throughout their marriage, publishing a weekly newspaper in support of his political endeavors. Bowen lived in South Carolina until her death in 1875.

A Marriage of Persuasion

"And so you refused him?"

"Yes, mamma."

"Without one word of hope?"

"Not one."

"Harshly? rudely?"

"I trust not. Finally and positively, I certainly did."

"Anna! I can't forgive you."

"My dear mamma, what have I done?"

"What have you done? Refused an excellent man; one whom any mother would be proud to see as her daughter's husband. Sent from the house the best friend I have—deprived us of our mainstay and support—insulted him—and—destroyed the great hope of my life!" The tears streamed from Mrs. Mansfield's eyes. She drew away her hand from her daughter's clasp, and tried to leave the room. Anna detained her.

"Dearest mother! you cannot be more grieved than I am. Mr. Gordon is a very worthy man—he has been a kind friend to us in adversity—he is, I believe, truly sincere in his love for me, and I regret very deeply that it should have brought us to this pass. I have not wounded him further than I could help, I assure you. He will return to visit us in his usual way, after a while; indeed, I hope to see so little change in our intercourse, that I would have spared you the annoyance of knowing this, had he not expressly desired that I should tell you."

"Ah, he is a forgiving and generous creature; a true Christian. Such a man as that to be so treated!"

Anna was silent.

"Anna," resumed her mother, with sudden energy, after a moment's pause, "do you love any one else? have you formed some absurd attachment which interferes with Mr. Gordon's undeniable claim to your affections?"

Miss Mansfield's noble and expressive face was calmly lifted to her mother's heated and excited gaze.

"No, mamma," she simply answered.

"Then, *why* can't you marry Mr. Gordon, and make me happy?"

"Because," and Anna's voice was firm, decided and honest. "Because I do not love him, and to marry him would make me very unhappy."

"Selfish as ever!" ejaculated Mrs. Mansfield. "Will you tell me what you dislike in him?" she pursued.

"I did not say I disliked Mr. Gordon, mamma."

"What you don't like, then? Why you don't love him?"

Anna smiled faintly. "Dear mamma! is there not a great difference between liking and being in love?"

"You are trifling with me most disrespectfully. Is it not enough that I should suffer this disappointment at your hands, and can you not spare me this beating about the bush? I wish a plain answer to a plain question. Is there anything about Mr. Gordon especially disagreeable to you? If so, what is it?"

"Nothing especially disagreeable, as a friend—as a man whom one sees three or four times a week; but as a husband, several things."

"May I, as only your mother—of course a very insignificant creature to wish or have your confidence—ask these several things?"

"In the first place, then, his appearance is not attractive to me."

"Gracious heaven!" cried Mrs. Mansfield, starting up; "do I live to hear my daughter express such a sentiment! His appearance! Do you not know that to think of such an objection is—the—the—very reverse

of modest? Where have you got such ideas? To a truly virtuous woman, what are a man's looks? I might expect such an objection from a girl of low mind and vicious ideas, but not from Anna Mansfield. So this is your reason for not marrying an excellent, kind—"

"Not my only one, mamma," Anna interrupted gently; "it is one of them, but not the greatest. I named it first because it is, I think, very important; and I cannot see the impropriety which strikes you." A slight blush rose to her cheek, as she continued, "I should not like to engage myself to pass my life with a man whose attentions would be repulsive to me, if he had the right to take my hand—or—excuse me, mamma, I don't like to say any more on this point;" and then as the color deepened, she added in a lower voice, "You saw Frederick yesterday put his arm around Maria's waist, as he lifted her from the saddle; and, not caring for the presence of you, his aunt, and us, his cousins, he—a bridegroom of three months—he kissed her pretty blooming cheek, and drew her close to him. She blushed, and said, 'don't Fred,' but evidently was not displeased. Now, could I endure?—Oh, mamma, pray don't talk about it. It makes me ill. I have named one of the smallest, and at the same time one of the greatest objections. Why dwell upon a difference of opinion, in many essential cases—a total want of congeniality—sympathy— taste, when this trivial reason (provided he possessed the others) is in itself so strong? Dear mamma, don't be angry—don't be disappointed. You would not wish to make me truly miserable? Perhaps in a year or two, Sally may be Mr. Gordon's choice; and Sally may take him as her beau ideal. Why do you want to get rid of me so soon?"

"Ah, my dear," said Mrs. Mansfield, "you know how poor we are now. Here I am with you four girls, and an income not much larger than in your dear father's time I spent upon my own dress. Is it wonderful that I long to see you settled? Heaven knows that I am not one of those mercenary mothers who would give their children to any man with money. No, indeed. I would not be so wicked. But when a gentleman like Norman Gordon—an honorable, trustworthy, generous creature—wishes to become my son, do you wonder that I should desire it too? I knew his father before him—I knew his mother—all good people; it is good blood, my child—the best dependence in the world. You are nearly twenty years old, and there are three younger than you; how can I help being anxious? And I who know what 'love-matches' are—how many a girl goes to her ruin by that foolish idea; marrying some boy in haste, and repenting at leisure—children—no money—bills to pay—oh! my dear Anna, where is the love then?"

"Mamma, am I making or thinking of making any such match?"

"But you may do it. I want to save you from this. I have a horror of these romantic 'love-matches.'"

"Did you not love my father, mamma?" Anna asked, in a low voice.

"Of course I did. All women should love their husbands. All proper, well-regulated women do love their husbands."

"And yet you wish me to marry without love!"

"Love comes after marriage—every woman with good principles loves her husband. She makes the best of her bargain. Life is a lottery, and if you draw a prize or a blank, you must accept it as it is and be satisfied. Then, when a woman has sworn, in the face of God and man, 'to love, honor and obey' her husband, how can she reconcile herself to not doing it?"

"But, if she should not? if she finds it impossible? Oh, think of that, mamma. Think of vowing solemnly in the face of heaven—and breaking one's oath! Swearing to love, where you feel indifference—promising to honor, where you see little to respect—and vowing to obey, where your reason tells you there is no judgment to make obedience possible! Taking upon your shoulders, *for life,* a burden you cannot bear, and which it is a crime to struggle under, or to cast aside!"

"You know nothing about it, Anna," Mrs. Mansfield said impatiently; "it is not proper for a young girl to think and speak in this wild way. Your mother is here to guide and direct you. No good ever comes of a child arguing and setting herself up in this manner, to teach those older and wiser than herself. The Bible says, 'Honor thy father and thy mother'—it don't say, 'dispute with them.' I tell you what I heard from *my* mother, and what every right-minded person knows. 'Make a good choice in life; marry, and love will come afterward.' Love comes with the—never mind. I will not say any more now. I hope sincerely you have been careful of poor Norman's feelings. But you are not apt to do that. You have lacerated mine enough, Heaven knows."

"Oh, mamma! when—how?"

"In this business. When it would be so easy for you to make us all happy, and you prefer your own notions, and willfully act up to them."

A flush of transient anger and indignation swept gustily over Miss Mansfield's face; but she conquered the emotion, and playfully taking a volume from a book-stand near, said, with perfect good homor, and meaningly, "May I read 'Clarissa Harlowe,' mamma?"

"No, put it down, Anna, and don't bother me with any further nonsense."

The daughter obediently withdrew, glad to escape so painful and so disagreeable an interview.

But although this was the first, it was by no means the last of such conversations. Every day the subject was renewed, but gradually Mrs. Mansfield changed her tactics. She no longer scolded or insisted; her reproaches were silent looks of misery—pathetic appeals to heaven "to grant her patience under her afflictions." She was very affectionate to her daughter—heart-rendingly so. Anna was called upon constantly to notice what a tender parent she was distressing. Each necessary privation in their reduced household (the father's honorable failure and death had brought them from affluence to comparative poverty,) was prologued and epilogued by sighs and suggestions. "If only Anna could"—and then a sudden pause and deep respiration.

"My own dear child," Mrs. Mansfield would sometimes say; "how I wish you had a new dress. That brown silk is very shabby; but we cannot, with our limited means, buy another, and yet I saw Jane Berryman sneering at it, with her flounced skirts spreading a mile behind her."

"Indeed, mamma, I don't care for Jane Berryman's sneers. It is very good of you to be anxious about it, but I think the old brown very becoming."

The next day a rich plaid silk, glossy and fresh, lay upon Anna's bed. "I could not stand it, my dear," said Mrs. Mansfield. "I must do without a new cloak this winter. A mother would rather starve with cold than see her daughter less handsomely dressed than she ought to be. Nothing is a sacrifice to *me*, for *you*, Anna."

In vain poor Anna protested and tried to return the silk, and exchange it for the very necessary cloak, whose purchase was now impossible. Mrs. Mansfield positively forbade her, and the thin black shawl which covered the widow's last year's bombazine was worn with a prolonged shiver, whenever Anna was near enough to hear and see.

Mr. Gordon soon returned to pay his usual visits—to offer his usual attentions—to make his usual presents, at stated times, of things which could permissibly be tendered. The visits Mrs. Mansfield received with great delight—the attentions were allowed; but the first basket of winter produce which arrived from Mr. Gordon's farm, she requested decidedly should be the last.

Clara, the youngest girl, a child of seven, cried lustily because her mamma said "These will be the last potatoes we shall ever eat." From the solemnity of the tone, the little thing fancied that potatoes—a very important item in her daily consumption—were tabooed forever. She desisted when she found that it was only the potatoes from the Gordon farm that fell under the restriction.

Day by day, week after week, this persecution continued. It was the unceasing drop of water that "stayed not itself" for a single instant. In despair, Anna went to consult an aunt, whose opinion she highly valued—whose principles were undoubted—an exemplary wife and mother, and a kind friend always to her niece. Anna recited her woes. "What must I do to escape this torment, my dear Aunt Mary? I feel and know my duty to mamma, I trust; but this life is wearing me out."

Aunt Mary smiled.

"And you don't like Mr. Gordon, dear?"

"I now detest him."

"Oh, for shame! How can you say so? Indeed, my child, I cannot but agree with your mother. This is an excellent match; and it seems to me that if you have no positive objection against his character and standing, you ought to reconsider Mr. Gordon's proposal."

"But, don't you understand that I don't in the least care for the man, except as an ordinary acquaintance. He is well enough as he is; but, do you too advocate a marriage made on such a foundation?"

"Anna! a love-match makes no marriage of love."

"*Violà une chanson dont je connais l'air!*" said Anna, smiling bitterly in her turn. "You will all force me to marry this man, actually to get rid of him."

"Well, you could not do a better thing, I think."

Anna returned home disconsolately; returned to the same wearying, petty, incessant, pin pricks, unencouraged by a single word. With all her affection for her mother, she could not but see her weakness in most cases; but on her aunt's judgment she relied, and what had been the result of the interview?—a decided approval of Mrs. Mansfield's wishes.

Let those who blame Anna Mansfield for her next step, pray to be kept from the same pit-fall. This is a mere sketch; but an outline to which all who choose may fill up the hints given. Those who believe that *they* would have been steadfast to the end, will have my admiration, if, when their day of trial comes, they hold firmly to the right; but—as we look around, have we not cause to think that there are many Mrs. Mansfields, and, alas! many Annas?

There came an evening, at length, when on Miss Mansfield's finger shone a great diamond, which dazzled tiny Clara's eyes and made her uncognizant of the tears in her sister's, as she asked wonderingly, "Where did you get such a beau-ti-ful ring?"

Mrs. Mansfield triumphantly said, "That is a secret, Clara."

"No secret for you, my little darling," Anna answered very low and gravely. "Mr. Gordon gave it to me as a pledge that I am to marry him."

"Do you love him, Annie?" Clara said, swallowing her surprise, with great, open, childish eyes.

"Don't ask foolish questions, Clara," her mother cried angrily. But the tears now rolled down the elder sister's white cheek, and she held the little girl close to her bosom, as she whispered, "you shall come and live with me, my own, and when you marry, I will not need, if God helps me, to ask *you* that question."

The day came—hurried on—and Anna Mansfield was Mrs. Norman Gordon. She was the owner of houses and lands—gold and silver—a perjured conscience and a bleeding heart. Very fine possessions were they, truly, and very proud Mrs. Mansfield was and is, of the hand she had in this righteous barter.

I see Mrs. Gordon frequently; she is very pale and cold, and kind. She has no children—Clara does live with her. Mr. Gordon is not happy, evidently; he has nothing to complain of in his wife. She is scrupulously polite to him, but there is not an atom of sympathy between them. He is prejudiced, uncultivated; and now that he has her, is terribly afraid of being ruled by her. It is a joyless household, and a very rich one. I watch Mrs. Mansfield's greedy gaze lighten broader and broader as the blaze of plate—the measured footfall of a train of servants—the luxurious profusion of their constant service, are spread out before her. She treads the "velvet pile" of carpets with a happy step, and adores her daughter's noble brow, when she sees shimmering upon it—reflecting a thousand lights—the mass of brilliants that binds, in its costly clasp, the struggling thoughts of what was once Anna Mansfield.

So we leave them. What of the end of all this? Is this grand automaton really dead, or does a heart, young and still untouched, lurk—strong, free and dangerous—in that quiet, unmoved and stately figure?

7. Sarah Grimké

(1792–1873)

Sarah Moore Grimké was born in Charleston, South Carolina, thirteen years before her youngest sister, Angelina, who, like Sarah, would become an outspoken proponent of the rights of women and blacks. The Grimké sisters were born into a prominent Episcopal family to parents who were strong supporters of the Old South tradition; the girls' father was a lieutenant colonel in the Revolutionary War and a chief justice of South Carolina, and he educated his children to be upholders of southern society. However, Sarah and Angelina both openly rebelled against their southern heritage, especially its support of slavery. Sarah left home first to move to Philadelphia and became a Quaker; Angelina followed her sister north soon after. Neither sister would ever live in the South again after 1829.

Despite the promise that a move north entailed for the sisters, they both quickly grew impatient with the Quakers' moderate views on slavery. Sarah and Angelina decided to condemn slavery publicly, a move that was unprecedented for women of their upbringing. The sisters quickly joined the lecture circuit, speaking out for the abolitionist movement.

Sarah's first publication, a pamphlet entitled *An Epistle to the Clergy of the Southern States* (1836), argues that if God created all men equal, a conflict exists between Christianity and slavery. That same year, Angelina published *Appeal to the Christian Women of the South* (1836). The pamphlet was met with severe hostility, for, in effect, it called women to civil disobedience, encouraging them to free their slaves and petition for emancipation. Angelina was warned never to return to Charleston; most of the pamphlets were destroyed as soon as they reached the South.

Angelina's most significant speech was presented in 1838 before a committee of Massachusetts legislators on the subject of slavery. Sarah was originally scheduled to give the speech but was kept away by illness; therefore, in front of the legislators and hundreds of spectators, Angelina became the first woman ever to address a legislative body in the United States. As they continued their lecturing in New England, the Grimké sisters were repeatedly attacked for their "unladylike" behavior.

Such criticism prompted them to add women's rights to their agenda; thus they became the first American women advocates of both abolitionism and women's rights. Adding the fight for women's rights to their platform, the sisters advocated that women were equal to men and so had an equal responsibility to fight for sexual and racial equality.

In her letters to Mary S. Parker, president of the Boston Female Anti-Slavery Society, Sarah Grimké continues the fight against slavery by focusing on the white woman's role in bringing about its end. The first significant statement supporting women's rights by an American woman, the letter anthologized here from *Letters on the Equality of the Sexes and the Condition of Woman, Addressed to Mary S. Parker, President of the Boston Female Anti-Slavery Society* (1838) emphasizes Grimké's interest in feminist issues. In the first letter, "The Original Equality of Women," Grimké carefully studies the creation story in Genesis to prove that there is no biblical basis for regarding women as subordinate to men. She extends this argument in Letter 8, "On the Condition of Women in the United States," by stressing the importance of education for women in improving inequalities, racial as well as social. Having grown up among what she describes as the "butterflies of the fashionable world," Grimké concludes that the traditional education of southern women was "miserably deficient."

The sisters ended their New England tour in 1838 with a lecture in Boston, attended by thousands. Later that year, Angelina married the man who had inspired and encouraged her for years, Theodore Weld, and two days later she gave her last speech in Philadelphia before a stone-throwing mob. Soon after, the Grimké sisters moved with Weld to New Jersey. They published *American Slavery As It Is* (1839) before retiring from active abolitionist work in 1840. Sarah Grimké spent the remainder of her life teaching in schools that she founded with her sister and brother-in-law. She died in 1873 in Hyde Park, Massachusetts.

From *Letters on the Equality of the Sexes and the Condition of Woman, Addressed to Mary S. Parker, President of the Boston Female Anti-Slavery Society* (Letter 8)

Brookline, [Mass.] 1837.

My Dear Sister,—

I have now taken a brief survey of the condition of women in various parts of the world. I regret that my time has been so much occupied by other things, that I have been unable to bestow that attention upon the subject which it merits, and that my constant change of place has prevented me from having access to books, which might probably have assisted me in this part of my work. I hope that the principles I have asserted will claim the attention of some of my sex, who may be able to bring into view, more thoroughly than I have done, the situation and degredation of woman. I shall now proceed to make a few remarks on the condition of women in my own country.

During the early part of my life, my lot was cast among the butterflies of the *fashionable* world; and of this class of women, I am constrained to say, both from experience and observation, that their education is miserably deficient; that they are taught to regard marriage as the one thing needful, the only avenue to distinction; hence to attract the notice and win the attentions of men, by their external charms, is the chief business of fashionable girls. They seldom think that men will be allured by intellectual acquirements, because they find, that where any mental superiority exists, a woman is generally shunned and regarded as stepping out of her "appropriate sphere," which, in their view, is to dress, to dance, to set out to the best possible advantage her person, to read the novels which inundate the press, and which do more to destroy her character as a rational creature, than any thing else. Fashionable women regard themselves, and are regarded by men, as pretty toys or as mere instruments of pleasure; and the vacuity of mind, the heartlessness, the frivolity which is the necessary result of this false and debasing estimate of women, can only be fully understood by those who have mingled in the folly and wickedness of fashionable life; and who have been called from such pursuits by the voice of the Lord Jesus, inviting their weary and heavy laden souls to come unto Him and learn of Him, that they may learn the high and holy purposes of their creation, and consecrate themselves unto the service of God; and not, as is now the case, to the pleasure of man.

There is another and much more numerous class in this country, who are withdrawn by education or circumstances from the circle of fashionable amusements, but who are brought up with the dangerous and absurd idea, that *marriage* is a kind of preferment; and that to be able to keep their husband's house, and render his situation comfortable, is the end of her being. Much that she does and says and thinks is done in reference to this situation; and to be married is too often held up to the view of girls as the sine qua non of human happiness and human existence. For this purpose more than for any other, I verily believe the majority of girls are trained. This is demonstrated by the imperfect education which is bestowed upon them, and the little pains taken to cultivate their minds, after they leave school, by the little time allowed them for reading, and by the idea being constantly inculcated, that although all household concerns should be attended to with scrupulous punctuality at particular seasons, the improvement of their intellectual capacities is only a secondary consideration, and may serve as an occupation to fill up the odds and ends of time. In most families, it is considered a matter of far more consequence to call a girl off from making a pie, or a pudding, than to interrupt her whilst engaged in her studies. This mode of training necessarily exalts, in their view, the animal above the intellectual and spiritual nature, and teaches women to regard themselves as a kind of machinery, necessary to keep the domestic engine in order, but of little value as the *intelligent* companions of men.

Let no one think, from these remarks, that I regard a knowledge of housewifery as beneath the acquisition of women. Far from it: I believe that a complete knowledge of household affairs is an indispensable requisite in a woman's education,—that by the mistress of a family, whether married or single, doing her duty thoroughly and *understandingly,* the happiness of the family is increased to an incalculable degree, as well as a vast amount of time and money saved. All I complain of is, that our education consists so almost exclusively in culinary and other manual operations. I do long to see the time, when it will no longer be necessary for women to spend so many hours in furnishing "a well spread table," but that their husbands will forego some of the accustomed indulgences in this way, and encourage their wives to devote some portion of their time to mental cultivation, even at the expense of having to dine sometimes on baked potatoes, or bread and butter.

I believe the sentiment expressed by the author of "Live and Let Live,"[1] is true:

> Other things being equal, a woman of the highest mental endowments will always be the best housekeeper, for domestic economy, is a science that brings into action the qualities of the mind, as well as the graces of the heart. A quick perception, judgment, discrimination, decision and order are high attributes of mind, and all are in a daily exercise in the well ordering of a family. If a sensible woman, an intellectual woman, a woman of genius, is not a good housewife, it is not because she is either, or all of those, but because there is some deficiency in her character, or some omission of duty which should make her very humble, instead of her indulging in any secret self-complacency on account of a certain superiority, which only aggravates her fault.

The influence of women over the minds and character of *children* of both sexes, is allowed to be far greater than that of men. This being the case by the very ordering of nature, women should be prepared by education for the performance of their sacred duties as mothers and as sisters. A late American writer, speaking on this subject,[2] says in reference to an article in the Westminster Review:

> I agree entirely with the writer in the high estimate which he places on female education, and have long since been satisfied, that the subject not only merits, but imperiously demands a thorough reconsideration. The whole scheme must, in my opinion, be reconstructed. The great elements of usefulness and duty are too little attended to. Women ought, in my view of the subject, to approach to the best education now given to men, (I except mathematics and the classics,) far more I believe than has ever yet been attempted. Give me a host of educated, pious mothers and sisters, and I will do more to revolutionize a country, in moral and religious taste, in manners and in social virtues and intellectual cultivation, than I can possibly do, in double or treble the time, with a similar host of educated men. I cannot but think that the miserable condition of the great body of the people in all ancient communities, is to be ascribed in a very great degree to the degradation of women.

There is another way in which the general opinion, that women are inferior to men, is manifested, that bears with tremendous effect on the laboring class, and indeed on almost all who are obliged to earn a subsistence, whether it be by mental or physical exertion—I allude to the disproportionate value set on the time and labor of men and of women. A man who is engaged in teaching, can always, I believe, command a higher price for tuition than a woman—even when he teaches the same branches, and is not in any respect superior to the woman. This I know is the case in boarding and other schools with which I have been acquainted, and it is so in every occupation in which the sexes engaged indiscriminately. As for example, in tailoring, a man has twice, or three times as much for making a waistcoat or pantaloons as a woman, although the work done by each may be equally good. In those employments which are peculiar to women, their time is estimated at only half the value of that of men. A woman who goes out to wash, works as hard in proportion as a wood sawyer, or a coal heaver, but she is not generally able to make more than half as much by a day's work. The low remuneration which women receive for their work, has claimed the attention of a few philanthropists, and I hope it will continue to do so until some remedy is applied for this enormous evil. I have known a widow, left with four or five children, to provide for, unable to leave home because her helpless babes demanded her attention, compelled to earn a scanty subsistence, by making coarse shirts at 12 ½ cents a piece, or by taking in washing, for which she was paid by some wealthy persons 12 ½ cents per dozen. All these things evince the low estimation in which woman is held. There is yet another and more disastrous consequence arising from this unscriptural notion—women being educated, from earliest childhood, to regard themselves as inferior creatures, have not that self-respect which conscious equality would engender, and hence when their virtue is assailed, they yield to temptation with facility, under the idea that it rather exalts than debases them, to be connected with a superior being.

There is another class of women in this country, to whom I cannot refer, without feelings of the deepest shame and sorrow. I allude to our female slaves. Our southern cities are whelmed beneath a tide of pollution; the virtue of female slaves is wholly at the mercy of irresponsible tyrants, and women are bought and sold in our slave markets, to gratify the brutal lust of those who bear the name of Christians. In our slave States, if amid all her degredation and ignorance, a woman desires to preserve her virtue unsullied, she is either bribed or whipped into compliance, or if she dares resist her seducer, her life by the laws of some of the slave States may be, and has actually been sacrificed to the fury of disappointed passion. Where such laws do not exist, the power which is necessarily vested in the master over his property, leaves the defenceless slave entirely at his mercy, and the sufferings of some females on this account, both physical and mental, are intense. Mr. [James H.] Gholson [New Brunswick County], in the House of Delegates of Virginia, in 1832, said, "He really had been under the impression that he owned his slaves. He had lately purchased four women and ten children, in whom he thought he had obtained a great bargain; for he supposed they were his own property, *as were his brood mares.*" But even if any laws existed in the United States, as in Athens formerly, for the protection of female slaves, they would be null and void, because the evidence of a colored person is not admitted against a white, in any of our Courts of Justice in the slave States. "In Athens, if a female slave had cause to complain of any want of respect to the laws of modesty, she could seek the protection of the temple, and demand a change of owners; and such appeals were never discountenanced, or neglected by the magistrate." In Christian America, the slave has no refuge from unbridled cruelty and lust.

S. A. Forrall, speaking of the state of morals at the South, says, "Negresses when young and likely, are often employed by the planter, or his friends, to administer to their sensual desires. This frequently is a matter of speculation, for if the offspring, a mulatto, be a handsome female, 800 or 1000 dollars may be obtained for her in the New Orleans market. It is an occurrence of no uncommon nature to see a Christian father sell his own daughter, and the brother his own sister." The following is copied by the N. Y. Evening Star from the Picayune, a paper published in New Orleans. "A very beautiful girl, belonging to the estate of John French, a deceased gambler at new Orleans, was sold a few days since for the round sum of $7,000. An ugly-looking bachelor named Gouch, a member of the Council of one of the Principalities, was the purchaser. The girl is a brunette; remarkable for her beauty and intelligence, and there was considerable contention, who should be the purchaser. She was, however, persuaded to accept Gouch, he having made her princely promises." I will add but one more from the numerous testimonies respecting the degredation of female slaves, and the licentiousness of the South. It is from the Circular of the Kentucky Union, for the moral and religious improvement of the colored race. "To the female character among our black population, we cannot allude but with feelings of the bitterest shame. A similar condition of moral pollution and utter disregard of a pure and virtuous reputation, is to be found *only without the pale of Christendom.* That such a state of society should exist in a Christian nation, claiming to be the most enlightened upon earth, without calling forth any *particular attention* to its existence, though ever before our eyes and *in our* families, is a moral phenomenon at once unaccountable and disgraceful." Nor does the colored woman suffer alone: the moral purity of the white woman is deeply contaminated. In the daily habit of seeing the virtue of her enslaved sister sacrificed without hesitancy or remorse, she looks upon the crimes of seduction and illicit intercourse without horror, and although not personally involved in the guilt, she loses that value for innocence in her own, as well as the other sex, which is one of the strongest safeguards to virtue. She lives in habitual intercourse with men, whom she knows to be polluted by licentiousness, and often is she compelled to witness in her own domestic circle, those disgusting and heart-sickening jealousies and strifes which disgraced and distracted the family of Abraham. In addition to all this, the female slaves suffer every species of degradation and cruelty, which the most wanton barbarity can inflict; they are indecently divested of their clothing, sometimes tied up and severely whipped, sometimes prostrated on the earth, while their naked bodies are torn by the scorpion lash.

> The whip on WOMAN'S shrinking flesh!
> Our soil yet reddening with the stains
> Caught from her scourging warm and fresh.

Can any American woman look at these scenes of shocking licentiousness and cruelty, and fold her hands in apathy and say, "I have nothing to do with slavery"? *She cannot and be guiltless.*

I cannot close this letter, without saying a few words on the benefits to be derived by men, as well as women, from the opinions I advocate relative to the equality of the sexes. Many women are now supported, in idleness and extravagance, by the industry of their husbands, fathers, or brothers, who are compelled to toil out their existence, at the counting house, or in the printing office, or some other laborious occupation, while the wife and daughters and sisters take no part in the support of the family, and appear to think that their sole business is to spend the hard bought earnings of their male friends. I deeply regret such a state of things, because I believe that if women felt their responsibility, for the support of themselves, or their families it would add strength and dignity to their characters, and teach them more true sympathy for their husbands, than is now generally manifested,—a sympathy which would be exhibited by actions as well as words. Our brethren may reject my doctrine, because it runs counter to common opinions, and because it wounds their pride; but I believe they would be "partakers of the benefit" resulting from the Equality of the Sexes, and would find that woman, as their equal, was unspeakably more valuable than woman as their inferior, both as a moral and an intellectual being.

Thine in the bonds of womanhood,
Sarah M. Grimké.

Notes

1. The author of *Live and Let Live,* Catharine Maria Sedgwick, was one of the most popular women writers of the antebellum period. She believed that a woman's place was in the home.
2. In the original printed version of this letter, "a late American writer" is identified as Thomas S. Grimké, Sarah's brother.

(1825–1911)

The only child of free black parents, Frances Ellen Watkins Harper was orphaned at three and raised in Baltimore by her uncle, Rev. William Watkins. Watkins ran a school for black children, through which he helped Frances acquire a solid education; in 1839, however, she left to work as a maid for a bookseller. By 1845 she had published her first collection of poetry and prose, *Forest Leaves,* which marked the beginning of an immensely successful literary career. She eventually became the best known black poet since Phillis Wheatley.

In 1850, Harper became a sewing teacher at Union Seminary in Ohio and then moved to Pennsylvania where she continued to teach. Dissatisfied with teaching, and keenly aware of the horror of slavery that she had been spared, Harper began speaking out for emancipation. The speech that made her career, "Education and the Elevation of the Colored Race," was delivered in New Bedford, Massachusetts, in 1854. Harper's best poetry served to enhance her lecturing career, especially her volume *Poems on Miscellaneous Subjects* (1854), a collection of antislavery poems (from which the following selections are taken). By 1871 the volume was in its twentieth edition and had sold more than fifty thousand copies. In the decade before the Civil War, Harper was most involved with her political work in the Maine Anti-Slavery Society, for which she traveled for two years, delivering lectures all over Maine. She remained active as a lecturer until her marriage in 1860 to Fenton Harper. When he died four years later, however, she began lecturing again, this time touring the South and focusing on the need for education and a high standard of morality among black people.

Although not as strong as her earlier work, two additional volumes of poetry were also published during Harper's lifetime, *Sketches of Southern Life* (1872) and *The Martyr of Alabama and Other Poems* (1894). Her long narrative poem, *Moses: A Story of the Nile* (1869), and her only novel, *Iola Leroy, or Shadows Uplifted* (1892), were very popular. She was also a frequent contributor to *Frederick Douglass' Paper,* in which she advocated free labor, and she was the first African-American to publish a short story, "The Two Offers," which was printed in the *Anglo-African Magazine* in 1859. Themes common to all of her works are white racial violence, women's rights, the importance of and need for education, and temperance; the poems anthologized here, while suggesting these issues, focus primarily on the concerns she found most pressing: freedom from slavery and social equality for African-Americans.

Harper continued working on social issues while she was writing. She served as the head of the Negro Division of the National Women's Christian Temperance Union from 1883 to 1890. In 1896 she organized the National Association of Colored Women and worked as a women's rights activist until her death in Philadelphia at the age of eighty-five.

Bible Defence of Slavery

Take sackcloth of the darkest dye,
    And shroud the pulpits round!
Servants of Him that cannot lie,
    Sit mourning on the ground.

Let holy horror blanch each cheek,
    Pale every brow with fears;
And rocks and stones, if ye could speak,
    Ye well might melt to tears!

Let sorrow breathe in every tone,
    In every strain ye raise;
Insult not God's majestic throne
    With th' mockery of praise.

A "reverend" man, whose light should be
    The guide of age and youth,
Brings to the shrine of Slavery
    The sacrifice of truth!

For the direst wrong by man imposed,
    Since Sodom's fearful cry,
The word of life has been unclos'd,
    To give your God the lie.

Oh! when ye pray for heathen lands,
    And plead for their dark shores,
Remember Slavery's cruel hands
    Make heathens at your doors!

An Appeal to My Countrywomen

You can sigh o'er the sad-eyed Armenian
　　Who weeps in her desolate home.
You can mourn o'er the exile of Russia
　　From kindred and friends doomed to roam.

You can pity the men who have woven
　　From passion and appetite chains
To coil with a terrible tension
　　Around their heartstrings and brains.

You can sorrow o'er little children
　　Disinherited from their birth,
The wee waifs and toddlers neglected,
　　Robbed of sunshine, music and mirth.

For beasts you have gentle compassion;
　　Your mercy and pity they share.
For the wretched, outcast and fallen
　　You have tenderness, love and care.

But hark! from our Southland are floating
　　Sobs of anguish, murmurs of pain,
And women heart-stricken are weeping
　　Over their tortured and their slain.

On their brows the sun has left traces;
　　Shrink not from their sorrow in scorn.
When they entered the threshold of being
　　The children of a King were born.

Each comes as a guest to the table
　　The hand of our God has outspread,
To fountains that ever leap upward,
　　To share in the soil we all tread.

When ye plead for the wrecked and fallen,
　　The exile from far-distant shores,
Remember that men are still wasting
　　Life's crimson around your own doors.

Have ye not, oh, my favored sisters,
  Just a plea, a prayer or a tear,
For mothers who dwell 'neath the shadows
  Of agony, hatred and fear?

Men may tread down the poor and lowly,
  May crush them in anger and hate,
But surely the mills of God's justice
  Will grind out the grist of their fate.

Oh, people sin-laden and guilty,
  So lusty and proud in your prime,
The sharp sickles of God's retribution
  Will gather your harvest of crime.

Weep not, oh my well-sheltered sisters,
  Weep not for the Negro alone,
But weep for your sons who must gather
  The crops which their fathers have sown.

Go read on the tombstones of nations
  Of chieftains who masterful trod,
The sentence which time has engraven,
  That they had forgotten their God.

'Tis the judgement of God that men reap
  The tares which in madness they sow,
Sorrow follows the footsteps of crime,
  And Sin is the consort of Woe.

Ethiopia

Yes! Ethiopia yet shall stretch
  Her bleeding hands abroad;
Her cry of agony shall reach
  The burning throne of God.

The tyrant's yoke from off her neck,
  His fetters from her soul,
The mighty hand of God shall break,
  And spurn the base control.

Redeemed from dust and freed from chains,
    Her sons shall lift their eyes;
From cloud-capt hills and verdant plains
    Shall shouts of triumph rise.

Upon her dark, despairing brow,
    Shall play a smile of peace;
For God shall bend unto her wo,
    And bid her sorrows cease.

'Neath sheltering vines and stately palms
    Shall laughing children play,
And aged sires with joyous psalms
    Shall gladden every day.

Secure by night, and blest by day,
    Shall pass her happy hours;
Nor human tigers hunt for prey
    Within her peaceful bowers.

Then, Ethiopia! stretch, oh! stretch
    Thy bleeding hands abroad;
Thy cry of agony shall reach
    And find redress from God.

Bury Me in a Free Land

Make me a grave where'er you will,
In a lowly plain, or a lofty hill;
Make it among earth's humblest graves,
But not in a land where men are slaves.

I could not rest if around my grave
I heard the steps of a trembling slave;
His shadow above my silent tomb
Would make it a place of fearful gloom.

I could not rest if I heard the tread
Of a coffle gang to the shambles led,
And the mother's shriek of wild despair
Rise like a curse on the trembling air.

I could not sleep if I saw the lash
Drinking her blood at each fearful gash,
And I saw her babes torn from her breast,
Like trembling doves from their parent nest.

I'd shudder and start if I heard the bay
Of bloodhounds seizing their human prey,
And I heard the captive plead in vain
As they bound afresh his galling chain.

If I saw young girls from their mothers' arms
Bartered and sold for their youthful charms,
My eye would flash with a mournful flame,
My death-paled cheek grow red with shame.

I would sleep, dear friends, where bloated might
Can rob no man of his dearest right;
My rest shall be calm in any grave
Where none can call his brother a slave.

I ask no monument, proud and high,
To arrest the gaze of the passers-by;
All that my yearning spirit craves,
Is bury me not in a land of slaves.

9. Harriet Jacobs

(1813–1897)

Writer of the first complete slave narrative by a woman, Harriet Jacobs was born on a slave plantation near Edenton, North Carolina. After her parents died, Jacobs's mistress taught her to read and write. But when Jacobs was eleven, her mistress died and she was willed to the young Mary Norcom, whose father, Dr. James Norcom, was a harsh and unsympathetic master. Though sexually harassed by Norcom for years, Jacobs fought off his advances; she did, however, have two children during her teenage years by a white lawyer, Samuel Sawyer. Soon after, she escaped from her master's home and was hidden by her grandmother, a freed slave, for nearly seven years. In the meantime, Sawyer bought the children and allowed them to live with Jacobs's grandmother; however, neither child received freedom through his efforts.

In 1842 Jacobs escaped to the North. The details of her life to this point are contained in the slave narrative *Incidents in the Life of a Slave Girl* (1861), written under the name Linda Brent. With her children, she settled in New York City, finding work as a nursemaid for the magazine editor Nathaniel P. Willis. Harassment by slaveholders and by James Norcom, who made repeated trips to New York to catch her, prompted Jacobs to move to Boston. After the death of his wife, Willis persuaded Jacobs to accompany him to London and care for his young daughter during their stay there. For a brief time after her return from England, Jacobs lived with her brother in Rochester, New York, and actively participated in the antislavery movement. In Rochester she met Amy Post, the Quaker abolitionist who became her close friend and to whom many of Jacobs's letters are addressed. Yet in 1850, Jacobs returned once again to New York City to work for Willis; this time, when she was again bothered by antiabolitionists, Willis bought and freed Jacobs and her children.

During the next decade, Jacobs began compiling her narrative. In 1858 she traveled to London to seek a publisher, but even with the support of both American and British abolitionists, she was unsuccessful. Two years later, however, abolitionists William C. Nell and L. Maria Child helped Jacobs publish the book herself as *Incidents in the Life of a Slave Girl*. In the past century, several critics have questioned the authenticity of Jacobs's narrative because her style is imitative of eighteenth-century novels and nineteenth-century sentimental fiction written by whites. In addition, her narrative provides an interesting contrast with others of its type; it is the only one to focus on sexual exploitation as a problem comparable to that of physical exploitation. The narrative also stresses the difference between the male and female slave story, for to Jacobs, slavery was "far more terrible for women."

With the outbreak of the Civil War, Jacobs was able to use the book in her work for emancipation. During the war, Jacobs worked in Washington, D.C., as a nurse for the Negro army. She remained there for the next thirty years, until her death in 1897. At her funeral, she was eulogized by the prominent abolitionist Rev. Francis Grimké, nephew of Angelina and Sarah Grimké.

Childhood

I was born a slave; but I never knew it till six years of happy childhood had passed away. My father was a carpenter, and considered so intelligent and skilful in his trade, that, when buildings out of the common line were to be erected, he was sent for from long distances, to be head workman. On condition of paying his mistress two hundred dollars a year, and supporting himself, he was allowed to work at his trade, and manage his own affairs. His strongest wish was to purchase his children; but, though he several times offered his hard earnings for that purpose, he never succeeded. In complexion my parents were a light shade of brownish yellow, and were termed mulattoes. They lived together in a comfortable home; and, though we were all slaves, I was so fondly shielded that I never dreamed I was a piece of merchandise, trusted to them for safe keeping, and liable to be demanded of them at any moment. I had one brother, William, who was two years younger than myself—a bright, affectionate child. I had also a great treasure in my maternal grandmother, who was a remarkable woman in many respects. She was the daughter of a planter in South Carolina, who, at his death, left her mother and his three children free, with money to go to St. Augustine, where they had relatives. It was during the Revolutionary War; and they were captured on their passage, carried back, and sold to different purchasers. Such was the story my grandmother used to tell me; but I do not remember all the particulars. She was a little girl when she was captured and sold to the keeper of a large hotel. I have often heard her tell how hard she fared during childhood. But as she grew older she evinced so much intelligence, and was so faithful, that her master and mistress could not help seeing it was for their interest to take care of such a valuable piece of property. She became an indispensable personage in the household, officiating in all capacities, from cook and wet nurse to seamstress. She was much praised for her cooking; and her nice crackers became so famous in the neighborhood that many people were desirous of obtaining them. In consequence of numerous requests of this kind, she asked permission of her mistress to bake crackers at night, after all the household work was done; and she obtained leave to do it, provided she would clothe herself and her children from the profits. Upon these terms, after working hard all day for her mistress, she began her midnight bakings, assisted by her two oldest children. The business proved profitable; and each year she laid by a little, which was saved for a fund to purchase her children. Her master died, and the property was divided among his heirs. The widow had her dower in the hotel, which she continued to keep open. My grandmother remained in her service as a slave; but her children were divided among her master's children. As she had five, Benjamin, the youngest one, was sold, in order that each heir might have an equal portion of dollars and cents. There was so little difference in our ages that he seemed more like my brother than my uncle. He was a bright, handsome lad, nearly white; for he inherited the complexion my grandmother had derived from Anglo-Saxon ancestors. Though only ten years old, seven hundred and twenty dollars were paid for him. His sale was a terrible blow to my grandmother; but she was naturally hopeful, and she went to work with renewed energy, trusting in time to be able to purchase some of her children. She had laid up three hundred dollars, which her mistress one day begged as a loan, promising to pay her soon. The reader probably knows that no promise or writing given to a slave is legally binding; for, according to Southern laws, a slave, *being* property, can *hold* no property. When my grandmother lent her hard earnings to her mistress, she trusted solely to her honor. The honor of a slaveholder to a slave!

To this good grandmother I was indebted for many comforts. My brother Willie and I often received portions of the crackers, cakes, and preserves, she made to sell; and after we ceased to be children we were indebted to her for many more important services.

Such were the unusually fortunate circumstances of my early childhood. When I was six years old, my mother died; and then, for the first time, I learned, by the talk around me, that I was a slave. My mother's mistress was the daughter of my grandmother's mistress. She was the foster sister of my mother; they were both nourished at my grandmother's breast. In fact, my mother had been weaned at three months old, that the babe of the mistress might obtain sufficient food. They played together as children; and, when they became women, my mother was a most faithful servant to her whiter foster sister. On her death-bed her mistress promised that her children should never suffer for any thing; and during her lifetime she kept her word. They all spoke kindly of my dead mother, who had been a slave merely in name, but in nature was noble and womanly. I grieved for her, and my young mind was troubled with the thought who would now take care of me and my little brother. I was told that my home was now to be with her mistress; and I found it a happy one. No toilsome or disagreeable duties were imposed upon me. My mistress was so kind to me that I was always glad to do her bidding, and proud to labor for her as much as my young years would permit. I would sit by her side for hours, sewing diligently, with a heart as free from care as that of any free-born white child. When she thought I was tired, she would send me out to run and jump; and away I bounded, to gather berries or flowers to decorate her room. Those were happy days—too happy to last. The slave child had no thought for the morrow; but there came that blight, which too surely waits on every human being born to be a chattel.

When I was nearly twelve years old, my kind mistress sickened and died. As I saw the cheek grow paler, and the eye more glassy, how earnestly I prayed in my heart that she might live! I loved her; for she had been almost like a mother to me. My prayers were not answered. She died, and they buried her in the little churchyard, where, day after day, my tears fell upon her grave.

I was sent to spend a week with my grandmother. I was now old enough to begin to think of the future; and again and again I asked myself what they would do with me. I felt sure I should never find another mistress so kind as the one who was gone. She had promised my dying mother that her children should never suffer for any thing; and when I remembered that, and recalled her many proofs of attachment to me, I could not help having some hopes that she had left me free. My friends were almost certain it would be so. They thought she would be sure to do it, on account of my mother's love and faithful service. But, alas! we all know that the memory of a faithful slave does not avail much to save her children from the auction block.

After a brief period of suspense, the will of my mistress was read, and we learned that she had bequeathed me to her sister's daughter, a child of five years old. So vanished our hopes. My mistress had taught me the precepts of God's Word: "Thou shalt love thy neighbor as thyself." "Whatsoever ye would that men should do unto you, do ye even so unto them." But I was her slave, and I suppose she did not recognize me as her neighbor. I would give much to blot out from my memory that one great wrong. As a child, I loved my mistress; and, looking back on the happy days I spent with her, I try to think with less bitterness of this act of injustice. While I was with her, she taught me to read and spell; and for this privilege, which so rarely falls to the lot of a slave, I bless her memory.

She possessed but few slaves; and at her death those were all distributed among her relatives. Five of them were my grandmother's children, and had shared the same milk that nourished her mother's children. Notwithstanding my grandmother's long and faithful service to her owners, not one of her children escaped the auction block. These God-breathing machines are no more, in the sight of their masters, than the cotton they plant, or the horses they tend.

The New Master and Mistress

Dr. Flint,[1] a physician in the neighborhood, had married the sister of my mistress, and I was now the property of their little daughter. It was not without murmuring that I prepared for my new home; and what added to my unhappiness, was the fact that my brother William was purchased by the same family. My father, by his nature, as well as by the habit of transacting business as a skilful mechanic, had more of the feelings of a freeman than is common among slaves. My brother was a spirited boy; and being brought up under such influences, he early detested the name of master and mistress. One day, when his father and his mistress had happened to call him at the same time, he hesitated between the two; being perplexed to know which had the strongest claim upon his obedience. He finally concluded to go to his mistress. When my father reproved him for it, he said, "You both called me, and I didn't know which I ought to go to first."

"You are *my* child," replied our father, "and when I call you, you should come immediately, if you have to pass through fire and water."

Poor Willie! He was now to learn his first lesson of obedience to a master. Grandmother tried to cheer us with hopeful words, and they found an echo in the credulous hearts of youth.

When we entered our new home we encountered cold looks, cold words, and cold treatment. We were glad when the night came. On my narrow bed I moaned and wept, I felt so desolate and alone.

I had been there nearly a year, when a dear little friend of mine was buried. I heard her mother sob, as the clods fell on the coffin of her only child, and I turned away from the grave, feeling thankful that I still had something left to love. I met my grandmother, who said, "Come with me,

Linda;" and from her tone I knew that something sad had happened. She led me apart from the people, and then said, "My child, your father is dead." Dead! How could I believe it? He had died so suddenly I had not even heard that he was sick. I went home with my grandmother. My heart rebelled against God, who had taken from me mother, father, mistress, and friend. The good grandmother tried to comfort me. "Who knows the ways of God?" said she. "Perhaps they have been kindly taken from the evil days to come." Years afterwards I often thought of this. She promised to be a mother to her grandchildren, so far as she might be permitted to do so; and strengthened by her love, I returned to my master's. I thought I should be allowed to go to my father's house the next morning; but I was ordered to go for flowers, that my mistress's house might be decorated for an evening party. I spent the day gathering flowers and weaving them into festoons, while the dead body of my father was lying within a mile of me. What cared my owners for that? he was merely a piece of property. Moreover, they thought he had spoiled his children, by teaching them to feel that they were human beings. This was blasphemous doctrine for a slave to teach; presumptuous in him, and dangerous to the masters.

The next day I followed his remains to a humble grave beside that of my dear mother. There were those who knew my father's worth, and respected his memory.

My home now seemed more dreary than ever. The laugh of the little slave-children sounded harsh and cruel. It was selfish to feel so about the joy of others. My brother moved about with a very grave face. I tried to comfort him, by saying, "Take courage, Willie; brighter days will come by and by."

"You don't know any thing about it, Linda," he replied. "We shall have to stay here all our days; we shall never be free."

I argued that we were growing older and stronger, and that perhaps we might, before long, be allowed to hire our own time, and then we could earn money to buy our freedom. William declared this was much easier to say than to do; moreover, he did not intend to *buy* his freedom. We held daily controversies upon this subject.

Little attention was paid to the slaves' meals in Dr. Flint's house. If they could catch a bit of food while it was going, well and good. I gave myself no trouble on that score, for on my various errands I passed my grandmother's house, where there was always something to spare for me. I was frequently threatened with punishment if I stopped there; and my grandmother, to avoid detaining me, often stood at the gate with something for my breakfast or dinner. I was indebted to *her* for all my comforts, spiritual or temporal. It was *her* labor that supplied my scanty wardrobe. I have a vivid recollection of the linsey-woolsey dress given me every winter by Mrs. Flint. How I hated it! It was one of the badges of slavery.

While my grandmother was thus helping to support me from her hard earnings, the three hundred dollars she had lent her mistress were never repaid. When her mistress died, her son-in-law, Dr. Flint, was appointed executor. When grandmother applied to him for payment, he said the estate was insolvent, and the law prohibited payment. It did not, however, prohibit him from retaining the silver candelabra, which had been purchased with that money. I presume thay will be handed down in the family, from generation to generation.

My grandmother's mistress had always promised her that, at her death, she should be free; and it was said that in her will she made good the promise. But when the estate was settled, Dr. Flint told the faithful old servant that, under existing circumstances, it was necessary she should be sold.

On the appointed day, the customary advertisement was posted up, proclaiming that there would be a "public sale of negroes, horses, &c." Dr. Flint called to tell my grandmother that he was unwilling to wound her feelings by putting her up at auction, and that he would prefer to dispose of her at private sale. My grandmother saw through his hypocrisy; she understood very well that he was ashamed of the job. She was a very spirited woman, and if he was base enough to sell her, when her mistress intended she should be free, she was determined the public should know it. She had for a long time supplied many families with crackers and preserves; consequently, "Aunt Marthy," as she was called, was generally known, and every body who knew her respected her intelligence and good character. Her long and faithful service in the family was also well known, and the intention of her mistress to leave her free. When the day of sale came, she took her place among the chattels, and at the first call she sprang upon the auction-block. Many voices called out, "Shame! Shame! Who is going to sell *you*, aunt Marthy? Don't stand there! That is no place for *you*." Without saying a word, she quietly awaited her fate. No one bid for her. At last, a feeble voice said, "Fifty dollars." It came from a maiden lady, seventy years old, the sister of my grandmother's deceased mistress. She had lived forty years under the same roof with my grandmother; she knew how faithfully she had served her owners, and how cruelly she had been defrauded of her rights; and she resolved to protect her. The auctioneer waited for a higher bid; but her wishes were respected; no one bid above her. She could neither read nor write; and when the bill of sale was made out, she signed it with a cross. But what consequence was that, when she had a big heart over-flowing with human kindness? She gave the old servant her freedom.

At that time, my grandmother was just fifty years old. Laborious years had passed since then; and now my brother and I were slaves to the man who had defrauded her of her money, and tried to defraud her of her freedom. One of my mother's sisters, called Aunt Nancy, was also a slave in his family. She was a kind, good aunt to me; and supplied the place of both housekeeper and waiting maid to her mistress. She was, in fact, at the beginning and end of every thing.

Mrs. Flint, like many southern women, was totally deficient in energy. She had not strength to superintend her household affairs; but her nerves were so strong, that she could sit in her easy chair and see a woman whipped, till the blood trickled from every stroke of the lash. She was a member of the church; but partaking of the Lord's supper did not seem to put her in a Christian frame of mind. If dinner was not served at the exact time on that particular Sunday, she would station herself in the kitchen, and wait till it was dished, and then spit in all the kettles and pans that had been used for cooking. She did this to prevent the cook and her children from eking out their meagre fare with the remains of the gravy and other scrapings. The slaves could get nothing to eat except what she chose to give them. Provisions were weighed out by the pound and ounce, three times a day. I can assure you she gave them no chance to eat wheat bread from her flour barrel. She knew how many biscuits a quart of flour would make, and exactly what size they ought to be.

Dr. Flint was an epicure. The cook never sent a dinner to his table without fear and trembling; for if there happened to be a dish not to his liking, he would either order her to be whipped, or compel her to eat every mouthful of it in his presence. The poor, hungry creature might not have objected to eating it; but she did object to having her master cram it down her throat till she choked.

They had a pet dog, that was a nuisance in the house. The cook was ordered to make some Indian mush for him. He refused to eat, and when his head was held over it, the froth flowed from his mouth into the basin. He died a few minutes after. When Dr. Flint came in, he said the mush had not been well cooked, and that was the reason the animal would not eat it. He sent for the cook, and compelled her to eat it. He thought that the woman's stomach was stronger than the dog's; but her sufferings afterwards proved that he was mistaken. This poor woman endured many cruelties from her master and mistress; sometimes she was locked up, away from her nursing baby, for a whole day and night.

When I had been in the family a few weeks, one of the plantation slaves was brought to town, by order of his master. It was near night when he arrived, and Dr. Flint ordered him to be taken to the work house, and tied up to the joist, so that his feet would just escape the ground. In that situation he was to wait till the doctor had taken his tea. I shall never forget that night. Never before, in my life, had I heard hundreds of blows fall, in succession, on a human being. His piteous groans, and his "O, pray don't, massa," rang in my ear for months afterwards. There were many conjectures as to the cause of this terrible punishment. Some said master accused him of stealing corn; others said the slave had quarrelled with his wife, in presence of the overseer, and had accused his master of being the father of her child. They were both black, and the child was very fair.

I went into the work house next morning, and saw the cowhide still wet with blood, and the boards all covered with gore. The poor man lived, and continued to quarrel with his wife. A few months afterwards Dr. Flint handed them both over to a slave-trader. The guilty man put their value into his pocket, and had the satisfaction of knowing that they were out of sight and hearing. When the mother was delivered into the trader's hands, she said, "You *promised* to treat me well." To which he replied, "You have let your tongue run too far; damn you!" She had forgotten that it was a crime for a slave to tell who was the father of her child.

From others than the master persecution also comes in such cases. I once saw a young slave girl dying soon after the birth of a child nearly white. In her agony she cried out, "O Lord, come and take me!" Her mistress stood by, and mocked at her like an incarnate fiend. "You suffer, do you?" she exclaimed. "I am glad of it. You deserve it all, and more too."

The girl's mother said, "The baby is dead, thank God; and I hope my poor child will soon be in heaven, too."

"Heaven!" retorted the mistress. "There is no such place for the like of her and her bastard."

The poor mother turned away, sobbing. Her dying daughter called her, feebly, and as she bent over her, I heard her say, "Don't grieve so, mother; God knows all about it; and HE will have mercy upon me."

Her sufferings, afterwards, became so intense, that her mistress felt unable to stay; but when she left the room, the scornful smile was still on her lips. Seven children called her mother. The poor black woman had but the one child, whose eyes she saw closing in death, while she thanked God for taking her away from the greater bitterness of life.

The Lover

Why does the slave ever love? Why allow the tendrils of the heart to twine around objects which may at any moment be wrenched away by the hand of violence? When separations come by the hand of death, the pious soul can bow in resignation, and say, "Not my will, but thine be done, O Lord!" But when the ruthless hand of man strikes the blow, regardless of the misery he causes, it is hard to be submissive. I did not reason thus when I was a young girl. Youth will be youth. I loved, and I indulged the hope that the dark clouds around me would turn out a bright lining. I forgot that in the land of my birth the shadows are too dense for light to penetrate. A land

> "Where laughter is not mirth; nor thought the mind;
> Nor words a language; nor e'en men mankind.
> Where cries reply to curses, shrieks to blows,
> And each is tortured in his separate hell."

There was in the neighborhood a young colored carpenter; a free born man. We had been well acquainted in childhood, and frequently met together afterwards. We became mutually attached, and he proposed to marry me. I loved him with all the ardor of a young girl's first love. But when I reflected that I was a slave, and that the laws gave no sanction to the marriage of such, my heart sank within me. My lover wanted to buy me; but I knew that Dr. Flint was too wilful and arbitrary a man to consent to that arrangement. From him, I was sure of experiencing all sorts of opposition, and I had nothing to hope from my mistress. She would have been delighted to have got rid of me, but not in that way. It would have relieved her mind of a burden if she could have seen me sold to some distant state, but if I was married near home I should be just as much in her husband's power as I had previously been,—for the husband of a slave has no power to protect her. Moreover, my mistress, like many others, seemed to think that slaves had no right to any family ties of their own; that they were created merely to wait upon the family of the mistress. I once heard her abuse a young slave girl, who told her that a colored man wanted to make her his wife. "I will have you peeled and pickled, my lady," said she, "if I ever hear you mention that subject again. Do you suppose that I will have you tending *my* children with the children of that nigger?" The girl to whom she said this had a mulatto child, of course not acknowledged by its father. The poor black man who loved her would have been proud to acknowledge his helpless offspring.

Many and anxious were the thoughts I revolved in my mind. I was at a loss what to do. Above all things, I was desirous to spare my lover the insults that had cut so deeply into my own soul. I talked with my grandmother about it, and partly told her my fears. I did not dare to tell her the worst. She had long suspected all was not right, and if I confirmed her suspicions I knew a storm would rise that would prove the overthrow of all my hopes.

This love-dream had been my support through many trials; and I could not bear to run the risk of having it suddenly dissipated. There was a lady in the neighborhood, a particular friend of Dr. Flint's, who often visited the house. I had a great respect for her, and she had always manifested a friendly interest in me. Grandmother thought she would have great influence with the doctor. I went to this lady, and told her my story. I told her I was aware that my lover's being a free-born man would prove a great objection; but he wanted to buy me; and if Dr. Flint would consent to that arrangement, I felt sure he would be willing to pay any reasonable price. She knew that Mrs. Flint disliked me; therefore, I ventured to suggest that perhaps my mistress would approve of my being sold, as that would rid her of me. The lady listened with kindly sympathy, and promised to do her utmost to promote my wishes. She had an interview with the doctor, and I believe she pleaded my cause earnestly; but it was all to no purpose.

How I dreaded my master now! Every minute I expected to be summoned to his presence; but the day passed, and I heard nothing from him. The next morning, a message was brought to me: "Master wants you in his study." I found the door ajar, and I stood a moment gazing at the hateful man who claimed a right to rule me, body and soul. I entered, and tried to appear calm. I did not want him to know how my heart was bleeding. He looked fixedly at me, with an expression which seemed to say, "I have half a mind to kill you on the spot." At last he broke the silence, and that was a relief to both of us.

"So you want to be married, do you?" said he, "and to a free nigger."

"Yes, sir."

"Well, I'll soon convince you whether I am your master, or the nigger fellow you honor so highly. If you *must* have a husband, you may take up with one of my slaves."

What a situation I should be in, as the wife of one of *his* slaves, even if my heart had been interested!

I replied, "Don't you suppose, sir, that a slave can have some preference about marrying? Do you suppose that all men are alike to her?"

"Do you love this nigger?" said he, abruptly.

"Yes, sir."

"How dare you tell me so!" he exclaimed, in great wrath. After a slight pause, he added, "I supposed you thought more of yourself; that you felt above the insults of such puppies."

I replied, "If he is a puppy I am a puppy, for we are both of the negro race. It is right and honorable for us to love each other. The man you call a puppy never insulted me, sir; and he would not love me if he did not believe me to be a virtuous woman."

He sprang upon me like a tiger, and gave me a stunning blow. It was the first time he had ever struck me; and fear did not enable me to control my anger. When I had recovered a little from the effects, I exclaimed, "You have struck me for answering you honestly. How I despise you!"

There was silence for some minutes. Perhaps he was deciding what should be my punishment; or, perhaps, he wanted to give me time to reflect on what I had said, and to whom I had said it. Finally, he asked, "Do you know what you have said?"

"Yes, sir; but your treatment drove me to it."

"Do you know that I have a right to do as I like with you,—that I can kill you, if I please?"

"You have tried to kill me, and I wish you had; but you have no right to do as you like with me."

"Silence!" he exclaimed, in a thundering voice. "By heavens, girl, you forget yourself too far! Are you mad? If you are, I will soon bring you to your senses. Do you think any other master would bear what I have borne from you this morning? Many masters would have killed you on the spot. How would you like to be sent to jail for your insolence?"

"I know I have been disrespectful, sir," I replied; "but you drove me to it; I couldn't help it. As for the jail, there would be more peace for me there than there is here."

"You deserve to go there," said he, "and to be under such treatment, that you would forget the meaning of the word *peace.* It would do you good. It would take some of your high notions out of you. But I am not ready to send you there yet, notwithstanding your ingratitude for all my kindness and forbearance. You have been the plague of my life. I have wanted to make you happy, and I have been repaid with the basest ingratitude; but though you have proved yourself incapable of appreciating my kindness, I will be lenient towards you, Linda. I will give you one more chance to redeem your character. If you behave yourself and do as I require, I will forgive you and treat you as I always have done; but if you disobey me, I will punish you as I would the meanest slave on my plantation. Never let me hear that fellow's name mentioned again. If I ever know of your speaking to him, I will cowhide you both; and if I catch him lurking about my premises, I will shoot him as soon as I would a dog. Do you hear what I say? I'll teach you a lesson about marriage and free niggers! Now go, and let this be the last time I have occasion to speak to you on this subject."

Reader, did you ever hate? I hope not. I never did but once; and I trust I never shall again. Somebody has called it "the atmosphere of hell;" and I believe it is so.

For a fortnight the doctor did not speak to me. He thought to mortify me; to make me feel that I had disgraced myself by receiving the honorable addresses of a respectable colored man, in preference to the base proposals of a white man. But though his lips disdained to address me, his eyes were very loquacious. No animal ever watched its prey more narrowly than he watched me. He knew that I could write, though he had failed to make me read his letters; and he was now troubled lest I should exchange letters with another man. After a while he became weary of silence; and I was sorry for it. One morning, as he passed through the hall, to leave the house, he contrived to thrust a note into my hand. I thought I had better read it, and spare myself the vexation of having him read it to me. It expressed regret for the blow he had given me, and reminded me that I myself was wholly to blame for it. He hoped I had become convinced of the injury I was doing myself by incurring his displeasure. He wrote that he had made up his mind to go to Louisiana; that he should take several slaves with him, and intended I should be one of the number. My mistress would remain where she was; therefore I should have nothing to fear from that quarter. If I merited kindness from him, he assured me that it would be lavishly bestowed. He begged me to think over the matter, and answer the following day.

The next morning I was called to carry a pair of scissors to his room. I laid them on the table, with the letter beside them. He thought it was my answer, and did not call me back. I went as usual to attend my young mistress to and from school. He met me in the street, and ordered me to stop at his office on my way back. When I entered, he showed me his letter, and asked me why I had not answered it. I replied, "I am your daughter's property, and it is in your power to send me, or take me, wherever you please." He said he was very glad to find me so willing to go, and that we should start early in the autumn. He had a large practice in the town, and I rather thought he had made up the story merely to frighten me. However that might be, I was determined that I would never go to Louisiana with him.

Summer passed away, and early in the autumn Dr. Flint's eldest son was sent to Louisiana to examine the country, with a view to emigrating. That news did not disturb me. I knew very well that I should not be sent with *him*. That I had not been taken to the plantation before this time, was owing to the fact that his son was there. He was jealous of his son; and jealousy of the overseer had kept him from punishing me by sending me into the fields to work. Is it strange that I was not proud of these protectors? As for the overseer, he was a man for whom I had less respect than I had for a bloodhound.

Young Mr. Flint did not bring back a favorable report of Louisiana, and I heard no more of that scheme. Soon after this, my lover met me at the corner of the street, and I stopped to speak to him. Looking up, I saw my master watching us from his window. I hurried home, trembling with fear. I was sent for, immediately, to go to his room. He met me with a blow. "When is mistress to be married?" said he, in a sneering tone. A shower of oaths and imprecations followed. How thankful I was that my lover was a free man! that my tyrant had no power to flog him for speaking to me in the street!

Again and again I revolved in my mind how all this would end. There was no hope that the doctor would consent to sell me on any terms. He had an iron will, and was determined to keep me, and to conquer me. My lover was an intelligent and religious man. Even if he could have obtained permission to marry me while I was a slave, the marriage would give him no power to protect me from my master. It would have made him miserable to witness the insults I should have been subjected to. And then, if we had children, I knew they must "follow the condition of the mother." What a terrible blight that would be on the heart of a free, intelligent father! For *his* sake, I felt that I ought not to link his fate with my own unhappy destiny. He was going to Savannah to see about a little property left him by an uncle; and hard as it was to bring my feelings to it, I earnestly entreated him not to come back. I advised him to go to the Free States, where his tongue would not be tied, and where his intelligence would be of more avail to him. He left me, still hoping the day would come when I could be bought. With me the lamp of hope had gone out. The dream of my girlhood was over. I felt lonely and desolate.

Still I was not stripped of all. I still had my good grandmother, and my affectionate brother. When he put his arms round my neck, and looked into my eyes, as if to read there the troubles I dared not tell, I felt that I still had something to love. But even that pleasant emotion was chilled by the reflection that he might be torn from me at any moment, by some sudden freak of my master. If he had known how we loved each other, I think he would have exulted in separating us. We often planned together how we could get to the north. But, as William remarked, such things are easier said than done. My movements were very closely watched, and we had no means of getting any money to defray our expenses. As for grandmother, she was strongly opposed to her children's undertaking any such project. She had not forgotten poor Benjamin's sufferings, and she was afraid that if another child tried to escape, he would have a similar or a worse fate. To me, nothing seemed more dreadful than my present life. I said to myself, "William *must* be free. He shall go to the north, and I will follow him." Many a slave sister has formed the same plans.

Note
1. The James Norcom family was the model for the Flint family.

The Civil

War South

(1861–1865)

In a diary entry dated March 4, 1861, Mary Boykin Chesnut described a slave woman she saw for sale on the auction block. The woman was "magnificently gotten up in silks and satins"; "ogling the bidders," she sometimes looked "quite coy and modest, but her mouth never relaxed from its expanded grin of excitement." Overwhelmed by what she saw, Chesnut took refuge in a local store where she "disciplined [her] wild thoughts"; a description of her sudden realization about slavery closes the diary entry: "You know how women sell themselves and are sold in marriage, from queens downward, eh? You know what the Bible says about slavery—and marriage. Poor women. Poor slaves" (*Mary Chesnut's Civil War* 15).

Historians and literary scholars have frequently read this passage as a feminist statement, and indeed, Chesnut does seem to believe that all women suffer in a slave society. Nevertheless, Chesnut's diary as a whole suggests that her principal concern was the "poisoning" of white children and wives in a system that promoted miscegenation to produce more slaves for the plantation society; "[t]he best way to take Negroes to your heart is to get as far away from them as possible," she wrote in March 1862 (199). Characterizing Chesnut as possessing "deep racial and sexual phobias," George Rable suggests in *Civil Wars* that she was more concerned with the morality of the masters than the suffering of the slaves (35–36). The ambivalence of Chesnut's view of slavery is reflected in the actions of many southern white women who, hoping to give the appearance of a congenial homelife, refused to acknowledge the inhumanity of the slave experience; like Chesnut, many looked the other way when slaves were physically and verbally abused or raped. One former slave from South Carolina said that his mistress would smile and pat the heads of young blacks, but she would walk away when her husband, the master, cursed them (Rable 33).

Oddly, whether motivated by self-interest, concern for their families, or concern for their slaves, the majority of women who wrote about slavery expressed nothing but hatred for the institution. Yet most of these women—perhaps feeling it was not their "place" to speak out, perhaps realizing that their own privileged position depended on slavery—confined their thoughts to journals and private letters. After the Civil War, one southern white woman wrote, "I was glad and thankful—on my own account when slavery ended, and I ceased to belong body and soul to my negroes." Another exclaimed that "in some mysterious way I had drunk in with my mother's milk . . . a detestation of the curse of slavery laid upon our beautiful southern land." Another wrote in her diary in 1859, "Southern white women are all, I believe, abolitionists" (all qtd. in Scott 1970, 48–50).

It is understandable, given the ambivalent attitudes of white women toward slavery, that historians are divided as to how they were affected by the war years. Anne Firor Scott sees "the challenge of war" and "the thoroughgoing social change" that the war brought to the lives of southerners as an opportunity for white women to become involved with new responsibilities, particularly as boundaries between genders were shifting (81, 102). Nevertheless, as Anne Goodwyn Jones explains in *Tomorrow Is Another Day,* under the influence of the Cult of True Womanhood, and perhaps subconsciously to quell apprehension in the "hearts of men who worried about the 'Amazon' and the 'strong-minded female,'" southern white women assimilated their new roles with the old. What resulted was an "oxymoronic ideal of the woman made of steel yet masked in fragility," a woman much like Margaret Mitchell's Melanie Wilkes (13). This new "Confederate Model" of southern womanhood was perpetuated as Confederate women took more responsibility for their own and their children's welfare, with husbands, lovers, brothers, and sons away at war. As in the Revolutionary War period, white women were working as nurses, sewing clothing, tents, and bandages, washing for men on the front lines, and raising money for the Confederacy on the home front. Equally affected by the war, many black women made their way across battle lines to serve in the same capacities for the federal army. But always linked to women's self-sufficiency was the horror of the massive destruction sweeping through the American landscape. Unlike most northern women, southern women faced war at their doorsteps, and they felt its effects firsthand: black women as they fled through battle lines to freedom in the north and as many were forced to return to the plantations they had fled; white women as they watched their homes and towns destroyed and as they fled with their families before marching troops. The war affected all races, both genders, and all socioeconomic levels.

Frustrated because she believed the Confederacy refused to use wisely one of its most valuable resources—its own women—Augusta Jane Evans Wilson was determined to follow her relatives into battle and to write southern propaganda. Likewise, Sarah Morgan Dawson exclaimed on the day the Yankees entered Baton Rouge, "O if I was only a man! Then I could don the breeches, and slay them with a will! If some few Southern women were in the ranks, they could set the men an example they would not blush to follow. Pshaw! there are *no* women here! We are *all* men!" (65). A similar description of the intensity of white women's convictions was given by the Englishman George A. Sala, who visited the United States in 1863 and wrote about his experiences in *My Diary in America in the Midst of War* (1865). He exclaimed that he found the women of both the North and the South to be "'unanimous' in their 'exasperation and implacability'": "I question whether either ancient or modern history can furnish an example of conflict which was so much of a 'woman's war' as this. The bitterest, most vengeful of politicians in this ensanguined controversy are the ladies" (359). Confederate white women were said to have exerted so much pressure on their men to enlist in the army that the Confederate leadership soon came to recognize them as "recruiting agents." One young woman even broke off an engagement to a boyfriend who was slow in enlisting by sending him a skirt, a petticoat, and a message reading, "Wear these or volunteer."

Other women were just as powerful, however, in getting men home from the front lines. As a result of the intensive letter-writing campaign launched by southern women, so many Confederate soldiers had returned home to care for their families that the Confederate leadership was forced to recognize the influence these women held. In 1863 Jefferson Davis stated publicly what should have been obvious: that the South needed its men on the lines to fight. A Florida newspaper editor echoed Davis's concern when he wrote, "The murmuring from suffering families at home is going up to the camps, and is doing more to dishearten our brave defenders than the balls and bayonets of the enemy" (qtd. in Simkins 227).

Letters, diaries, and journals of the bellum period tell much about women's perspectives on the war. Probably the best known is Mary Boykin Chesnut's diary, which she later revised for a book published as *A Diary from Dixie* (1906). As she battled her helplessness as a woman both in war and in the political realm of her husband, Chesnut found the written word a source of power. Elizabeth Keckley demonstrated a similar power when she divulged little-known details of the life of the Lincolns during the war years in Washington, D.C., in her *Behind the Scenes, or Thirty Years a Slave and Four Years in the White House* (1868). Before the war, women often kept diaries that they hoped might serve as instructive tools for their daughters and granddaughters; after the war, many women found that their accounts of war and Reconstruction sold well to northern publishers. Many such personal stories were published as southerners and northerners struggled to understand what had happened to the divided nation and as women struggled to find financial support for their families. Collections of poetry and war songs were especially popular in the years following the war, the most notable being William Gilmore Simms's *War Poetry of the South* (1866) and William Shepperson's *War Songs of the South* (1862). Margaret Junkin Preston's poems, anthologized in both collections, memorialized not only the heroic deeds of the Confederate leadership but also the sacrifices of the white woman and the common foot soldier. As a tribute to the endurance of the Confederate woman, Preston dedicated her poem *Beechenbrook* (1865) to "Every Southern Woman, who has been widowed by the war" as "a faint memorial of suffering, of which there can be no forgetfulness."

Novels and short stories had become the genres of choice for white women writers publishing in the 1830s through the 1850s. During the war, white southerners who supported the Confederacy were unable to publish as extensively as they did before the war because of the lack of publishing houses in the South and the limited production of those in the North. They were surpassed by the writers of slave narratives, which, although at the height of production and popularity in the 1850s, continued to be published in the war years as support for the northern cause. Because attention was focussed on the war effort, publications by black and white women were generally limited to accounts of slavery and Civil War battles and descriptions of life on the home front. Often these accounts were published to promote either the southern cause or the northern cause. Augusta Jane Evans Wilson dedicated her novel *Macaria* (1863) to those "who have delivered the South from despotism," and in it she presents an idealized portrait of faithful slaves and kind masters and mistresses and celebrates southern war victories. Legend has it that one Confederate soldier was saved when he was called into battle and quickly placed the book in his breast pocket; the book stopped a bullet that would have pierced his heart. Whether or not the tale is true, it suggests the power of the old southern myth to sustain the Confederate Army.

The war provided white women with experiences that brought them out of their sheltered environments and face to face with the social and racial problems of the South. Yet at the end of the war, although many white women were vacillating in their support of the Confederacy, they rarely questioned the gender, racial, or class inequalities around them. In addition, despite the extra burdens Confederate women shouldered to support the war effort, those of the upper and middle classes were incapable of envisioning themselves divorced from the traditional passive, ladylike role. The absurdity of this situation is illustrated by Sarah Morgan Dawson, who put her health at risk in order to maintain this ideal. Dawson tells of visiting a Confederate army camp and falling from her buggy when the horses were frightened by gunfire. Although she realized her lower spine was seriously injured, she knew she could not mention such a private spot to the men who came to her aid, and her primary concern was making sure that her feet were not exposed (334–36). "Active courage was for men; stoic suffering fell to women," George

Rable explains (50). To pay his respect to the white woman's "stoic suffering," Jefferson Davis dedicated his memoirs to Confederate ladies, "whose fortitude sustained them under all the privations to which they were subjected."

Whether or not women like Wilson and Dawson challenged their southern world, their world was indeed changing. Slavery was ended, and the mask of southern social harmony was lifted. Many whites were left clinging to the myths of the Old South, alarmed that their slaves would no longer be there to care for their needs. Several days before the Confederate surrender, one mistress, Eliza Andrews, was horrified when the family cook Lizzie said she would not fix a meal "fur Jesus Christ today" and certainly not for two of her mistress's friends. Another ex-slave told of her mistress's confrontation with General Ulysses S. Grant: "Den she went back to the general, an' begged an' cried, and hel' out her han's, and say 'General dese han's never was in dough—I never made a cake o' bread in my life; please let me have my cook!'" (qtd. in J. Jones 48). Elizabeth Fox-Genovese explains in her introduction to Parthenia Antoinette Hague's Civil War journal, *A Blockaded Family: Life in Southern Alabama during the Civil War*, that when Hague describes privileged white women learning to spin, card, and weave textiles, she neglects "a longstanding tradition of household textile work" by African-American women (Hague xxi). In other words, white women often failed to recognize the value and skill of the work of African-American women. Certainly many southern white women were self-sufficient and able to piece together their homes despite the loss of slaves; certainly not all were "abandoned," for black servants became as common to the postbellum portrait as slaves to the antebellum. But these examples illuminate a strength in black women—and a weakness in white—that justifies postwar anxieties.

Although adjusting to life without their slaves often proved difficult for white women, certainly black women faced far greater struggles as they attempted to provide for themselves and their families. Like many Confederate women, black women often joined their husbands on the front lines rather than remain behind on plantations or risk separation from their families, for northern army camps represented freedom to blacks. One Louisiana woman brought her dead child's body to a northern camp "to be buried, as she said, *free*" (qtd. in J. Jones 49). Emancipation offered freedom only on paper, however, for prejudices and social restrictions held black women back in both the South and the North. Moreover, during the war, black male slaves were often taken behind Confederate lines by retreating slaveholders who tended to leave the women, children, and elderly on plantations overtaken by federal troops. The war thus tore apart black families just as slavery had, with black mothers often left to serve as the sole caretakers and sources of support for their children. The postwar period was also marked by years of devastation and poverty for many southern women, but especially for newly freed blacks. According to E. Merton Coulter, in antebellum Charleston the mortality rates of blacks and whites were comparable, but after the war the rate of black deaths was roughly double that of white deaths.

Because of the suffering of black and white women, because of the hatred between races and regions, women's lives remained in flux for years after the war. For emotional and spiritual support, women turned to each other. Church, community betterment, and memorial organizations brought women together in larger communities, but these communities were still segregated by race and class. As black and white families traveled in search of those separated from them by slavery or in search of the graves of loved ones, as blacks struggled to recover from years of poverty and degredation, the memory and the tragedies of slavery and war were to replay themselves again and again. The recuperation would be long (and many would argue still incomplete today), but for women, both black and white, the war was only the beginning of a long struggle for individual freedoms.

10. *Mary Boykin Chesnut*

(1823–1886)

Born in Statesburg, North Carolina, Chesnut was the daughter of Mary Boykin and Stephen Decatur Miller, the U.S. senator who became the nullification governor of South Carolina. Although Mary's father gave her a solid education at home, it was her grandmother who taught her the management and care of a large plantation. When her family left for the Mississippi frontier in 1835, Mary was sent to a French boarding school in Charleston. Her education there was interrupted for a year, however, when her father found out that his thirteen-year-old daughter was seeing James Chesnut, a recent graduate of Princeton and son of one of the wealthiest planters in the state. When Mary reentered school in Charleston, her mother and sisters moved there with her.

In 1840 Mary married James Chesnut and moved to his parents' plantation south of Camden. Although she was very outgoing and intelligent, Chesnut found no outlet for her energy on the plantation as her husband's mother and sisters took full charge of domestic affairs. In addition, the Chesnuts had no children, so Mary turned to her husband's political career to occupy her time. When James was elected U.S. senator, the couple moved to Washington, D.C., where Chesnut became very popular for her ability to entertain southern politicians; she became close friends with both Varina Davis and Mary Custis Lee, and she worked with her husband for the Confederate cause. However, James resigned in 1860 because of his disapproval of Lincoln, and the couple returned to the Chesnut plantation.

Back in Camden, Chesnut began keeping a journal, describing in detail her many acquaintances and activities during the war. Though at her best when in the fashionable political society, Chesnut rarely had such opportunities. The family lost everything in the war, leaving them so poor that Chesnut had to sell butter and eggs in order to survive. She drafted three novels, also in hopes of making money, but none were successfully completed. She then returned to her journal, planning to revise it for publication ("Overlooking it—copying—leaving myself out," she explained to Varina Davis, who she wished might read the journal). But Chesnut's poor health and the pressures of running a dairy farm and caring for ailing relatives made it impossible for her to complete the work before she died in 1886.

Chesnut's friends Isabella D. Martin and Myrta L. Avary first published a version of Chesnut's journal in 1905 with the title *A Diary from Dixie.* Martin, however, took a heavy hand in editing the book; she insisted that any passages that did not concur with the contemporary version of the Confederate legend be omitted. For example, Martin left in a mention of a Mrs. Witherspoon's death, but cut any mention of her slaves' involvement in her death. An edition twice the size of the 1905 version came out in 1949, containing almost two-thirds of the material from the earlier version in addition to gossip and rumors Chesnut's friends feared would damage the reputations of many southern people. Finally, in 1980, C. Vann Woodward published *Mary Chesnut's Civil War,* a scholarly edition of Chesnut's journal that Woodward claims Chesnut kept "under lock and key, and . . . clearly intended for no eyes but her own" (xix). The selections included here are from that version.

The journal in its various versions has proven to be a valuable source for the study of social and psychological history. Because her husband held such a high position, and because Chesnut herself was extremely personable, many notable people confided in her; the result is a fascinating portrait of the South during the Civil War and a candid evaluation of the administrative problems that contributed to its defeat.

Nation in the Making[1]

February 19, 1861. I left the brand-new Confederacy making—or remodeling—its Constitution. Everybody wanted Mr. Davis[2] to be general in chief or president.

Keitt and Boyce[3] and a party preferred Howell Cobb[4] for president. And the fire-eaters per se wanted Barnwell Rhett.[5]

Today at dinner, Stephen[6] brought in the officers of the Montgomery Blues.

"Very soiled Blues," they said, apologizing for their rough condition.

Poor fellows! they had been a month before Fort Pickens and not allowed to attack it. They said Colonel Chase[7] built it and he was sure it was impregnable.

Colonel Lomax[8] telegraphed to Governor Moore[9] "if he might try, Chase or no Chase," and got for his answer no.

"And now," say the Blues, "we have worked like niggers—and when the fun and the fighting begins, they send us home and put regulars there."

They have an immense amount of powder along. The wheel of the car in which it was took fire. There was an escape for you!

We are packing a hamper of eatables for them. If they fight as they eat, they are Trojans indeed. Just now they are enjoying a quiet game of billiards.

Colonel Chase insulted them by blazing out a road behind them, in case of a sudden necessity for retreat.

It was not needed, for Stephen took one of his men with him to whom cannon was new. A double-barreled gun was his only experience in firearms. He saw the huge mouth of the cannon, and at the firing of the evening gun he dashed for home, straight as the crow flies, and was there by breakfast, cured forever of all weaknesses for soldiering. Fifty miles or more!

I am despondent once more. If I thought them in earnest because they put their best in front, *at first*—what now? We have to meet tremendous odds by pluck, activity, zeal, dash, endurance of the toughest, military instinct. We had to choose the born leaders of men, people who could attract love and trust. Everywhere political intrigue is as rife as in Washington.

Somebody likened it to the boys who could not catch up with the carriage, calling out to the coachman, "cut behind," to dislodge the luckier ones. <At any rate, I hear it said, "Surely if they believed a war inevitable, very different would be their choice"—and that gives us some hope.> Cecil's saying of Sir Walter Raleigh "I know he can labor terribly" is an electric touch.[10]

Clarendon's portraits. These are idlers—they only talk. "Hampden, who was of an industry and vigilance not to be tired out or wearied by the most laborious, and of parts not to be imposed on by the most subtile and sharp, and of a personal courage equal to his best parts. Falkland, who was so severe an adorer of truth that he could as easily have given himself leave to steal as to dissemble."

Above all, let the men to save South Carolina be young and vigorous. While I was cudgeling my brain to say what kind of men we ought to choose, I fell on Clarendon, and it was easy to construct my man out of this material. What has been may be again. So it need not be a purely ideal type.

❧

We keep each other in countenance and exasperate by emulation the frenzy of the time. The shield against the stinging of conscience is the universal practice of our contemporaries.[11]

—*Emerson*

Aye—aye—sir—

Mr. Toombs[12] told us a story of General Scott[13] and himself a few days before I left Montgomery. He said he was dining in Washington with General Scott, who seasoned every dish and every glass of wine with the eternal refrain "Save the Union"—"The Union must be preserved."

Toombs remarked that he knew why the Union was so dear to the general and illustrated by a steamboat anecdote. An explosion, of course; and while the passengers were struggling in the water, a woman ran up and down the bank, crying, "Oh, save the redheaded man!" The redhead man was saved, and his preserver, after landing him, noticed with surprise how little interest in him the woman who had made such moving appeals seemed to feel. He asked her, "Why did you make that pathetic outcry?" "Oh, he owes me ten thousand dollars." "Now, general, the U.S.A. or the Union owes you seventeen thousand a year."

I can imagine the scorn of old Scott's face.

My husband writes in fine spirits, but the daily bulletins are very contradictory.

Down here they did not like the president's message.[14]

February 25, 1861. Montgomery. Found them working very hard here. The cars were so overheated and disagreeable yesterday. As I dozed on the sofa last night could hear scratch, scratch of my husband's pen as he wrote at the table until midnight. After church today Captain Ingraham[15] called. He left me so uncomfortable. He dared to express his regret that he had to leave the U.S. Navy. He was stationed in the Mediterranean, where he likes to be; expected to be there two years. He expected to take those lovely daughters of his to Florence. Then came that ogre Lincoln and rampant Black Republicanism—and he must lay down his life for South Carolina. He, however, does not make any moan. He says we lack everything necessary of naval gear to retake Fort Sumter. Of course he only expects the navy to take it. He is a fish out of water here. He is one of the finest sea captains, so I suppose they will soon give him a ship and send him back to his own element.

At dinner Judge Withers[16] was loudly abusive of the [Provisional] Congress (already?). He said: "They had trampled the Constitution underfoot. They have provided President Davis with a house." It is hardly worth while wasting time in quarrels about nonessentials. He was disgusted with the folly of parading the president at the inauguration in a coach drawn by four white horses. (I thought that all right.) Then someone said Mrs. Fitzpatrick[17] was the only lady who sat with the Congress—and after the inaugural poked Jeff Davis in the back with her parasol, that he might turn and speak to her. "I am sure that was demo-cratic enough," said someone.

Governor Moore came in with the latest news. A telegram from Gov-ernor Pickens to the president. "That a war steamer is lying off the bar, laden with reinforcements for Fort Sumter—What must we do?" Answer: "Use your own discretion."

There is faith for you. After all said and done, it is believed there is some discretion still left in South Carolina, fit for use.

Everybody who comes here wants an office. And the many who of course are disappointed raise the cry, against the few who are successful, of corruption. And I thought we had left all that in Washington. Nobody is willing to be out of sight. And they take any office. Ex-Governor Man-ning[18] said he was an ambassador to Louisiana and quite pleased with his position, but Slidell[19] welcomed him coolly, as one of those "itinerant commissioners," and he felt himself held in contempt. Bonham[20] declared he did not mean to be fobbed off with any trashy commission of that sort. They were making merry over their woes, when Governor Moore gravely inquired of Mr. McQueen[21] if they were a party of disap-pointed office seekers.

Judge Withers denounced the people of South Carolina as fools and knaves—especially the people of Kershaw District. Mr. Chesnut said, "You represent those people. If I thought as you do, I would not stay here a day. I would not represent such a people."

Angry words ensued, and I was awfully frightened. Why will the man be so harsh and abusive of everybody?

Constitution Browne[22] says he is going to Washington for twenty-four hours.

I mean to send by him to Mary Garnett[23] for a bonnet ribbon. If they take him up as a traitor, he may cause a civil war. War is now our dread. Mr. C told him not to make himself a bone of contention.

Tom Taylor[24] and Malley Howell[25] called. Asked me when I was going home. "When this thing breaks up." "But you are not respectful to our Congress! Treason!" cried Alabama Tom Taylor.

"I am from South Carolina. That answers all. The more tenderfooted of you rebels must be more cautious in your speech."

Trescot[26] writes, "That clever, learned creature, naturalist, mathe-matician, &c&c, John McCrady[27] wants to be made a captain of regu-lars." So everybody means to go in the army.

If Sumter is attacked, then Jeff Davis's trouble begins.

The Judge says a military despotism would be best for us, anything to prevent a triumph of the Yankees.

All right, but every man objects to any despot but himself.

Read *Framley Parsonage* in *Cornhill*.[28] Don't care for elderly loves, so found Miss Dunstable and Dr. Thorne dull because I wanted to see how the young lovers were getting on.

How much I owe of the pleasure of my life to these much reviled writers of fiction.

Mr. Chesnut, in high spirits, dines today with the Louisiana delegation.

Stephen in higher spirits. The Montgomery Blues have presented him with a silver dipper in grateful remembrance of his hospitality.

Breakfasted with Constitution Browne, who is appointed assistant secretary of state. And so does not go to Washington.

Also there was at table the man who advertised for a wife—with the wife so obtained. She was not pretty. <<She was ugly as sin.>>

We dine at Mr. Pollard's[29] and go to a ball afterwards at Judge Bibb's.[30]

The *Herald*[31] says Lincoln stood before Washington's picture at his inauguration. Taken by the country as a good sign. Always frantic for a sign.

Let us pray that a Caesar or a Napoleon may be sent us. That would be our best sign of success.

But they still say no war. Peace let it be, kind Heaven!

Mr. Barnwell[32] brought a letter from Wigfall.[33] It was enclosed to him, though addressed to Jeff Davis. Before handing it to the president, Mr. Barnwell was to read it to Mr. C and Robert Barnwell Rhett. It accused the *Mercury*[34] of doing incalculable mischief—insulting and irritating the border states, who held back, saying, "South Carolina apparently was going to secede from the new Confederacy."

&

"Charitably take him aside and whisper in his ear that little comes of real knowledge but modesty—and doubt of self." Camden DeLeon, M.D.,[35] called, fresh from Washington. Says General Scott is using all of his power and influence to prevent officers from the South from resigning their commissions.

Among other things, promising that they should never be sent against us in case of war.

Captain Ingraham, in his short, curt way, said: "That will never do. If they take their government pay, they must do its fighting."

A brilliant dinner at the Pollards'. Mr. Barnwell took me down to dinner.

Came home and found Judge Withers and Governor Moore waiting to go with me to the Bibbs'.

And they say it is dull in Montgomery!!

Clayton,[36] fresh from Washington, was at the party—told us, "There was to be peace."

February 28, 1861. In the drawing room a literary lady began a violent attack upon this mischief-making South Carolina. She told me she was a successful writer in the magazines of the day. But when I found she used "incredible" for "incredulous," I said not a word in defense of my native land. I left her "incredible." Another person came in while she was pouring upon me home truths and asked her if she did not know I was a Carolinian. Then she gracefully reversed her engine and took the other tack—sounded our praises. But I left her incredible—and I remained incredulous, too.

Brewster[37] says the war specs are growing in size. Nobody at the North nor in Virginia believes we are in earnest. They think that we are sulking and that Jeff Davis and Stephens[38] are getting up a very pretty little comedy.

The Virginia delegates were insulted at the peace conference. Brewster said "kicked out."[39]

The *Herald* said today, "Hon. James Chesnut was the only son of one of the wealthiest men in Carolina, his father owning a thousand slaves, and found it impossible to ride across his estate in a day."[40]

There is accurate information for you!

I asked Brewster how his friend Wigfall liked being left alone with the Black Republicans.

He replied: "Wigfall chafes at the restraints of civil life. He likes to be where he can be as rude as he pleases, and he is indulging himself now to the fullest extent, apparently."

Mr. Keitt called. He complained of the *Mercury.* It calls everybody a submissionist but R. B. Rhett.

Mr. Mallory[41] then called. <<Seemed to have so high an opinion of me, but Captain Ingraham told Mr. Chesnut that he was so notoriously dissolute that a woman was compromised to be much seen with him.>> Fortunately the Judge likes him better than anyone here—thinks him so pleasant and witty. The Senate has not yet confirmed him as secretary of the navy.

Found a capital bookstore here. Got from there *Evan Harrington— Or He Would Be a Tailor.*[42] Rather a discouraging name, but it turns out to be an extremely clever book.

The Judge thought Jeff Davis rude to him when the latter was secretary of war. Mr. C persuaded the Judge to forego his private wrong for the public good, so he voted for him. Now his old grudge has come back with an increased venomousness.

What a pity to bring the spites of the old Union into this new one. It seems to me already men are willing to risk an injury to our cause if they may in so doing hurt Jeff Davis.

March 1, 1861. Dined today with Mr. Hill from Georgia and his wife. After he left us she told me he was the celebrated individual who for Christian scruples refused to fight a duel with Stephens.[43] She seemed very proud of him for his conduct in the affair.

Ignoramus that I am, I had not heard of it.

I am having all kinds of experiences. Drove today with a lady who fervently wished her husband would go down to Pensacola and be shot. I was dumb with amazement, of course.

Telling my story to one who knew the parties, was informed, "Don't you know he beats her?"

So I have seen a man "who lifts his hand against a woman in aught save kindness."

Brewster says Lincoln passed through Baltimore, disguised and at night—and that he did well—for just now Baltimore is dangerous ground. He says he hears from all quarters that the vulgarity of Lincoln, his wife, and his son is beyond credence—a thing you must see before you can believe it. Sen. Stephen Douglas[44] told Mr. C that Lincoln was awfully clever and that he had found him a heavy handful.

Went to pay my respects to Mrs. Jefferson Davis.[45]

She met me with open arms. We did not allude to anything by which we are surrounded. We eschewed politics and our changed relations. <<What a chat that was—*two* hours. She told me all Washington news.>>

She described the Prince of Wales's visit.[46] The various pieces of information she had derived from the noblemen who accompanied the Prince.

Lord St. Germans[47] told her who Sydney Smith was and also Sir Henry Holland,[48] and informed her furthermore that as a statesman they did not think highly of Mr. Calhoun[49] in England.

A girl inquired of a Sir Somebody Elliott[50] if he were a relative of the Carolina Elliotts.

The marchioness of Chandos[51] condemned Mrs. Gwin's[52] extravagance. Her velvet dress was cut up and pinked so it could never be used again for anything else.

And that "Oh, uncommon fine!" was king's English, for the Prince said so at every turn.

Dr. Manly,[53] the celebrated Baptist minister, was very much interested in me as soon as he found out I was the granddaughter of that famous good sister (Baptist) Mrs. Burwell Boykin.[54]

. . .

March 4, 1861. . . . So I have seen a Negro woman sold—up on the block—at auction. I was walking. The woman on the block overtopped the crowd. I felt faint—seasick. The creature looked so like my good little Nancy. She was a bright mulatto with a pleasant face. She was magnificently gotten up in silks and satins. She seemed delighted with it all— sometimes ogling the bidders, sometimes looking quite coy and modest, but her mouth never relaxed from its expanded grin of excitement. I daresay the poor thing knew who would buy her.

I sat down on a stool in a shop. I disciplined my wild thoughts. I tried it Sterne fashion.[55]

You know how women sell themselves and are sold in marriage, from queens downward, eh?

You know what the Bible says about slavery—and marriage. Poor women. Poor slaves. Sterne with his starling. What did he know? He only thought—he did not feel.

&

Evan Harrington: "Like a true English female she believed in her own inflexible virtue but never trusted her husband out of sight."[56]

New York *Herald* says, "Lincoln's carriage is not bombproof, so he does not drive out."

Two flags and a bundle of sticks have been sent him as a gentle reminder. The sticks are to break our heads.

The English are gushingly unhappy as to our family quarrel.

Magnanimous of them—for it is their opportunity.

. . .

<<*March 7, 1861.* . . . Dr. Tom Taylor was saying how stiff it was at the reception yesterday until I got there—and I went in like a ray of warmth and sunshine. Pretty good for a woman of my years. Saw a flag with stars and stripes, floating in the breeze, and told Miss Tyler, as she seemed head of the flag committee, to have it taken down.>>

. . .

March [no day] 1861. . . . In the hotel parlor we had a scene.

Mrs. Scott[57] was describing Lincoln, who is of the cleverest Yankee type, she said. "Awfully ugly—even grotesque in appearance, the kind who are always at corner stores, sitting on boxes, whittling sticks. And telling stories as funny as they are vulgar."

Here I interposed to sigh, "But Douglas said one day to Mr. Chesnut, 'Lincoln is the hardest fellow to handle I have ever encountered yet.'" Mr. Scott is from California. He said: "Lincoln is an utterly American specimen, coarse, tough, and strong. A good-natured, kindly creature.

"As pleasant-tempered as he is clever. And if this country can be joked and laughed out of its rights, he is the kind-hearted fellow to do it. Now, if there be a war and it pinches the Yankee pocket instead of filling it—"

Here a shrill voice came from the next room (which opened upon the one we were in by folding doors, thrown wide open):

"Yankees are no more mean and stingy than you are. People at the North are as good as people at the South."

The speaker advanced upon us in great wrath. Mrs. Scott apologized and made some smooth, polite remarks, though evidently much embarrassed. But the vinegar face and curly pate refuse to receive any concession. She said, "That comes with a very bad grace after what you were saying." And she harangued us loudly for several minutes. Someone in the other room giggled outright. We were quiet as mice.

Nobody wanted to hurt her feelings. She was one against so many. If I were at the North I should expect them to belabor us—and should hold my tongue. We separated because of incompatibility of temper. We are divorced, North from South, because we hated each other so. If we could only separate—a "séparation à l'agréable," as the French say it, and not a horrid fight for divorce.

This poor exile had already been insulted, she said. She was playing "Yankee Doodle" on the piano before breakfast to soothe her wounded spirits. The Judge came in and calmly requested her to leave out the Yankee while she played the Doodle. The Yankee end of it did not suit our climate. Was totally out of place. Had got out of its latitude, &c&c.

Mrs. Davis does not like her husband being made president. People are hard to please. She says general of all the armies would have suited his temperament better.

And then Mrs. Watson[58] came in to deplore her husband's having been made adjutant general of the Alabama contingent.

· · ·

<<*March 15, 1861.* Walked to see Mrs. Bethea[59] with Mr. Chesnut, who, however, rushed home and left me at the door. . . . Went to the party with the Brownes. At first we stood alone and were gazed at. . . . I know my

dress is the prettiest in the room. Then we saw Mr. Clayton, and the remark was made: what a party when we are glad to see Mr. Clayton! Then Mr. Curry[60] walked off with Mrs. Browne. Mr. B and I had a good time. All sorts of stupid people came to interrupt us. . . . I want to tell Mrs. Browne that the effect upon me last night was not unlike the impression made by my first visit to Washington. The people I thought one mass of vulgarity and finery and horror. How differently I felt when I had been there long enough to separate the wheat from the tares. . . . I think old Governor Moore was jealous. He said quite peevishly that he must take lessons in the art of pleasing from Mr. M[allory].

<<Poor Mrs. Browne. How she hated my coming. Actually shed tears. <I can make anybody love me if I choose. I would get tired of it. Mr. B, too—how excessively complimentary he was that night at the party,>[61] and so nicely done. Any woman might have been proud of my three attendants that night. . . .>>

• • •

March 18, 1861. . . . <<I wonder if it be a sin to think slavery a curse to any land. Sumner[62] said not one word of this hated institution which is not true. Men and women are punished when their masters and mistresses are brutes and not when they do wrong—and then we live surrounded by prostitutes. An abandoned woman is sent out of any decent house elsewhere. Who thinks any worse of a negro or mulatto woman for being a thing we can't name? God forgive us, but ours is a *monstrous* system and wrong and iniquity. Perhaps the rest of the world is as bad— this *only* I see. Like the patriarchs of old our men live all in one house with their wives and their concubines, and the mulattoes one sees in every family exactly resemble the white children—and every lady tells you who is the father of all the mulatto children in everybody's household, but those in her own she seems to think drop from the clouds, or pretends so to think. Good women we have, *but* they talk of all *nastiness*—tho' they never do wrong, they talk day and night of [*erasures illegible save for the words* "all unconsciousness"] my disgust sometimes is boiling over—but they are, I believe, in conduct the purest women God ever made. Thank God for my countrywomen—alas for the men! No worse than men everywhere, but the lower their mistresses, the more degraded they must be.

<<My mother-in-law told me when I was first married not to send my female servants in the street on errands. They were then tempted, led astray—and then she said placidly, so they told *me* when I came here, and I was very particular, *but you see with what result.*

<<Mr. Harris said it was so patriarchal. So it is—flocks and herds and

slaves—and wife Leah does not suffice. Rachel must be *added,* if not *married.*[63] And all the time they seem to think themselves patterns—models of husbands and fathers.>>

. . .

March 25, 1861. <<Today, forlorn and weak and miserable, I am slowly packing to be off to town. . . .>>

I was mobbed yesterday by my own house servants. Some of them are at the plantation, some hired out at the Camden hotel. Some here at Mulberry.[64]

They agreed to come in a body and beg me to stay at home—to keep my own house once more, as I ought not to have them scattered and distributed every which way.

I have not been a month in Camden since 1858. So a house here would be for their benefit solely, not mine. I asked my cook if she lacked anything on the plantation at the Hermitage.

"Lack anything?" said she. "I lack everything. What is cornmeal and bacon, milk and molasses? Would that be all you wanted? Ain't I bin living and eating exactly as you does all these years? When I cook for you, didn't I have some of all? Dere now."

So she doubled herself up laughing.

They all shouted, "Missis, we is crazy for you to stay home."

Armsted, my butler, said he hated the hotel. Besides, he heard a man there abusing "Marster," but Mr. Clyburn[65] took it up and made him stop short. Armsted said he wanted Marster to know Mr. Clyburn was his friend and would let nobody say a word behind his back against him, &c&c.

Stay here? Not if I can help it.

"Festers in provincial sloth." That's Tennyson's way of putting it.[66]

Mary

Boykin

Chesnut

&

109

Notes

1. All subsequent notes are from C. Vann Woodward's text, although occasionally the editors have clarified a reference; these additions are indicated by brackets. The following symbols have been used:

 & To indicate Chesnut's original space breaks within entries. (A centered ellipsis indicates material omitted from the original by the editors of this volume.)

<> To enclose effaced or erased passages Woodward restored.

<< >> To enclose excerpts from other versions inserted in the text. Unless identified in the footnotes as being from some other version, these passages are from the 1860s journal, which is housed at the South Caroliniana Library at the University of South Carolina.

2. Jefferson Davis would serve as president of the Confederacy.

3. Lawrence Massillon Keitt of Orangeburg and William Waters Boyce of Edgefield, S.C. Both men were former U.S. congressmen and delegates to the Montgomery convention.

4. Howell Cobb, a former congressman, governor of Ga., and secretary of the treasury in the Buchanan administration, was chairman of the Montgomery convention and president of the Provisional Confederate Congress.

5. Barnwell Rhett, South Carolina's most prominent secessionist agitator and a member of the S.C. delegation to the Montgomery convention.

6. Stephen Decatur Miller, Jr., Chesnut's younger brother.

7. William H. Chase, a retired U.S. Army Corps of Engineers officer who held a military commission from the state of Fla.

8. Col. Tennent Lomax, commander of the Montgomery Blues, was a lawyer and a newspaper editor born in S.C.

9. Andrew Barry Moore, governor of Ala.

10. M. B. C. [Mary Boykin Chesnut] took this line and the following paragraph from Ralph Waldo Emerson, "The Uses of Great Men," *Representative Men* (1850). Emerson himself had paraphrased the descriptions of Hampden and Falkland from Edward Hyde, Earl of Clarendon, *History of the Rebellion and Civil Wars in England* (1702–04), book 7, sections 84 and 224.

11. Also quoted from "The Uses of Great Men."

12. Robert Augustus Toombs of Ga., a disappointed aspirant for the Confederate presidency, resigned his seat in the U.S. Senate early in Feb. and became Confederate secretary of state at the end of the month.

13. Winfield Scott, a native of Va. and an unsuccessful Whig presidential candidate in 1852, was general chief of the U.S. Army.

14. Jefferson Davis's address at his inauguration as Provisional Confederate president on Feb. 18.

15. Duncan Nathaniel Ingraham of Charleston resigned as a U.S. Navy commander in Jan. 1861 and was commissioned captain in the Confederate States Navy (C.S.N.) in March.

16. Common-law judge Thomas Jefferson Withers of Camden, a delegate to the S.C. secession convention and a member of the Provisional Congress, was M. B. C.'s uncle and former guardian.

17. A friend of the Chesnuts from their days in Washington, Aurelia (Blassingame) Fitzpatrick was the second wife of former Ala. governor and U.S. senator Benjamin Fitzpatrick.

18. John Laurence Manning of Clarendon District, governor of S.C. from 1852 to 1854, was one of the wealthiest men in the South. The

owner of 648 slaves on plantations in S.C. and La., he valued his holdings at more than two million dollars in 1860. Manning served in the S.C. state legislature and secession convention and went to La. to urge that state to join the Confederacy.

19. John Slidell, former U.S. senator from La. and a leading secessionist.

20. Milledge Luke Bonham of Edgefield District, S.C., had resigned his seat in the U.S. Congress in Dec. 1860.

21. John McQueen of Marlboro District, S.C., resigned from the U.S. Congress in Dec. 1860 and served as a commissioner to Tex. to secure that state's secession.

22. William Montague Browne of Washington, D.C., was the Irish-born editor of the Buchanan administration newspaper, the Washington *Constitution*. His commission as colonel in the C.S.A. [Confederate States Army] and his title, assistant secretary of state, were the result of his friendship with Howell Cobb and Jefferson Davis.

23. Mary (Stevens) Garnett, daughter of J. C.'s [James Chesnut] cousin, Edwin Stevens of N.J. She had lived with the Chesnuts in Washington the year before her marriage to Congressman Muscoe Garnett of Va. in 1860.

24. Thomas B. Taylor, a physician who moved from Richland District, S.C., to Ala. in the 1830s. Taylor's uncle, John Taylor, governor of S.C. from 1826 to 1828, married J.C.'s aunt Sarah Cantey (Chesnut) Taylor. One of Taylor's first cousins, James Madison Taylor, was the husband of M. B. C.'s aunt Charlotte (Boykin) Taylor. M. B. C. probably calls Taylor "Alabama Tom" to distinguish him from his cousin, Thomas Taylor of Richland District, whom she later encounters. Compounded kinship in S.C. often transcends terminology!

25. Jesse Malachi Howell, a planter with interests in Richland District and Miss., was Thomas B. Taylor's second cousin.

26. William Henry Trescot of Beaufort District, S.C., a slaveholder, historian, and author of *The Position and Course of the South* (1850), had resigned as U.S. assistant secretary of state but remained in Washington as an unofficial adviser to the S.C. commissioners negotiating the fate of the Federal forts at Charleston.

27. John McCrady, professor of mathematics and zoology at the College of Charleston, served as an engineer in the C.S.A.

28. Anthony Trollope's *Framley Parsonage* (1861) appeared as a serial in the English *Cornhill Magazine* in 1860-61.

29. The home of Charles T. Pollard, a prominent Montgomery merchant and railroad owner, and his wife, Emily Virginia (Scott) Pollard.

30. The home of Montgomery County Court judge Benajah Bibb and his wife, Sophia (Gilmer) Bibb.

31. The New York *Herald.*

32. Robert Woodward Barnwell, senior member of the S.C. delegation to the Provisional Congress, was a moderate rather than a fire-eater like his cousin, Robert Barnwell Rhett, Sr. In his long public career, he had served as a U.S. congressman, a U.S. senator, president of S.C. College, and member of the S.C. secession convention from St. Helena's Parish, Charleston.

33. Louis Trezevant Wigfall, a South Carolinian, moved to Tex. after a duel and became an important secessionist agitator and a U.S. senator from 1859 to 1861. With the approval of Jefferson Davis, Wigfall remained in Washington after the secession of Tex. to buy arms and recruit men for the Confederacy.

34. The Charleston *Mercury* had opposed the Provisional Confederate government from the beginning, fearing that it would promote sectional reconciliation. When the Confederate Congress voted to prohibit the slave trade and retain a protective tariff—measures designed to attract support in still undecided border states—the *Mercury* charged, "South Carolina is about to be saddled with every grievance except abolition for which she has long struggled [*sic*] and just withdrawn from the United States government."

35. David Camden DeLeon, a native of Camden, resigned as a U.S. Army surgeon on Feb. 19 and soon became the first surgeon general of the Confederacy.

36. Phillip Clayton of Ga. had resigned as assistant secretary of the U.S. Treasury. He held the same post in the Confederate government.

37. Born in S.C., Henry Percy Brewster became secretary of war of the Texas Republic and a prominent lawyer in Tex. and Washington, D.C.

38. Former congressman Alexander Hamilton Stephens of Ga. was elected vice-president of the Confederacy on Feb. 6.

39. On Feb. 4, a peace conference requested by the Va. legislature brought representatives from twenty-one of the thirty-three states to Washington in a last attempt to find a solution to the sectional crisis. The "insult" to the Virginians was apparently the selection as second temporary chairman of Christopher Walcott, Ohio's attorney general, who had allegedly moved to adjourn a state court in honor of John Brown. The Va. delegation had not been expelled from the convention, however.

40. This sketch of James Chesnut, Jr., and his father appeared in a column entitled "The Members of the Southern Congress" in the

New York *Herald,* Feb. 23, 1861. The owner of 448 slaves in 1860, old Mr. Chesnut was indeed one of the wealthiest men in S.C. and the South. But J. C. shared little of this wealth in his own name.

41. Stephen Russell Mallory of Fla. had resigned from the U.S. Senate in Jan.

42. Actually George Meredith's *Evan Harrington; or, He Would Be A Gentleman* (1860), describing the career of a socially ambitious tailor.

43. During a debate in 1856, Benjamin Harvey Hill called Alexander Stephens "Judas Iscariot." Challenged, Hill declined to face "a man who has neither conscience nor family." Hill, who was married to Caroline (Holt) Hill, served as a delegate to the Montgomery convention, even though he opposed secession.

44. Stephen Arnold Douglas of Ill.

45. Varina Anne (Howell) Davis of Miss., granddaughter of a Revolutionary War governor of N.J., became Davis's second wife in 1845. A socially accomplished woman of the planter class, she was an ambitious supporter of her husband. Her friendship with M. B. C. began in Washington when their husbands were in the U.S. Senate.

46. In 1860, Queen Victoria sent her son, Edward Albert, on a tour of Canada and the U.S. Mrs. Davis probably saw the Prince in Washington, where he stayed three days at the White House.

47. Edward Granville Eliot, third earl of St. Germans and lord steward of the royal household.

48. Sydney Smith was a founder of the *Edinburgh Review* and canon of St. Paul's until his death in 1845. Sir Henry Holland, a fashionable London doctor and physician to Queen Victoria, was Smith's son-in-law.

49. John Caldwell Calhoun of S.C.

50. Lord St. Germans.

51. Caroline Harvey, wife of the keeper of the privy seal to the Prince of Wales.

52. Mary (Bell) Gwin was the second wife of William McKendree Gwin, U.S. senator from Calif.

53. Basil Manly, Sr., a native of S.C., was pastor of the First Baptist Church in Montgomery and chaplain at the inauguration of Jefferson Davis.

54. Mary (Whitaker) Boykin, second wife of Burwell Boykin.

55. In Laurence Sterne's "The Passport. The Hotel at Paris," *A Sentimental Journey through France and Italy* (1768), Mr. Yorick, reasoning away the evils of captivity in the Bastille, hears a caged starling say, "I can't get out—I can't get out." Yorick struggles unsuccessfully

to free the bird and concludes, "Disguise thyself as thou wilt, still slavery!"

56. A paraphrase from chapter 22.

57. Anne (Vivian) Scott of Ala. was the wife of Charles Lewis Scott, a Virginia-born congressman from Calif. Early in March, Scott left Congress, went to Ala. with his wife, and enlisted as a private in the C.S.A.

58. Hugh P. Watson, adjutant general of Ala. militia through the war.

59. Eugenia (Bethea) Bethea, wife of Montgomery planter and politician Tristram B. Bethea.

60. Jabez Lamar Monroe Curry of Ala., a member of the Provisional Confederate Congress, had belonged to the Chesnuts' Washington mess while serving in the U.S. Congress.

61. Here the brackets < > indicate erasures recovered.

62. Charles Sumner, U.S. senator from Mass.

63. In Genesis 29-30, Jacob, unhappy with his wife Leah, also marries her sister Rachel. He has children by both women and by their handmaidens as well. M. B. C. apparently believed old Mr. Chesnut had children by a slave whom she calls "Rachel" (p. 72) [see p. 72 in Woodward's text]. She confesses no such suspicions of her husband.

64. James Chesnut's house slaves were distributed in this manner when he sold his house and went to Washington in 1858.

65. William Craig Clyburn, a planter of Kershaw District.

66. M. B. C. is probably misquoting a line from Tennyson's *In Memoriam* (1850), part 27, stanza 3: "The heart that never plighted troth / But stagnates in the weeds of sloth."

11. Augusta Jane Evans Wilson

(1835–1909)

Augusta Jane Evans Wilson was born into a wealthy southern family in Wynnton, Georgia. Shortly after her birth, Wilson's father built Sherwood Hall, a mansion the family occupied for the next few years. But in the early 1840s the Evans family went bankrupt and then fell further into poverty until they were forced to give up their home and move to Texas in hopes of a stable income. From 1845 to 1849 the family moved from place to place in Texas. Unable to attain success anywhere, Wilson's father finally settled the family in Mobile, Alabama. Because they were so often moving, the Evans children received little formal education but instead were taught by their mother.

Wilson began writing seriously when she was fifteen years old. Her first novel, about emigrants to Texas, was published in 1855. *Inez: A Tale of the Alamo* was an ambitious work, but it was considered overly moralistic and sentimental. Issues of faith, however, continued to permeate Wilson's works, more successfully in her second novel, *Beulah* (1859), which focuses on the difficulty of sustaining religious faith. This novel was extremely popular, bringing Wilson not only critical attention but also considerable wealth. Just prior to the Civil War, Wilson broke off an engagement to James Spalding, a New York journalist with "unacceptable Yankee views." Then, with the outbreak of war, Wilson organized an army hospital, followed relatives to battle on several occasions, and consistently published southern propaganda.

Macaria; or, Altars of Sacrifice (1863) was written as a means of encouraging the southern soldiers; it describes the greatness of the South through realistic depictions of the war. Because the novel was so popular and so damaging to northern morale, northern troops were prohibited from reading it. The story revolves around two families, the Huntingdons and the Aubreys. Leonard Huntingdon, a wealthy, landed gentleman, was in love with Russell Aubrey's mother, Amy, when she married Russell's father. Amy had accepted Huntingdon's proposal of marriage but then decided that she instead loved Aubrey, who was "poor, but honest, highly cultivated, and, in every sense of that much-abused word, a gentleman." Because Huntingdon would not release Amy from her promise, she eloped with Aubrey, never to be forgiven by

Huntingdon or her parents for the marriage. When their son, Russell, was still very young, Aubrey was pursued by a creditor, whom he ultimately killed. Aubrey was sent to jail and sentenced to death; he committed suicide before the hanging could take place. The chapter anthologized here takes place years later, during the Civil War, when Russell Aubrey is a young man and much in love with Irene, Leonard Huntingdon's daughter.

Wilson's next novel, *St. Elmo* (1866), is, like *Beulah,* about the power of virtue and prayer. It was equally successful and was adapted for the stage and film in the following years. In 1868 Augusta married her neighbor, Col. Lorenzo Wilson, and took on the management of her husband's property. Although finding time for writing became more difficult, Wilson still managed to complete *Vashti* in 1869 and *Infelice* in 1875. After her husband died in 1891, Wilson moved to Mobile to live with her brother. While there she wrote *A Speckled Bird* (1902), which opposed women's suffrage, as well as *Devota* (1907), a novel attacking the Populist movement. Wilson suffered a heart attack in 1908 and died in the following year.

From *Macaria; or, Altars of Sacrifice* (Chapter 30)

Picking his way to avoid trampling the dead, Russell saw Major Huntingdon at a little distance, trying to drag himself toward a neighboring tree. The memory of his injuries crowded up—the memory of all that he had endured and lost through that man's prejudice—the sorrow that might have been averted from his blind mother—and his vindictive spirit rebelled at the thought of rendering him aid. But as he paused and struggled against his better nature, Irene's holy face, as he saw it last, lifted in prayer for him, rose, angel-like, above all that mass of death and horrors. The sufferer was Irene's father; she was hundreds of miles away; Russell set his lips firmly, and, riding up to the prostrate figure, dismounted. Exhausted by his efforts, Major Huntingdon had fallen back in the dust, and an expression of intolerable agony distorted his features as Russell stooped over him, and asked, in a voice meant to be gentle:

"Can I do anything for you? Could you sit up, if I placed you on my horse?"

The wounded man scowled as he recognized the voice and face, and turned his head partially away, muttering:

"What brought you here?"

"There has never been any love between us, Major Huntingdon; but we are fighting in the same cause for the first time in our lives. You are badly wounded, and, as a fellow-soldier, I should be glad to relieve your sufferings, if possible. Once more, for humanity's sake, I ask, can you ride my horse to the rear if I assist you to mount?"

"No. But for God's sake, give me some water!"

Russell knelt, raised the head, and unbuckling his canteen, put it to his lips, using his own wounded arm with some difficulty. Half of the contents was eagerly swallowed, and the remainder Russell poured slowly on the gaping ghastly wound in his side. The proud man eyed him steadily till the last cool drop was exhausted, and said, sullenly:

"You owe me no kindness, Aubrey. I hate you, and you know it. But you have heaped coals of fire on my head. You are more generous than I thought you. Thank you, Aubrey; lay me under that tree yonder and let me die."

"I will try to find a surgeon. Who belongs to your regiment?"

"Somebody whom I never saw till last week. I won't have him hacking about me. Leave me in peace."

"Do you know anything of your servant? I saw him as I came on the field."

"Poor William! he followed me so closely that he was shot through the head. He is lying three hundred yards to the left, yonder. Poor fellow! he was faithful to the last."

A tear dimmed the master's eagle eye as he muttered, rather than spoke, these words.

"Then I will find Dr. Arnold at once, and send him to you."

It was no easy matter, on that crowded, confused Aceldama, and the afternoon was well nigh spent before Russell, faint and weary, descried Dr. Arnold busily using his instruments in a group of wounded. He rode up, and, having procured a drink of water and refilled his canteen, approached the surgeon.

"Doctor, where is your horse? I want you."

"Ho, Cyrus! bring him up. What is the matter, Aubrey? You are hurt."

"Nothing serious, I think. But Major Huntingdon is desperately wounded—mortally, I am afraid. See what you can do for him."

"You must be mistaken! I have asked repeatedly for Leonard, and they told me he was in hot pursuit, and unhurt. I hope to heaven you are mistaken!"

"Impossible; I tell you I lifted him out of a pool of his own blood. Come; I will show you the way."

At a hard gallop they crossed the intervening woods, and without difficulty Russell found the spot where the mangled form lay still. He had swooned, with his face turned up to the sky, and the ghastliness of death had settled on his strongly-marked, handsome features.

"God pity Irene!" said the doctor, as he bent down and examined the horrid wound, striving to press the red lips together.

The pain caused from handling him roused the brave spirit to consciousness, and, opening his eyes, he looked around wonderingly.

"Well, Hiram! it is all over with me, old fellow."

"I hope not, Leonard; can't you turn a little, and let me feel for the ball?"

"It is of no use; I am torn all to pieces. Take me out of this dirt, on the fresh grass somewhere."

"I must first extract the ball. Aubrey, can you help me raise him a little?"

Administering some chloroform, he soon succeeded in taking out the ball, and, with Russell's assistance, passed a bandage round the body.

"There is no chance for me, Hiram; I know that. I have few minutes to live. Some water."

Russell put a cup to his white lips, and, calling in the assistance of Cyrus, who had followed his master, they carried him several yards farther, and made him comfortable, while orders were despatched for an ambulance.

"It will come after my corpse. Hiram, see that I am sent home at once. I don't want my bones mixed here with other people's; and it will be some comfort to Irene to know that I am buried in sight of home. I could not rest in a ditch here. I want to be laid in my own vault. Will you see to it?"

"Yes."

"Hiram, come nearer, where I can see you better. Break the news gently to Irene. Tell her I did my duty; that will be her only comfort, and best. Tell her I fell in the thickest of the battle, with my face to Washington; that I died gloriously, as a Huntingdon and a soldier should. Tell her I sent her my blessing, my love, and a last kiss."

He paused, and tears glided over his wan cheeks as the picture of his far-off home rose temptingly before him.

"She is a brave child; she will bear it, for the sake of the cause I died in. Take care of her, Arnold; tell Eric I leave her to his guardianship. Harris has my will. My poor lonely child! it is bitter to leave her. My Queen! my golden-haired, beautiful Irene!"

He raised his hand feebly, and covered his face.

"Don't let it trouble you, Leonard. You know how I love her; I promise you I will watch over her as long as I live."

"I believe you. But if I could see her once more, to ask her not to remember my harshness—long ago. You must tell her for me; she will understand. Oh! I—"

A horrible convulsion seized him at this moment, and so intense was the agony that a groan burst through his set teeth, and he struggled to rise. Russell knelt down and rested the haughty head against his shoulder, wiping off the cold drops that beaded the pallid brow. After a little while, lifting his eyes to the face bending over him, Major Huntingdon gazed into the melancholy black eyes, and said, almost in a whisper:

"I little thought I should ever owe you thanks. Aubrey, forgive me all my hate; you can afford to do so now. I am not a brute; I know magnanimity when I see it. Perhaps I was wrong to visit Amy's sins on you; but I could not forgive her. Aubrey, it was natural that I should hate Amy's son."

Again the spasm shook his lacerated frame, and twenty minutes after his fierce, relentless spirit was released from torture; the proud, ambitious, dauntless man was with his God.

Dr. Arnold closed the eyes with trembling fingers, and covered his face with his hands to hide the tears that he could not repress.

"A braver man never died for freedom. He cheered me on, as my regiment charged over the spot where he lay," said Russell, looking down at the stiffening form.

"He had his faults, like the rest of us, and his were stern ones; but, for all that, I was attached to him. He had some princely traits. I would rather take my place there beside him, than have to break this to Irene. Poor desolate child! what an awful shock for her! She loves him with a devotion which I have rarely seen equalled. God only knows how she will bear it. If I were not so needed here, I would go to her to-morrow."

"Perhaps you can be spared."

"No; it would not be right to leave so much suffering behind."

He turned to Cyrus, and gave directions about bringing the body into camp, to his own tent; and the two mounted and rode slowly back.

For some moments silence reigned; then Dr. Arnold said, suddenly:

"I am glad you were kind to him, Aubrey. It will be some consolation to that pure soul in W——, who has mourned over and suffered for his violent animosity. It was very generous, Russell."

"Save your commendation for a better occasion; I do not merit it now. I had, and have, as little magnanimity as my old enemy, and what I did was through no generous oblivion of the past."

Glancing at him as these words were uttered gloomily, the doctor noticed his faint, wearied appearance, and led the way to his temporary hospital.

"Come in, and let me see your arm. Your sleeve is full of blood."

An examination discovered a painful flesh-wound—the minie ball having glanced from the shoulder and passed out through the upper part of the arm. In removing the coat to dress the wound, the doctor exclaimed:

"Here is a bullet-hole in the breast, which must have just missed your heart! Was it a spent-ball?"

A peculiar smile disclosed Russell's faultless teeth an instant, but he merely took the coat, laid it over his uninjured arm, and answered:

"Don't trouble yourself about spent-balls—finish your job. I must look after my wounded."

As soon as the bandages were adjusted he walked away, and took from the inside pocket of the coat a heavy square morocco case containing Irene's ambrotype. When the coat was buttoned, as on that day, it rested over his heart; and during the second desperate charge of General Beauregard's lines Russell felt a sudden thump, and, above all the roar of that scene of carnage, heard the shivering of the glass which covered the likeness. The morocco was torn and indented, but the ball was turned aside harmless, and now, as he touched the spring, the fragments of glass fell at his feet. It was evident that his towering form had rendered him a conspicuous target; some accurate marksman had aimed at his heart, and the ambrotype-case had preserved his life. He looked at the uninjured, radiant face till a mist dimmed his eyes; nobler aspirations, purer aims possessed him, and, bending his knees, he bowed his forehead on the case and he reverently thanked God for his deliverance. With a countenance pale from physical suffering, but beaming with triumphant joy for the Nation's first great victory, he went out among the dead and dying, striving to relieve the wounded, and to find the members of his own command. Passing from group to group, he heard a feeble, fluttering voice pronounce his name, and saw one of his men sitting against a tree, mortally wounded by a fragment of shell.

"Well, Colonel, I followed that black feather of yours as long as I could. I am glad I had one good chance at the cowardly villains before I got hurt. We've thrashed them awfully, and I am willing to die now."

"I hope you are not so badly hurt. Cheer up, Martin; I will bring a doctor to dress your leg, and we will soon have you on crutches."

"No, Colonel; the doctor has seen it, and says there is nothing to be done for me. I knew it before; everybody feels when death strikes them. Dr. Arnold gave me something that has eased me of my pain, but he can't save me. Colonel, they say my captain is killed; and, as I may not see any of our company boys, I wish you would write to my poor wife, and tell her all about it. I have n't treated her as well as I ought; but a wife forgives everything, and she will grieve for me, though I did act like a brute when I was drinking. She will be proud to know that I fought well for my country, and died a faithful Confederate soldier; and so will my boy, Philip, who wanted to come with me. Tell Margaret to send him to take my place just as soon as he is old enough. The boy will revenge me; he has a noble spirit. And, Colonel, be sure to tell her to tell Miss Irene that I kept my promise to her—that I have not touched a drop of liquor since the day she talked to me before I went out to build Mr. Huntingdon's gin-house. God bless her sweet, pure soul! I believe she saved me from a drunkard's grave, to fill that of a brave soldier. I know she will never let my Margaret suffer, as long as she lives."

"Is there anything else I can do for you, Martin?"

"Nothing else, unless I could get a blanket, or something, to put under my head. I am getting very weak."

"Leavens, pick up one of those knapsacks scattered about, and bring a blanket. I promise you, Martin, I will write to your wife; and when I go home, if I outlive this war, I will see that she is taken care of. I am sorry to lose you, my brave fellow. You were one of the best sergeants in the regiment. But remember that you have helped to win a great battle, and your country will not forget her faithful sons who fell at Manassas."

"Good-by, Colonel; I should like to follow you to Washington. You have been kind to us all, and I hope you will be spared to our regiment. God bless you, Colonel Aubrey, wherever you go."

Russell changed him from his constrained posture to a more comfortable one, rested his head on a knapsack and blanket, placed his own canteen beside him, and, with a long, hard gripe of hands, and faltering "God bless you!" the soldiers parted. The day of horrors was shuddering to its close; glazing eyes were turned for the last time to the sun which set in the fiery West; the din and roar of the pursuit died away in the distance; lowering clouds draped the sky; the groans and wails of the wounded rose mournfully on the reeking air; and night and a drizzling rain came down on the blanched corpses on the torn, trampled, crimson plain of Manassas.

> "I hate the dreadful hollow behind the little wood.
> Its lips in the field above are dabbled with blood-red heath,
> The red-ribbed ledges drip with a silent horror of blood,
> And Echo there, whatever is asked her, answers 'Death!'"

But all of intolerable torture centred not there, awful as was the scene. Throughout the length and breadth of the Confederacy telegraphic despatches told that the battle was raging; and an army of women spent that 21st upon their knees, in agonizing prayer for husbands and sons who wrestled for their birthright on the far-off field of blood.

Gray-haired pastors and curly-haired children alike besought the God of Justice to bless the Right, to deliver our gallant band of patriots from the insolent hordes sent to destroy us; and to that vast trembling volume of prayer which ascended from early morning from the altars of the South, God lent his ear, and answered.

The people of W—— were subjected to painful suspense as hour after hour crept by, and a dense crowd collected in front of the telegraph office, whence floated an ominous red flag. Andrew waited on horseback to carry to Irene the latest intelligence, and during the entire afternoon she paced the colonnade, with her eyes fixed on the winding road. At half-past five o'clock the solemn stillness of the sultry day was suddenly broken by a wild, prolonged shout from the town; cheer after cheer was caught up by the hills, echoed among the purple valleys, and finally lost in the roar of the river. Andrew galloped up the avenue with an extra, yet damp from the printing-press, containing the joyful tidings that McDowell's army had been completely routed, and was being pursued toward Alexandria. Meagre was the account—our heroes, Bee and Bartow, had fallen. No other details were given, but the premonition, "Heavy loss on our side," sent a thrill of horror to every womanly heart, dreading to learn the price of victory. Irene's white face flushed as she read the despatch, and, raising her hands, exclaimed:

"Oh, thank God! thank God!"

"Shall I go back to the office?"

"Yes; I shall certainly get a despatch from Father some time to-night. Go back, and wait for it. Tell Mr. Rogers, the operator, what you came for, and ask him I say please to let you have it as soon as it arrives. And, Andrew, bring me any other news that may come before my despatch."

Tediously time wore on: the shadows on the lawn and terrace grew longer and thinner; the birds deserted the hedges; the pigeons forsook the colonnade and steps; Paragon, tired of walking after Irene, fell asleep on the rug; and the slow, drowsy tinkle of cow-bells died away among the hills.

Far off to the east the blue was hidden by gray thunderous masses of rain-cloud, now and then veined by lightning; and as Irene watched their jagged, grotesque outlines they took the form of battling hosts. Cavalry swept down on the flanks, huge forms heaved along the centre, and the lurid furrows, ploughing the whole from time to time, seemed indeed death-dealing flashes of artillery. She recalled the phantom cloud-battle in the Netherlandish vision, and shuddered involuntarily as, in imagination, she

> "Heard the heavens fill with shouting, and there rained a ghastly dew
> From the nations airy navies grappling in the central blue."

Gradually the distant storm drifted southward, the retreat passed the horizon, a red sunset faded in the west; rose and amber and orange were quenched, and sober blue, with starry lights, was over all. How the serene regal beauty of that summer night mocked the tumultuous throbbing, the wild joy, and great exultation of the national heart! Mother Earth industriously weaves and hangs about the world her radiant lovely tapestries, pitiless of man's wails and requiems, deaf to his paeans. Irene had earnestly endeavored to commit her father and Russell to the merciful care and protection of God, and to rest in faith, banishing apprehension; but a horrible presentiment, which would not "down" at her bidding, kept her nerves strung to their utmost tension. As the night advanced her face grew haggard and the wan lips fluttered ceaselessly. Russell she regarded as already dead to her in this world, but for her father she wrestled desperately in spirit. Mrs. Campbell joined her, uttering hopeful, encouraging words, and Nellie came out, with a cup of tea on a waiter.

"Please drink your tea, just to please me, Queen. I can't bear to look at you. In all your life I never saw you worry so. Do sit down and rest; you have walked fifty miles since morning."

"Take it away, Nellie. I don't want it."

"But, child, it will be time enough to fret when you know Mass' Leonard is hurt. Don't run to meet trouble; it will face you soon enough. If you won't take the tea, for pity's sake let me get you a glass of wine."

"No; I tell you I can't swallow anything. If you want to help me, pray for Father."

She resumed her walk, with her eyes strained in the direction of the town.

Thus passed three more miserable hours; then the clang of the iron gate at the foot of the avenue fell on her aching ear; the tramp of horses' hoofs and roll of wheels came up the gravelled walk.

"Bad news! they are coming to break it to me!" said she hoarsely, and, pressing her hands together, she leaned heavily against one of the guardian statues which had stood so long before the door, like ancient Hermae at Athens. Was the image indeed prescient? It tilted from its pedestal and fell with a crash, breaking into fragments. The omen chilled her, and she stood still, with the light from the hall-lamp streaming over her. The carriage stopped; Judge Harris and his wife came up the steps, followed slowly by Andrew, whose hat was slouched over his eyes. As they approached, Irene put out her hands wistfully.

"We have won a glorious victory, Irene, but many of our noble soldiers are wounded. I knew you would be anxious, and we came—"

"Is my father killed?"

"Your father was wounded. He led a splendid charge."

"Wounded! No! he is killed! Andrew, tell me the truth—is Father dead?"

The faithful negro could no longer repress his grief and sobbed convulsively, unable to reply.

"Oh, my God! I knew it! I knew it!" she gasped.

The gleaming arms were thrown up despairingly, and a low, dreary cry wailed through the stately old mansion as the orphan turned her eyes upon Nellie and Andrew—the devoted two who had petted her from childhood.

Judge Harris led her into the library, and his weeping wife endeavored to offer consolation, but she stood rigid and tearless, holding out her hand for the despatch. Finally they gave it to her, and she read:

> *"Charles T. Harris:*
> *"Huntingdon was desperately wounded at three o'clock to-day, in making a charge. He died two hours ago. I was with him. The body leaves to-morrow for W——.*
>
> *"Hiram Arnold."*

The paper fell from her fingers; with a dry sob she turned from them and threw herself on the sofa, with her face of woe to the wall. So passed the night.

12. *Margaret Junkin Preston*

(1820–1897)

The daughter of a Presbyterian minister and educator, Margaret Junkin Preston was highly educated in both classics and biblical studies. She was born in Milton, Pennsylvania, but grew up in Lexington, Virginia, where her father was the head of Washington College (now Washington and Lee University); she lived in Lexington most of her life. Preston's life was not an easy one. When she was twenty-one years old, her eyes began to fail and she was forced to spend seven years inside in dimly lighted rooms. Also, as a young woman she experienced the deaths of her mother, brother, and sister.

In 1857 Margaret married a widowed professor, Colonel J. T. L. Preston, who taught Latin and belles-lettres at the Virginia Military Institute and who encouraged his new wife in her studies and writing. Because the death of Col. Preston's first wife left him with the care of his seven children—and the couple then had two more of their own—Margaret's life was dominated by her domestic affairs.

Preston was considered a "woman of letters," for she corresponded with several important writers, wrote prose occasionally, and became a successful writer of poetry. Her letters and journals are excerpted in Elizabeth Preston Allen's *Life and Letters of Margaret Junkin Preston,* published in 1903. Preston's best-known poetry was that written for special occasions, especially weddings, births, and deaths. *Beechenbrook; A Rhyme of the War* (1865) was perhaps her most popular poem; describing the South and its suffering during the war, the poem is dedicated to "Every Southern Woman, who has been widowed by the war" and moves toward the heroic with its many classical and biblical references.

Silverwood (1856), a partially autobiographical novel, focuses on the domestic life of the genteel South in the midst of poverty. Other works include *Centennial Poems For Washington and Lee University* (1885), *Colonial Ballads, Sonnets, and Other Verse* (1887), and *Chimes for Church Children* (1889). Her *Cartoons,* published in Boston in 1875, were extremely popular. Although she never considered herself a poet or a writer of merit, one favorable critic of her time claims that she "takes her place beside Lanier . . . in fertility, wealth of fancy, culture, and rhythmical melodiousness of expression and feeling."

In 1862 Preston returned to Lexington with her husband so that he could continue his teaching career. She soon became known there for her poems written in honor of Confederate leaders, such as those written for *Century* commemorating Lee and Jackson, and she was even named "Poet Laureate" of Lexington's schools. Preston's husband died in 1890, and she moved to Baltimore to live the remainder of her life with her eldest son.

From *Beechenbrook; A Rhyme of the War*

[Alice's husband is away at war. The poem describes life on the home front, at Beechenbrook Cottage.]

II.

The feathery foliage has broadened its leaves,
And June, with its beautiful mornings and eves,
Its magical atmosphere, breezes and blooms,
Its woods all delicious with thousand perfumes,—
First-born of the Summer,— spoiled pet of the year,—
June, delicate queen of the seasons, is here!

The sadness has passed from the dwelling away,
And quiet serenity brightens the day:
With innocent prattle, her toils to beguile,
In the midst of her children, the mother *must* smile.
With matronly cares,— those relentless demands
On the strength of her heart and the skill of her hands,—
The hours come tenderly, ceaselessly fraught,
And leave her small space for the broodings of thought.
Thank God!—busy fingers a solace can find,
To lighten the burden of body or mind;
And Eden's old curse proves a blessing instead,—
"In the sweat of they brow shalt thou toil for thy bread."
For the bless'd relief in all labours that lurk,
Aye, thank Him, unhappy ones,— thank Him for work!

Thus Alice engages her thoughts and her powers,
And industry kindly lends wings to the hours:
Poor, petty employments they sometimes appear,
And on her bright needle there plashes a tear,—

Half shame and half passion;—what would she not dare
Her fervid compatriots' struggles to share?
It irks her,—the weakness of womanhood then,—
Yet such are the tears that make heroes of men!

She feels the hot blood of the nation beat high;
With rapture she catches the rallying cry:
From mountain and valley and hamlet they come!
On every side echoes the roll of the drum.
A people as firm, as united, as bold,
As ever drew blade for the blessings they hold,
Step sternly and solemnly forth in their might,
And swear on their altars to die for the right!

The clangor of muskets,—the flashing of steel,—
The clatter of spurs on the stout-booted heel,—
The waving of banners,—the resonant tramp
Of marching battalions,—the fiery stamp
Of steeds in their war-harness, newly decked out,—
The blast of the bugle,—the hurry, the shout,—
The terrible energy, eager and wild,
That lights up the face of man, woman and child,—
That burns on all lips, that arouses all powers;
Did ever we dream that such times would be ours?

One thought is absorbing, with giant control,—
With deadliest earnest, the national soul:—
"The right of self-government, crown of our pride,—
Right, bought with the sacredest blood,—is denied!
Shall we tamely resign what our enemy craves?
No! martyrs we *may* be!—we *cannot* be slaves!"

Fair women who naught but indulgence have seen,
Who never have learned what denial could mean,—
Who deign not to slipper their own dainty feet,
Whose wants swarthy handmaids stand ready to meet,
Whose fingers decline the light kerchief to hem,—
What aid in this struggle is hoped for from them?

Yet see! how they haste from their bowers of ease,
Their dormant capacities fired,—to seize
Every feminine weapon their skill can command,—

To labor with head, and with heart, and with hand.
They stitch the rough jacket, they shape the coarse shirt,
Unheeding though delicate fingers be hurt;
They bind the strong haversack, knit the grey glove,
Nor falter nor pause in their service of love.

When ever were people subdued, overthrown,
With women to cheer them on, brave as our own?
With maidens and mothers at work on their knees,
When ever were soldiers as fearless as these?

June's flower-wreathed sceptre is dropped with a sigh,
And forth like an empress steps stately July:
She sits all unveiled, amidst sunshine and balms,
As Zenobia sat in her City of Palms!

Not yet has the martial horizon grown dun,
Not yet has the terrible conflict begun:
But the tumult of legions,— the rush and the roar,
Break over our borders, like waves on the shore.
Along the Potomac, the confident foe
Stands marshalled for onset,— prepared, at a blow,
To vanquish the daring rebellion, and fling
Utter ruin at once on the arrogant thing!

How sovran the silence that broods o'er the sky,
And ushers the twenty-first morn of July;
—Date, written in fire on history's scroll,—
—Date, drawn in deep blood-lines on many a soul!

There is quiet at Beechenbrook: Alice's brow
Is wearing a Sabbath tranquility now,
As softly she reads from the page on her knee,—
"Thou wilt keep him in peace who is stayed upon Thee!"
When Sophy bursts breathlessly into the room,—
"Oh! mother! we hear it,—we hear it!. . . the boom
Of the fast and the fierce cannonading!—it shook
The ground till it trembled, along by the brook."

One instant the listener sways in her seat,—
The paralysed heart has forgotten to beat;
The next, with the speed and the frenzy of fear,
She gains the green hillock, and pauses to hear.

Again and again the reverberant sound
Is fearfully felt in the tremulous ground;
Again and again on their senses it thrills,
Like thunderous echoes astray in the hills.

On tip-toe,—the summer wind lifting his hair,
With nostril expanded, and scenting the air
Like a mettled young war-horse that tosses his mane,
And frettingly champs at the bit and the rein,—
Stands eager, exultant, a twelve-year-old boy,
His face all aflame with a rapturous joy.

"*That's* music for heroes in battle array!
Oh, mother! I feel like a Roman to-day!
The Romans I read of in Plutarch;—Yes, men
Thought it noble to die for their liberties then!
And I've wondered if soldiers were ever so bold,
So gallant and brave, as those heroes of old.
—There!—listen!—that volley peals out the reply;
They prove it is sweet for their country to die:
How grand it must be! what a pride! what a joy!
—And *I* can do nothing: I'm only a boy!"

The fervid hand drops as he ceases to speak,
And the eloquent crimson fades out on his cheek.

"Oh, Beverly!—brother! It never would do!
Who comforts mamma, and who helps her like you?
She sends to the battle her darlingest one,—
She could not give both of them,—husband and son;
If she lose *you,* what's left her in life to enjoy?
—Oh, no! I am *glad* you are only a boy."
And Sophy looks up with her tenderest air,
And kisses the fingers that toy with her hair.

For her, who all silent and motionless stands,
And over her heart locks her quivering hands,
With white lips apart, and with eyes that dilate,
As if the low thunder were sounding her fate,—
What racking suspenses, what agonies stir,
What spectres these echoes are rousing for her!
Brave-natur'd, yet quaking,—high-souled, yet so pale,—
Is it thus that the wife of a soldier should quail,

And shudder and shrink at the boom of a gun,
As only a faint-hearted girl should have done?
Ah! wait until custom has blunted the keen,
Cutting edge of that sound, and no woman, I ween,
Will hear it with pulses more equal, more free
From feminine terrors and weakness, than she.

The sun sinks serenely; a lingering look
He flings at the mists that steal over the brook,
Like nuns that come forth in the twilight to pray,
Till their blushes are seen through their mantles of grey.

The gay-hearted children, but lightly oppressed,
Find perfect relief on their pillow of rest:
For Alice, no bless'd forgetfulness comes;—
The wail of the bugles,—the roll of the drums,—
The musket's sharp crack,—the artillery's roar,—
The flashing of bayonets dripping with gore,—
The moans of the dying,—the horror, the dread,
The ghastliness gathering over the dead,—
Oh! these are the visions of anguish and pain,—
The phantoms of terror that troop through her brain!

She pauses again and again on the floor,
Which the moonlight has brightened so mockingly o'er;
She wrings her cold hands with a groan of despair;
—"Oh, God! have compassion!—my darling is there!"

All placidly, dewily, freshly, the dawn
Comes stealing in pulseless tranquility on:
More freely she breathes, in its balminess, though
The forehead it kisses is pallid with woe.

Through the long summer sunshine the Cottage is stirred
By passers, who brokenly fling them a word:
Such tidings of slaughter! "The enemy cowers;"—
"He breaks!"—"He is flying!"—"Manassas is ours!"

'Tis evening: and Archie, alone on the grass,
Sits watching the fire-flies gleam as they pass,
When sudden he rushes, too eager to wait,—
"Mamma! there's an ambulance stops at the gate!"

Suspense then is past: he is borne from the field,—
"God help me! . . . God grant it be *not* on his shield!"
And Alice, her passionate soul in her eyes,
And hope and fear winging each quicken'd step, flies,—
Embraces, with frantical wildness, the form
Of her husband, and finds . . . it is living, and warm!

13. Elizabeth Keckley

(1825–1905)

Elizabeth Keckley was born a slave in Dinwiddie, Virginia. When she was eighteen years old she was given to (or possibly married to) a white man, Alexander Kirkland, with whom she had one son, George. After Kirkland died, she moved with her former master to St. Louis, Missouri, where she began working as a seamstress and dressmaker. She was allowed to marry again, this time to James Keckley, who claimed to be a free man; he was actually a fugitive slave, however, and proved to be more of a burden than a helpmate for Keckley. Because she was so successful with her sewing, Keckley was able to save money; in 1855 she borrowed $1200, added it to her savings, and purchased freedom for herself and her son. Soon afterward, she left her husband and departed for Washington, D.C., a free and self-educated woman.

Soon after establishing herself as a seamstress in Washington, Keckley opened her own shop, where she employed as many as twenty women. Among her most frequent customers was Varina Davis, wife of Jefferson Davis. With the outbreak of the Civil War in 1861, working conditions in Washington grew increasingly difficult, and Mary Todd Lincoln invited Keckley to become her personal maid and seamstress in the White House. Keckley's son, who was at the time a student at Wilberforce University, enlisted in the Union Army and was killed at the Battle of Wilson Creek. Through this experience, and through Mary Todd Lincoln's efforts to secure Keckley's pension, the two women grew to be intimate friends and Mrs. Lincoln became much more supportive of black rights. When Keckley founded the Contraband Relief Association, an organization established to aid former slaves in the Washington area, Mary Todd Lincoln became a strong contributor.

Even after the war, Keckley and Lincoln remained close friends, but their relationship abruptly ended with the publication of *Behind the Scenes, or Thirty Years a Slave and Four Years in the White House* in 1868. Though it was apparently an accurate portrayal of the Lincolns during their stay in the White House, complete with letters sent to Keckley by Mary Todd Lincoln, the book was harshly criticized for its revealing depiction of the Lincolns. The chapter anthologized here describes not only the everyday lives of the Lincolns but also Keckley's observations of the living conditions of southern blacks who fled to Washington, D.C., during the war years.

Keckley's business sharply declined after 1868, and she never again knew the comfort and security of former years. She was for years very active in the Fifteenth Street Presbyterian Church, which most likely supported her in her later years; this church was pastored for years by Francis Grimké, who stood behind Keckley when her authorship of *Behind the Scenes* was questioned. In 1892 and 1893, she was able to secure a position teaching domestic art at Wilberforce University but lived most of the remainder of her life off her son's pension. Having helped to found the Home for Destitute Women and Children, Keckley died there in 1907.

From *Behind the Scenes, or Thirty Years a Slave and Four Years in the White House* (Chapter 7)

Washington in 1862–3
In the summer of 1862, freedmen began to flock into Washington from Maryland and Virginia. They came with a great hope in their hearts, and with all their worldly goods on their backs. Fresh from the bonds of slavery, fresh from the benighted regions of the plantation, they came to the Capital looking for liberty, and many of them not knowing it when they found it. Many good friends reached forth kind hands, but the North is not warm and impulsive. For one kind word spoken, two harsh ones were uttered; there was something repelling in the atmosphere, and the bright joyous dreams of freedom to the slave faded—were sadly altered, in the presence of that stern, practical mother, reality. Instead of flowery paths, days of perpetual sunshine, and bowers hanging with golden fruit, the road was rugged and full of thorns, the sunshine was eclipsed by shadows, and the mute appeals for help too often were answered by cold neglect. Poor dusky children of slavery, men and women of my own race—the transition from slavery to freedom was too sudden for you! The bright dreams were too rudely dispelled; you were not prepared for the new life that opened before you, and the great masses of the North learned to look upon your helplessness with indifference—learned to speak of you as an idle, dependent race. Reason should have prompted kinder thoughts. Charity is ever kind.

One fair summer evening I was walking the streets of Washington, accompanied by a friend, when a band of music was heard in the distance. We wondered what it could mean, and curiosity prompted us to find out its meaning. We quickened our steps, and discovered that it came from the house of Mrs. Farnham. The yard was brilliantly lighted, ladies and gentlemen were moving about, and the band was playing some of its sweetest airs. We approached the sentinel on duty at the gate, and asked what was going on. He told us that it was a festival given for the benefit of the sick and wounded soldiers in the city. This suggested an idea to me. If the white people can give festivals to raise funds for the relief of suffering soldiers, why should not the well-to-do colored people go to work to do something for the benefit of the suffering blacks? I could not rest. The thought was ever present with me, and the next Sunday I made a suggestion in the colored church, that a society of colored people be formed to labor for the benefit of the unfortunate freedmen. The idea proved popular, and in two weeks "the Contraband Relief Association" was organized, with forty working members.

In September of 1862, Mrs. Lincoln left Washington for New York, and requested me to follow her in a few days, and join her at the Metropolitan Hotel. I was glad of the opportunity to do so, for I thought that in New York I would be able to do something in the interests of our society. Armed with credentials, I took the train for New York, and went to the Metropolitan, where Mrs. Lincoln had secured accommodations for me. The next morning I told Mrs. Lincoln of my project; and she immediately headed my list with a subscription of $200. I circulated among the colored people, and got them thoroughly interested in the subject, when I was called to Boston by Mrs. Lincoln, who wished to visit her son Robert, attending college in that city. I met Mr. Wendell Phillips, and other Boston philanthropists, who gave me all the assistance in their power. We held a mass meeting at the Colored Baptist Church. Rev. Mr. Grimes, in Boston, raised a sum of money, and organized there a branch society. The society was organized by Mrs. Grimes, wife of the pastor, assisted by Mrs. Martin, wife of Rev. Stella Martin. This branch of the main society, during the war, was able to send us over eighty large boxes of goods, contributed exclusively by the colored people of Boston. Returning to New York, we held a successful meeting at the Shiloh Church, Rev. Henry Highland Garnet, pastor. The Metropolitan Hotel, at that time as now, employed colored help. I suggested the object of my mission to Robert Thompson, Steward of the Hotel, who immediately raised quite a sum of money among the dining-room waiters. Mr. Frederick Douglass contributed $200, besides lecturing for us. Other prominent colored men sent in liberal contributions. From England a large quantity of stores was received. Mrs. Lincoln made frequent contributions, as also did the President. In 1863 I was re-elected President of the Association, which office I continue to hold.

For two years after [the Lincolns' son] Willie's death the White House was the scene of no fashionable display. The memory of the dead boy was duly respected. In some things Mrs. Lincoln was an altered woman. Sometimes, when in her room, with no one present but myself, the mere mention of Willie's name would excite her emotion, and any trifling memento that recalled him would move her to tears. She could not bear to look upon his picture; and after his death she never crossed the threshold of the Guest's Room in which he died, or the Green Room in which he was embalmed. There was something supernatural in her dread of these things, and something that she could not explain. Tad's nature was the opposite of Willie's, and he was always regarded as his father's favorite child. His black eyes fairly sparkled with mischief.

The war progressed, fair fields had been stained with blood, thousands of brave men had fallen, and thousands of eyes were weeping for the fallen at home. There were desolate hearthstones in the South as well as in the North, and as the people of my race watched the sanguinary struggle, the ebb and flow of the tide of battle, they lifted their faces Zionward, as if they hoped to catch a glimpse of the Promised Land beyond the sulphureous clouds of smoke which shifted now and then but to reveal ghastly rows of new-made graves. Sometimes the very life of the nation seemed to tremble with the fierce shock of arms. In 1863 the Confederates were flushed with victory, and sometimes it looked as if the proud flag of the Union, the glorious old Stars and Stripes, must yield half its nationality to the tri-barred flag that floated grandly over long columns of gray. These were sad, anxious days to Mr. Lincoln, and those who saw the man in privacy only could tell how much he suffered. One day he came into the room where I was fitting a dress on Mrs. Lincoln. His step was slow and heavy, and his face sad. Like a tired child he threw himself upon a sofa, and shaded his eyes with his hands. He was a complete picture of dejection. Mrs. Lincoln, observing his troubled look, asked:

"Where have you been, father?"

"To the War Department," was the brief, almost sullen answer.

"Any news?"

"Yes, plenty of news, but no good news. It is dark, dark everywhere."

He reached forth one of his long arms, and took a small Bible from a stand near the head of the sofa, opened the pages of the holy book, and soon was absorbed in reading them. A quarter of an hour passed, and on glancing at the sofa the face of the President seemed more cheerful. The dejected look was gone, and the countenance was lighted up with new resolution and hope. The change was so marked that I could not but wonder at it, and wonder led to the desire to know what book of the Bible afforded so much comfort to the reader. Making the search for a missing article an excuse, I walked gently around the sofa, and looking into the open book, I discovered that Mr. Lincoln was reading that divine comforter, Job. He read with Christian eagerness, and the courage and hope that he derived from the inspired pages made him a new man. I almost imagined that I could hear the Lord speaking to him from out the whirlwind of battle: "Gird up thy loins now like a man: I will demand of thee, and declare thou unto me." What a sublime picture was this! A ruler of a mighty nation going to the pages of the Bible with simple Christian earnestness for comfort and courage, and finding both in the darkest hours of a nation's calamity. Ponder it, O ye scoffers at God's Holy Word, and then hang your heads for very shame!

Frequent letters were received warning Mr. Lincoln of assassination, but he never gave a second thought to the mysterious warnings. The letters, however, sorely troubled his wife. She seemed to read impending danger in every rustling leaf, in every whisper of the wind.

"Where are you going now, father?" she would say to him, as she observed him putting on his overshoes and shawl.

"I am going over to the War Department, mother, to try and learn some news."

"But, father, you should not go out alone. You know you are surrounded with danger."

"All imagination. What does any one want to harm me for? Don't worry about me, mother, as if I were a little child, for no one is going to molest me;" and with a confident, unsuspecting air he would close the door behind him, descend the stairs, and pass out to his lonely walk.

For weeks, when trouble was anticipated, friends of the President would sleep in the White House to guard him from danger.

Robert would come home every few months, bringing new joy to the family circle. He was very anxious to quit school and enter the army, but the move was sternly opposed by his mother.

"We have lost one son, and his loss is as much as I can bear, without being called upon to make another sacrifice," she would say, when the subject was under discussion.

"But many a poor mother has given up all her sons," mildly suggested Mr. Lincoln, "and our son is not more dear to us than the sons of other people are to their mothers."

"That may be; but I cannot bear to have Robert exposed to danger. His services are not required in the field, and the sacrifice would be a needless one."

"The services of every man who loves his country are required in this war. You should take a liberal instead of a selfish view of the question, mother."

Argument at last prevailed, and permission was granted Robert to enter the army. With the rank of Captain and A.D.C. he went to the field, and remained in the army till the close of the war.

I well recollect a little incident that gave me a clearer insight into Robert's character. He was at home at the time the Tom Thumb combination was at Washington. The marriage of little Hop-o'-my-thumb— Charles Stratton—to Miss Warren created no little excitement in the world, and the people of Washington participated in the general curiosity. Some of Mrs. Lincoln's friends made her believe that it was the duty of Mrs. Lincoln to show some attention to the remarkable dwarfs. Tom Thumb had been caressed by royalty in the Old World, and why should not the wife of the President of his native country smile upon him also? Verily, duty is one of the greatest bugbears in life. A hasty reception was arranged, and cards of invitation issued. I had dressed Mrs. Lincoln, and she was ready to go below and receive her guests, when Robert entered his mother's room.

"You are at leisure this afternoon, are you not, Robert?"

"Yes, mother."

"Of course, then, you will dress and come down-stairs."

"No, mother, I do not propose to assist in entertaining Tom Thumb. My notions of duty, perhaps, are somewhat different from yours."

Robert had a lofty soul, and he could not stoop to all of the follies and absurdities of the ephemeral current of fashionable life.

Mrs. Lincoln's love for her husband sometimes prompted her to act very strangely. She was extremely jealous of him, and if a lady desired to court her displeasure, she could select no surer way to do it than to pay marked attention to the President. These little jealous freaks often were a source of perplexity to Mr. Lincoln. If it was a reception for which they were dressing, he would come into her room to conduct her downstairs, and while pulling on his gloves ask, with a merry twinkle in his eyes:

"Well, mother, who must I talk with to-night—shall it be Mrs. D.?"

"That deceitful woman! No, you shall not listen to her flattery."

"Well, then, what do you say to Miss C.? She is too young and handsome to practise deceit."

"Young and handsome, you call her! You should not judge beauty for me. No, she is in league with Mrs. D., and you shall not talk with her."

"Well, mother, I must talk with some one. Is there any one that you do not object to?" trying to button his glove, with a mock expression of gravity.

"I don't know as it is necessary that you should talk to anybody in particular. You know well enough, Mr. Lincoln, that I do not approve of your flirtations with silly women, just as if you were a beardless boy, fresh from school."

"But, mother, I insist that I must talk with somebody. I can't stand around like a simpleton, and say nothing. If you will not tell me who I may talk with, please tell me who I may *not* talk with."

"There is Mrs. D. and Miss C. in particular. I detest them both. Mrs. B. also will come around you, but you need not listen to her flattery. These are the ones in particular."

"Very well, mother; now that we have settled the question to your satisfaction, we will go down-stairs;" and always with stately dignity, he proffered his arm and led the way.

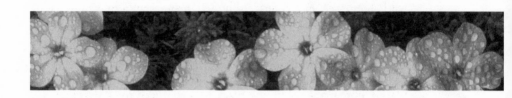

The

Postbellum

South

(1866–1917)

Not until 1885, when a *Boston Herald* story recounted the meeting of Mary Murfree and her editor, did readers realize that the widely published "strapping six-foot Tennessean" Charles Egbert Craddock was actually a "delicate looking lady." The Appalachian setting of her stories was indeed unusual for a woman writing in the postbellum South, so Murfree had assumed a masculine name to create a persona that would seem capable of writing about the wild Tennessee mountains. Although many southern women were writing and publishing before the war, they typically focused their stories on concerns of the home and domestic life, subject matter American audiences deemed suitable for women writers. Even slave narratives by women, such as Harriet Jacobs's *Incidents in the Life of a Slave Girl,* placed more emphasis on the black woman's need to establish a home for herself and her children than on the necessity of freedom. But with the end of the war, emancipation, and the southern woman's growing freedom to seek employment outside the home and to make money, the literature written by postbellum women increasingly reflected experiences and influences beyond the confines of the home. Although sometimes hesitant to reveal their identities, southern women writers like Murfree were eager to write of their changing lives.

Having been active participants in the war effort, many postbellum women believed that the next step was the right to vote. When asked why she deserved this right, one Verbena, Alabama, woman explained that she was "as much a citizen as [her] brother": "With an equal amount of patriotism and politics we sang together 'The Bonny Blue Flag.' He marched off to the tune of Dixie, and I stayed at home to scrape lint and sew sand bags. I was a patriot then, and I am one now" (qtd. in Henry 360). Despite their seeming desire for progress and change, many white southerners—particularly in the years right after the war—saw this right as a means to maintain control over the newly freed slaves. The "patriotism" and assertiveness of some such women are often blamed for slowing reconciliation of the North and South. Stubbornly loyal to the Confederacy, these women formed societies whose members vowed never to speak to a Federal soldier. Joseph E. Brown, who served as governor of Georgia from 1857 to 1865, believed that if southern women would only give up these loyalties, the South would be able to rejoin the nation on a stronger economic level: "25,000 women [could be] selected in the South to-day," he stated in 1867, "who could reconstruct this Government in twelve months, and cause tens of thousands of people to come to the South and bring tens of millions of dollars to aid and build up and develop it." Yet eight years after the end of the war, Jefferson Davis claimed he had never met a reconstructed southern white woman (qtd. in Coulter 178).

Despite the resistance to the new South by many white women, the war was the impetus for changes in the lives of southern black women who were left to deal with the problems that came with their emancipation. Nominally, the freedoms for which they struggled before the war had been achieved through a proclamation, but postwar prejudices became increasingly destructive as southern whites attempted to regain power over blacks. In her poetry, alongside the joys of freedom and of establishing a home life, Alice Dunbar-Nelson records the difficulties of being both black and female, exposed to poverty and lynchings, rape and denigration. Frances E. W. Harper, perhaps even more influential as a writer and lecturer in these years than she was before the war, emphasized the frustration of women like Dunbar-Nelson in an article entitled "Colored Women of America" (1878). In order to gain an education or to support their children, Harper explains, many former slave women managed plantations virtually single-handedly, only to be subjected to physical abuse by black men. For such women, as for all women in the South, the postbellum period was characterized by harrowing contradictions.

Many of the difficulties faced by women during the postwar years resulted from reconstructing their lives without husbands or brothers from whom they had been separated by slavery or by death. Additionally, the heavy casualties of the war meant that many women were remaining single, so families became more likely to provide their daughters with educations and to put them to work outside the home. In 1891 the president of a flourishing southern women's college wrote that one-fourth of the students at his institution "look[ed] to supporting themselves" after graduation because of the "enforced impoverishment of the Southern woman" (qtd. in Tillett 14). Many educated women became teachers, some became writers, a few became editors. Less privileged women found it necessary to enter the industrial labor force that was growing in the South. C. Vann Woodward notes that between 1885 and 1895 the number of women working in Alabama factories increased by 75 percent. The number of female factory workers under age eighteen increased by 158 percent. Shops in Charleston, South Carolina, were said to employ "well-born, well-educated girl[s] side by side in the least attractive pursuits with the 'cracker'" (qtd. in Woodward 226). Ironically, however, the introduction of factory-produced goods led to a better way of life for many privileged women by the turn of the century. The sewing machine, for example, became a valuable tool for the southern woman, who could now more easily produce clothing from fabric that was readily available in stores and thus enjoy more leisure time. In effect, "modern" conveniences like the sewing machine freed one group of women from the labors of the home while forcing another group out of their homes and into factories.

Grace King illustrates this new, sometimes forced, independence of women in her writings about Louisiana, and in doing so she stresses the problem of male inadequacies. In her stories, men frequently desert their women, suffer from acute illness, or die prematurely. In the introduction to one of her later novels, *The Pleasant Ways of St. Medard* (1916), King explains that as a result of the Civil War, the roles of the sexes were turned upside down. According to King, the South was rapidly becoming a matriarchy, moving away from the patriarchal society of the antebellum years; her women find a salvation in the solidarity among themselves that her male characters do not possess. King's perspective is understandable in light of the state of the South after the war. A severe shortage of men grew as black men migrated northward and white men moved westward in hopes of beginning anew. One woman, Caroline Merrick, explained that "the women in every community seemed to far outnumber the men; and the empty sleeve and the crutch made men who had unflinchingly faced death in battle impotent to face their future" (qtd. in A. Jones 32).

At the turn of the century, as they joined male organizations such as the Grange and the Farmers' Alliance and also formed their own organizations, southern women became more active politically and more interested in attaining the vote. Josephine Henry explained in 1895 that the battle for women's suffrage almost became another civil war: "There is nothing in history so pathetic as woman's struggle for freedom. Men of the Old South, armed with all the implements of war, and supplied with the wealth of states, fought for empire based on slavery, and lost. The women of the new South, armed with clear-cut, unanswerable argument alone, are struggling for liberty based on justice, and will win. The failure of the former left our section in ruin and despair; the triumph of the latter will bring progress and hope" (Henry 357).

Well into the twentieth century, women continued the struggle against gender prejudices. In 1910, Mary Johnston, the popular novelist and author of *Hagar* (1913), wrote to Thomas Nelson Page, a widely read romance writer of the South, with the hope of enlisting his support for the "Woman's Movement." Johnston explained that the leaders of the Virginia Movement hoped to enlist the aid of other Virginia "writers, thinkers, and educators." Page replied with a letter stating, "I can only say that I wish you would let woman-suffrage alone with all the self-chaining to benches, etc. and chain yourself to that work which has given you your fame and Virginia so wonderful an example of intellectual and imaginative womanhood among her unvoting daughters. What care you for what these other women are scabbling for? Let others write her ballot-extension arguments and even her laws—and you write her Romances. There are thousands who are your equals at the one, but not one who is your equal at the other" (qtd. in Roberson 290). Needless to say, Page withheld his support of the movement.

Josephine Henry describes in "New Woman of the New South" the women "who stand on higher intellectual ground, who realize their potentialities, and who have the courage to demand a field of thought and action commensurate with their aspirations" (353–54). Despite the resistance to gender equality, changes in domestic relations occasioned by the war and reflected upon in literature suggest the emergence of a "new woman." However, this "new woman" was not the moving force in the South that she had become in the North, for the image of the "southern lady" still remained very powerful. The pre–Civil War woman writer of the sentimental novel asserts, according to Ann Douglas Wood, that "only a fool (or a man) would want to be anywhere but in the kitchen or at the altar when such titillating and stirring events apparently daily take place there" (10). But in the local color tradition of the postwar United States, Wood continues, the house is "also in part an iconographical representation of the womb, but of the womb in a new and destructive guise." The house is "no longer a garden of delights, but a bed of weeds; it is not rampantly fertile, but barren, and even poisonous" (22). Women expecting better education, more financial independence, and more political power upset the orderly southern world, infecting it with their "modern" ideas.

The new woman emerging in the South, making great strides in establishing her social position, can certainly be credited with helping to usher in a new world. But in many ways she was often unwilling or unable to relinquish her pedestal—most notably in her treatment of black women, whose fight for equality far surpassed that of white women in intensity and suffering. In their zeal for self-promotion, white women's associations were guilty of promoting racist sentiment to further their cause. Near the end of the century, for example, the Memphis Equal Suffrage Club compiled a list of reasons that the members of the organization wanted the ballot. These explanations ranged from "We mothers want an equal partnership in our children" and "We educated women want the power to offset the illiterate vote of our state" to "Being sane, we object to being classed with the *lunatic*" (Henry 357–58). But at the same time, other women argued that they should be given the right to vote so that the white race could stay in control of southern polling places. Henry quotes a Beaumont, Texas, woman who said that "the Southern woman has now the choice to inherit her land or pass into a tradition": "The women of the South should be the very first to work for the ballot, to preserve its homes, its institutions and its individuality from the great influx of opposing forces from the North, East and West, from the foreigner and negro" (362).

To this insistence on the vote for white women, Frances Watkins Harper had but one reply: It was voters who tortured, burned, and lynched black people. Certainly black women, too, wanted the vote, but equality with whites, and solidarity among themselves, came first. Harper, who had been speaking out on behalf of her people since long before the war, became a leader in the black women's movement shortly after the war came to a close. In 1869 she attacked the leaders of the American Equal Rights Association, Susan B. Anthony and Elizabeth Cady Stanton, for asserting that "[i]f intelligence, justice, and morality are to be placed in the government, then let the question of woman be brought up first and that of the negro last" (qtd. in Carby 67). Among the many black women who joined Harper's crusade were southerners Anna Julia Cooper and Ida B. Wells, who directed their energies toward exposing racism in women's organizations dominated by white women and toward the betterment of black women *and* men—and for all of humanity. In 1895 the First National Conference of the Colored Women of America convened, and by 1896 the National Association of Colored Women was formed.

Although generally overlooked by literary critics, so many black women were writing and publishing between 1890 and 1910 that Henry Louis Gates refers to these years as "The Black Woman's Era." In fact, according to Gates, more fiction by black women was published during that twenty years than had been published in the previous half-century by black men (Gates xvi). And the era was well represented by southerners, most notably Cooper, Wells, Harper, and Dunbar-Nelson, who provided inspiration and paved the way for the black woman's literary tradition of the twentieth century. As Gates contends, the roots of these early writers "have branched luxuriantly" (xvii), particularly in the works of such writers as Zora Neale Hurston, Margaret Walker, Sonia Sanchez, and Alice Walker.

Similarly, modern feminist literature owes a great debt to the writing of Kate Chopin. Although her involvement in the women's movement is an issue of considerable debate (she tended to shy away from the suffrage organizations), most of her fiction is devoted to questions of gender definition and female sexuality. When reprinted for the first time in 1969, *The Awakening* immediately became a classic within the women's movement for its frank treatment of female sexuality and its concern with a woman's individual freedoms. Yet even this "modern" novel contains a degree of racism that confirms Chopin's conventional southern attitude toward race, which is echoed in the works of her contemporaries such as Grace King. The paths to progress for white and black women too rarely intersected and too often diverged, even among the most forward-looking women of the postbellum South.

The literature by women in the postbellum years, growing out of and depicting the changing face of the South, suggests a decided movement into the modern world. Before the war, writing had been a popular occupation for women, because as Ann Douglas Wood explains, a woman could sit down at her kitchen table to take a break from household chores and the caretaking of children in order to address a letter to an editor and mail out a manuscript (7). That image of women writers rapidly faded after the war. Local color stories and romances were the most common of the literature written by southern women right after the war, but by the turn of the century the voices of Alice Dunbar-Nelson and Kate Chopin passionately expounded the cause of freedom. Their biting works, exposing the psychological and emotional turmoil that results from the constant fight against racial and gender suppression, could not be ignored. With the work of these women, then, we move into the Southern Renaissance, a period that brought southern literature a status comparable to the literature of New England in the days of Hawthorne and Dickinson.

14. Katherine McDowell (Sherwood Bonner)

(1849–1883)

Katherine Bonner McDowell began writing as a young girl in Holly Springs, Mississippi. Quite an ambitious writer, she published her first story when she was just fifteen years old. Growing up in a cotton-growing family, McDowell lived on the family farm and attended Holly Springs Female Institute. During the Civil War, Union forces occupied Holly Springs, and the constant conflict provided Katherine with much material for her writing. In 1864 her first story, "Laura Capello, A Leaf from a Traveler's Notebook," was published in the *Massachusetts Ploughman;* the publisher, Nahum Capen, recognized her talent and helped her publish two additional stories five years later. Her work was interrupted in 1871 when she married Edward McDowell, an unsuccessful speculator who cared little for his wife's literary ability. The couple had a child the next year, and McDowell was forced to concern herself with domestic affairs.

Unhappy in marriage and eager to return to her work, McDowell left her husband in 1873 to move to Boston with their young daughter. She was able to live with the family of Nahum Capen, through whom she became acquainted with a large literary circle. After serving as Longfellow's literary assistant, McDowell left for Europe in 1876 with a contract to write travel letters for the *Boston Times.* By then she had also published several short stories under the pseudonym Sherwood Bonner.

McDowell's works focused on life in the South. Her family did own slaves, and as a young girl she was well acquainted with the tales, customs, and dialect of the blacks who lived on her family's plantation; the "Gran'mammy" of these stories was actually McDowell's childhood nurse. The stories were collected in 1884 in *Suwanee River Tales.* ("Why Gran'mammy Didn't Like Pound-Cake" was originally published in *Wide Awake Pleasure Book* 2 [September 1880].) Though her characters are often considered stereotypical, McDowell is important as a writer of local color. Likewise, McDowell's only novel, *Like Unto Like,* is a study of the Deep South at the end of Reconstruction. It was dedicated to Longfellow and published by Harper and Brothers in 1878. Her *From*

'60 to '65, an autobiographical memoir of the Civil War, explains her dedication to the southern cause.

In 1878 McDowell returned to the South in order to care for her dying brother and father. She then tried reconciling with her husband twice, but unsuccessfully, and in 1881 she moved to Illinois to file for divorce. Though she hoped to establish a life for herself and her daughter there, illness drove her back to Holly Springs where she died of cancer at age thirty-four.

Gran'mammy

In our Southern home we were very fond of our old colored mammy, who had petted and scolded and nursed and coddled,—yes, and spanked us,—from the time we were born.

She was not a "black mammy," for her complexion was the color of clear coffee; and we did not call her "mammy," but "gran'mammy," because she had nursed our mother when a little delicate baby,—loving her foster child, I believe, more than her own, and loving us for our dear mother's sake.

She was all tenderness when we were wee toddlers, not more than able to clutch at the great gold hoops in her ears, or cling to her ample skirts like little burrs; but she showed a sharper side as we grew old enough to "bother round the kitchen," with inquisitive eyes and fingers and tongues. I regret to say that she sometimes called us "limbs," and would wonder, with many a groan and shake of the head, how we contrived to hold so much of the Evil One in our small frames.

"I never seed sich chillern in all my born days," she cried one day, when Ruth interrupted her in the midst of custard-making, to beg leave to get into the kettle of boiling soap that she might be clean once for all, and never need another bath; while Sam, on the other side, entreated that she would make three "points" of gravy with the fried chicken for dinner. (Sam always came out strong on pronunciation; his very errors leaned to virtue's side.)

"I clar to gracious," said poor gran'mammy, "you'll drive all de sense clean outen my head. How Miss Mary 'xpec's me ter git a dinner fitten fur white folks ter eat, wid you little onruly sinners *furever* under foot, is mo' dan I kin say. An' here's Leah an' Rachel, my own gran'chillern, a no mo' use ter me dan two tar-babies!"

She looked very threatening as she shook her rolling-pin at her two idle grandchildren. They only grinned in an aggravating way; for to them as well as to us, the great wide kitchen, with its roomy fire-place, where the back-log glowed and the black kettle swung, was the pleasantest place in the world.

As gran'mammy grew older, her manner softened; her love was less fluctuating. It was she to whom we ran to tell of triumphs and sorrows; she, whose sympathy, ash-cakes, and turnover-pies never failed us! It was she who hung over our sick-beds; who told us stories more beautiful than we read in any books; who sang to us old-fashioned hymns of praise and faith; and who talked to us with childlike simplicity of the God whom she loved.

During the troubled four years that swept like the hot breath of the simoon over our country, she was true to the family. Her love, her courage, her faithful work, helped us to bear up under our heavy trials. And when the gentle mother whose life had been set to such sweet music that her spirit broke in the discords of dreadful war, sank out of life, it was in gran'mammy's arms that she died; and neither husband nor children mourned more tenderly for the beautiful life cut short.

Like most of her race, gran'mammy told a story well. Among the earliest that I remember, is one told to us when we were very small children, so complete, so näive, so crowded with moral, as to deserve a chapter all to itself.

Why Gran'mammy Didn't Like Pound-Cake

There had been a birthday party at our house, and, owing to a recent fit of illness, gran'mammy had been unable to take any part in the festivity. So the day after the party we piled up a basket with good things and started off, swinging it on a long pole, of which Ruth held one end and I the other. Gran'mammy's cabin was quite at the end of the negro quarter; a pretty log-house with roses growing over it and shaded by fine hickory trees. Evidently she was getting well fast; for we heard her singing. Long before we reached her house the swift wind bore to our ears these very queer words, sung to a see-saw tune:—

"You may *back-bite* me
Jes' *as much as you please*.
Jes' *gi' me deliverin' grace,*
An' *I'll sail away*
On *de golden seas*.
Jes' *gi' me deliverin' grace!*
O Lord! *han' down my crown!*
O Lord! *han' doown my crown!*"

There sat gran'mammy, rocking back and forth in a great chair that Uncle Ned had made for her, warranted not to break down under her weight; for she was fat.

"Tell you what, I *tips* things I stan's on!" she used to say.

There was a legend in the family that our grandfather had bought our old mammy for her weight in silver dollars. She was a slim young girl then. She was worth her weight in gold now; but only a Bonanza or a Golconda man could have bought her.

"Lor, chillern!" she said, kissing us all round, "I's powerful glad ter see you. 'Pears like I gits lonesome wid on'y de birds an' dat little trash on de flo' fur company."

"Dat little trash on de flo'" consisted of half-a-dozen sprawling black babies, left in gran'mammy's charge, while their mothers were in the cotton field.

"We've brought you some of my birthday, grammy," said Sam, with an air of importance.

"So you did manage ter make out a party widout me!" cried gran'mammy. "Well! well!" with innocent pride, "Becky is a tollerbul fust-class cook. I learnt her all she knows!"

We unpacked the basket,—turkey and jelly, and light bread, and wafers grey with sugar and rolled round in the most delicate curves, and fruit-cake and cup-cake, and a whole half of a pound-cake loaf.

"Why, chillern!" she cried with a start, "don't you know dat I don't love pound-cake?"

"Don't like pound-cake!" cried Sam, his eyes distended. "Well, I do!" And he took a great bite out of the loaf in an absent-minded sort of way.

"Why, gran'mammy?" said I, "why don't you?"

"I'll tell you why, chillern, an' let de warnin' sink inter you deep as a track inter de snow; but don't you let it melt away cause you lives in de sunshine!"

So saying, gran'mammy lit a cob-pipe, settled herself comfortably and began:—

"Long time ago, my blessin's, I was a little gal. An' I wus a limb—I wus. Ole Mis', she had an *awful* time wid me. 'Pears as if imps hed possession o' me. Howmsoever, she kept a-b'arin' wid me, an' a-b'arin' wid me, till de time come when she couldn't bar *no mo'*. An' de way it happened wus dis. Dar wus a pretty young lady in de nex' county from us who went an' got married. An' ole Mis' had a keard ter de weddin'. Well now, as luck would have it, she wus took sick de very day ov de weddin'. She wus bilious I recollec', and jes' de color ov clover cream she wus! So she could n't go. An' she sont *me*—fur I wus her little maid—wid a gret basket ov jerponicas an' vi'lets an' geraniums. It wus winter, an' flowers wus skeerce; so dat wus a very pretty gi't for de young Miss dat wus about ter marry.

"Bless you, chillern! did n't I enjoy myse'f? I rid in a waggin ter de weddin',—for it wus a matter of ten mile or so in de country. An' when we got dar, all de groun's wus lighted wid pine knots burnin' in forked sticks high as a man's head. Nothin' like dat beauty an' gorgeousness in dese days! Pooh! ef you had seen one weddin' like dat o' Miss Josephine Dandridge, you would n't roll off a log ter look at one now!

"Miss Josephine, she wus as white an' shinin' an' smilin' as an angel, but when she led off de dance, she blushed like a sweet rose. An' *sich* a weddin' supper! I et as much as I could fur de excitement; but my eyes was so eager to see all dat wus a-goin' on, an' my heart wus a-beatin' so fas' to de sound ov de music, dat I did n't do no manner of justice to de feast. More's de pity too! fur dat's one reason why I fell from grace de nex' day.

"Miss Josephine was gwine to her husband's house acrost de line of de State fur de *infair*. Ever heard ov an *infair*, chillern? Well, dat's de gret, gret cillybration give by de young man's folks to de bridle an' de broom—"

"De bridle an' de broom?" echoed Sam, vaguely.

"In course, boy. What else should I call de young pa'r?" said gran'mammy, with severity.

"Well, in all de hurry of gittin' off, Miss Josephine writ a note to my ole Mis' a-thankin' her fur de flowers, an' a-sendin' her a big slice o' weddin'-cake; an' den she says:—

"'Why, ma! here's a poun'-cake dat has n't ben cut! S'pose we sen' it ter Mis' Rout',—dat was my Mis'.

"So, honeys, dey done up dat poun'-cake in silver paper, an' put it in a basket, an' give it to me wid dese words:—

"'Take dat to your mistis, Mariar.'

"'Yes'm,' says I.

"But lor, chillern! I wus a *limb*!

"I tell you, I smelt dat poun'-cake all de way home, an' a v'ice, as close ter my ear as a flower in a young lady's hair, kep' sayin':

"'Molly, you little goose, jes' *eat* dat cake. You'll never have sich anudder chance.'

"Ter be short wid it, chillern, I listened ter de v'ice, an' when I got home, I handed de slice o' weddin'-cake to ole Mis', an' told her all about de weddin', lookin' as innercent as a lily; an' all de time wus dat poun'-cake hid away under de waggin seat.

"Jes' as soon as night fell, I stole up de stairs to ole Mis's room, an' I snuggled under de bed, an' I *et de poun'*-cake! De fust bite tasted as if all de stars had turned to cake an' was a-meltin' in my mouth; but to tell you de trufe,—an', Sam, you listen,—I had ter sort o' *push* de las' piece down.

"But eat it I did, to de las' crumb. Den I laid down, kind o' composed, an' went ter sleep. I was waked up by de mos' awful kind o' gripin' pain,—struck me somewhar inside like lightnin',—an' I jumped up an' screamed. Ole Mis', she came a-runnin' up,—seventy years ole do she wus,—an' says:—

"'What's de matter, you little screech-owl?' She always called me by some pet-name, ole Mis' did.

"An' seein' me all doubled up wid pain, she rings de bell, an' she says to little weakly Partridge, who answered it, 'Tell Uncle Dowdy to git on de fastest mule an' go fer de doctor, *quick*!'

"Den she turned ter me, a-squirmin' an' a-howlin' like a baby, on de flo', an' she says ter me, as still an' terrible as de pestilence:—

"'What has you been eatin', Mariar?'

"It was n't no use tryin' ter lie, my chillern; so I says, weak-like:—

"'I *et* a whole poun'-cake dat Miss Josephine sent ter you.'

"'I shall whip you for dat falsehood,' says ole Mis', 'as soon as you is recovered. It is impossible dat a chile of your age could eat a whole poun'-cake. You might as well talk of a toad swallowin' a cat.'

"Den I give anudder screech, fur it seemed as if dat cake had turned to a cat, an' wus clawin' me.

"Arter about a million years o' sufferin', de doctor got dar; and he says:—

"'Seems as if dis chile's stomach is been overloaded.'"

"I jes' rolled my eyes up at him. I was tu fur gone ter speak.

"Well, he wrestled, wid me *all night,* chillern; an' de nex' mornin' dar I wus, gaspin' like a fish out of water, but saved. Ole Mis', she handed de doctor somethin' folded up in an envelope, an' he went a-sailin' off. Den she looked at me. I wus powerful weak, so I went off kind o' faint-like.

"She nussed me like a baby; an' when I got well she never said one word ter me, excep' jes' dis:—

"'Mariar, you need n't ter come ter my Sunday-school class ter-morrer.'

"I bu'st out a-cryin' at dat, an' I said:—

"'Mis' Jane, I owns up. I et de cake, an' I'm a miserbel sinner; but if you will try me agin, I'll try to do a better part.'

Katherine

McDowell

❧

151

"And den, honeys, she jes' knelt down, wid her little white han' on my head, and she prayed fur me, soft an' solemn.

"Well, I ain't never wanted to steal nothin' sence dat hour; an' I never has been able to look at a piece o' poun'-cake."

Silence.

"Anyhow," said Sam, "pound-cake is good."

"Yes, my boy," said our dear old gran'mammy; "but many a good thing is turned ter poison if you take it on de sly. You's mighty safe ter pend on dat ar trufe!"

15. Mary Noailles Murfree (Charles Egbert Craddock)

(1850–1922)

Mary Noailles Murfree was born on a plantation outside of Murfreesboro, Tennessee, a town named for her great-grandfather. Determined to provide his daughters with a solid education, Murfree's father taught the children at home or hired a tutor for them when they were not attending school. At Nashville Female Academy and at home the girls learned French, Spanish, and Latin. When the Civil War broke out, the Murfrees attempted to relocate to Grantland, their plantation in Mississippi, but military tensions prohibited their move. Shortly afterward, Grantland was destroyed. In 1867 the Murfree girls were sent to Chegaray Institute in Philadelphia to complete their education.

In 1869 the family was hit with financial problems as the price of cotton sank, so Murfree returned home to live with her parents. To amuse themselves during the difficult years, Murfree and her father wrote stories together; the result was several fine works, such as Murfree's first published story, "Flirts and Their Ways" (1874). Murfree also attempted to write a novel, but the first chapter was so good by itself that it was published by *Atlantic Monthly* in 1878. This story, "The Dancin' Party at Harrison's Cove," remains one of her best works. The story's large white frame hotel set high on a mountainside was based on a resort at Beersheba Springs, a hotel that her family visited often. It was during these trips to the mountains that Murfree learned about Appalachia and its people.

From this point on, Murfree became an avid writer. The editor of the *Atlantic* was very encouraging, especially of her mountain stories, and he published several more; eight of them (including "The Dancin' Party") are included in the collection *In the Tennessee Mountains* (1884), a book that gained immediate popularity. Her novel of postwar Tennessee, *Where the Battle Was Fought* (1884), was followed by another novel, *The Prophet of the Great Smoky Mountains* (1885).

Murfree received even more attention, and became an extremely popular writer, with the disclosure of her identity. The editor of the *Atlantic,* Thomas Bailey Aldrich, assumed he had been working for years with a man named Charles Egbert Craddock, and when Murfree traveled to Boston to visit him in 1885, the disclosure attracted national attention. For the next several years Murfree was compared to the best local colorists, and everything she wrote was immediately published. Her novels tended to focus on the mountain people, either in conflict with strangers or with townspeople, but by the 1890s she seemed to have exhausted her material. Her stories remain fresh, however, because of her successful blend of romance and realism, which grew from her love of nineteenth-century novels coupled with her commitment to precise and accurate detail. A complete collection of her stories was published in 1895 as *The Phantoms of the Foot-Bridge and Other Stories.*

In 1889 Murfree returned with her family to Murfreesboro after several years in St. Louis. She continued to experiment with new ideas, completing her first historical novel, *The Story of Old Fort Loudon,* in 1899; her first "St. Louis" novel, *The Champion,* in 1902; and her first novel about the Delta region, *The Fair Mississippian,* in 1908. In all she wrote twenty-five books and was able to support her family with her writing until her death. Shortly before her death she was awarded a Doctor of Letters degree by the University of the South.

The Dancin' Party at Harrison's Cove

"Fur ye see, Mis' Darley, them Harrison folks over yander ter the Cove hev determinated on a dancin' party."

The drawling tones fell unheeded on old Mr. Kenyon's ear, as he sat on the broad hotel piazza of the New Helvetia Springs, and gazed with meditative eyes at the fair August sky. An early moon was riding, clear and full, over this wild spur of the Alleghanies; the stars were few and very faint; even the great Scorpio lurked, vaguely outlined, above the wooded ranges; and the white mist, that filled the long, deep, narrow valley between the parallel lines of mountains, shimmered with opalescent gleams.

All the world of the watering-place had converged to that focus, the ball-room, and the cool, moonlit piazzas were nearly deserted. The fell determination of the "Harrison folks" to give a dancing party made no impression on the preoccupied old gentleman. Another voice broke his reverie,—a soft, clear, well-modulated voice,—and he started and turned his head as his own name was called, and his niece, Mrs. Darley, came to the window.

"Uncle Ambrose,—are you there? So glad! I was afraid you were down at the summer-house, where I hear the children singing. Do come here a moment, please. This is Mrs. Johns, who brings the Indian peaches to sell,—you know the Indian peaches?"

Mr. Kenyon knew the Indian peaches, the dark crimson fruit streaked with still darker lines, and full of blood-red juice, which he had meditatively munched that very afternoon. Mr. Kenyon knew the Indian peaches right well. He wondered, however, what had brought Mrs. Johns back in so short a time, for although the principal industry of the mountain people about the New Helvetia Springs is selling fruit to the summer sojourners, it is not customary to come twice on the same day, nor to appear at all after nightfall.

Mrs. Darley proceeded to explain.

"Mrs. Johns's husband is ill and wants us to send him some medicine."

Mr. Kenyon rose, threw away the stump of his cigar, and entered the room. "How long has he been ill, Mrs. Johns?" he asked, dismally.

Mr. Kenyon always spoke lugubriously, and he was a dismal-looking old man. Not more cheerful was Mrs. Johns; she was tall and lank, and with such a face as one never sees except in these mountains,—elongated, sallow, thin, with pathetic, deeply sunken eyes, and high cheekbones, and so settled an expression of hopeless melancholy that it must be that naught but care and suffering has been her lot; holding out wasted hands to the years as they pass,—holding them out always, and always empty. She wore a shabby, faded calico, and spoke with the peculiar expressionless drawl of the mountaineer. She was a wonderful contrast to Mrs. Darley, all furbelows and flounces, with her fresh, smooth face and soft hair, and plump, round arms half-revealed by the flowing sleeves of her thin, black dress. Mrs. Darley was in mourning, and therefore did not affect the ballroom. At this moment, on benevolent thoughts intent, she was engaged in uncorking sundry small phials, gazing inquiringly at their labels, and shaking their contents.

In reply to Mr. Kenyon's question, Mrs. Johns, sitting on the extreme edge of a chair and fanning herself with a pink calico sun-bonnet, talked about her husband, and a misery in his side and in his back, and how he felt it "a-comin' on nigh on ter a week ago." Mr. Kenyon expressed sympathy, and was surprised by the announcement that Mrs. Johns considered her husband's illness "a blessin', 'kase ef he war able ter git out'n his bed, he 'lowed ter go down ter Harrison's Cove ter the dancin' party, 'kase Rick Pearson war a-goin' ter be thar, an' hed said ez how none o' the Johnses should come."

"What, Rick Pearson, that terrible outlaw!" exclaimed Mrs. Darley,

Mary

Noailles

Murfree

ॐ

with wide open blue eyes. She had read in the newspapers sundry thrilling accounts of a noted horse thief and outlaw, who with a gang of kindred spirits defied justice and roamed certain sparsely-populated mountainous counties at his own wild will, and she was not altogether without a feeling of fear as she heard of his proximity to the New Helvetia Springs,—not fear for life or limb, because she was practical-minded enough to reflect that the sojourners and employés of the watering-place would far outnumber the outlaw's troop, but fear that a pair of shiny bay ponies, Castor and Pollux, would fall victims to the crafty wiles of the expert horse thief.

"I think I have heard something of a difficulty between your people and Rick Pearson," said old Mr. Kenyon. "Has a peace never been patched up between them?"

"No-o," drawled Mrs. Johns; "same as it always war. My old man'll never believe but what Rick Pearson stole that thar bay filly we lost 'bout five year ago. But I don't believe he done it; plenty other folks around is ez mean ez Rick, leastways mos' ez mean; plenty mean enough ter steal a horse, ennyhow. Rick *say* he never tuk the filly; say he war a-goin' ter shoot off the nex' man's head ez say so. Rick say he'd ruther give two bay fillies than hev a man say he tuk a horse ez he never tuk. Rick say ez how he kin stand up ter what he does do, but it's these hyar lies on him what kills him out. But ye know, Mis' Darley, ye know yerself, he never give nobody two bay fillies in this world, an' what's more he's never goin' ter. My old man an' my boy Kossute talks on 'bout that thar bay filly like she war stole yestiddy, an' 't war five year ago an' better; an' when they hearn ez how Rick Pearson hed showed that red head o' his'n on this hyar mounting las' week, they war fightin' mad, an' would hev lit out fur the gang sure, 'ceptin' they hed been gone down the mounting fur two days. An' my son Kossute, he sent Rick word that he had better keep out'n gunshot o' these hyar woods; that he did n't want no better mark than that red head o' his'n, an' he could hit it two mile off. An' Rick Pearson, he sent Kossute word that he would kill him fur his sass the very nex' time he see him, an' ef he don't want a bullet in that pumpkin head o' his'n he hed better keep away from that dancin' party what the Harrisons hev laid off ter give, 'kase Rick say he's a-goin' ter it hisself, an' is a-goin' ter dance too; he ain't been invited, Mis' Darley, but Rick don't keer fur that. He is a-goin' ennyhow, an' he say ez how he ain't a-goin' ter let Kossute come, 'count o' Kossute's sass an' the fuss they've all made 'bout that bay filly that war stole five year ago,—'t war five year an' better. But Rick say ez how he is goin', fur all he ain't got no invite, an' is a-goin' ter dance too, 'kase you know, Mis' Darley, it's a-goin' ter be a dancin' party; the Harrisons hev determined on that. Them gals of theirn air mos' crazed 'bout a dancin' party. They ain't been a bit of account sence they went ter Cheatham's Cross-Roads ter see thar gran'mother, an' picked up all them queer new notions. So the Harrisons hev determinated on a dancin' party; an' Rick say ez how he is goin' ter dance too; but Jule, *she* say ez how she know thar ain't a gal on the mounting ez would dance with him; but I ain't so sure 'bout that, Mis' Darley; gals air cur'ous critters, ye know yerself; thar's no sort o' countin' on 'em; they'll do one thing one time, an' another thing nex' time; ye can't put no dependence in 'em. But Jule say if he kin git Mandy Tyler ter dance with him, it's the mos' he kin do, an' the gang'll be no whar. Mebbe he kin git Mandy ter dance with him, 'kase the other boys say ez how none o' them is a-goin' ter ax her ter dance, 'count of the trick she played on 'em down ter the Wilkins settlemint—las' month, war it? no, 't war two month ago, an' better; but the boys ain't forgot how scandalous she done 'em, an' none of 'em is a-goin ter ax her ter dance."

"Why, what did she do?" exclaimed Mrs. Darley, surprised. "She came here to sell peaches one day, and I thought her such a nice, pretty, well-behaved girl."

"Waal, she hev got mighty quiet say-nuthin' sort'n ways, Mis' Darley, but that thar gal do behave *rediculous*. Down thar ter the Wilkins settlemint,—ye know it's 'bout two mile or two mile 'n a half from hyar,—waal, all the gals walked down thar ter the party an hour by sun, but when the boys went down they tuk thar horses, ter give the gals a ride home behind 'em. Waal, every boy axed his gal ter ride while the party war goin' on, an' when 't war all over they all set out fur ter come home. Waal, this hyar Mandy Tyler is a mighty favo*rite* 'mongst the boys,—they ain't got no sense, ye know, Mis' Darley,—an' stiddier one of 'em axin' her ter ride home, thar war five of 'em axed her ter ride, ef ye'll believe me, an' what do ye think she done, Mis' Darley? She tole all five of 'em yes; an' when the party war over, she war the last ter go, an' when she started out'n the door, thar war all five of them boys a-standin' thar waitin' fur her, an' every one a-holdin' his horse by the bridle, an' none of 'em knowed who the others war a-waitin' fur. An' this hyar Mandy Tyler, when she got ter the door an' seen 'em all a-standin' thar, never said one word, jest walked right through 'mongst 'em, an' set out fur the mounting on foot with all them five boys a-followin' an' a-leadin' thar horses an' a-quarrelin' enough ter take off each others' heads 'bout which one war a-goin' ter ride with her; which none of 'em did, Mis' Darley, fur I hearn ez how the whole lay-out footed it all the way ter New Helveshy. An' thar would hev been a fight 'mongst 'em, 'ceptin' her brother, Jacob Tyler, went along with 'em, an' tried ter keep the peace atwixt 'em. An' Mis' Darley, all them married folks down thar at the

party—them folks in the Wilkins settlemint is the biggest fools, sure—
when all them married folks come out ter the door, an' see the way
Mandy Tyler hed treated them boys, they jest hollered and laffed an'
thought it war mighty smart an' funny in Mandy; but she never say a
word till she kem up the mounting, an' I never hearn ez how she say
ennything then. An' now the boys all say none of 'em is a-goin' ter ax her

ter dance, ter pay her back fur them fool airs of hern. But Kossute say
he'll dance with her ef none the rest will. Kossute he thought 't war all
mighty funny too,—he's sech a fool 'bout gals, Kossute is,—but Jule, she
thought ez how 't war scandalous."

Mrs. Darley listened in amused surprise; that these mountain wilds
could sustain a first-class coquette was an idea that had not hitherto
entered her mind; however, "that thar Mandy" seemed, in Mrs. Johns's
opinion at least, to merit the unenviable distinction, and the party at
Wilkins settlement and the prospective gayety of Harrison's Cove awakened the same sentiments in her heart and mind as do the more ambitious germans and kettledrums of the lowland cities in the heart and
mind of Mrs. Grundy. Human nature is the same everywhere, and the
Wilkins settlement is a microcosm. The metropolitan centres, stripped
of the civilization of wealth, fashion, and culture, would present only the
bare skeleton of humanity outlined in Mrs. Johns's talk of Harrison's
Cove, the Wilkins settlement, the enmities and scandals and sorrows and
misfortunes of the mountain ridge. As the absurd resemblance developed, Mrs. Darley could not forbear a smile. Mrs. Johns looked up with
a momentary expression of surprise; the story presented no humorous
phase to her perceptions, but she too smiled a little as she repeated,
"Scandalous, ain't it?" and proceeded in the same lack-lustre tone as
before.

"Yes,—Kossute say ez how he'll dance with her ef none the rest will,
fur Kossute say ez how he hev laid off ter dance, Mis' Darley; an' when I
ax him what he thinks will become of his soul ef he dances, he say the
devil may crack away at it, an' ef he kin hit it he's welcome. Fur soul or
no soul he's a-goin' ter dance. Kossute is a-fixin' of hisself this very minit
ter go; but I am verily afeard the boy 'll be slaughtered, Mis' Darley, 'kase
thar is goin' ter be a fight, an' ye never in all yer life hearn sech sass ez
Kossute and Rick Pearson done sent word ter each other."

Mr. Kenyon expressed some surprise that she should fear for so
young a fellow as Kossute. "Surely," he said, "the man is not brute
enough to injure a mere boy; your son is a mere boy."

"That's so," Mrs. Johns drawled. "Kossute ain't more 'n twenty year
old, an' Rick Pearson is double that ef he is a day; but ye see it's the fire-
arms ez makes Kossute more 'n a match fur him, 'kase Kossute is the

best shot on the mounting, an' Rick knows that in a shootin' fight Kossute's better able ter take keer of hisself an' hurt somebody else nor ennybody. Kossute's more likely ter hurt Rick nor Rick is ter hurt him in a shootin' fight; but ef Rick did n't hurt him, an' he war ter shoot Rick, the gang would tear him ter pieces in a minit; and 'mongst 'em I'm actually afeard they'll slaughter the boy."

Mr. Kenyon looked even graver than was his wont upon receiving this information, but said no more; and after giving Mrs. Johns the febrifuge she wished for her husband, he returned to his seat on the piazza.

Mrs. Darley watched him with some little indignation as he proceeded to light a fresh cigar. "How cold and unsympathetic uncle Ambrose is," she said to herself. And after condoling effusively with Mrs. Johns on her apprehensions for her son's safety, she returned to the gossips in the hotel parlor, and Mrs. Johns, with her pink calico sunbonnet on her head, went her way in the brilliant summer moon light.

The clear lustre shone white upon all the dark woods and chasms and flashing waters that lay between the New Helvetia Springs and the wide, deep ravine called Harrison's Cove, where from a rude log hut the vibrations of a violin, and the quick throb of dancing feet, already mingled with the impetuous rush of a mountain stream close by and the weird night-sounds of the hills,—the cry of birds among the tall trees, the stir of the wind, the monotonous chanting of frogs at the water side, the long, drowsy drone of the nocturnal insects, the sudden faint blast of a distant hunter's horn, and the far baying of hounds.

Mr. Harrison had four marriageable daughters, and had arrived at the conclusion that something must be done for the girls; for, strange as it may seem, the prudent father exists even among the "mounting folks." Men there realize the importance of providing suitable homes for their daughters as men do elsewhere, and the eligible youth is as highly esteemed in those wilds as is the much scarcer animal at a fashionable watering-place. Thus it was that Mr. Harrison had "determinated on a dancin' party." True, he stood in bodily fear of the judgment day and the circuit-rider; but the dancing party was a rarity eminently calculated to please the young hunters of the settlements round about, so he swallowed his qualms, to be indulged at a more convenient season, and threw himself into the vortex of preparation with an ardor very gratifying to the four young ladies, who had become imbued with sophistication at Cheatham's Cross-Roads.

Not so Mrs. Harrison; she almost expected the house to fall and crush them, as a judgment on the wickedness of a dancing party; for so heinous a sin, in the estimation of the greater part of the mountain people, had not been committed among them for many a day. Such trifles as killing a man in a quarrel, or on suspicion of stealing a horse, or wash-tub, or anything that came handy, of course, does not count; but a dancing party! Mrs. Harrison could only hold her idle hands, and dread the heavy penalty that must surely follow so terrible a crime.

It certainly had not the gay and lightsome aspect supposed to be characteristic of such a scene of sin: the awkward young mountaineers clogged heavily about in their uncouth clothes and rough shoes, with the stolid-looking, lack-lustre maids of the hill, to the violin's monotonous iteration of The Chicken in the Bread-Trough, or The Rabbit in the Pea-Patch,—all their grave faces as grave as ever. The music now and then changed suddenly to one of those wild, melancholy strains sometimes heard in old-fashioned dancing tunes, and the strange pathetic cadences seemed more attuned to the rhythmical dash of the waters rushing over their stone barricades out in the moonlight yonder, or to the plaintive sighs of the winds among the great dark arches of the primeval forests, than to the movement of the heavy, coarse feet dancing a solemn measure in the little log cabin in Harrison's Cove. The elders, sitting in rush-bottomed chairs close to the walls, and looking on at the merriment, well-pleased despite their religious doubts, were somewhat more lively; every now and then a guffaw mingled with the violin's resonant strains and the dancers' well-marked pace; the women talked to each other with somewhat more animation than was their wont, under the stress of the unusual excitement of a dancing party, and from out the shed-room adjoining came an anticipative odor of more substantial sin than the fiddle or the grave jiggling up and down the rough floor. A little more cider too, and a very bad article of illegally-distilled whiskey, were ever and anon circulated among the pious abstainers from the dance; but the sinful votaries of Terpsichore could brook no pause nor delay, and jogged up and down quite intoxicated with the mirthfulness of the plaintive old airs and the pleasure of other motion than following the plow or hoeing the corn.

And the moon smiled right royally on her dominion: on the long, dark ranges of mountains and mist-filled valleys between; on the woods and streams, and on all the half-dormant creatures either amongst the shadow-flecked foliage or under the crystal waters; on the long, white, sandy road winding in and out through the forest; on the frowning crags of the wild ravine; on the little bridge at the entrance of the gorge, across which a party of eight men, heavily armed and gallantly mounted, rode swiftly and disappeared amid the gloom of the shadows.

The sound of the galloping of horses broke suddenly on the music and the noise of the dancing; a moment's interval, and the door gently opened and the gigantic form of Rick Pearson appeared in the aperture.

He was dressed, like the other mountaineers, in a coarse suit of brown jeans somewhat the worse for wear, the trowsers stuffed in the legs of his heavy boots; he wore an old soft felt hat, which he did not remove immediately on entering, and a pair of formidable pistols at his belt conspicuously challenged attention. He had auburn hair, and a long full beard of a lighter tint reaching almost to his waist; his complexion was much tanned by the sun, and roughened by exposure to the inclement mountain weather; his eyes were brown, deep-set, and from under his heavy brows they looked out with quick, sharp glances, and occasionally with a roguish twinkle; the expression of his countenance was rather good-humored,— a sort of imperious good-humor, however,— the expression of a man accustomed to have his own way and not to be trifled with, but able to afford some amiability since his power is undisputed.

He stepped slowly into the apartment, placed his gun against the wall, turned, and solemnly gazed at the dancing, while his followers trooped in and obeyed his example. As the eight guns, one by one, rattled against the wall, there was a startled silence among the pious elders of the assemblage, and a sudden disappearance of the animation that had characterized their intercourse during the evening. Mrs. Harrison, who by reason of flurry and a housewifely pride in the still unrevealed treasures of the shed-room had well-nigh forgotten her fears, felt that the anticipated judgment had even now descended, and in what terrible and unexpected guise! The men turned the quids of tobacco in their cheeks and looked at each other in uncertainty; but the dancers bestowed not a glance upon the newcomers, and the musician in the corner, with his eyes half-closed, his head bent low upon the instrument, his hard, horny hand moving the bow back and forth over the strings of the crazy old fiddle, was utterly rapt by his own melody. At the supreme moment when the great red beard had appeared portentously in the doorway and fear had frozen the heart of Mrs. Harrison within her at the ill-omened apparition, the host was in the shed-room filling a broken-nosed pitcher from the cider-barrel. When he re-entered, and caught sight of the grave sunburned face with its long red beard and sharp brown eyes, he too was dismayed for an instant, and stood silent at the opposite door with the pitcher in his hand. The pleasure and the possible profit of the dancing party, for which he had expended so much of his scanty store of this world's goods and risked the eternal treasures laid up in heaven, were a mere phantasm; for, with Rick Pearson among them, in an ill frame of mind and at odds with half the men in the room, there would certainly be a fight, and in all probability one would be killed, and the dancing party at Harrison's Cove would be a text for the bloody-minded sermons of the circuit-rider for all time to come.

However, the father of four marriageable daughters is apt to become crafty and worldly-wise; only for a moment did he stand in indecision; then, catching suddenly the small brown eyes, he held up the pitcher with a grin of invitation. "Rick!" he called out above the scraping of the violin and the clatter of the dancing feet, "slip round hyar ef ye kin, I've got somethin' for ye;" and he shook the pitcher significantly.

Not that Mr. Harrison would for a moment have thought of Rick Pearson in a matrimonial point of view, for even the sophistication of the Cross-Roads had not yet brought him to the state of mind to consider such a half loaf as this better than no bread, but he felt it imperative from every point of view to keep that set of young mountaineers dancing in peace and quiet, and their guns idle and out of mischief against the wall. The great red beard disappeared and reappeared at intervals, as Rick Pearson slipped along the gun-lined wall to join his host and the cider-pitcher, and after he had disposed of the refreshment, in which the gang shared, he relapsed into silently watching the dancing and meditating a participation in that festivity.

Now, it so happened that the only young girl unprovided with a partner was "that thar Mandy Tyler," of Wilkins settlement renown; the young men had rigidly adhered to their resolution to ignore her in their invitations to dance, and she had been sitting since the beginning of the festivities, quite neglected, among the married people, looking on at the amusement which she had been debarred sharing by that unpopular bit of coquetry at Wilkins settlement. Nothing of disappointment or mortification was expressed in her countenance; she felt the slight of course,— even a "mounting" woman is susceptible of the sting of wounded pride; all her long-anticipated enjoyment had come to naught by this infliction of penance for her ill-timed jest at the expense of those five young fellows dancing with their triumphant partners and bestowing upon her not even a glance; but she looked the express image of immobility as she sat in her clean pink calico, so carefully gotten up for the occasion, her short black hair curling about her ears, and watched the unending reel with slow, dark eyes. Rick's glance fell upon her, and without further hesitation he strode over to where she was sitting and proffered his hand for the dance. She did not reply immediately, but looked timidly about her at the shocked pious ones on either side, who were ready but for mortal fear to aver that "dancin' ennyhow air bad enough, the Lord knows, but dancin' with a horse thief air jest scandalous!" Then, for there is something of defiance to established law and prejudice in the born flirt everywhere, with a sudden daring spirit shining in her brightening eyes, she responded, "Don't keer ef I do," with a dimpling half-laugh; and the next minute the two outlaws were flying down the middle together.

While Rick was according grave attention to the intricacies of the mazy dance and keeping punctilious time to the scraping of the old fiddle, finding it all a much more difficult feat than galloping from the Cross-Roads to the "Snake's Mouth" on some other man's horse with the sheriff hard at his heels, the solitary figure of a tall gaunt man had followed the long winding path leading deep into the woods, and now began the steep descent to Harrison's Cove. Of what was old Mr. Kenyon thinking, as he walked on in the mingled shadow and sheen? Of St. Augustin and his Forty Monks, probably, and what they found in Britain. The young men of his acquaintance would gladly have laid you any odds that he could think of nothing but his antique hobby, the ancient church. Mr. Kenyon was the most prominent man in St. Martin's church in the city of B——, not excepting the rector. He was a lay-reader, and officiated upon occasions of "clerical sore-throat," as the profane denominate the ministerial summer exodus from heated cities. This summer, however, Mr. Kenyon's own health had succumbed, and he was having a little "sore-throat" in the mountains on his own account. Very devout was Mr. Kenyon. Many people wondered that he had never taken orders. Many people warmly congratulated themselves that he never had; for drier sermons than those he selected were surely never heard, and a shuddering imagination shrinks appalled from the problematic mental drought of his ideal original discourse. But he was an integrant part of St. Martin's; much of his piety, materialized into contributions, was built up in its walls and shone before men in the costliness of its decorations. Indeed, the ancient name had been conferred upon the building as a sort of tribute to Mr. Kenyon's well-known enthusiasm concerning apostolic succession and kindred doctrines.

Dull and dismal was Mr. Kenyon, and therefore it may be considered a little strange that he should be a notable favorite with men. They were of many different types, but with one invariable bond of union: they had all at one time served as soldiers; for the war, now ten years passed by, its bitterness almost forgotten, had left some traces that time can never obliterate. What a friend was the droning old churchman in those days of battle and bloodshed and suffering and death! Not a man sat within the walls of St. Martin's who had not received some signal benefit from the hand stretched forth to impress the claims of certain ante-Augustin British clergy to consideration and credibility; not a man who did not remember stricken fields where a good Samaritan went about under shot and shell, succoring the wounded and comforting the dying; not a man who did not applaud the indomitable spirit and courage that cut his way from surrender and safety, through solid barriers of enemies, to deliver the orders on which the fate of an army depended; not a man whose memory did not harbor fatiguing recollections of long, dull sermons read for the souls' health of the soldiery. And through it all,—by the camp-fires at night, on the long white country-roads in the sunshiny mornings; in the mountains and the morasses; in hilarious advance and in cheerless retreat; in the heats of summer and by the side of frozen rivers, the ancient British clergy went through it all. And, whether the old churchman's premises and reasoning were false, whether his tracings of the succession were faulty, whether he dropped a link here or took in one there, he had caught the spirit of those staunch old martyrs, if not their falling churchly mantle.

The mountaineers about the New Helvetia Springs supposed that Mr. Kenyon was a regularly ordained preacher, and that the sermons which they had heard him read were, to use the vernacular, out of his own head. For many of them were accustomed on Sunday mornings to occupy humble back benches in the ball-room, where on week-day evenings the butterflies sojourning at New Helvetia danced, and on the Sabbath metaphorically beat their breasts, and literally avowed that they were "miserable sinners," following Mr. Kenyon's lugubrious lead.

The conclusion of the mountaineers was not unnatural, therefore, and when the door of Mr. Harrison's house opened and another uninvited guest entered, the music suddenly ceased. The half-closed eyes of the fiddler had fallen upon Mr. Kenyon at the threshold, and, supposing him a clergyman, he immediately imagined that the man of God had come all the way from New Helvetia Springs to stop the dancing and snatch the revelers from the jaws of hell. The rapturous bow paused shuddering on the string, the dancing feet were palsied, the pious about the walls were racking their slow brains to excuse their apparent conniving at sin and bargaining with Satan, and Mr. Harrison felt that this was indeed an unlucky party and it would undoubtedly be dispersed by the direct interposition of Providence before the shed-room was opened and the supper eaten. As to his soul—poor man! these constantly recurring social anxieties were making him callous to immortality; this life was about to prove too much for him, for the fortitude and tact even of a father of four marriageable young ladies has a limit. Mr. Kenyon, too, seemed dumb as he hesitated in the door-way, but when the host, partially recovering himself, came forward and offered a chair, he said with one of his dismal smiles that he hoped Mr. Harrison had no objection to his coming in and looking at the dancing for a while. "Don't let me interrupt the young people, I beg," he added, as he seated himself. The astounded silence was unbroken for a few moments. To be sure he was not a circuit-rider, but even the sophistication of Cheatham's Cross-Roads had never heard of a preacher who did not object to dancing. Mr. Harrison could not believe his ears, and asked for a more explicit expression of opinion.

"Ye say ye don't keer ef the boys an' gals dance?" he inquired. "Ye don't think it's sinful?"

And after Mr. Kenyon's reply, in which the astonished "mounting folks" caught only the surprising statement that dancing if properly conducted was an innocent, cheerful, and healthful amusement, supplemented by something about dancing in the fear of the Lord, and that in all charity he was disposed to consider objections to such harmless recreations a tithing of mint and anise and cummin, whereby might ensue a neglect of weightier matters of the law; that clean hands and clean hearts—hands clean of blood and ill-gotten goods, and hearts free from falsehood and cruel intention—these were the things well-pleasing to God,—after his somewhat prolix reply, the gayety recommenced. The fiddle quavered tremulously at first, but soon resounded with its former vigorous tones, and the joy of the dance was again exemplified in the grave joggling back and forth.

Meanwhile Mr. Harrison sat beside this strange new guest and asked him questions concerning his church, being instantly, it is needless to say, informed of its great antiquity, of the journeying of St. Augustin and his Forty Monks to Britain, of the church they found already planted there, of its retreat to the hills of Wales under its oppressors' tyranny, of many cognate themes, side issues of the main branch of the subject, into which the talk naturally drifted, the like of which Mr. Harrison had never heard in all his days. And as he watched the figures dancing to the violin's strains, and beheld as in a mental vision the solemn gyrations of those renowned Forty Monks to the monotone of old Mr. Kenyon's voice, he abstractedly hoped that the double dance would continue without interference till a peaceable dawn.

His hopes were vain. It so chanced that Kossuth Johns, who had by no means relinquished all idea of dancing at Harrison's Cove and defying Rick Pearson, had hitherto been detained by his mother's persistent entreaties, some necessary attentions to his father, and the many trials which beset a man dressing for a party who has very few clothes, and those very old and worn. Jule, his sister-in-law, had been most kind and complaisant, putting on a button here, sewing up a slit there, darning a refractory elbow, and lending him the one bright ribbon she possessed as a neck-tie. But all these things take time, and the moon did not light Kossuth down the gorge until she was shining almost vertically from the sky, and the Harrison Cove people and the Forty Monks were dancing together in high feather. The ecclesiastic dance halted suddenly, and a watchful light gleamed in old Mr. Kenyon's eyes as he became silent and the boy stepped into the room. The moon-light and the lamp-light fell mingled on the calm, inexpressive features and tall, slender form of the young mountaineer. "Hy're, Kossute!" A cheerful greeting from many voices met him. The next moment the music ceased once again, and the dancing came to a standstill, for as the name fell on Pearson's ear he turned, glanced sharply toward the door, and drawing one of his pistols from the belt advanced to the middle of the room. The men fell back; so did the frightened women, without screaming, however, for that indication of feminine sensibility had not yet penetrated to Cheatham's Cross-Roads, to say nothing of the mountains.

"I told ye that ye war n't ter come hyar," said Rick Pearson imperiously, "and ye've got ter go home ter year mammy, right off, or ye'll never git thar no more, youngster."

"I've come hyar ter put *you* out, ye cussed red-headed horse thief!" retorted Kossuth, angrily; "ye hed better tell me whar that thar bay filly is, or light out, one."

It is not the habit in the mountains to parlay long on these occasions. Kossuth had raised his gun to his shoulder as Rick, with his pistol cocked, advanced a step nearer. The outlaw's weapon was struck upward by a quick, strong hand, the little log cabin was filled with flash, roar, and smoke, and the stars looked in through a hole in the roof from which Rick's bullet had sent the shingles flying. He turned in mortal terror and caught the hand that had struck his pistol,—in mortal terror, for Kossuth was the crack shot of the mountains and he felt he was a dead man. The room was somewhat obscured by smoke, but as he turned upon the man who had disarmed him, for the force of the blow had thrown the pistol to the floor, he saw that the other hand was over the muzzle of young Johns's gun, and Kossuth was swearing loudly that by the Lord Almighty if he did n't take it off he would shoot it off.

"My young friend," Mr. Kenyon began, with the calmness appropriate to a devout member of the one catholic and apostolic church; but then, the old Adam suddenly getting the upper-hand, he shouted out in irate tones, "If you don't stop that noise, I'll break your head! Well, Mr. Pearson," he continued, as he stood between the combatants, one hand still over the muzzle of young Johns's gun, the other, lean and sinewy, holding Pearson's powerful right arm with a vise-like grip, "well, Mr. Pearson, you are not so good a soldier as you used to be; you did n't fight boys in the old times."

Rick Pearson's enraged expression suddenly gave way to a surprised recognition. "Ye may drag me through hell an' beat me with a soot-bag ef hyar ain't the old fightin' preacher agin!" he cried.

"I have only one thing to say to you," said Mr. Kenyon. "You must go. I will not have you here shooting boys and breaking up a party."

Rick demurred. "See hyar, now," he said, "ye've got no business meddlin'."

"You must go," Mr. Kenyon reiterated.

"Preachin's yer business," Rick continued; "'pears like ye don't 'tend to it, though."

"You must go."

"S'pose I say I won't," said Rick, good-humoredly; "I s'pose ye'd say ye'd make me."

"You must go," repeated Mr. Kenyon. "I am going to take the boy home with me, but I intend to see you off first."

Mr. Kenyon had prevented the hot-headed Kossuth from firing by keeping his hand persistently over the muzzle of the gun; and young Johns had feared to try to wrench it away lest it should discharge in the effort. Had it done so, Mr. Kenyon would have been in sweet converse with the Forty Monks in about a minute and a quarter. Kossuth had finally let go the gun, and made frantic attempts to borrow a weapon from some of his friends, but the stern authoritative mandate of the belligerent peacemaker had prevented them from gratifying him, and he now stood empty-handed beside Mr. Kenyon, who had shouldered the old rifle in an absent-minded manner, although still retaining his powerful grasp on the arm of the outlaw.

"Waal, parson," said Rick at length, "I'll go, jest ter pleasure you-uns. Ye see, I ain't forgot Shiloh."

"I am not talking about Shiloh now," said the old man. "You must get off at once,—all of you," indicating the gang, who had been so whelmed in astonishment that they had not lifted a finger to aid their chief.

"Ye say ye'll take that—that"—Rick looked hard at Kossuth while he racked his brains for an injurious epithet—"that sassy child home ter his mammy?"

"Come, I am tired of this talk," said Mr. Kenyon; "you must go."

Rick walked heavily to the door and out into the moonlight. "Them was good old times," he said to Mr. Kenyon, with a regretful cadence in his peculiar drawl; "good old times, them War days. I wish they was back agin,—I wish they was back agin. I ain't forgot Shiloh yit, though, and I ain't a-goin' ter. But I'll tell ye one thing, parson," he added, his mind reverting from ten years ago to the scene just past, as he unhitched his horse and carefully examined the saddle-girth and stirrups, "ye're a mighty queer preacher, ye air, a-sittin' up an' lookin' at sinners dance an' then gittin' in a fight that don't consarn ye,—ye're a mighty queer preacher! Ye ought ter be in my gang, that's whar ye ought ter be," he exclaimed with a guffaw, as he put his foot in the stirrup; "ye've got a damned deal too much grit fur a preacher. But I ain't forgot Shiloh yit, an' I don't mean ter, nuther."

A shout of laughter from the gang, an oath or two, the quick tread of horses' hoofs pressing into a gallop, and the outlaw's troop were speeding along the narrow paths that led deep into the vistas of the moonlit summer woods.

As the old churchman, with the boy at his side and the gun still on his shoulder, ascended the rocky, precipitous slope on the opposite side of the ravine above the foaming waters of the wild mountain stream, he said but little of admonition to his companion; with the disappearance of the flame and smoke and the dangerous ruffian his martial spirit had cooled; the last words of the outlaw, the highest praise Rick Pearson could accord to the highest qualities Rick Pearson could imagine—he had grit enough to belong to the gang—had smitten a tender conscience. He, at his age, using none of the means rightfully at his command, the gentle suasion of religion, must needs rush between armed men, wrench their weapons from their hands, threatening with such violence that an outlaw and desperado, recognizing a parallel of his own belligerent and lawless spirit, should say that he ought to belong to the gang! And the heaviest scourge of the sin-laden conscience was the perception that, so far as the unsubdued old Adam went, he ought indeed.

He was not so tortured, though, that he did not think of others. He paused on reaching the summit of the ascent, and looked back at the little house nestling in the ravine, the lamplight streaming through its open doors and windows across the path among the laurel bushes where Rick's gang had hitched their horses.

"I wonder," said the old man, "if they are quiet and peaceable again; can you hear the music and dancing?"

"Not now," said Kossuth. Then, after a moment, "Now, I kin," he added, as the wind brought to their ears the oft-told tale of the rabbit's gallopade in the pea-patch. "They're a-dancin' now, and all right agin."

As they walked along, Mr. Kenyon's racked conscience might have been in a slight degree comforted had he known that he was in some sort a revelation to the impressible lad at his side, that Kossuth had begun dimly to comprehend that a Christian may be a man of spirit also, and that bravado does not constitute bravery. Now that the heat of anger was over, the young fellow was glad that the fearless interposition of the warlike peace-maker had prevented any killing, " 'kase ef the old man hed n't hung on ter my gun like he done, I'd have been a murderer like he said, an' Rick would hev been dead. An' the bay filly ain't sech a killin' matter nohow; ef it war the roan three-year-old now, 't would be different."

16. Grace King

(1851?–1932)

Grace Elizabeth King was raised in the Creole society of New Orleans, the city of her birth. During the Civil War her family lost their home, and because her father refused to pledge allegiance to the Union, he lost his law practice. Despite the financial difficulties that her family faced, King was able to attend the Institut St. Louis and the school of Heloise Cenas, where she became very skilled in French language and literature.

King launched her writing career through a challenge made by George Washington Cable. In response to an attack on his depiction of Creole society, he invited any writer to do better. The result was "Monsieur Motte" (1886), King's first story, which was published in *New Princeton Review*. Charles Dudley Warner, who helped get the story published, invited King to Connecticut in 1887, where she met Mark Twain (Samuel Clemens) and his wife, Olivia. Living in the North, King was able to devote much of her time to writing, publishing several stories in *Harper's, Century,* and *Harper's Bazaar.*

By 1888 her first collection of stories, *Monsieur Motte,* was printed; a second, *Tales of a Time and Place,* followed in 1892. This collection contains one of King's best works, "Bayou L'Ombre," a somewhat autobiographical story about three sisters left on their isolated family plantation during the Civil War under the guardianship of "Uncle Jim," a trusted family slave. The girls fantasize that they are soldiers; "Ah, if we were only men!" they sigh. In a recent study of King's work, Helen Taylor describes the betrayal of the girls by their cousin Beau, who poses as a Federal captain, as "a paradigm of the betrayal by men, northern as well as southern, of the hopes and ideals of their women" (62).

King's best works are collected in *Balcony Stories* (1893), which includes "The Little Convent Girl." First published in *Century Magazine* (August 1893), this story shocks the reader more than all others in the collection. Critic Helen Taylor calls the little convent girl "a grotesque parody of the [southern] feminine ideal," and she finds the ending of the story "abrupt and uncompromising": it is one of "assertive action" rather than of passive timidity (70). The central figure in the story, though a young girl, resembles Chopin's Edna Pontellier from *The Awakening* in her quiet determination.

While working on *Tales of a Time and Place* and *Balcony Stories,* King was able to spend a few years in Europe, particularly in France and with Samuel Clemens and his family outside of Florence, Italy. King's interest in French writers is reflected in the realism of her short works, but it also provided her with a job writing about the French authors for Warner's *Library of the World's Best Literature* (1896–97).

Interested in the history of the South, King devoted much of her writing to histories of Louisiana. A biography of the Canadian founder of New Orleans, *Jean Baptiste le Moyne* (1892), and two social histories of the area, *New Orleans: The Place and the People* (1895) and *Creole Families of New Orleans* (1921), strive for historical accuracy while *The Pleasant Ways of St. Médard* (1916) presents a more personal history of her own experience during Reconstruction. For these works, as well as for her fiction, she received an honorary degree from Tulane University, the Palmes d'Officier de l'Instruction Publique from the French government, and recognition from the Louisiana Historical Society.

King's research and writing kept her busy until she died in 1932. *Memories of a Southern Woman of Letters* (1932) is an excellent source for a study of her life and opinions.

The Little Convent Girl

She was coming down on the boat from Cincinnati, the little convent girl. Two sisters had brought her aboard. They gave her in charge of the captain, got her a state-room, saw that the new little trunk was put into it, hung the new little satchel up on the wall, showed her how to bolt the door at night, shook hands with her for good-by (good-bys have really no significance for sisters), and left her there. After a while the bells all rang, and the boat, in the awkward elephantine fashion of boats, got into mid-stream. The chambermaid found her sitting on the chair in the state-room where the sisters had left her, and showed her how to sit on a chair in the saloon. And there she sat until the captain came and hunted her up for supper. She could not do anything of herself; she had to be initiated into everything by some one else.

She was known on the boat only as "the little convent girl." Her name, of course, was registered in the clerk's office, but on a steamboat no one thinks of consulting the clerk's ledger. It is always the little widow, the fat madam, the tall colonel, the parson, etc. The captain, who pronounced by the letter, always called her the little con*vent* girl. She was the beau-ideal of the little convent girl. She never raised her eyes except when spoken to. Of course she never spoke first, even to the chambermaid, and when she did speak it was in the wee, shy, furtive voice one might imagine a just-budding violet to have; and she walked with such soft, easy, carefully calculated steps that one naturally felt the penalties that must have secured them—penalties dictated by a black code of deportment.

She was dressed in deep mourning. Her black straw hat was trimmed with stiff new crape, and her stiff new bombazine dress had crape collar and cuffs. She wore her hair in two long plaits fastened around her head tight and fast. Her hair had a strong inclination to curl, but that had been taken out of it as austerely as the noise out of her footfalls. Her hair was as black as her dress; her eyes, when one saw them, seemed blacker than either, on account of the bluishness of the white surrounding the pupil. Her eyelashes were almost as thick as the black veil which the sisters had fastened around her hat with an extra pin the very last thing before leaving. She had a round little face, and a tiny pointed chin; her mouth was slightly protuberant from the teeth, over which she tried to keep her lips well shut, the effort giving them a pathetic little forced expression. Her complexion was sallow, a pale sallow, the complexion of a brunette bleached in darkened rooms. The only color about her was a blue taffeta ribbon from which a large silver medal of the Virgin hung over the place where a breastpin should have been. She was so little, so little, although she was eighteen, as the sisters told the captain; otherwise they would not have permitted her to travel all the way to New Orleans alone.

Unless the captain or the clerk remembered to fetch her out in front, she would sit all day in the cabin, in the same place, crocheting lace, her spool of thread and box of patterns in her lap, on the handkerchief spread to save her new dress. Never leaning back—oh no! always straight and stiff, as if the conventual back board were there within call. She would eat only convent fare at first, notwithstanding the importunities of the waiters, and the jocularities of the captain, and particularly of the clerk. Every one knows the fund of humor possessed by a steamboat clerk, and what a field for display the table at meal-times affords. On Friday she fasted rigidly, and she never began to eat, or finished, without a little Latin movement of the lips and a sign of the cross. And always at six o'clock of the evening she remembered the angelus, although there was no church bell to remind her of it.

She was in mourning for her father, the sisters told the captain, and she was going to New Orleans to her mother. She had not seen her mother since she was an infant, on account of some disagreement between the parents, in consequence of which the father had brought her to Cincinnati, and placed her in the convent. There she had been for twelve years, only going to her father for vacations and holidays. So long as the father lived he would never let the child have any communication with her mother. Now that he was dead all that was changed, and the first thing that the girl herself wanted to do was to go to her mother.

The mother superior had arranged it all with the mother of the girl, who was to come personally to the boat in New Orleans, and receive her child from the captain, presenting a letter from the mother superior, a facsimile of which the sisters gave the captain.

It is a long voyage from Cincinnati to New Orleans, the rivers doing their best to make it interminable, embroidering themselves *ad libitum* all over the country. Every five miles, and sometimes oftener, the boat would stop to put off or take on freight, if not both. The little convent girl, sitting in the cabin, had her terrible frights at first from the hideous noises attendant on these landings—the whistles, the ringings of the bells, the running to and fro, the shouting. Every time she thought it was shipwreck, death, judgment, purgatory; and her sins! her sins! She would drop her crochet, and clutch her prayer-beads from her pocket, and relax the constraint over her lips, which would go to rattling off prayers with the velocity of a relaxed windlass. That was at first, before the captain took to fetching her out in front to see the boat make a landing. Then she got to liking it so much that she would stay all day just where the captain put her, going inside only for her meals. She forgot herself at times so much that she would draw her chair a little closer to the railing, and put up her veil, actually, to see better. No one ever usurped her place, quite in front, or intruded upon her either with word or look; for every one learned to know her shyness, and began to feel a personal interest in her, and all wanted the little convent girl to see everything that she possibly could.

And it was worth seeing—the balancing and *chasséeing* and waltzing of the cumbersome old boat to make a landing. It seemed to be always attended with the difficulty and the improbability of a new enterprise; and the relief when it did sidle up anywhere within rope's-throw of the spot aimed at! And the roustabout throwing the rope from the perilous end of the dangling gang-plank! And the dangling roustabouts hanging like drops of water from it—dropping sometimes twenty feet to the land, and not infrequently into the river itself. And then what a rolling of barrels, and shouldering of sacks, and singing of Jim Crow songs, and pacing of Jim Crow steps; and black skins glistening through torn shirts, and white teeth gleaming through red lips, and laughing, and talking and—bewildering! entrancing! Surely the little convent girl in her convent walls never dreamed of so much unpunished noise and movement in the world!

The first time she heard the mate—it must have been like the first time woman ever heard man—curse and swear, she turned pale, and ran quickly, quickly into the saloon, and—came out again? No, indeed! not with all the soul she had to save, and all the other sins on her conscience. She shook her head resolutely, and was not seen in her chair on deck again until the captain not only reassured her, but guaranteed his reassurance. And after that, whenever the boat was about to make a landing, the mate would first glance up to the guards, and if the little convent girl was sitting there he would change his invective to sarcasm, and politely request the colored gentlemen not to hurry themselves— on no account whatever; to take their time about shoving out the plank; to send the rope ashore by post-office—write him when it got there; begging them not to strain their backs; calling them mister, colonel, major, general, prince, and your royal highness, which was vastly amusing. At night, however, or when the little convent girl was not there, language flowed in its natural curve, the mate swearing like a pagan to make up for lost time.

The captain forgot himself one day: it was when the boat ran aground in the most unexpected manner and place, and he went to work to express his opinion, as only steamboat captains can, of the pilot, mate, engineer, crew, boat, river, country, and the world in general, ringing the bell, first to back, then to head, shouting himself hoarser than his own whistle—when he chanced to see the little black figure hurrying through the chaos on the deck; and the captain stuck as fast aground in midstream as the boat had done.

In the evening the little convent girl would be taken on the upper deck, and going up the steep stairs there was such confusion, to keep the black skirts well over the stiff white petticoats; and, coming down, such blushing when suspicion would cross the unprepared face that a rim of white stocking might be visible; and the thin feet, laced so tightly in the glossy new leather boots, would cling to each successive step as if they could never, never make another venture; and then one boot would (there is but that word) hesitate out, and feel and feel around, and have such a pause of helpless agony as if indeed the next step must have been wilfully removed, or was nowhere to be found on the wide, wide earth.

It was a miracle that the pilot ever got her up into the pilot-house; but pilots have a lonely time, and do not hesitate even at miracles when there is a chance for company. He would place a box for her to climb to the tall bench behind the wheel, and he would arrange the cushions, and open a window here to let in air, and shut one there to cut off a draft, as if there could be no tenderer consideration in life for him than her comfort. And he would talk of the river to her, explain the chart, pointing out eddies, whirlpools, shoals, depths, new beds, old beds, cut-offs, caving banks, and making banks, as exquisitely and respectfully as if she had been the River Commission.

It was his opinion that there was as great a river as the Mississippi flowing directly under it—an underself of a river, as much a counterpart of the other as the second story of a house is of the first; in fact, he said they were navigating through the upper story. Whirlpools were holes in the floor of the upper river, so to speak; eddies were rifts and cracks. And deep under the earth, hurrying toward the subterranean stream, were other streams, small and great, but all deep, hurrying to and from that great mother-stream underneath, just as the small and great overground streams hurry to and from their mother Mississippi. It was almost more than the little convent girl could take in: at least such was the expression of her eyes; for they opened as all eyes have to open at pilot stories. And he knew as much of astronomy as he did of hydrology, could call the stars by name, and define the shapes of the constellations; and she, who had studied astronomy at the convent, was charmed to find that what she had learned was all true. It was in the pilot-house, one night, that she forgot herself for the first time in her life, and stayed up until after nine o'clock. Although she appeared almost intoxicated at the wild pleasure, she was immediately overwhelmed at the wickedness of it, and observed much more rigidity of conduct thereafter. The engineer, the boiler-men, the firemen, the stokers, they all knew when the little convent girl was up in the pilot-house: the speaking-tube became so mild and gentle.

With all the delays of river and boat, however, there is an end to the journey from Cincinnati to New Orleans. The latter city, which at one time to the impatient seemed at the terminus of the never, began, all of a sudden, one day to make its nearingness felt; and from that period every other interest paled before the interest in the immanence of arrival into port, and the whole boat was seized with a panic of preparation, the little convent girl with the others. Although so immaculate was she in person and effects that she might have been struck with a landing, as some good people might be struck with death, at any moment without fear of results, her trunk was packed and repacked, her satchel arranged and rearranged, and, the last day, her hair was brushed and plaited and smoothed over and over again until the very last glimmer of a curl disappeared. Her dress was whisked, as if for microscopic inspection; her face was washed; and her finger-nails were scrubbed with the hard convent nail-brush, until the disciplined little tips ached with a pristine soreness. And still there were hours to wait, and still the boat added up delays. But she arrived at last, after all, with not more than the usual and expected difference between the actual and the advertised time of arrival.

There was extra blowing and extra ringing, shouting, commanding, rushing up the gangway and rushing down the gangway. The clerks, sitting behind tables on the first deck, were plied, in the twinkling of an eye, with estimates, receipts, charges, countercharges, claims, reclaims, demands, questions, accusations, threats, all at topmost voices. None but steamboat clerks could have stood it. And there were throngs composed of individuals every one of whom wanted to see the captain first and at once; and those who could not get to him shouted over the heads of the others; and as usual he lost his temper and politeness, and began to do what he termed "hustle."

"Captain! Captain!" a voice called him to where a hand plucked his sleeve and a letter was thrust toward him. "The cross, and the name of the convent." He recognized the envelope of the mother superior. He read the duplicate of the letter given by the sisters. He looked at the woman—the mother—casually, then again and again.

The little convent girl saw him coming, leading some one toward her. She rose. The captain took her hand first, before the other greeting, "Good-by, my dear," he said. He tried to add something else, but seemed undetermined what. "Be a good little girl—" It was evidently all he could think of. Nodding to the woman behind him, he turned on his heel, and left.

One of the deck-hands was sent to fetch her trunk. He walked out behind them, through the cabin, and the crowd on deck, down the stairs, and out over the gangway. The little convent girl and her mother went with hands tightly clasped. She did not turn her eyes to the right or left, or once (what all passengers do) look backward at the boat which, however slowly, had carried her surely over dangers that she wot not of. All looked at her as she passed. All wanted to say good-by to the little convent girl, to see the mother who had been deprived of her so long. Some expressed surprise in a whistle; some in other ways. All exclaimed audibly, or to themselves, "Colored!"

It takes about a month to make the round trip from New Orleans to Cincinnati and back, counting five days' stoppage in New Orleans. It was a month to a day when the steamboat came puffing and blowing up to the wharf again, like a stout dowager after too long a walk; and the same scene of confusion was enacted, as it had been enacted twelve times a year, at almost the same wharf for twenty years; and the same calm, a death calmness by contrast, followed as usual the next morning.

The decks were quiet and clean; one cargo had just been delivered, part of another stood ready on the levee to be shipped. The captain was there waiting for his business to begin, the clerk was in his office getting his books ready, the voice of the mate could be heard below, mustering the old crew out and a new crew in; for if steamboat crews have a single principle,—and there are those who deny them any,—it is never to ship twice in succession on the same boat. It was too early yet for any but roustabouts, marketers, and church-goers; so early that even the river was still partly mist-covered; only in places could the swift, dark current be seen rolling swiftly along.

"Captain!" A hand plucked at his elbow, as if not confident that the mere calling would secure attention. The captain turned. The mother of the little convent girl stood there, and she held the little convent girl by the hand. "I have brought her to see you," the woman said. "You were so kind—and she is so quiet, so still, all the time, I thought it would do her a pleasure."

She spoke with an accent, and with embarrassment; otherwise one would have said that she was bold and assured enough.

"She don't go nowhere, she don't do nothing but make her crochet and her prayers, so I thought I would bring her for a little visit of 'How d' ye do' to you."

There was, perhaps, some inflection in the woman's voice that might have made known, or at least awakened, the suspicion of some latent hope or intention, had the captain's ear been fine enough to detect it. There might have been something in the little convent girl's face, had his eye been more sensitive—a trifle paler, maybe, the lips a little tighter drawn, the blue ribbon a shade faded. He may have noticed that, but— And the visit of "How d' ye do" came to an end.

They walked down the stairway, the woman in front, the little convent girl—her hand released to shake hands with the captain—following, across the bared deck, out to the gangway, over to the middle of it. No one was looking, no one saw more than a flutter of white petticoats, a show of white stockings, as the little convent girl went under the water.

The roustabout dived, as the roustabouts always do, after the drowning, even at the risk of their good-for-nothing lives. The mate himself jumped overboard; but she had gone down in a whirlpool. Perhaps, as the pilot had told her whirlpools always did, it may have carried her through to the underground river, to that vast, hidden, dark Mississippi that flows beneath the one we see; for her body was never found.

(1851–1904)

Kate O'Flaherty Chopin was born in St. Louis, Missouri, to an Irish father and a French Creole mother. When she was four years old her father died in a train wreck, so Chopin was raised by her mother, grandmother, and great-grandmother. Though quite young, Chopin began formulating her opinions while a student at the Academy of the Sacred Heart, a school that strongly supported the South and the Catholic faith. Her aristocratic upbringing, however, also cultivated her social graces, and when she graduated from the Academy in 1868, both well read and musically adept, she entered the St. Louis social world with ease. In 1870 she married Oscar Chopin, a cotton manufacturer from Louisiana. The couple moved to New Orleans, and in the ten years that they lived there the Chopins had six children. These years were spent in considerable wealth, traveling in Europe and vacationing at a resort off the coast of Louisiana. But in 1879 Oscar Chopin's business failed, and after moving his family to central Louisiana to run a general store, he died in 1882.

Returning to St. Louis, Chopin began her writing career as a woman in her late thirties. Her first published work, the poem "If It Might Be," was published in 1889; short stories followed, first in local papers and then in national magazines. "Desiree's Baby" was one of these early stories, published by *Vogue* in 1893. Several others soon appeared in *Atlantic Monthly* and *Century*. The primary influence on Chopin's writing was Guy de Maupassant, whose works she read, translated, and imitated. The precision of Maupassant's style as well as his stark realism shaped even Chopin's early stories. At the same time, Chopin is considered a local-color writer because she often focused on the Creole and black communities of southern Louisiana; *Bayou Folk* (1894), her first collection of short stories, contains tales and sketches firmly grounded in this southern setting.

Even her early tales characteristically portray women in search of freedom, love, and art, or they explore social tradition with a questioning eye. What makes these subjects distinctive, however, is her controversial manner of dealing with them. Chopin's first novel, *At Fault* (1890), shocked its American audience as Chopin refused to criticize divorce, entertaining the possibility that at times it may be preferable to marriage. Chopin's "A Respectable Woman," first published in *Vogue* (February 15, 1894) and later included in the collection *A Night in Acadie* (1897), deals with many of the issues Chopin would later address in *The Awakening* (1899); yet its ending sharply contrasts with Edna Pontellier's suicide. Chopin's masterpiece, *The Awakening,* so damaged her reputation that she was not again seriously considered as a writer of merit until the 1960s. This novel proves that Chopin was far more than a local-color writer, as it not only addresses a woman's dissatisfaction with marriage and motherhood but also contemplates the unsettling consequences of that dissatisfaction, such as adultery or suicide.

Chopin spent the final years of her life in St. Louis, writing very little. She died of a brain hemorrhage when she was fifty-one years old.

A Respectable Woman

Mrs. Baroda was a little provoked to learn that her husband expected his friend, Gouvernail, up to spend a week or two on the plantation.

They had entertained a good deal during the winter; much of the time had also been passed in New Orleans in various forms of mild dissipation. She was looking forward to a period of unbroken rest, now, an undisturbed tête-a-tête with her husband, when he informed her that Gouvernail was coming up to stay a week or two.

This was a man she had heard much of but never seen. He had been her husband's college friend; was now a journalist, and in no sense a society man or "a man about town," which were, perhaps, some of the reasons she had never met him. But she had unconsciously formed an image of him in her mind. She pictured him tall, slim, cynical; with eyeglasses, and his hands in his pockets; and she did not like him. Gouvernail was slim enough, but he wasn't very tall nor very cynical; neither did he wear eyeglasses nor carry his hands in his pockets. And she rather liked him when he first presented himself.

But why she liked him she could not explain satisfactorily to herself when she partly attempted to do so. She could discover in him none of those brilliant and promising traits which Gaston, her husband, had often assured her that he possessed. On the contrary, he sat rather mute and receptive before her chatty eagerness to make him feel at home and in face of Gaston's frank and wordy hospitality. His manner was as courteous toward her as the most exacting woman could require; but he made no direct appeal to her approval or even esteem.

Once settled at the plantation he seemed to like to sit upon the wide portico in the shade of one of the big Corinthian pillars, smoking his cigar lazily and listening attentively to Gaston's experience as a sugar planter.

"This is what I call living," he would utter with deep satisfaction, as the air that swept across the sugar field caressed him with its warm and scented velvety touch. It pleased him also to get on familiar terms with the big dogs that came about him, rubbing themselves sociably against his legs. He did not care to fish, and displayed no eagerness to go out and kill grosbecs when Gaston proposed doing so.

Gouvernail's personality puzzled Mrs. Baroda, but she liked him. Indeed, he was a lovable, inoffensive fellow. After a few days, when she could understand him no better than at first, she gave over being puzzled and remained piqued. In this mood she left her husband and her guest, for the most part, alone together. Then finding that Gouvernail took no manner of exception to her action, she imposed her society upon him, accompanying him in his idle strolls to the mill and walks along the batture. She persistently sought to penetrate the reserve in which he had unconsciously enveloped himself.

"When is he going—your friend?" she one day asked her husband. "For my part, he tires me frightfully."

"Not for a week yet, dear. I can't understand; he gives you no trouble."

"No. I should like him better if he did; if he were more like others, and I had to plan somewhat for his comfort and enjoyment."

Gaston took his wife's pretty face between his hands and looked tenderly and laughingly into her troubled eyes. They were making a bit of toilet sociably together in Mrs. Baroda's dressing-room.

"You are full of surprises, ma belle," he said to her. "Even I can never count upon how you are going to act under given conditions." He kissed her and turned to fasten his cravat before the mirror.

"Here you are," he went on, "taking poor Gouvernail seriously and making a commotion over him, the last thing he would desire or expect."

"Commotion!" she hotly resented. "Nonsense! How can you say such a thing? Commotion, indeed! But, you know, you said he was clever."

"So he is. But the poor fellow is run down by overwork now. That's why I asked him here to take a rest."

"You used to say he was a man of ideas," she retorted, unconciliated. "I expected him to be interesting, at least. I'm going to the city in the morning to have my spring gowns fitted. Let me know when Mr. Gouvernail is gone; I shall be at my Aunt Octavie's."

That night she went and sat alone upon a bench that stood beneath a live oak tree at the edge of the gravel walk.

She had never known her thoughts or her intentions to be so confused. She could gather nothing from them but the feeling of a distinct necessity to quit her home in the morning.

Mrs. Baroda heard footsteps crunching the gravel; but could discern in the darkness only the approaching red point of a lighted cigar. She knew it was Gouvernail, for her husband did not smoke. She hoped to remain unnoticed, but her white gown revealed her to him. He threw away his cigar and seated himself upon the bench beside her, without a suspicion that she might object to his presence.

"Your husband told me to bring this to you, Mrs. Baroda," he said, handing her a filmy, white scarf with which she sometimes enveloped her head and shoulders. She accepted the scarf from him with a murmur of thanks, and let it lie in her lap.

He made some commonplace observation upon the baneful effect of the night air at that season. Then as his gaze reached out into the darkness, he murmured, half to himself:

"'Night of south winds—night of the large few stars!
Still nodding night—'"

She made no reply to this apostrophe to the night, which indeed, was not addressed to her.

Gouvernail was in no sense a diffident man, for he was not a self-conscious one. His periods of reserve were not constitutional, but the result of moods. Sitting there beside Mrs. Baroda, his silence melted for the time.

He talked freely and intimately in a low, hesitating drawl that was not unpleasant to hear. He talked of the old college days when he and Gaston had been a good deal to each other; of the days of keen and blind ambitions and large intentions. Now there was left with him, at least, a philosophic acquiescence to the existing order—only a desire to be permitted to exist, with now and then a little whiff of genuine life, such as he was breathing now.

Her mind only vaguely grasped what he was saying. Her physical being was for the moment predominant. She was not thinking of his words, only drinking in the tones of his voice. She wanted to reach out her hand in the darkness and touch him with the sensitive tips of her fingers upon the face or the lips. She wanted to draw close to him and whisper against his cheek—she did not care what—as she might have done if she had not been a respectable woman.

The stronger the impulse grew to bring herself near him, the further, in fact, did she draw away from him. As soon as she could do so without an appearance of too great rudeness, she rose and left him there alone.

Before she reached the house, Gouvernail had lighted a fresh cigar and ended his apostrophe to the night.

Mrs. Baroda was greatly tempted that night to tell her husband—who was also her friend—of this folly that had seized her. But she did not yield to the temptation. Beside being a respectable woman she was a very sensible one, and knew there are some battles in life which a human being must fight alone.

When Gaston arose in the morning, his wife had already departed. She had taken an early morning train to the city. She did not return till Gouvernail was gone from under her roof.

There was some talk of having him back during the summer that followed. That is, Gaston greatly desired it, but this desire yielded to his wife's strenuous opposition.

However, before the year ended, she proposed, wholly from herself, to have Gouvernail visit them again. Her husband was surprised and delighted with the suggestion coming from her.

"I am glad, chère amie, to know that you have finally overcome your dislike for him; truly he did not deserve it."

"Oh," she told him, laughingly, after pressing a long, tender kiss upon his lips, "I have overcome everything! you will see. This time I shall be very nice to him."

Julia Mood Peterkin

(1880–1961)

Julia Mood Peterkin was born in Laurens County, South Carolina, in 1880 and was raised by her father and by a black nurse, "Mauma," after the death of her mother later in that same year. Her early education was a dual one: her nurse taught Julia the dialect, customs, and attitudes of the southern black community while her father so demanded intellectual growth that the girl received her master's degree when she was sixteen years old. After graduating from Converse College in 1896, Julia left home to teach in a small rural school in Fort Motte, South Carolina. There she met her husband, a wealthy planter whose family owned most of the land in that part of the state. After her marriage, Peterkin found life on the plantation extremely demanding, for she was expected to attend to the nearly five hundred sharecroppers that farmed the land; typically, this would involve providing simple medical care and sometimes clothing. She was also an avid gardener herself and kept busy with community work through the Daughters of the American Revolution and the United Daughters of the Confederacy.

When her husband fell ill, the management of the plantation fell to Peterkin. Almost overwhelmed by her responsibilities, she turned to music lessons as an escape from the daily pressures and hardships. Because her music instructor was also a fine writer, he encouraged Peterkin to try writing down some of the stories she told him about her life on the plantation. Later, he brought Carl Sandburg to meet her, and the two men convinced her to send her sketches to H. L. Mencken, surely the toughest critic of the day. Mencken, however, was delighted with her work and immediately published one sketch. Shortly after, in 1921, she sent the others to the *Reviewer,* which accepted every one and published "Over the River" in January 1924; it is reprinted here from *Collected Short Stories of Julia Peterkin* (1970).

In that same year, her first collection of sketches and stories, *Green Thursday,* was published. Though its stark realism was harshly criticized by her white audience, Peterkin was praised by black readers and by literary critics. Her fiction is distinguished by its excellent depiction of the Gullahs of the South Carolina coastal region. In fact, it is because of stories like "Over the River" that Peterkin gained a reputation as a pioneer in the portrayal of blacks as human beings. Just as she created her black characters as complete and nonstereotypical, so too did she present the complexities of women's minds and emotions both realistically and thoughtfully.

The next ten years were ones of tremendous literary production for Peterkin. She published *Black April* in 1927 and received an honorary degree from Converse College that same year. Peterkin reached her peak with *Scarlet Sister Mary* (1928), which won the 1929 Pulitzer Prize and was immediately adapted for the stage. Her next novel, *Bright Skin* (1932), was not as strong, and by the time she produced *Roll, Jordan, Roll* (1933), Peterkin seemed to be merely reworking old material. After the publication of *A Plantation Christmas* in 1934, Peterkin returned to managing the plantation full-time, and, with the exception of one year of teaching creative writing in Bennington, Vermont, she continued doing so until her death at age eighty.

Over the River

A lone black woman walked steadily along the railroad track keeping to the middle where the vines and weeds did not grow so profusely. Her slim bare feet stepped mechanically yet firmly, on the cross-ties.

She carried a clumsy, cloth-tied bundle on her head and it shaded her eyes from the glaring overhead sun, but their soft depths had an anxious, uneasy expression as she gazed steadfastly into the forward distance. Her full purple lips were parted. From time to time she moistened them nervously with her tongue.

Blue and brown lizards slipped under the rails, and crickets and grasshoppers skipped to a safer distance, when her blue home-spun skirt fluttered near them. But she was intent on something ahead and did not heed them at all.

When the track made a sudden swift curve and changed to a trestle she stopped short. Should she go on?

The river bridge could not be very far ahead now. Walking over high places always made her head swim. The swamp in front of her looked dark and gloomy and mysterious. Should she go on and try to cross it?

Where the earth fell away the track seemed very narrow. The trestle was long. Dizzy high. Could she walk those cross-ties without losing her balance and falling?

She took a few steps forward and looked down. Sluggish yellow streams wound logily far beneath her. Stagnant pools hid under thick green slime. Rough black cypress roots pushed up out of the earth, then thrust down again out of sight. She thought of snakes and shivered.

Pointed saw-palmetto leaves glistened in the sunshine, and in the top of a tall ash tree not far above the level of the track was a cluster of orange colored blossoms flaunting gayly. A determined vine had climbed. Struggled up. When it reached the top of the tree it bloomed! Yes, bloomed. She'd go on. She'd shed her fear. It was her only way to get to him.

He was yonder, somewhere yonder over the river. When he went away he told her that was where he lived. If she wanted him, she would have to go over there to find him.

He pointed this way to show her the direction. He made signs to show her plainly where he was going. She was deaf. She could not hear words. But his signs were easy to understand.

When the days were clear that low line of faint blue hills was plain. Many a time when she wanted him, *wanted* him, it somehow comforted her to look away at those hills. He was there. There, over the river.

She might not know just where to find him when she got over there, but the time had come to her when she had to find him. Had to! She wasn't able to work for herself any longer now, let alone for another. She had to get to him and tell him. Had to let him work for her, take care of her, of her child, his child, until she was strong and ready to work for herself again.

He would do it. Yes, he would be glad to do it. He loved her.

She would like to stop and rest a little while in the shade and think. The sun was scorching hot. The bundle on her head was heavy. Her neck was tired. The cross-ties were splintery and stung the soles of her feet.

But if she was going to get to him in time she must not tarry.

Her time, the child's time, was almost come. The moon would change maybe tonight. She must hurry on.

She must have come most of the distance. She was far from home. Farther than she had ever been in her life before.

Suppose she did now turn and go back. There was nobody to go to. Nobody to care whether she lived or died. And he—he was yonder on the other side of the river. Somewhere yonder where the track dimmed and faded into the smoky haze.

She must not wait here. She must go on. She must not be afraid. She must keep thinking about him. Thinking that she was going to him, and then she would not be afraid.

Nothing would hurt her anyway unless she stumbled and fell—or a train should slip up behind her before she saw it—or a snake coiled up on the track to sun would strike her foot—

She'd watch close. She'd make her eyes see more today than they ever did before.

If she could only hear! She had never yearned to know what sound was like before. And not for herself. Now. No. Alone, she could manage. But now she had his child to think of. To take care of. His child—yes— and hers—

Its weight, its restless turning, kept her from walking fast. But she must try to make haste. She must be patient with her jaded feet. She must comfort the ache in her tired neck and back. For she was taking his child to him!

How pleased he would be when he knew. He'd throw his head back and laugh in the happy way she loved. He'd come hurrying to meet her with his light straight stride! He'd take her where she would be safe. He'd provide for her needs, hers and his child's—Yes—she was sure he would.

She shifted the weight of the bundle further back on her head so its pressing on her forehead would be less. She brushed away drops of sweat that trickled over her eyelids and stepped forward on the trestle.

Her heart thumped in her breast. She was afraid. Not of anything she saw but of the loneliness, the strangeness of it all.

This morning before sunrise she had started out lighthearted, proud, full of hope. Her feet almost wanted to dance with joy that she was going to him. And now, before noon was even near, before the day was half gone, before her journey was nearly ended, she was ready to turn back. She was afraid and sad, and tired—discouraged.

She must watch her feet. They seemed inclined to stumble. They'd make a misstep and she'd fall.

Breathing seemed harder here somehow. The hot air, mixed as it was with the smell of rank, lush swamp growth and with steam from the oozy, yellow mud and black, rotting wood, was almost suffocating.

The very leaves on the trees were limp and drooping.

A wisp of smoke trailed into view. She faltered, half-halted, then she hurried on to a little shelf built out at one side of the track. A train was coming. She'd wait there until it passed.

The trestle quivered, shook, as the long freight came nearer. A black fireman leaned out of his cab and waved a cheerful arm at her. Steadying the bundle with one hand she waved timidly at him.

It was good to see a face. Even a strange face. It gave her comfort.

She turned and watched the train rushing away on the trembly track carrying its cloud of sooty smoke and dust with it. Trains always held her fascinated. She had never ridden on one. There had never been any- where for her to go. And besides, it took money to ride on trains.

Today, if she had even a few pieces of money, she could ride over the river on a train. They crossed like this every day. But she did not have one piece left. Not one.

She worked. Yes, she had always worked. But she got her pay in orders for things at the cross-roads store. Food. Clothes. Sometimes a bit of candy or cake or a ribbon. Never money.

Work had always seemed good until lately. Her body had got heavy and slow. Nobody wanted her to work for them now. They all shook their heads and told her not to come back.

All her life until this year she had worked in the fields. Nobody could hoe or pick cotton any better. She couldn't hear and she couldn't talk and she didn't waste time.

This year she got a job helping the cook at a saw-mill. That was a good job. Always there was plenty to eat. Scraps, sometimes, but good food. Washing dishes was not hard to do. Her hands were quick. She hardly ever dropped a dish and broke it. Once or twice at first, when she didn't know just how to hold them, she did, but since she learned to hold them firm and light too, she never broke any at all.

She met *him* at the saw-mill. He came there to work in the off season when his crop was laid by over the river. Saw-mill wages were good. He made some money—then he went back home—

He put money in her hand the last time she saw him. She kept it until yesterday, then she spent it all. She spent it for things she had to have. For charms. Two of them. Two that were good and strong.

As she walked she fingered the two little bags tied to a string around her neck. One of them held a charm made of the charred bones of an owl. That would make child-birth easy for her. The other held the tip of a buzzard's claw. That would make her baby teethe easy.

She touched the tips of her own white teeth together and smiled. Her baby's teeth—somehow the thought of them thrilled her heart. *His* teeth were white as rice grains! And even—Her baby's teeth would be like them. Of course they would be like his. He was her baby's father.

How happy he always was! Always laughing, playing, joking, teasing—Her baby would be like that.

Charms cost money, but she was right to spend what she had for these two. They were not for herself. They were for the child. His child. And he had given the money to her.

She had come to the wide yellow river. There it was, lying quiet in its bed, but she knew how it rose up and flooded and ruined low-lying fields when it was tired resting.

This river divided her world. And he—he was yonder on the other side.

She couldn't be very far from him now. When she got over there she'd take the first road she saw and follow it until she met somebody. Then she'd make signs to ask where he lived.

How could she make a stranger understand whom she meant? She pondered this seriously.

He was tall, yes. She could hold an arm high to show that. He was black. Her own skin could show that. But many men were tall and slim and black.

How was she to tell a stranger that he had the most beautiful face in the world, and the tenderest smile—How?

His teeth and his mouth were different. Yes, different from every other man's. Nobody had teeth white as his. That was the way she could tell people whom she wanted to find.

She was finally across. The deep woods began to give way to open spaces. Small clearings held fields of cotton and corn.

Soon there would be a road. Maybe it would lead quickly to a house where she could stop and ask about him and rest.

She was tired. She had been walking since before day was clear this morning, when the morning star shone bright. She had not stopped once to blow.

On the side of a shallow slope a dim path straggled through woods and disappeared. It went somewhere. She'd follow it and see where.

She left the track and soon there were trees on both sides of her. The sky barely shone through the branches overhead. The path, cool and moist, led her on to a little clear spring bubbling with good clean water. Thank God!

She put her bundle carefully down on the ground and knelt and drank thirstily. Her face was steamy with heat and sweat. She cupped her hands and dipped water up and laved it and cooled it. Thank God for water!

She sat on the ground and dabbled her dusty feet in the stream and her tired eyes rested themselves with watching dreamily the white sand rising and stirring and settling in the water that flowed out from under it.

Her thirst was quenched but she was hungry and sleepy. She had nothing to eat. Stretching out on the wet ground to sleep would not be good. She'd just sit here a little. The child seemed glad to be still.

It must be nearly noon. Maybe quite noon. Here, where the trees hid the sun, it was hard to tell exactly. One small bright spot of light fell into the water. She looked up to see where it came from. Yes, it came from straight overhead. It was noon. Time to rest. People who work by the day in the field all stop and rest at noon. She had walked far this morning. She was due to rest, too.

It was hard to realize that she was on the same side of the river with him. The deep yellow river no longer ran between them. It wouldn't take long to find him now—to tell him why she had come.

For his sake she was sorry to be deaf. But he had never seemed to mind. He laughed at the signs she made to him as if he liked them. He'd laugh with surprise today when he saw her here—when he knew about their little child—

A purple flower hanging by a slender stem over the shining water trembled as a dusty yellow bee hovered wavering over it, then settled to suck its honey. She bent forward a little to watch it better. She leaned her chin in her hand. Her eyelids grew heavy. It was so peaceful here. The air is so fresh. The light so quiet and dim. The child must be sleeping too....

When something roused her, startled, confused, she could not think at first where she was. She tried to get to her feet. A mule's great shaggy neck was almost brushing her shoulder. His big loose lips sucked up water close beside her. His great hoofs were sinking into the soft wet earth not far from her bare feet.

Black plowmen stood staring at her while other mules drank. They had come from the fields near by. It was noon. They came here with their mules to drink. She was over the river. She remembered.

Maybe they knew him, and could tell her where to find him. She'd try to ask them. To make them understand by signs.

They were speaking to her. They were asking her questions. She could tell by the look on their faces. By their moving lips.

Her own lips and throat struggled to form words. She pointed to tell them she had come from over the river. They understood.

They saw she was deaf. They were saying so to each other. They were laughing. Laughing at her. She could see it.

One of them, one with thick ugly lips, and eyes that flickered through narrow slitted lids, was saying something to her. She couldn't tell his words but she knew what they were by the look on his face. By the way the others laughed and scolded and shamed him.

He cared for nothing they said. He stood looking at her with bold mean eyes.

She tried to look away from him. To pretend she did not understand him. It was hard to do. She dropped her eyes to the ground. Then turned to look far away—and—there he was! He was coming!

He came riding a mule along the path to the spring. He laughed as he came and kicked the mule in the sides with his strong bare heels. He was shouting to the others. She could see his lips move. The muscles in his big throat quivered with his voice. It was *he*. Yes—here—

Her throat strained and strove to call him. To tell him she was here looking for him. Her lips twisted and wrung with trying to speak words.

He saw her. He looked right at her. He looked straight into her eyes.

And he turned away to the others. Maybe——Maybe—he didn't know her—

He had turned away. He did not know her.

She knew she was changed. Yes. That her body was different. But altered so much he did not know her?

The big, ugly man was laughing. Was making sport of her. And he—he was listening and laughing too—laughing at her—making sport of her—How could he—how could he?

Her forehead felt burning hot all of a sudden. Chills went up and down her spine. Her knees got weak and shaky. A dark mist came before her eyes. She couldn't see him—or anything.

A pain, sharp, brutal, like a butcher knife plunged through her insides, made her stagger forward. Her weight made her clumsy. Awkward.

Her body squeezed itself into a tight, dumb knot of pain. She put out a hand to keep herself from falling. Her fingers felt the shaggy rough hair of the mule, then the leaves on the damp earth where she fell. She tried to reach out. Maybe she would feel the touch of his hand. She would feel the touch of his hand. She would know it even in the darkness. . . .

The next morning a thin black old woman with sunken eyes leaned over the bed where she lay and stared her hard in the face. How shriveled and puckered the old features were. But the dim eyes were gentle, pitying.

A trembling warm hand was patting her shoulder. The quilt was being drawn back. A shaky old hand was motioning her to look at the child there on the bed beside her. The hand patted her and motioned again. It shook her and made quick impatient signs. She must turn and look, it was saying.

She was too tired to look at anything. She wanted just to lie still and sleep. Sleep on and on.

The old hand was bent on having its way. It pulled at her and jerked her. She may as well do as it bade. It would not let her rest.

She opened her eyes and followed where it pointed. Her baby was close by her on the bed. It was wrapped in one of her own petticoats, and sleeping. She raised up on an elbow to see better. Ah— With a finger she stroked its tiny head. Its small wrinkled face. Her little baby was sleeping as if there was no trouble in the world, while its father— wouldn't own it or her.

The old hand began making signs again. It pointed to her breasts. It told her the child must be fed. Fed now.

She clutched at the quilt and drew it up over her.

She turned away from the child and with her face to the shabby, dingy, brown wall she tried to recover what had happened.

She had seen him and he had not owned her. Over and over the thought milled through her mind. He had not owned her. After she had come all this way to bring him his child, he did not care. He had laughed at her! She thought he'd be proud—when he saw her—She was a fool! Yes.

Tears hid the rain-stained walls from her eyes. If she could only die! Why hadn't she died! The misery in her heart was too much to bear—too much—It was keener than her body's pain had been.

He—he—It was the loss of him that was eating into her very insides. Her lips began trying to cry out words. If she could only say words! They would help. Her throat almost burst with the effort to say them. Her breath choked back with sobs.

He had refused to own her! He wouldn't even own that he knew her! Before her own eyes—Before all the strange men—He scorned her—He made sport of her. It was too much!

The old hand patted her shoulder gently, then stroked her forehead. It drew the quilt up around her and coaxed her to be quiet.

How could she be quiet again as long as she lived? Everything was gone from her. She had nothing to live for. Why did she ever come to look for him? Why didn't she stay where she was? She would never have known how cruel he could be. She would always have believed he loved her. But now—now—that she knew—how could she bear to live on?

A mosquito disturbed by her moving flitted close to her face, then settled on the wall right in front of her eyes. His body was puffed with food. With blood. He had been feeding on somebody. She had not felt his stinging. Maybe he had bitten her baby. How dared he?

She turned to see if the child's face was stung. Not that she could see. The light was very dim. The door and the windows were closed and there was only the feeble fire light flickering in the chimney, and the thin pale lines of light that showed through the cracks.

She touched the baby's soft wrinkled cheek with an unsteady fingertip.

This was her child. Hers. Yet his too. Nothing could keep it from being his. Together they had formed it. He and she—and life—they all three had a part in making it.

Once there had been love between them. Now he had only shame. And here was the child—Oh, who was to blame? What was it that made him forget and change—made him ashamed to own he knew her?

Poor little baby. Helpless. Naked. Friendless. Yet sleeping so sound. Sleep is good. If she herself could go to sleep and never wake up any more. That would be like death! Yes, death. If she and the child both would die.

If she never did feed the little baby it would sleep on and on. It would never wake up. Without food it could not live—it would die!

Should she let it die? Why not? He cared nothing for it. Nothing for her. It was better off asleep than awake—Dead than living.

The old woman was back at the bedside again, motioning to her to put the child to her breast. Pointing and gesturing and talking and insisting.

Her breasts were ready. She could feel them swollen, feverish, filled.

Should she let them give the child food? Should she wake it now? He had denied it and her. She'd let it sleep on and die. Yes, die.

Then she would die herself. She couldn't die now, but when the baby was dead she'd go somewhere in the woods, away off by herself. She'd stretch her length on the ground and die. Yes, she would make herself die.

The old woman shook her and pointed to a cupboard whose open door showed a pan holding pieces of corn-bread. The shelf near it held a bucket of water and on a nail hung a long-handled gourd.

The old woman said something else, then took up a basket and a sun-bonnet. She was going somewhere. Yes, she was putting the sunbonnet on her head, and getting ready to leave the cabin—to leave her—here—alone. The old woman came back to the bed and pointed to the child. She said it must be fed. Foolish old woman!

When the old woman went out and closed the door behind her, the fire died lower and lower. The shadows wavered dim over the dingy walls until at last they were still. Only a few coals gleamed in the ashes.

The little baby woke. Its arms made quick jerky signs. It was asking for something. It was hungry and asking for food.

She leaned low and peered into its face. It was ugly and twisted with crying. Poor little thing. Better cry now and have it over with than to live on and on with something in your heart that cries always. Yes, let it cry.

She couldn't look at it. She turned back to the wall and closed her eyes. She was tired—tired—If she could only sleep!

The bed quivered a little with the baby's crying. She was glad she couldn't hear it. Yes.

When she opened her eyes the day seemed spent. No light came through the cracks. She got up and opened the cabin door. The night outside was black. Smothering black. The darkness pushed itself into the room. She could hardly see the bed except for the baby's little fluttering hands. They still made signs. Signs for something to eat.

Maybe if she gave it water it would rest and sleep again.

She found a piece of wood and threw it on the coals, then knelt and blew on them until flames fluttered up yellow.

The long-handled gourd seemed big for a baby's mouth but no cup was in sight. She dipped up a little water and held it for the baby to drink. It couldn't drink. No, it didn't know how.

She took it up and wrapped the petticoat close around it. She carried it where the fire-light could fall on its face.

How like him it was. But, so little and so grieved. It couldn't help being like him. She had thought of nothing but him since he went away from her months ago.

Was it—was it a boy-child? She had never thought to see. Yes, it was. Of course it would be. He, so strong, so full of life, would never get girl-children. No, not he.

Pain, fierce, pitiless, clutched at her heart. Her breath seemed cut off. She loved him—loved him—and he—Ah—

She put the child back on the bed and covered it up with the quilt. She would sit there by the fire until day-light. Maybe its pitiful gesturing would be still before morning came. Maybe it would go back to sleep.

Her own weariness brought a kind of peace with it. A resignation. When at last day shone through the cracks, everything seemed quiet. The child? Yes, it was quiet too.

She uncovered its face. The eyelids were closed.

The mouth where white teeth were to grow and show with laughing—was slightly open—but the lips were blue. Still. Cold.

With earnest eyes she followed the curve of the tender cheek and chin. It was asleep for good. It wouldn't wake and flutter its little clenched fists any more. Not any more.

Another day was here. She must be moving. There was much to do before the old woman came back. She must hurry.

She went out of the door and looked for something to use for digging. Her baby had to be buried before she went away. Was there a hoe any-where—or an axe?

The dull old axe by the wood-pile had a poor cracked handle but it would do. The earth was sandy. It would give. The grave need not be very deep—or large—

Where should she make it?

She looked for a place. A vegetable garden had hand-split clapboards around it. Grass and weeds and a few green collards were inside. There, in the corner, would be a safe place. Safe from dogs and possums and cats. Yes, that was a safe place. Safe from the dogs and possums and cats. Yes, that was where she would put her child.

It didn't take very long. Her strokes were quick and the earth yielded easily. Gladly.

How could she put it in—cover it—with heavy, stifling dirt—but it wouldn't wake—it couldn't—it never would know it was not on the bed covered up with the soft light quilt—it wouldn't know.

Tears almost kept her from seeing what she did. They poured out of her eyes and her nose and into her mouth. But at last she was finished. There was nothing else to do now but to tie up her bundle and start back over the river. She couldn't stay here. Not here. No.

As the sun showed above the tree tops she closed the cabin door behind her and started on the path to the little clear spring that bubbled with good clean water. Thank God for water.

She knelt and drank thirstily, then took up her bundle and went on. It wasn't far to the railroad track. Soon she'd be back. Back, over the river.

19. Alice Dunbar-Nelson

(1875–1935)

Alice Moore grew up in a black middle-class New Orleans family that was able to support her musical and literary interests. She attended Straight College, and upon graduation in 1892 she took a teaching position in the city. For the next few years, she kept busy by participating in a number of musical groups and social clubs and by working on her writing. In 1895 her first book, *Violets and Other Tales,* was privately published; the volume collects her poems, sketches, stories, and essays.

Seeking additional education, in 1896 Alice moved to the Northeast and took courses at the University of Pennsylvania and at Cornell University, where she received a master of arts degree in English literature and education. Although a promising literary scholar, she did not devote her time to research but instead took a position teaching at the White Rose Mission in New York City, an institution that she helped found. The prominent black poet Paul Laurence Dunbar became interested in her after seeing her picture and poetry in a Boston newspaper. After several months of corresponding, the two writers met and were married in 1898. During this time, Alice was also working on a collection of short stories about Creole life in New Orleans, *The Goodness of St. Rocque and Other Stories,* which was published in the following year.

Living with Dunbar in Washington, D.C., was not easy, however. The competition between the two writers, as well as Dunbar's instability, made for a difficult marriage. After their separation in 1902, Alice moved to Wilmington, Delaware, and began teaching English at Howard High School. There she also helped found the Industrial School for Colored Girls. While she was living there, Paul Dunbar died of tuberculosis. It was several years before Alice produced additional works, though she kept busy working for the rights of women. She helped organize the Middle Atlantic women's suffrage group in 1915 and was also active in the National Association of Colored Women and the League of Independent Political Action. Through these organizations, Alice became intimately acquainted with several black women, specifically Edwina Kruse, with whom she remained close for the rest of her life; an unpublished novel, *The Lofty Oak,* was based on the life of this friend.

After a brief marriage in 1912 to a man twelve years her junior, she met the widowed journalist and political activist Robert Nelson. The two married in 1916 and spent several years working together; from 1920 to 1922, the Nelsons published the *Wilmington Weekly,* a progressive black newspaper. In addition, Dunbar-Nelson became the first black woman to serve on the State Republican Committee of Delaware in 1920, and she served as the executive secretary for the Interracial Peace Committee in the late 1920s. Her journalistic writing can also be found in a weekly column she wrote for the *Washington Eagle* from 1926 to 1930.

Dunbar-Nelson continued writing and publishing poetry throughout the twenties and was recognized in part because of the Harlem Renaissance going on at the time. She also wrote and collected speeches and performance material, publishing two anthologies, *Masterpieces of Negro Eloquence: The Best Speeches Delivered by the Negro From the Days of Slavery to the Present Time* (1913) and *The Dunbar Speaker and Entertainer* (1920).

The poems in this volume are all included in *The Works of Alice Dunbar-Nelson* (1988). "Sonnet" was first published in *Caroling Dusk* (1927); "April Is on the Way," in *Ebony and Topaz* (1927); "Cano—I Sing," in *American Inter-Racial Peace Committee Bulletin* (October 1929); and "The Proletariat Speaks," in *The Crisis* (1929).

Dunbar-Nelson died in Philadelphia in 1935. The story of her life can also be traced through *Give Us Each Day: The Diary of Alice Dunbar-Nelson* (1984).

Sonnet

I had no thought of violets of late,
The wild, shy kind that spring beneath your feet
In wistful April days, when lovers mate
And wander through the fields in raptures sweet.
The thought of violets meant florists' shops,
And bows and pins, and perfumed papers fine;
And garish lights, and mincing little fops
And cabarets and songs, and deadening wine.
So far from sweet real things my thoughts had strayed,
I had forgot wide fields, and clear brown streams;
The perfect loveliness that God has made,—
Wild violets shy and Heaven-mounting dreams.
And now—unwittingly, you've made me dream
Of violets, and my soul's forgotten gleam.

April Is on the Way

April is on the way!
I saw the scarlet flash of a blackbird's wing
As he sang in the cold, brown February trees;
And children said that they caught a glimpse of the sky on a bird's wing
    from the far South.
(Dear God, was that a stark figure outstretched in the bare branches
Etched brown against the amethyst sky?)

April is on the way!
The ice crashed in the brown mud-pool under my tread,
The warning earth clutched my bloody feet with great fecund fingers.
I saw a boy rolling a hoop up the road,
His little bare hands were red with cold,
But his brown hair blew backward in the southwest wind.
(Dear God! He screamed when he saw my awful woe-spent eyes.)

April is on the way!
I met a woman in the lane;
Her burden was heavy as it is always, but today her step was light,
And a smile drenched the tired look away from her eyes.
(Dear God, she had dreams of vengeance for her slain mate,
Perhaps the west wind has blown the mist of hate from her heart,
The dead man was cruel to her, you know that, God.)

April is on the way!
My feet spurn the ground now; instead of dragging on the bitter road.
I laugh in my throat as I see the grass greening beside the patches of
    snow
(Dear God, those were wild fears. Can there be hate when the southwest
    wind is blowing?)

April is on the way!
The crisp brown hedges stir with the bustle of bird wings.
There is business of building, and songs from brown thrust throats
As the bird-carpenters make homes against Valentine Day.
(Dear God, could they build me a shelter in the hedge from the icy
    winds that will come with the dark?)

April is on the way!
I sped through the town this morning. The florist shops have put yellow
    flowers in the windows,

Daffodils and tulips and primroses, pale yellow flowers
Like the tips of her fingers when she waved me that frightened farewell.
And the women in the market have stuck pussy willows in the
    long necked bottles on their stands.
(Willow trees are kind, Dear God. They will not bear a body on
    their limbs.)

April is on the way!
The soul within me cried that all the husk of indifference to sorrow
    was but the crust of ice with which winter disguises life;
It will melt, and reality will burgeon forth like the crocuses in the glen,
(Dear God! Those thoughts were from long ago. When we read
    poetry after the day's toil, and got religion together at the revival
    meeting.)

April is on the way!
The infinite miracle of unfolding life in the brown February fields.
(Dear God, the hounds are baying!)
Murder and wasted love, lust and weariness, deceit and vainglory—what
    are they but the spent breath of the runner?
(God, you know he laid hairy red hands on the golden loveliness
    of her little daffodil body.)
Hate may destroy me, but from my brown limbs will bloom
    the golden buds with which we once spelled love.
(Dear God! How their light eyes glow into black pin points
    of hate!)

April is on the way!
Wars are made in April, and they sing at Easter time of the Resurrection.
Therefore I laugh in their faces.
(Dear God, give her the strength to join me before her golden petals are
    fouled in the slime!)
April is on the way!

Cano—I Sing

Let others sing in their intricate strophes
        Of sorrow and grim despair
And wail of the snares that beset the race,
        Of the hate that befouls the air;
Let them beat their breasts at the lynching tree,
        And clench their fists at the sky—

My soul sinks, too, but I will not wail,
    I know there's a God on high.

So it's hope again, trust again, sing again,
    A whine is a weakling's plea;
The stars have not changed in their courses,
    The moon still orders the sea.

There's murder and hate in the Balkans;
    There's vengeance in far Cathay;
Injustice and tyranny threaten
    Where men and greed have their sway;
They're lynching my sisters in Texas,
    They're flogging my sons on the farm;
But I know that Omnipotence watches,
    That God has a far-flung arm.

So it's hope again, trust again, sing again,
    Step proudly, your face to the skies,
Though the curtain of midnight fold you,
    At the dawning, the sun will arise.

Let despairing youth carve in their cameos,
    Black, lurid, and hellish hate;
Paint a Japanese couplet to emblazon the screed
    That Christ came to earth too late;
'Twas ever the way of the young to forget
    That Love is the one great rule;
Through ultimate tears this lesson is drilled,
    For this God sends us to school.

So it's hope again, trust again, sing again,
    For hate is the wild beast's yelp;
Though the pack of the jungle be at our heels,
    Omnipotent Love is our help.

The Proletariat Speaks

I love the beautiful things:
Great trees, bending green winged branches to a velvet lawn,
Fountains sparkling in white marble basins,
Cool fragrance of lilacs and roses and honeysuckle.

Or exotic blooms, filling the air with heart-contracting odors;
Spacious rooms, cool and gracious with statues and books,
Carven seats and tapestries, and old masters
Whose patina shows the wealth of centuries.

And so I work
In a dusty office, whose grimed windows
Look out in an alley of unbelievable squalor,
Where mangy cats, in their degradation, spurn
Swarming bits of meat and bread;
Where odors, vile and breath taking, rise in fetid waves
Filling my nostrils, scorching my humid, bitter cheeks.

I love beautiful things:
Carven tables laid with lily-hued linen
And fragile china and sparking irridescent glass;
Pale silver, etched with heraldies,
Where tender bits of regal dainties tempt,
And soft-stepped service anticipates the unspoken wish.

And so I eat
In the food-laden air of a greasy kitchen,
At an oil-clothed table:
Plate piled high with food that turns my head away,
Lest a squeamish stomach reject too soon
The lumpy gobs it never needed.
Or in a smoky cafeteria, balancing a slippery tray
To a table crowded with elbows
Which lately the bus boy wiped with a grimy rag.

I love beautiful things:
Soft linen sheets and silken coverlet,
Sweet coolth of chamber opened wide to fragrant breeze;
Rose shaded lamps and golden atomizers,
Spraying Parisian fragrance over my relaxed limbs,
Fresh from a white marble bath, and sweet cool spray.

And so I sleep
In a hot hall-room whose half opened window,
Unscreened, refuses to budge another inch;
Admits no air, only insects, and hot choking gasps,
That make me writhe, nun-like, in sack-cloth sheets and lumps of straw.

And then I rise
To fight my way to a dubious tub,
Whose tiny, tepid stream threatens to make me late;
And hurrying out, dab my unrefreshed face
With bits of toiletry from the ten cent store.

The

Modern

South

(1918–1960)

In a description of American literature written after World War II, critic Alfred Kazin claims that "American society is remarkable for its degree of loneliness," a loneliness created by the "mass age" that forces the individual to turn inward and be concerned primarily with self-identity (208). Alienation—from God and from society—had become associated with the human condition in the modern world and, as Flannery O'Connor says, had permeated the literature of the age: "Alienation was once a diagnosis, but in much of the fiction of our time it has become an ideal. The modern hero is the outsider. His experience is rootless. He can go anywhere. He belongs nowhere. Being alien to nothing, he ends up being alienated from any kind of community based on common tastes and interests. The borders of his country are the sides of his skull" (O'Connor 199–200). Though O'Connor generally protected herself from this isolation by clinging to her southern and Catholic roots, as a writer she understood it and recreated it poignantly in the lives of her characters. Like O'Connor, women writers of the modern South faced multiple layers of alienation, for in addition to being confined to their age, they belonged to a region set apart from the rest of the nation, and they were of a gender, and in many cases a race, still struggling for its place in American society.

In the literature of the period, the educated woman or the woman artist of the South is often transformed into a grotesque, lonely figure, probably best exemplified by Hulga in O'Connor's short story "Good Country People." Hulga has a Ph.D. in philosophy, a wooden leg, a bad heart, and a disposition her mother believes is sure to frighten away any visitor to their backwoods southern farm. In *The Golden Apples* (1949), Eudora Welty considers the artist's similar isolation in the character of Miss Eckhart, the piano teacher, who will always be set apart from the Morgana community because of her exceptional talent and ambition, which are seen as a little odd, perhaps a little unladylike. Welty even notes in *One Writer's Beginnings* that she "came to feel oddly in touch" with Miss Eckhart, unable to fit herself to the feminine ideal represented by the tradition of the southern belle (101). Ironically, what at first seems to be freeing—that is, the increased education of women in the modern world—only serves to isolate Hulga and Miss Eckhart, O'Connor and Welty.

In the midst of the modern era the Southern Renaissance arose. That literary awakening produced a body of literature of quality and in quantity never before generated, in a region that H. L. Mencken once called the "Sahara of the Bozart." The term *modern,* then, defines the span of time (1918–1960), and *renaissance* describes the quality of the literature written in that period. This body of literature is generally recognized by its predominant traits, most notably a concern with the past as it shaped the present; a preoccupation with the lingering effects of the injustices and evils of slavery; a fascination with the grotesque and the eccentric; a focus on land and community; and a struggle to flee from the "Brahmins" of the Old South or the Southern Myth. Certainly many factors worked together to prompt this outpouring of literature, but the Southern Renaissance is often linked to key historical circumstances. Young southerners of the first several decades of the twentieth century grew up hearing the stories of the pre–Civil War South and of the war itself from a direct source—their grandparents; however, not having experienced the Old South firsthand, they approached the topic from a very different perspective. In addition, by traveling to other parts of the country and the world, southerners such as Katherine Anne Porter and Caroline Gordon were beginning to reevaluate their lives in the region from an outside perspective, much as young men returning from Europe after World War I did. Finally, the debate over the teaching of evolution that raged in Dayton, Tennessee, in 1925, emphasized the clash of worldviews represented by the "Old South" and the "New."

Despite common characteristics of the literature of the Renaissance, often the writers themselves—female and male, black and white—were divided by our traditional ways of defining the literary movement. Indeed, as southern culture itself has been segregated, so too have its renaissances. In the 1920s, many southern blacks were living, working, and writing in Harlem, including Zora Neale Hurston. Although many of these writers were southern, they are typically identified with the Harlem Renaissance rather than the Southern, and the movement in Harlem is discussed as an aside in most southern literature textbooks and scholarship. Furthermore, most scholars date the beginning of the Southern Renaissance as 1920, when the Fugitive poets at Vanderbilt University, including Robert Penn Warren, Allen Tate, and John Crowe Ransom, began meeting to read and discuss poetry. But Ellen Glasgow, who is considered a "modern" writer, was publishing long before 1920. Was she a precursor of the Southern Renaissance, or was she its first significant writer? In addition, in the recently published *History of Southern Literature* (1985), Edgar E. MacDonald writes of the literary revival in turn-of-the-century Richmond. He identifies the most important writers in this group as Ellen Glasgow, James Branch Cabell, Mary Johnston, and Amelie Rives, "who exhibit the first really important break with the aesthetics, social attitudes, and community assumptions of the older, late-Victorian South, and who speak with voices that are recognizably of the emerging twentieth century rather than the nineteenth" (264). Why haven't these writers gained a larger role in our southern literary history? Notably, the majority were women.

In 1922 the Fugitives published the first issue of their poetry magazine, *Fugitive,* which included few works by women writers. The literary groups identified as most influential in shaping the Renaissance—the Fugitives, the Agrarians, who published their manifesto *I'll Take My Stand* (1930) in support of an agrarian way of life, and the New Critics— were all notably white male groups. Even the 1981 publication of *Why the South Will Survive* (an update on the Agrarians' work) does not contain a single essay by a woman. Thus although the term "Renaissance," or "rebirth," seems aptly suited to describing the developments in southern literature of the first half of the twentieth century, the typically identified boundaries and influences of the Renaissance have done much to stifle our celebration of the southern voices of women and persons of color.

Accordingly, much of the work of the period focuses on the writer's struggle to know self and seek order, and thus often on the writer's attempts to find her place in the southern culture and in the literary world. Yet even those writers who were forced to leave the South for jobs or education or who left in self-proclaimed exile were typically drawn back to write about the South. Like Caroline Gordon and her husband Allen Tate, Harriet Arnow and her husband, the writer Harold Arnow, attempted to combine their writing with the agrarian life. Although they bought a farm in southern Kentucky planning to farm and write, the Arnows soon found that farming was a full-time job that left little extra time for their creative work, and the couple had to give up their rural experience to make a living in Detroit. Arnow's desire to hold on to her homeplace in the midst of city living is reflected in her best novel, *The Dollmaker,* the story of a Kentucky woman who is displaced to Detroit with her family and must adjust to the changes of living in the North.

In contrast to Arnow, Evelyn Scott chose to exile herself from the South. During her college years at Sophie Newcomb College in New Orleans, she became involved with a professor of tropical diseases from Tulane University. The two fled to Brazil where they worked at building and farming a plantation, but their struggle only resulted in poverty and despair. Upon returning to the United States after six years in the jungle, Scott turned back to the region she fled and began to consider once again her early years in Clarksville, Tennessee; out of this "backward glance" came her autobiographical novel *Background in Tennessee,* published in 1937.

The 1930s, in particular, saw the production of a number of "back-ward glances" in novels about the Civil War. With the deaths of ex-slaves and those who fought the war and supported the Confederacy on the homefront, the American public became increasingly interested in reading about the war and about southern culture. Scott's novel *The Wave* was one of the first of these Civil War novels, published in 1929. Although *The Wave* did not receive long-lived acclaim, the book is now being rediscovered as a unique portrayal of diverse perspectives on the war. Scott's characters range from northern homemakers to southern soldiers to a foreign correspondent for a European newspaper. A substantially greater influence on our country's popular awareness of the war, however, is Margaret Mitchell's *Gone With the Wind* (1936), which revived the sentimental novel tradition of life in the Old South.

The modern period was also a time when southern writers addressed the tensions between families and between generations as a new South emerged. In her play *The Little Foxes* (1939), Lillian Hellman points to the conflicts between the worlds of the old and the new—the decayed gentility of the Old South and the materialism of Ben and Oscar Hubbard of the New South, who resemble the members of William Faulkner's Snopes family. Caroline Gordon's *Penhally* (1931) also portrays a southern family in conflict while spanning more than a hundred years of southern culture, from the antebellum period through the rise of the modern South. Roughly a century after their grandfather settled the land, brothers Nick and Chance Llewellyn clash over its fate. Nick, a banker, sells the house and property to the hunting club; Chance, a farmer who finds his way of life irrevocably changed by this action, kills his brother. The book ends in a complete rejection of familial ties.

The modern South also brought with it new concerns about the roles of blacks and whites and the problems of prejudice in the South. A native Floridian, Zora Neale Hurston was primarily concerned with making an anthropological study of the black residents of Florida, collecting their folklore and recording their spoken language in *Mules and Men* (1935) and "The Eatonville Anthology" (1926). Perhaps most powerfully, however, Hurston's novel *Their Eyes Were Watching God* (1937) chronicles the lives of southern blacks from the point of view of Janie Crawford, whose storytelling frames the novel. Besides describing the violence and hardships faced by black women during the 1930s, Hurston vividly portrays the emotional and sexual fulfillment possible for a middle-aged black woman who would not be defeated by the difficulties of her life. During Hurston's lifetime *Their Eyes Were Watching God* was harshly criticized, most openly by black critics; Richard Wright, for example, saw in the novel Hurston's pandering to "a white audience whose chauvinistic tastes she [knew] how to satisfy" (22). More recently, however, black feminist scholars have transformed the novel's reputation with such analyses as that of June Jordan, who sees the novel as "the prototypical Black novel of affirmation" (6).

Black writers were not alone in their attempts to reveal the racial conditions of the modern South, for at least one white southern writer, Lillian Smith, wrestled with the issue throughout her life and in many of her works, both fiction and nonfiction. As the daughter of what she called "two old-generation southerners," growing up in a rapidly changing South, Smith defines her childhood experience in terms of alienation; her parents taught her "to split [her] body from [her] mind and both from [her] soul" and taught her to "split [her] conscience from [her] acts and Christianity from the southern tradition" (Smith 27). Smith spent her life attempting to reconcile these elements of her identity through social and psychoanalytical studies of the "mind" of the South. *Strange Fruit,* a highly controversial novel, explores the romantic relationship between a black woman and a white man and the complexity of the suffering, most notably by the black community, that inevitably ensues.

With southern writers' increasing concerns about both racial and sexual equality also came attempts to retrieve the "lost voices" of both the feminine and the black pasts and to capture and preserve the African-American and southern cultures. The search for identity had become a growing concern of the southern woman not only because of the change in her gender role in southern society but also because the southerner was quickly losing or had lost her link to the past, whether she considered that past to be in Africa or on the southern homeplace. Just as the major social upheaval and change of civil war brought about new historical periods in southern literature, so too did the change and conflict of the early stirrings of the civil rights movement and the feminist movement in the late 1950s and early 1960s bring the Renaissance to a close for the woman writer in the South. As the modern period saw the most radical developments in technology, travel, and communications that the South and the entire nation have yet experienced, the character of the traditional southern landscape quickly faded. A number of influences would bring about significant change to the region, including World War II, increased land and air transportation, and the space program. The Old South was quickly being transformed into the "Sun Belt," complete with air conditioning; widespread audiences for television and radio were producing an increased homogeneity in American language and culture; and the family structure was being altered by a job market that employed more and more women. As Doris Betts said of

Welty's Mississippi, "Welty's place is now parked full of mobile homes, which are crammed full of televisions and plastic utensils" (Betts 4).

As they traveled to other parts of the country and other parts of the world, as the South of their youth underwent changes that would bring it fully into the realm of the industrialized United States, these modern writers carried a sense of their southernness with them. In her essay "Place in Fiction," Eudora Welty refers to this sense of place as "the ball of golden thread" that is able "to carry us there and back and in every sense of the word to bring us home" (129). So long as women tell their stories of the South, then, the South will remain a unique place. And although the influences and pressures of a world beyond the South have dramatically shaped its contemporary literature, have threatened the very existence of a distinct "southern" literature, the South of the Renaissance years remains vital and distinct. The women writers of this period undoubtedly excelled in telling their stories, and they kept the South alive by producing some of its finest literature.

20. *Evelyn Scott*

(1893–1963)

Born Elsie Dunn in Clarksville, Tennessee, Scott was a self-proclaimed feminist by the time she reached fifteen. When only seventeen years old, Scott began serving as the secretary of Louisiana's Women's Suffrage Party. One year later her family moved to New Orleans where she entered Sophie Newcomb College, but she soon dropped out, electing to educate herself at home. In 1913 she ran off to Brazil with a professor of tropical diseases from Tulane University, Frederick Wellman, and the two changed their names to Cyril and Evelyn Scott. They lived in the jungle for six years, never free from the hardships caused by poverty, illness, and extreme isolation. In 1920 the Scotts gave up their work in Brazil to move to New York's Greenwich Village and then lived briefly in Cape Cod before separating. Scott recorded her experiences in Brazil, including the birth of her son, the writer and painter Creighton Scott, in *Escapade* (1923).

Scott began writing poetry while in Brazil; her first collection, *Precipitations* (1920), reflects the influence of the Imagist poets on her work. She was also a fluent writer of fiction, completing two trilogies over the next decade. Her first one, which chronicles three generations of a family, includes *The Narrow House* (1921), *Narcissus* (1922), and *The Golden Door* (1925). Her second trilogy is perhaps better known as a social history, describing the South during the years 1850-1918. Along with *Migrations* (1927) and *A Calendar of Sin* (1932), the trilogy includes *The Wave* (1929), now considered her best work. Mosaic-like in its depiction of more than one hundred episodes, the novel portrays the perversions of the Civil War and the people forced to experience them. In the 1920s Scott was also interested in literary criticism, writing articles on William Faulkner and James Joyce, both of whom she imitated in her fiction; the structure of *The Wave* has often been compared to the innovative styles of these writers.

In 1928 Scott married Australian novelist John Metcalfe, who was then serving in the Royal Air Force. They lived in Canada for a time but returned to London when he was demobilized. Financial troubles there made writing difficult for Scott, but she was able to complete several additional works, including a second volume of poetry, *The Winter*

Alone (1930); a second autobiography that focused on the post–Civil War South, *Background in Tennessee* (1937); and a final novel, *The Shadow of the Hawk* (1941). In many of her works, Scott attacked traditional marriage, femininity, and domesticity, believing that women were free only when unleashed from the expectations of society. Though such novels as *Eva Gay* (1933) present hope for such a world, *The Shadow of the Hawk* more pessimistically suggests that women can never escape the oppression of society. Scott's contemporary Lillian Smith praised her as the most "brilliant and profound" woman writing in the 1930s. After the publication of her last novel, Scott found little time for writing, never completing several promised works. In the 1950s she moved to New York City and lived there until her death.

From *The Wave* (Chapter 1)

Henry Clay had once heard Mamma say that Aunt Amanda, "poor little creature," was already beginning to have an "old maid" look. Mamma had remarked, then, that Aunt Amanda's throat was "stringy," and Henry Clay had resented it. He had stared. When Aunt Amanda turned her head, slowly, the skin on her neck made little bags. It was the first time that Henry Clay had observed this, and it upset him. He disliked Mamma for having told him. Previously, he had regarded Aunt Amanda as, of course, a "grown-up" lady, but much, much, and forever, younger than his father and his mother who were married people.

Aunt Amanda wore blue dresses. In the winter they would be brocade and velvet and very fashionably wide, but in the summer, in India muslins and sashes, with the short puff sleeves and the low neck, and the garden hat, she often put off hoops. Then she was like a strange little girl in a long gown. There was something alert and frightened in her expression, which never altered, and Henry Clay, though he loved her, and was sorry for her because she was so very little, would experience just the smallest shiver of discomfort when he met her glance. She was "like a doll," with her frizzly blond hair that no amount of bandoline could keep in place. And she was too gay. He understood what it was that he had been trying to say about her when his mother called her "hystericky."

Aunt Amanda was Papa's sister. Henry Clay had no little sisters of his own, and he had "helped Papa" to take care of Aunt Amanda ever since she had come to live with him. But she was not young enough after all, he realized, when his mamma told him sharply she was twenty-eight.

Something to do with the war that had come, had made Aunt Amanda change. And it was the war coming, and Papa going to Richmond to join the army, that had made everybody "different." Mamma was "very nice" to Aunt Amanda, yet spoke of her in a tone of voice which Henry Clay called "indignant." And when Aunt Amanda talked of Papa being a "hero" and an officer, she did so "crowingly," as though she had been made glad by it. Mamma was a "Yankee." When Aunt Amanda whispered to Henry Clay, softly, that Mamma's brothers in Boston were "Black Republicans," Henry Clay waited a minute before replying, then, his heart beating terribly because this was something he did *not* want to know, he answered steadily, "I don't believe it, Aunt Amanda, because I've seen the miniatures that Mamma keeps in her dresser, and they're *not* black."

He was sorry for Mamma because her brothers were Black Republicans. He had to admit, finally, when he understood things better, that a man could be a Black Republican and not look like his own body-servant, Jesse, who would belong to him when he grew up. Henry Clay thought long and secretly before he understood these matters. Papa's army was going to "whip" the Yankees. Black Republicans, if they were ever found, would receive no mercy. It must make Mamma both ashamed and sad. But Henry Clay would not blame his father, so he blamed his uncles. He considered that it would be a good thing for Mamma if the Black Republican brothers who humiliated her were "wiped out." He did not tell her so, directly, but played a game with Jesse in which Jesse was a Black Republican who was to be executed. Henry Clay kept his ideas on safeguarding Mamma entirely to himself. When Aunt Amanda said, "Poor Mamma, Henry Clay—she is in a very distressing situation and we must try not to make it hard for her, not to make her feel it," he glanced at Aunt Amanda cautiously, and, somehow, though her voice was so low and sweet, he did not believe that she was as anxious to save Mamma trouble as she pretended to be. Always, however, when he would be deciding that he simply never could forgive her, she would snatch up the guitar with the white ribbon, draw him quickly beside her upon the sofa, and sing songs to him.

He liked *Gathering up the Shells on the Seashore*, though it was sad, and he was glad when she had finished it and sang *Jim Crack Corn* or something funny. There were pier-glasses in the parlour, and Aunt Amanda, when she played on her guitar, always seated herself so she could see in them. There was a picture of the hill and the river, made by the reflection in the mirror which faced the window. When Papa had gone to Richmond, Henry Clay had left off crying to see the tiny, "really-truly" boat sail by in it. He had not believed that he could see it, but Aunt Amanda had persuaded him, and, sure enough, through the bare trees, and down, down past the sheep that were cropping the lawn to keep it trim and neat, the steamboat had swum away like a little fish, and the trail of smoke, like a little puff of wool, had floated off, outside the mirror's frame. He had not gone with Mamma to the steamer landing, but it had been much, much more wonderful to behold his papa steaming off to Richmond just inside the pier-glass. The tears had stopped while he gazed. Then he had sprung up from the sofa suddenly, and had been shocked, had been disappointed. It was only a trick after all. There was the river, greasy-looking and white, at the bottom of the garden, and the *real* boat was like a little trail of smut upon it, going out of sight.

When Aunt Amanda sat in front of the mirror, she looked at herself. And when she looked at herself, picking the guitar strings with her little white hand, her little finger crooked so delicately, she would be smiling and smiling in a peculiar manner, as if she were very satisfied with what she saw. She made nice little faces at herself. Henry Clay would notice, and would pretend that he was unobservant. For, if ever she found him looking at her at such times, she would start, become grave, abruptly, and that queer, secret, suspecting gaze would return to her eyes. She was happiest when Papa was about. Then she talked a great deal and laughed too much, and too merrily. But if Mama entered the room, Aunt Amanda would say: "There, I must leave off such nonsense. Hannah already finds me too frivolous, Gordon."

Aunt Amanda often talked a long time to Henry Clay about his papa. "You must be proud," she would declare, "that your papa is a gallant officer who would give all for the cause that he believes in, and loves the South." Mamma was proud of Papa, too, but it was not agreeable of Mamma to assert so glumly that she had no opinions about the war, and that she would be just as loyal to Papa if he were an Abolitionist. Mamma was a Protestant, and Aunt Amanda was a Roman Catholic, and that made "friction," Henry Clay had quoted. Aunt Amanda had one criticism to make of Papa. He was not a "good" Catholic. He did not do his duty by Henry Clay, who was receiving only his mamma's religious instructions while he was growing up. When Henry Clay's education had been discussed with Papa, Aunt Amanda had "spoken out." And Henry Clay had been wretched. He did not see why his mamma should object to having him a Catholic if it would make Aunt Amanda content to see him so. But when Aunt Amanda informed him, surreptitiously, that his prayers were the only thing that could keep his papa safe in battle, he felt angry. He hated them both—Mamma, who came from Massachusetts, and was *not* a Christy; and Aunt Amanda who tried to frighten him unfairly because he did not say his catechism properly.

"Pray hard for us, Honey," Aunt Amanda whispered in her sweet, queer, little breaking voice, when she stole into his room at night.

Henry Clay, in the smudged dimness made by the bedroom candle, did not look at her. Her arm was about him, and her "smell," of lavender and orris, was in his nostrils. He shivered in his nightshirt, and his heart grew hard and his body stiff against her. She made him feel like a baby which was what he hated. He wanted her *not* to touch him. If she would stay away from him, he could do it better. But he kept his eyes shut, and repeated hastily the *Our Fathers* and the *Hail Marys*, while she annoyed him with prompting. His hands fumbled for the beads stealthily. Aunt Amanda said: "Don't stop, Honey. We must tell God how much we love dear Papa that he may be spared to us. Your father wants it, Precious. We can't deprive you of the benefits of the Church because your mother's brothers in Boston are scientific men."

Mamma prayed, also. It was a relief to find it out. He heard her, when, his own prayers said, he climbed from the trundle bed and went noiselessly into the hall to fetch himself a drink of water from the pail out there. The door into Mamma's bedroom was ajar, and he spied on her just a little bit. When he "forgot" and dropped the dipper he was holding, there was a clatter. Mamma, startled, straightened up beside the bed, and he thought that she was as embarrassed as he was when Aunt Amanda would caution him to go on quickly with his *Hail Marys*. He went away before she could come out into the hall. But why was she such a liar? When, the next night, she discovered the prayerbook under his pillow, he said, "Don't tell Aunt Amanda that you found the prayer-book," and he felt desperate, and began to weep bitterly without knowing why. Then Mamma squeezed his ribs tight, and he was glad, and felt he ought not to be, until she whispered, "It's so degrading, Henry Clay—so undignified—but *don't* be a Roman Catholic—please don't be. And don't believe all that Aunt Amanda tells you about your uncles. It's bad enough to have to give up Papa—and we must do our duty."

Henry Clay became silent. He was so still that his mother imagined him asleep.

When she had spread the quilts over him and tiptoed away, the necessity to deceive her ended. He opened his eyes again. His eyeballs felt hot. Horrid prickly feelings came in his stomach and his "bread-basket." He seemed to hear, in his head, words that he had listened to *them* saying:

"You know I did it for love of the child, Hannah."

"You teach the child to be ashamed of his mother and his uncles and you call that 'love.' You do this and ignore one of the greatest tenets of your own religion—to love your enemies."

Aunt Amanda's small face, on her thin neck, had gone up. The strange, frightened sparkle had become more brilliant in her pale blue,

wide eyes. Henry Clay remembered the two women like rocks, and himself ignored. Nobody loved him. "I won't defend myself, Hannah. I am
devoted to my brother, and to your son, too, Hannah. If it is a crime to
teach a child to ask God to protect his father's life, then I am guilty. That
is the last thing I would deny. If I had known how bitter your sentiments
were—but after all you *married* a Virginian and a Catholic."

"If you did not think that I objected, why did you not attempt to con-
vert Henry Clay openly?" Mamma's face, as it came back, was bold and
cold, and it was black and white. That made it alarming. Aunt Amanda
wore flounces and ruchings that Henry Clay liked, but Mamma was
"plain," in her grey merino with her stiff white cuffs and collar, and her
hair as Papa preferred it, in "Grecian bandeau," though Henry Clay did
not care for that much. Aunt Amanda called Mamma's severity of dress
"an attitude." It was adopted, Aunt Amanda reckoned, because Mamma
wished to be "taken for a bluestocking." Or, Aunt Amanda has conjec-
tured, "It's because she disapproves of me so much."

"I did not anticipate direct interference, Hannah, but I anticipated
ridicule. I believe in the Church and in the Miracles of the Church.
When I came here, I subjected myself to your flippant comment on matters that are sacred to me. In the future—I will keep hands off the
child—unless Gordon—who is as much a Catholic and a Southerner as
I am—"

Mamma had interrupted. Henry Clay remembered her face growing
"ugly," while she smiled sarcastically. "*I* flippant," Mamma seemed to be
saying, drawing her breath in sharply. "*I* who have done my duty if ever
wife did! And you *dare* to say such a thing to me. *I* flippant."

Henry Clay turned over sidewise in his bed and looked at the moon.
The cedar trees on the lawn were like silver bears. Above them, a big
gold claw, like the claw on the balls on the parlour furniture, clutched
fiercely at its own round shadow. He thought he would like to go to war
on Papa's horse. He didn't care about the religious part of it—if Mamma
would only let him go to war and wear a Confederate uniform. Mamma
was "mean," she was "wicked" when she would not let him talk about
the war too much. But if he gave up "religion," Aunt Amanda would be
"broken-hearted."

He tossed. It was troubling here at home. He looked at the moon
again, and pretended it was a silver-golden cannon ball that was sailing
down to get him. All at once he was frightened, and grew quiet, in the
whitened sheets, trembling. He had forgotten about God, and what
God might do to his papa if he did not pray enough.

"Mamma?" Henry Clay lifted himself on one quivering elbow, and
called to her shrilly, demandingly. Even the sound of his own voice left,

in his confused mind, the echo of his own uneasiness. She did not hear him. He gave up. His hot head fell back on his pillow. He *was going* to war, when he got big enough, and if the war hurt people he was glad— *not* sorry. He was a "mean" boy—almost as mean as a Yankee (and his mother was a Yankee anyhow)—and he *liked* war.

The power and the glory everlasting, it said somewhere. In the silence, he could hear the trees brushing outside the window. It was a creeping, quiet sound. He longed for something that would go off suddenly, and wake his mother up. It was so still in the house. The boards creaked. Jesse was a "nigger," and a coward. Jesse belonged to him. He would like to send Jesse to the battle front and *make* him fight the Yankees. It was Jesse who had told him all about the devil, "wif green eyes gogglin'." But the devil was less than God whom you could not see—more insignificant.

Suddenly, Henry Clay began to sob helplessly, coughing, sputtering, his thin ribs racked by his incessant sighs. I wish I was dead. I wish I was dead, he told himself, surprised that this was what he wanted. It seemed so much better, with all this horror around him, to get the worst over with.

After a time, he stifled his agitation in the thick heat of the pillow. He grew, little by little, *so* still, inside his heart, inside his mind, that he wondered, stricken pleasurably by the fancy, if he *could* be already dead. It wasn't true. God had not listened. Mammy Nancy slept in the room behind the nursery, and he could detect her stirring as she left her pallet. She was often restless, and would potter about the house at night.

An owl passed, noiseless, like a cloud of dust, between him and the moon. That round glare bored into his eyes, bored craftily into the quivering exhaustion of his mind. He began to fancy the explosion. He waited for the big *boom,* that would send the silver splinters of the cedars right into his face. If it would only "crunch" them all. The war was coming nearer every minute, and he wanted the moon to burst so loud, so violently, that his mother and his Aunt Amanda could not argue any longer. Nobody—not a single person in the world—should hear another noise. He shivered. He felt weak and "wicked."

21. Katherine Anne Porter

(1890–1980)

Born Callie Russell Porter in Indian Creek, Texas, Katherine Anne Porter was raised by her father and grandmother after her mother's death. She was educated in convents and private schools, where she enjoyed music, dancing, and horseback riding. Although she had no formal instruction in writing, Porter read extensively, and writing came quite naturally for her. When she was sixteen years old she ran away from home and was married. The marriage lasted for nine years; she divorced her husband in 1915 and lived for a time in Chicago before returning to Texas.

Although she began working on short stories when she was a young woman, her professional career did not begin until 1917 when she became a journalist for the *Critic,* a weekly newspaper in Fort Worth; she then spent two years working for the *Rocky Mountain News* in Denver. Porter left her journalistic work to live in Mexico and study art, and while there she published several articles about Mexico. Finally, in 1930, her first collection of stories, *Flowering Judas,* was published. The success of these stories earned Porter a Guggenheim Fellowship, which allowed her to write in Europe. She traveled through Switzerland and Germany before settling down in France; *Hacienda; A Story of Mexico* (1934) was written while Porter was living in Paris. She was also married while in Europe but divorced in 1937.

Shortly after she returned to the States, *Pale Horse, Pale Rider* (1939) was published; this collection of three novellas earned Porter considerable critical praise and established her as a writer comparable to Henry James and Nathaniel Hawthorne. The novellas are unified by their development of the character Miranda, who struggles to come to terms with her southern heritage. This character had already appeared in "The Journey," first published as "The Old Order" in *Southern Review* (Winter 1936); it was first collected in *The Leaning Tower and Other Stories* (1944). It is a nostalgic look at the relationship between a white woman and a black woman, Miranda's grandmother and Aunt Nannie. This story takes on the semblance of a quilt as the two women sit and sew and reminisce about their past experiences, piecing together their lives and friendship.

In 1938 Porter married Albert Erskine, then a professor of English and the editor of the *Southern Review* and later an editor at Random House. Porter lived in Baton Rouge with Erskine until their separation in 1940; they were divorced in 1942. In 1943 Porter received outstanding recognition when she was elected to the National Institute of Arts and Letters. She received additional support throughout the 1950s for her work, including a Ford Foundation grant and a Fulbright lectureship, which took her to Belgium, University of Virginia, and Washington and Lee University. She also began teaching frequently, at schools such as Stanford University, the University of Chicago, and the University of Michigan. In 1962, the same year that her only full-length novel, *Ship of Fools,* was published, Porter won an O. Henry Award; ironically, O. Henry (Sidney Porter) was Porter's father's second cousin. Always known as a master of the short story, Porter received both a Pulitzer Prize and a National Book Award for her *Collected Stories* (1965). In addition, thirty years of Porter's reviews and essays were published in 1952 as *The Days Before,* and *Collected Essays and Occasional Writings of Katherine Anne Porter* was published in 1970. Though she continued to write until a few years before her death, Porter was constantly in ill physical and mental health. She died in Silver Spring, Maryland.

The Journey

In their later years, the Grandmother and old Nannie used to sit together for some hours every day over their sewing. They shared a passion for cutting scraps of the family finery, hoarded for fifty years, into strips and triangles, and fitting them together again in a carefully disordered patchwork, outlining each bit of velvet or satin or taffeta with a running briar stitch in clear lemon-colored silk floss. They had contrived enough bed and couch covers, table spreads, dressing table scarfs, to have furnished forth several households. Each piece as it was finished was lined with yellow silk, folded, and laid away in a chest, never again to see the light of day. The Grandmother was the great-granddaughter of Kentucky's most famous pioneer: he had, while he was surveying Kentucky, hewed out rather competently a rolling pin for his wife. This rolling pin was the Grandmother's irreplaceable treasure. She covered it with an extraordinarily complicated bit of patchwork, added golden tassels to the handles, and hung it in a conspicuous place in her room. She was the daughter of a notably heroic captain in the War of 1812. She had his razors in a shagreen case and a particularly severe-looking daguerreotype taken in his old age, with his chin in a tall stock and his black satin waistcoat smoothed over a still-handsome military chest. So she fitted a patchwork case over the shagreen and made a sort of envelope of cut velvet and violet satin, held together with briar stitching, to contain the portrait. The rest of her handiwork she put away, to the relief of her grandchildren, who had arrived at the awkward age when Grandmother's quaint old-fashioned ways caused them acute discomfort.

In the summer the women sat under the mingled trees of the side garden, which commanded a view of the east wing, the front and back porches, a good part of the front garden and a corner of the small fig grove. Their choice of this location was a part of their domestic strategy. Very little escaped them: a glance now and then would serve to keep them fairly well informed as to what was going on in the whole place. It is true they had not seen Miranda the day she pulled up the whole mint bed to give to a pleasant strange young woman who stopped and asked her for a sprig of fresh mint. They had never found out who stole the giant pomegranates growing too near the fence: they had not been in time to stop Paul from setting himself on fire while experimenting with a miniature blowtorch, but they had been on the scene to extinguish him with rugs, to pour oil on him, and lecture him. They never saw Maria climbing trees, a mania she had to indulge or pine away, for she chose tall ones on the opposite side of the house. But such casualties were so minor a part of the perpetual round of events that they did not feel defeated nor that their strategy was a failure. Summer, in many ways so desirable a season, had its drawbacks. The children were everywhere at once and the Negroes loved lying under the hackberry grove back of the barns playing seven-up, and eating watermelons. The summer house was in a small town a few miles from the farm, a compromise between the rigorously ordered house in the city and the sprawling old farmhouse which Grandmother had built with such pride and pains. It had, she often said, none of the advantages of either country or city, and all the discomforts of both. But the children loved it.

During the winters in the city, they sat in Grandmother's room, a large squarish place with a small coal grate. All the sounds of life in the household seemed to converge there, echo, retreat, and return. Grandmother and Aunt Nannie knew the whole complicated code of sounds, could interpret and comment on them by an exchange of glances, a lifted eyebrow, or a tiny pause in their talk.

They talked about the past, really—always about the past. Even the future seemed like something gone and done with when they spoke of it. It did not seem an extension of their past, but a repetition of it. They would agree that nothing remained of life as they had known it, the world was changing swiftly, but by the mysterious logic of hope they insisted that each change was probably the last; or if not, a series of changes might bring them, blessedly, back full-circle to the old ways they had known. Who knows why they loved their past? It had been bitter for them both, they had questioned the burdensome rule they lived by every day of their lives, but without rebellion and without expecting an answer. This unbroken thread of inquiry in their minds contained no doubt as to the utter rightness and justice of the basic laws of human existence, founded as they were on God's plan; but they wondered perpetually, with only a hint now and then to each other of the uneasiness of their hearts, how so much suffering and confusion could have been built up and maintained on such a foundation. The Grandmother's role was authority, she knew that; it was her duty to portion out activities, to urge or restrain where necessary, to teach morals, manners, and religion, to punish and reward her own household according to a fixed code. Her own doubts and hesitations she concealed, also, she reminded herself, as a matter of duty. Old Nannie had no ideas at all as to her place in the world. It had been assigned to her before birth, and for her daily rule she had all her life obeyed the authority nearest to her.

So they talked about God, about Heaven, about planting a new hedge of rose bushes, about the new ways of preserving fruit and vegetables, about eternity and their mutual hope that they might pass it happily together, and often a scrap of silk under their hands would start them on long trains of family reminiscences. They were always amused to notice again how the working of their memories differed in such important ways. Nannie could recall names to perfection; she could always say what the weather had been like on all important occasions, what certain ladies had worn, how handsome certain gentlemen had been, what there had been to eat and drink. Grandmother had masses of dates in her mind, and no memories attached to them: her memories of events seemed detached and floating beyond time. For example, the 26th of August, 1871, had been some sort of red-letter day for her. She had said to herself then that never would she forget that date; and indeed, she remembered it well, but she no longer had the faintest notion what had happened to stamp it on her memory. Nannie was no help in the matter; she had nothing to do with dates. She did not know the year of her birth, and would never have had a birthday to celebrate if Grandmother had not, when she was still Miss Sophia Jane, aged ten, opened a calendar at random, closed her eyes, and marked a date unseen with a pen. So it turned out that Nannie's birthday thereafter fell on June 11, and the year, Miss Sophia Jane decided, should be 1827, her own birth-year, making Nannie just three months younger than her mistress.

Sophia Jane then made an entry of Nannie's birth-date in the family Bible, inserting it just below her own. "Nannie Gay," she wrote, in stiff careful letters, "(black)," and though there was some uproar when this was discovered, the ink was long since sunk deeply into the paper, and besides no one was really upset enough to have it scratched out. There it remained, one of their pleasantest points of reference.

They talked about religion, and the slack way the world was going nowadays, the decay of behavior, and about the younger children, whom these topics always brought at once to mind. On these subjects they were firm, critical, and unbewildered. They had received educations which furnished them an assured habit of mind about all the important appearances of life, and especially about the rearing of young. They relied with perfect acquiescence on the dogma that children were conceived in sin and brought forth in iniquity. Childhood was a long state of instruction and probation for adult life, which was in turn a long, severe, undeviating devotion to duty, the largest part of which consisted in bringing up children. The young were difficult, disobedient, and tireless in wrong-doing, apt to turn unkind and undutiful when they grew up, in spite of all one had done for them, or had tried to do: for small painful doubts rose in them now and again when they looked at their completed works. Nannie couldn't abide her new-fangled grandchildren. "Wuthless, shift-less lot, jes plain scum, Miss Sophia Jane; I cain't undahstand it aftah all the raisin' dey had."

The Grandmother defended them, and dispraised her own second generation—heartily, too, for she sincerely found grave faults in them—which Nannie defended in turn. "When they are little, they trample on your feet, and when they grow up they trample on your heart." This was about all there was to say about children in any generation, but the fascination of the theme was endless. They said it thoroughly over and over with thousands of small variations, with always an example among their own friends or family connections to prove it. They had enough material of their own. Grandmother had borne eleven children, Nannie thirteen. They boasted of it. Grandmother would say, "I am the mother of eleven children," in a faintly amazed tone, as if she hardly expected to be believed, or could even quite believe it herself. But she could still point to nine of them. Nannie had lost ten of hers. They were all buried in Kentucky. Nannie never doubted or expected anyone else to doubt she had children. Her boasting was of another order. "Thirteen of 'em," she would say, in an appalled voice, "yas, my Lawd and my Redeemah, thirteen!"

The friendship between the two old women had begun in early childhood, and was based on what seemed even to them almost mythical events. Miss Sophia Jane, a prissy, spoiled five-year-old, with tight black ringlets which were curled every day on a stick, with her stiffly pleated lawn pantalettes and tight bodice, had run to meet her returning father, who had been away buying horses and Negroes. Sitting on his arm, clasping him around the neck, she had watched the wagons filing past on the way to the barns and quarters. On the floor of the first wagon sat two blacks, male and female, holding between them a scrawny, half-naked black child, with a round nubbly head and fixed bright monkey eyes. The baby Negro had a potbelly and her arms were like sticks from wrist to shoulder. She clung with narrow, withered, black leather fingers to her parents, a hand on each.

"I want the little monkey," said Sophia Jane to her father, nuzzling his cheek and pointing. "I want that one to play with."

Behind each wagon came two horses in lead, but in the second wagon there was a small shaggy pony with a thatch of mane over his eyes, a long tail like a brush, a round, hard barrel of a body. He was standing in straw to the knees, braced firmly in a padded stall with a Negro holding his bridle. "Do you see that?" asked her father. "That's for you. High time you learned to ride."

Sophia Jane almost leaped from his arm for joy. She hardly recognized her pony or her monkey the next day, the one clipped and sleek, the other clean in new blue cotton. For a while she could not decide which she loved more, Nannie or Fiddler. But Fiddler did not wear well. She outgrew him in a year, saw him pass without regret to a small brother, though she refused to allow him to be called Fiddler any longer. That name she reserved for a long series of saddle horses. She had named the first in honor of Fiddler Gay, an old Negro who made the music for dances and parties. There was only one Nannie and she outwore Sophia Jane. During all their lives together it was not so much a question of affection between them as a simple matter of being unable to imagine getting on without each other.

Nannie remembered well being on a shallow platform out in front of a great building in a large busy place, the first town she had ever seen. Her father and mother were with her, and there was a thick crowd around them. There were several other small groups of Negroes huddled together with white men bustling them about now and then. She had never seen any of these faces before, and she never saw but one of them again. She remembered it must have been summer, because she was not shivering with cold in her cotton shift. For one thing, her bottom was still burning from a spanking someone (it might have been her mother) had given her just before they got on the platform, to remind her to keep still. Her mother and father were field hands, and had never lived in white folks' houses. A tall gentleman with a long narrow face and very high curved nose, wearing a great-collared blue coat and immensely long light-colored trousers (Nannie could close her eyes and see him again, clearly, as he looked that day) stepped up near them suddenly, while a great hubbub rose. The red-faced man standing on a stump beside them shouted and droned, waving his arms and pointing at Nannie's father and mother. Now and then the tall gentleman raised a finger, without looking at the black people on the platform. Suddenly the shouting died down, the tall gentleman walked over and said to Nannie's father and mother, "Well, Eph! Well, Steeny! Mister Jimmerson comin' to get you in a minute." He poked Nannie in the stomach with a thickly gloved forefinger. "Regular crowbait," he said to the auctioneer. "I should have had lagniappe with this one."

"A pretty worthless article right now, sir, I agree with you," said the auctioneer, "but it'll grow out of it. As for the team, you won't find a better, I swear."

"I've had an eye on 'em for years," said the tall gentleman, and walked away, motioning as he went to a fat man sitting on a wagon tongue, spitting quantities of tobacco juice. The fat man rose and came over to Nannie and her parents.

Nannie had been sold for twenty dollars: a gift, you might say, hardly sold at all. She learned that a really choice slave sometimes cost more than a thousand dollars. She lived to hear slaves brag about how much they had cost. She had not known how little she fetched on the block until her own mother taunted her with it. This was after Nannie had gone to live for good at the big house, and her mother and father were still in the fields. They lived and worked and died there. A good worming had cured Nannie's potbelly, she thrived on plentiful food and a species of kindness not so indulgent, maybe, as that given to the puppies; still it more than fulfilled her notions of good fortune.

The old woman often talked about how strangely things come out in this life. The first owner of Nannie and her parents had gone, Sophia Jane's father said, hog-wild about Texas. It was a new Land of Promise, in 1832. He had sold out his farm and four slaves in Kentucky to raise the money to take a great twenty-mile stretch of land in southwest Texas. He had taken his wife and two young children and set out, and there had been no more news of him for many years. When Grandmother arrived in Texas forty years later, she found him a prosperous ranchman and district judge. Much later, her youngest son met his granddaughter, fell in love with her, and married her—all in three months.

The judge, by then eighty-five years old, was uproarious and festive at the wedding. He reeked of corn liquor, swore by God every other breath, and was rearing to talk about the good old times in Kentucky. The Grandmother showed Nannie to him. "Would you recognize her?" "For God Almighty's sake!" bawled the judge. "Is that the strip of crow-bait I sold to your father for twenty dollars? Twenty dollars seemed like a fortune to me in those days!"

While they were jolting home down the steep rocky road on the long journey from San Marcos to Austin, Nannie finally spoke out about her grievance. "Look lak a jedge might had better raisin'," she said, gloomily, "look lak he didn't keer how much he hurt a body's feelins."

The Grandmother, muffled down in the back seat in the corner of the old carryall, in her worn sealskin pelisse, showing coffee-brown at the edges, her eyes closed, her hands wrung together, had been occupied once more in reconciling herself to losing a son, and, as ever, to a girl and a family of which she could not altogether approve. It was not that there was anything seriously damaging to be said against any of them; only— well, she wondered at her sons' tastes. What had each of them in turn found in the wife he had chosen? The Grandmother had always had in mind the kind of wife each of her sons needed; she had tried to bring about better marriages for them than they had made for themselves. They had merely resented her interference in what they considered strictly their personal affairs. She did not realize that she had spoiled and pampered her youngest son until he was in all probability unfit to be any kind of a husband, much less a good one. And there was something about her new daughter-in-law, a tall, handsome, firm-looking young woman, with a direct way of speaking, walking, talking, that seemed to promise that the spoiled Baby's days of clover were ended. The Grand-mother was annoyed deeply at seeing how self-possessed the bride had been, how she had had her way about the wedding arrangements down to the last detail, how she glanced now and then at her new husband with calm, humorous, level eyes, as if she had already got him sized up. She had even suggested at the wedding dinner that her idea of a honey-moon would be to follow the chuck-wagon on the round-up, and help in the cattle-branding on her father's ranch. Of course she may have been joking. But she was altogether too Western, too modern, something like the "new" woman who was beginning to run wild, asking for the vote, leaving her home and going out in the world to earn her own living . . .

The Grandmother's narrow body shuddered to the bone at the thought of women so unsexing themselves; she emerged with a start from the dark reverie of foreboding thoughts which left a bitter taste in her throat. "Never mind, Nannie. The judge just wasn't thinking. He's very fond of his good cheer."

Nannie had slept in a bed and had been playmate and work-fellow with her mistress; they fought on almost equal terms, Sophia Jane defending Nannie fiercely against any discipline but her own. When they were both seventeen years old, Miss Sophia Jane was married off in a very gay wedding. The house was jammed to the roof and everybody present was at least fourth cousin to everybody else. There were forty carriages and more than two hundred horses to look after for two days. When the last wheel disappeared down the lane (a number of the guests lingered on for two weeks), the larders and bins were half empty and the place looked as if a troop of cavalry had been over it. A few days later Nannie was married off to a boy she had known ever since she came to the family, and they were given as a wedding present to Miss Sophia Jane.

Miss Sophia Jane and Nannie had then started their grim and terrible race of procreation, a child every sixteen months or so, with Nannie nursing both, and Sophia Jane, in dreadful discomfort, suppressing her milk with bandages and spirits of wine. When they each had produced their fourth child, Nannie almost died of puerperal fever. Sophia Jane nursed both children. She named the black baby Charlie, and her own child Stephen, and she fed them justly turn about, not favoring the white over the black, as Nannie felt obliged to do. Her husband was shocked, tried to forbid her; her mother came to see her and reasoned with her. They found her very difficult and quite stubborn. She had already begun to develop her implicit character, which was altogether just, humane, proud, and simple. She had many small vanities and weaknesses on the surface: a love of luxury and a tendency to resent criticism. This tendency was based on her feeling of superiority in judgment and sensibility to almost everyone around her. It made her very hard to manage. She had a quiet way of holding her ground which convinced her antagonist that she would really die, not just threaten to, rather than give way. She had learned now that she was badly cheated in giving her children to another woman to feed: she resolved never again to be cheated in just that way. She sat nursing her child and her foster child, with a sensual warm pleasure she had not dreamed of, translating her natural physical relief into something holy, God-sent, amends from heaven for what she had suffered in childbed. Yes, and for what she missed in the marriage bed, for there also something had failed. She said to Nannie quite calmly, "From now on, you will nurse your children and I will nurse mine," and it was so. Charlie remained her special favorite among the Negro children. "I understand now," she said to her older sister Keziah, "why the black mammies love their foster children. I love mine." So Charlie was brought up in the house as a playmate for her son Stephen, and exempted from hard work all his life.

Sophia Jane had been wooed at arm's length by a mysteriously attractive young man whom she remembered well as rather a snubby little boy with curls like her own, but shorter, a frilled white blouse and kilts of the Macdonald tartan. He was her second cousin and resembled her so closely they had been mistaken for brother and sister. Their grandparents had been first cousins, and sometimes Sophia Jane saw in him, years after they were married, all the faults she had most abhorred in her elder brother: lack of aim, failure to act at crises, a philosophic detachment from practical affairs, a tendency to set projects on foot and then leave them to perish or to be finished by someone else; and a profound conviction that everyone around him should be happy to wait upon him hand and foot. She had fought these fatal tendencies in her brother, within the bounds of wifely prudence she fought them in her husband, she was long after to fight them again in two of her sons and in several of her grandchildren. She gained no victory in any case, the selfish, careless, unloving creatures lived and ended as they had begun. But the Grandmother developed a character truly portentious under the discipline of trying to change the characters of others. Her husband shared with her the family sharpness of eye. He disliked and feared her deadly willfulness, her certainty that her ways were not only right but beyond criticism, that her feelings were important, even in the lightest matter, and must not be tampered with or treated casually. He had disappeared at the critical moment when they were growing up, had gone to college and then for travel; she forgot him for a long time, and when she saw him again forgot him as he had been once for all. She was gay and sweet and decorous, full of vanity and incredibly exalted daydreams which threatened now and again to cast her over the edge of some mysterious forbidden frenzy. She dreamed recurrently that she had lost her virginity (her virtue, she called it), her sole claim to regard, consideration, even to existence, and after frightful moral suffering which masked altogether her physical experience she would wake in a cold sweat, disordered and terrified. She had heard that her cousin Stephen was a little "wild," but that was to be expected. He was leading, no doubt, a dashing life full of manly indulgences, the sweet dark life of the knowledge of evil which caused her hair to crinkle on her scalp when she thought of it. Ah, the delicious, the free, the wonderful, the mysterious and terrible life of men! She thought about it a great deal. "Little daydreamer," her mother or father would say to her, surprising her in a brown study, eyes moist, lips smiling vaguely over her embroidery or her book, or with hands fallen on her lap, her face turned away to a blank wall. She memorized and saved for these moments scraps of high-minded poetry, which she instantly quoted at them when they offered her a penny for her thoughts;

or she broke into a melancholy little song of some kind, a song she knew they liked. She would run to the piano and tinkle the tune out with one hand, saying, "I love this part best," leaving no doubt in their minds as to what her own had been occupied with. She lived her whole youth so, without once giving herself away; not until she was in middle age, her husband dead, her property dispersed, and she found herself with a houseful of children, making a new life for them in another place, with all the responsibilities of a man but with none of the privileges, did she finally emerge into something like an honest life: and yet, she was passionately honest. She had never been anything else.

Sitting under the trees with Nannie, both of them old and their long battle with life almost finished, she said, fingering a scrap of satin, "It was not fair that Sister Keziah should have had this ivory brocade for her wedding dress, and I had only dotted swiss . . ."

"Times was harder when you got married, Missy," said Nannie. "Dat was de yeah all de crops failed."

"And they failed ever afterward, it seems to me," said Grandmother.

"Seems to me like," said Nannie, "dotted swiss was all the style when you got married."

"I never cared for it," said Grandmother.

Nannie, born in slavery, was pleased to think she would not die in it. She was wounded not so much by her state of being as by the word describing it. Emancipation was a sweet word to her. It had not changed her way of living in a single particular, but she was proud of having been able to say to her mistress, "I aim to stay wid you as long as you'll have me." Still, Emancipation had seemed to set right a wrong that stuck in her heart like a thorn. She could not understand why God, Whom she loved, had seen fit to be so hard on a whole race because they had got a certain kind of skin. She talked it over with Miss Sophia Jane. Many times. Miss Sophia Jane was always brisk and opinionated about it: "Nonsense! I tell you, God does not know whether a skin is black or white. He sees only souls. Don't be getting notions, Nannie—of course you're going to Heaven."

Nannie showed the rudiments of logic in a mind altogether untutored. She wondered, simply and without resentment, whether God, Who had been so cruel to black people on earth, might not continue His severity in the next world. Miss Sophia Jane took pleasure in reassuring her; as if she, who had been responsible for Nannie, body and soul in this life, might also be her sponsor before the judgment seat.

Miss Sophia Jane had taken upon herself all the responsibilities of her tangled world, half white, half black, mingling steadily and the confusion growing ever deeper. There were so many young men about the place, always, younger brothers-in-law, first cousins, second cousins, nephews. They came visiting and they stayed, and there was no accounting for them nor any way of controlling their quietly headstrong habits. She learned early to keep silent and give no sign of uneasiness, but whenever a child was born in the Negro quarters, pink, worm-like, she held her breath for three days, she told her eldest granddaughter, years later, to see whether the newly born would turn black after the proper interval . . . It was a strain that told on her, and ended by giving her a deeply grounded contempt for men. She could not help it, she despised men. She despised them and was ruled by them. Her husband threw away her dowry and her property in wild investments in strange territories: Louisiana, Texas; and without protest she watched him play away her substance like a gambler. She felt that she could have managed her affairs profitably. But her natural activities lay elsewhere, it was the business of a man to make all decisions and dispose of all financial matters. Yet when she got the reins in her hands, her sons could persuade her to this and that enterprise or investment; against her will and judgment she accepted their advice, and among them they managed to break up once more the stronghold she had built for the future of her family. They got from her their own start in life, came back for fresh help when they needed it, and were divided against each other. She saw it as her natural duty to provide for her household, after her husband had fought stubbornly through the War, along with every other man of military age in the connection; had been wounded, had lingered helpless, and had died of his wound long after the great fervor and excitement had faded in hopeless defeat, when to be a man wounded and ruined in the War was merely to have proved oneself, perhaps, more heroic than wise. Left so, she drew her family together and set out for Louisiana, where her husband, with her money, had bought a sugar refinery. There was going to be a fortune in sugar, he said; not in raising the raw material, but in manufacturing it. He had schemes in his head for operating cotton gins, flour mills, refineries. Had he lived . . . but he did not live, and Sophia Jane had hardly repaired the house she bought and got the orchard planted when she saw that, in her hands, the sugar refinery was going to be a failure.

She sold out at a loss, and went on to Texas, where her husband had bought cheaply, some years before, a large tract of fertile black land in an almost unsettled part of the country. She had with her nine children, the youngest about two, the eldest about seventeen years old; Nannie and her three sons, Uncle Jimbilly, and two other Negroes, all in good health, full of hope and greatly desiring to live. Her husband's ghost persisted in her, she was bitterly outraged by his death almost as if he had willfully deserted her. She mourned for him at first with dry eyes, angrily. Twenty years later, seeing after a long absence the eldest son of her favorite daughter, who had died early, she recognized the very features and look of the husband of her youth, and she wept.

During the terrible second year in Texas, two of her younger sons, Harry and Robert, suddenly ran away. They chose good weather for it, in mid-May, and they were almost seven miles from home when a neighboring farmer saw them, wondered and asked questions, and ended by persuading them into his gig, and so brought them back.

Miss Sophia Jane went through the dreary ritual of discipline she thought appropriate to the occasion. She whipped them with her riding whip. Then she made them kneel down with her while she prayed for them, asking God to help them mend their ways and not be undutiful to their mother; her duty performed, she broke down and wept with her arms around them. They had endured their punishment stoically, because it would have been disgraceful to cry when a woman hit them, and besides, she did not hit very hard; they had knelt with her in a shamefaced gloom, because religious feeling was a female mystery which embarrassed them, but when they saw her tears they burst into loud bellows of repentance. They were only nine and eleven years old. She said in a voice of mourning, so despairing it frightened them: "Why did you run away from me? What do you think I brought you here for?" as if they were grown men who could realize how terrible the situation was. All the answer they could make, as they wept too, was that they had wanted to go back to Louisiana to eat sugar cane. They had been thinking about sugar cane all winter. . . . Their mother was stunned. She had built a house large enough to shelter them all, of hand-sawed lumber dragged by ox-cart for forty miles, she had got the fields fenced in and the crops planted, she had, she believed, fed and clothed her children; and now she realized they were hungry. These two had worked like men; she felt their growing bones through their thin flesh, and remembered how mercilessly she had driven them, as she had driven herself, as she had driven the Negroes and the horses, because there was no choice in the matter. They must labor beyond their strength or perish. Sitting there with her arms around them, she felt her heart break in her breast. She had thought it was a silly phrase. It happened to her. It was not that she was incapable of feeling afterward, for in a way she was more emotional, more quick, but griefs never again lasted with her so long as they had before. This day was the beginning of her spoiling her children and being afraid of them. She said to them after a long dazed silence, when they began to grow restless under her arms: "We'll grow fine ribbon cane here. The soil is perfect for it. We'll have all the sugar we want. But we must be patient."

By the time her children began to marry, she was able to give them each a good strip of land and a little money, she was able to help them buy more land in places they preferred by selling her own, tract by tract, and she saw them all begin well, though not all of them ended so. They went about their own affairs, scattering out and seeming to lose all that sense of family unity so precious to the Grandmother. They bore with her infrequent visits and her advice and her tremendous rightness, and they were impatient of her tenderness. When Harry's wife died—she had never approved of Harry's wife, who was delicate and hopelessly inadequate at housekeeping, and who could not even bear children successfully, since she died when her third was born—the Grandmother took the children and began life again, with almost the same zest, and with more indulgence. She had just got them brought up to the point where she felt she could begin to work the faults out of them—faults inherited, she admitted fairly, from both sides of the house—when she died. It happened quite suddenly one afternoon in early October after a day spent in helping the Mexican gardener of her third daughter-in-law to put the garden to rights. She was on a visit in far western Texas and enjoying it. The daughter-in-law was exasperated but apparently so docile, the Grandmother, who looked upon her as a child, did not notice her little moods at all. The son had long ago learned not to oppose his mother. She wore him down with patient, just, and reasonable argument. She was careful never to venture to command him in anything. He consoled his wife by saying that everything Mother was doing could be changed back after she was gone. As this change included moving a fifty-foot adobe wall, the wife was not much consoled. The Grandmother came into the house quite flushed and exhilarated, saying how well she felt in the bracing mountain air—and dropped dead over the doorsill.

22. Caroline Gordon

(1895–1981)

Born at Merry Mount Farm in Kentucky, the home of her mother's family, Caroline Gordon was educated by her father, a teacher and a scholar of classical literature. A sort of portrait of the artist as a young woman, Gordon's story "The Petrified Woman" is largely autobiographical, set in the Kentucky locale of her youth. When Gordon was ten years old, her father enrolled her in his boy's preparatory school, which she attended until she entered Bethany College in West Virginia. In 1916 she received her degree and taught high school for the next four years; she then quit in order to pursue a career in journalism by joining the staff of the *Chattanooga News*.

Writing about the Fugitive poets at Vanderbilt for the *Chattanooga News,* Gordon was noticed by Allen Tate and other members of the group. Tate, whom she married in 1924, encouraged her early fiction writing, as did Ford Madox Ford who, though employing Gordon as his literary secretary, began taking dictation from her in order to get her to write. The result was her first novel, *Penhally* (1931), which chronicles the tragic decline of a Tennessee family in the nineteenth century. After spending 1928 and 1929 in Europe on Guggenheim Fellowships, the Tates moved to Benfolly Farm in Tennessee where they raised their only daughter, Nancy. There Gordon completed her second novel, *Aleck Maury, Sportsman* (1934), which depicts a classics teacher devoted to hunting and fishing, a character Gordon modeled after her father. In that same year, her short story "Old Red" received an O. Henry Award. Always interested in history, Gordon immediately began working on her third novel, this one about the Civil War, *None Shall Look Back* (1937).

In 1938, Gordon began teaching again, but this time as the first writer-in-residence at Women's College, University of North Carolina. She continued to publish novels, and by 1946 she had been awarded her first of three honorary degrees, this one from Bethany College. Gordon was converted to Roman Catholicism in 1947, and her later novels suggest that this action substantially influenced her writing. Her major concerns had always been the religious and cultural heritage of the South, but in *The Strange Children* (1951) and in *The Malefactors* (1956) she specifically addresses the issue of grace and presents hope for the redemption of the South through Catholicism. These two novels, together with *The Women on the Porch* (1944), comprise a sort of Christian comedy set in the context of southern history.

The selection anthologized here, "The Petrified Woman," was originally published in *Mademoiselle* (September 1947); it later appeared in *Old Red and Other Stories* (1963).

The Tates collaborated on *The House of Fiction: An Anthology of the Short Story with Commentary* (1950), which explains the development of the short story from a New Critical approach. Much like Gordon's later work, *How to Read a Novel* (1957), the anthology propounds a specific method of reading designed to derive the maximum benefits from fiction. Although the Tates were divorced in 1959 (actually their second divorce), they completed a revision of *The House of Fiction* for a 1960 publication.

Gordon's last published novel was *The Glory of Hera* (1972). She was living in Mexico with her daughter, Nancy, and working on her final novel, *A Narrow Heart: The Portrait of a Woman,* when she died in 1981.

The Petrified Woman

We were sitting on the porch at the Fork—it is where two creeks meet—after supper, talking about our family reunion. It was to be held at a place called Arthur's Cave that year (it has the largest entrance in the world, though it is not so famous as Mammoth), and there was to be a big picnic dinner, and we expected all our kin and connections to come, some of them from as far off as California.

Hilda and I had been playing in the creek all afternoon and hadn't had time to wash our legs before we came in to supper, so we sat on the bottom step where it was dark. Cousin Eleanor was in the porch swing with Cousin Tom. She had on a long white dress. It brushed the floor a little every time the swing moved. But you had to listen hard to hear it, under the noise the creek made. Wherever you were in that house you could hear the creek running over the rocks. Hilda and I used to play in it all day long. I liked to stay at her house better than at any of my other cousins'. But they never let me stay there long at a time. That was because she didn't have any mother, just her old mammy, Aunt Rachel—till that spring, when her father, Cousin Tom, married a lady from Birmingham named Cousin Eleanor.

A mockingbird started up in the juniper tree. It was the same one sang all night long that summer; we called him Sunny Jim. Cousin Eleanor got up and went to the end of the porch to try to see him.

"Do they always sing when there's a full moon?" she asked.

"They're worse in August," Cousin Tom said. "Got their crops laid by and don't give a damn if they do stay up all night."

"And in August the Fayerlees repair to Arthur's Cave," she said. "Five hundred people repairing en masse to the womb—what a sight it must be."

Cousin Tom went over and put his arm about her waist. "Do they look any worse than other folks, taking them by and large?" he asked.

The mockingbird burst out as if he was the one who would answer, and I heard Cousin Eleanor's dress brushing the floor again as she walked back to the swing. She had on tiny diamond earrings that night and a diamond cross that she said her father had given her. My grandmother said that she didn't like her mouth. I thought that she was the prettiest person ever lived.

"I'd rather not take them by and large," she said. "Do we *have* to go, Tom?"

"Hell!" he said. "I'm contributing three carcasses to the dinner. I'm going, to get my money's worth."

"One thing, I'm not going to let Cousin Edward Barker kiss me tomorrow," Hilda said. "He's got tobacco juice on his mustaches."

Cousin Tom hadn't sat down in the swing when Cousin Eleanor did. He came and stood on the step above us. "I'm going to shave off my mustache," he said, "and then the women won't have any excuse."

"Which one will you start with?"

"Marjorie Wrenn. She's the prettiest girl in Gloversville. No, she isn't. I'm going to start with Sally. She's living in town now. . . . Sally, you ever been kissed?"

"She's going to kiss me good night right this minute," Cousin Eleanor said, and got up from the swing and came over and bent down and put her hand on each of our shoulders and kissed us, French fashion, she said, first on one cheek and then on the other. We said good night and started for the door. Cousin Tom was there. He put his arms about our waists and bumped our heads together and kissed Hilda first, on the mouth, and then he kissed me and he said, "What about Joe Larrabee now?"

After we got in bed Hilda wanted to talk about Joe Larrabee. He was nineteen years old and the best dancer in town. That was the summer we used to take picnic suppers to the cave, and after supper the band would play and the young people would dance. Once, when we were sitting there watching, Joe Larrabee stopped and asked Hilda to dance, and after that she always wanted to sit on that same bench and when he went past, with Marjorie Wrenn or somebody, she would squeeze my hand tight, and I knew that she thought that maybe he would stop and ask her again. But I didn't think he ever would, and anyway I didn't feel like talking about him that night, so I told her I had to go to sleep.

I dreamed a funny dream. I was at the family reunion at the cave. There were a lot of other people there, but when I'd look into their faces it would be somebody I didn't know and I kept thinking that maybe I'd gone to the wrong picnic, when I saw Cousin Tom. He saw me too, and he stood still till I got to where he was and he said, "Sally, this is Tom." He didn't say Cousin Tom, just Tom. I was about to say something but somebody came in between us, and then I was in another place that wasn't like the cave and I was wondering how I'd ever get back when I heard a *knock, knock, knock,* and Hilda said, "Come on, let's get up."

The knocking was still going on. It took me a minute to know what it was: the old biscuit block was on the downstairs back porch right under our room, and Jason, Aunt Rachel's grandson, was pounding the dough for the beaten biscuits that we were going to take on the picnic.

We got to the cave around eleven o'clock. They don't start setting the dinner out till noon, so we went on down into the hollow, where Uncle Jack Dudley and Richard were tending the fires in the barbecue pits. A funny-looking wagon was standing over by the spring, but we didn't know what was in it, then, so we didn't pay any attention, just watched them barbecuing. Thirteen carcasses were roasting over the pits that day. It was the largest family reunion we ever had. There was a cousin named Robert Dale Owen Fayerlee who had gone off to St. Louis and got rich and he hadn't seen any of his kin in a long time and wanted everybody to have a good time, so he had chartered the cave and donated five cases of whiskey. There was plenty of whiskey for the Negroes too. Every now and then Uncle Jack would go off into the bushes and come back with tin cups that he would pass around. I like to be around Negroes, and so does Hilda. We were just sitting there watching them and not doing a thing, when Cousin Tom came up.

There are three or four Cousin Toms. They keep them straight by their middle names, usually, but they call him Wild Tom. He is not awfully old and has curly brown hair. I don't think his eyes would look so light if his face wasn't so red. He is out in the sun a lot.

He didn't see us at first. He went up to Uncle Jack and asked, "Jack, how you fixed?" Uncle Jack said, "Mister Tom, I ain't fooling you. I done already fixed." "I ain't going to fool with you, then," Cousin Tom said, and he was pulling a bottle out of his pocket when he saw us. He is a man that is particular about little girls. He said, "Hilda, what are you doing here?" and when we said we weren't doing a thing he said, "You go right on up the hill."

The first person I saw up there was my father. I hadn't expected to see him because before I left home I heard him say, "All those mediocre people, getting together to congratulate themselves on their mediocrity! I ain't going a step." But I reckon he didn't want to stay home by himself and, besides, he likes to watch them making fools of themselves.

My father is not connected. He is Professor Aleck Maury and he had a boys' school in Gloversville then. There was a girls' school there too, Miss Robinson's, but he said that I wouldn't learn anything if I went there till I was blue in the face, so I had to go to school with the boys. Sometimes I think that that is what makes me so peculiar.

It takes them a long time to set out the dinner. We sat down on a top rail of one of the benches with Susie McIntyre and watched the young people dance. Joe Larrabee was dancing with Marjorie Wrenn. She had on a tan coat-suit, with buttons made out of brown braid. Her hat was brown straw, with a tan ribbon. She held it in her hand, and it flopped up and down when she danced. It wasn't twelve o'clock, but Joe Larrabee already had whiskey on his breath. I smelled it when they went past.

Susie said for us to go out there and dance too. She asked me first, and I started to, and then I remembered last year when I got off on the wrong foot and Cousin Edward Barker came along and stepped on me, and I thought it was better not to try than to fail, so I let Hilda go with Susie.

I was still sitting there on top of the bench when Cousin Tom came along. He didn't seem to remember that he was mad at us. He said, "Hello, Bumps." I am not Bumps. Hilda is Bumps, so I said, "I'm just waiting for Hilda . . . want me to get her?"

He waved his hand and I smelled whiskey on his breath. "Well, hello, anyhow," he said, and I thought for a minute that he was going to kiss me. He is a man that you don't so much mind having him kiss you, even when he has whiskey on his breath. But he went on to where Cousin Eleanor was helping Aunt Rachel set out the dinner. On the way he knocked into a lady and when he stepped back he ran into another one, so after he asked them to excuse him he went off on tiptoe. But he lifted his feet too high and put one of them down in a basket of pies. Aunt Rachel hollered out before she thought, "Lord God, he done ruint my pies!"

Cousin Eleanor just stood there and looked at him. When he got almost up to her and she still didn't say anything, he stopped and looked at her a minute and then he said, "All right!" and went off down the hill.

Susie and Hilda came back and they rang a big bell and Cousin Sidney Grassdale (they call them by the names of their places when there are too many of the same name) said a long prayer, and they all went in.

My father got his plate helped first and then he turned around to a man behind him and said, "You stick to me and you can't go wrong. I know the ropes."

The man was short and fat and had on a cream-colored Palm Beach suit and smiled a lot. I knew he was Cousin Robert Dale Owen Fayerlee, the one that gave all the whiskey.

I didn't fool with any of the barbecue, just ate ham and chicken. And then I had some chicken salad, and Susie wanted me to try some potato salad, so I tried that too, and then we had a good many hot rolls and some stuffed eggs and some pickles and some coconut cake and some chocolate cake. I had been saving myself up for Aunt Rachel's chess pies and put three on my plate when I started out, but by the time I got to them I wasn't really hungry and I let Susie eat one of mine.

After we got through, Hilda said she had a pain in her stomach and we sat down on a bench till it went away. My grandmother and Aunt Maria came and sat down too. They had on white shirtwaists and black skirts and they both had their palm-leaf fans.

Cousin Robert D. Owen got up and made a speech. It was mostly about his father. He said that he was one of nature's noblemen. My grandmother and Aunt Maria held their fans up before their faces when he said that, and Aunt Maria said, "Chh! *Jim* Fayerlee!" and my grandmother said that all that branch of the family was boastful.

Cousin Robert D. Owen got through with his father and started on back. He said that the Fayerlees were descended from Edward the Confessor and Philippe le Bel of France and the grandfather of George Washington.

My father was sitting two seats down, with Cousin Edward Barker. "Now ain't that tooting?" he said.

Cousin Edward Barker hit himself on the knee. "I be damn if I don't write to the *Tobacco Leaf* about that," he said. "The Fayerlees have been plain, honest countrymen since 1600. Don't that fool know anything about his own family?"

Susie touched me and Hilda on the shoulder, and we got up and squeezed past my grandmother and Aunt Maria. "Where you going?" my grandmother asked.

"We're just going to take a walk, Cousin Sally," Susie said.

We went out to the gate. The cave is at the foot of a hill. There are some long wooden steps leading up to the top of the hill, and right by the gate that keeps people out if they haven't paid is a refreshment stand. I thought that it would be nice to have some orange pop, but Susie said, "No, let's go to the carnival."

"There isn't any carnival," Hilda said.

"There is, too," Susie said, "but it costs a quarter."

"I haven't got but fifteen cents," Hilda said.

"Here comes Giles Allard," Susie said. "Make out you don't see him."

Cousin Giles Allard is a member of our family connection who is not quite right in the head. He doesn't have any special place to live, just roams around. Sometimes he will come and stay two or three weeks with you and sometimes he will come on the place and not come up to the house, but stay down in the cabin with some darky that he likes. He is a little warped-looking man with pale blue eyes. I reckon that before a family reunion somebody gives him one of their old suits. He had on a nice gray suit that day and looked just about like the rest of them.

He came up to us and said, "You all having a good time?" and we said, "Fine," and thought he would go on, but he stood and looked at us. "My name is Giles Allard," he said.

We couldn't think of anything to say to that. He pointed his finger at me. "You're named for your grandmother," he said, "but your name ain't Fayerlee."

"I'm Sally Maury," I said, "Professor Maury's daughter." My father being no kin to us, they always call me and my brother Sally Maury and Frank Maury, instead of plain Sally and Frank, the way they would if our blood was pure.

"Let's get away from him," Susie whispered, and she said out loud, "We've got to go down to the spring, Cousin Giles," and we hurried on as fast as we could. We didn't realize at first that Cousin Giles was coming with us.

"There comes Papa," Hilda said.

"He looks to me like he's drunk," Susie said.

Cousin Tom stood still till we got up to him, just as he did in my dream. He smiled at us then and put his hand on Hilda's head and said, "How are you, baby?" Hilda said, "I'm all right," and he said, "You are three sweet, pretty little girls. I'm going to give each one of you fifty cents," and he stuck his hand in his pocket and took out two dollar bills, and when Hilda asked how we were going to get the change out, he said, "Keep the change."

"Whoopee!" Susie said. "Now we can go to the carnival. You come, too, Cousin Tom," and we all started out toward the hollow.

The Negroes were gone, but there were still coals in the barbecue pits. That fat man was kneeling over one, cooking something.

"What you cooking for, fellow?" Cousin Tom asked. "Don't you know this is the day everybody eats free?"

The fat man turned around and smiled at us.

"Can we see the carnival?" Susie asked.

The fat man jumped up. "Yes, *ma'am*," he said, "you sure can see the carnival," and he left his cooking and we went over to the wagon.

On the way the fat man kept talking, kind of singsong: "You folks are in luck. . . . Wouldn't be here now but for a broken wheel . . . but one man's loss is another man's gain . . . I've got the greatest attraction in the world . . . yes, sir. Behind them draperies of pure silk lies the world's greatest attraction."

"Well, what is it?" Cousin Tom asked.

The fat man stopped and looked at us and then he began shouting:

"Stell-a, Stell-a, the One and Only Stella!
Not flesh, not bone,
But calkypyrate stone,
Sweet Sixteen a Hundred Years Ago
And Sweet Sixteen Today!"

A woman sitting on a chair in front of the wagon got up and ducked around behind it. When she came out again she had on a red satin dress, with ostrich feathers on the skirt, and a red satin hat. She walked up to us and smiled and said, "Will the ladies be seated?" and the man got some little stools down, quick, from where they were hooked on to the end of the wagon, and we all sat down, except Cousin Giles Allard, and he squatted in the grass.

The wagon had green curtains draped at each end of it. Gold birds were on the sides. The man bent down and pushed a spring or something, and one side of the wagon folded back, and there, lying on a pink satin couch, was a girl.

She had on a white satin dress. It was cut so low that you could see her bosom. Her head was propped on a satin pillow. Her eyes were shut. The lashes were long and black, with a little gold on them. Her face was dark and shone a little. But her hair was gold. It waved down on each side of her face and out over the green pillow. *The pillow had gold fringe on it! . . . lightly prest . . . in palace chambers . . . far apart . . . The fragrant tresses are not stirred . . . that lie upon her charmèd heart . . .*

The woman went around to the other side of the wagon. The man was still shouting:

"Stell-a, Stell-a
The One and Only Stell-a!"

Cousin Giles Allard squeaked like a rabbit. The girl's eyes had opened. Her bosom was moving up and down.

Hilda got hold of my hand and held it tight. I could feel myself breathing . . . But *her* breathing *is not heard . . . in palace chambers, far apart.* Her eyes were no color you could name. There was a veil over them.

The man was still shouting:

"You see her now
As she was then,
Sweet Sixteen a Hundred Years Ago,
And Sweet Sixteen Today!"

"How come her bubbies move if she's been dead so long?" Cousin Giles Allard asked.

Cousin Tom stood up, quick. "She's a pretty woman," he said, "I don't know when I've seen a prettier woman . . . lies quiet, too. . . . Well, thank you, my friend," and he gave the man two or three dollars and started off across the field.

I could tell that Susie wanted to stay and watch the girl some more, and it did look like we could, after he had paid all that money, but he was walking straight off across the field and we had to go after him. Once, before we caught up with him, he put his hand into his pocket, and I saw the bottle flash in the sun as he tilted it, but he had it back in his pocket by the time we caught up with him.

"You reckon she is sort of mummied, Cousin Tom, or is she just turned to pure rock?" Susie asked.

He didn't answer her. He was frowning. All of a sudden he opened his eyes wide, as if he had just seen something he hadn't expected to see. But there wasn't anybody around or anything to look at, except that purple weed that grows all over the field. He turned around. He hollered, the way he hollers at the hands on the place: "You come on here, Giles Allard!" and Cousin Giles came running. Once he tried to turn back, but Cousin Tom wouldn't let him go till we were halfway up to the cave. He let him slip off into the bushes then.

The sun was in all our eyes. Hilda borrowed Susie's handkerchief and wiped her face. "What made you keep Cousin Giles with us, Papa?" she asked. "I'd just as soon not have him along."

Cousin Tom sat down on a rock. The sun's fiery glare was full on his face. You could see the pulse in his temple beat. A little red vein was spreading over one of his eyeballs. He pulled the bottle out of his pocket. "I don't want him snooping around Stella," he said.

"How could he hurt her, Papa, if she's already dead?" Hilda asked.

Cousin Tom held the bottle up and moved it so that it caught the sun. "Maybe she isn't dead," he said.

Susie laughed out.

Cousin Tom winked his red eye at Susie and shook the bottle. "Maybe she isn't dead," he said again. "Maybe she's just resting."

Hilda stamped her foot on the ground. "*Papa*! I believe you've had too much to drink."

He drank all there was in the bottle and let it fall to the ground. He stood up. He put his hand out, as if he could push the sun away. "And what business is that of yours?" he asked.

"I just wondered if you were going back to the cave, where everybody is," Hilda said.

He was faced toward the cave then, but he shook his head. "No," he said, "I'm not going up to the cave," and he turned around and walked off down the hill.

We stood there a minute and watched him. "Well, anyhow, he isn't going up there where everybody is," Susie said.

"Where Mama is," Hilda said. "It just drives her crazy when he drinks."

"She better get used to it," Susie said. "All the Fayerlee men drink."

The reunion was about over when we got up to the cave. I thought I had to go back to my grandmother's—I was spending the summer there—but Hilda came and said I was to spend the night at the Fork.

"But you got to behave yourselves," Aunt Rachel said. "Big doings tonight."

We rode back in the spring wagon with her and Richard and the ice-cream freezers and what was left of the dinner. Cousin Robert D. Owen and his wife, Cousin Marie, were going to spend the night at the Fork too, and they had gone on ahead in the car with the others.

Hilda and I had long-waisted dimity dresses made just alike that summer. I had a pink sash and she had a blue one. We were so excited while we were dressing for supper that night that we couldn't get our sashes tied right. "Let's get Mama to do it," Hilda said, and we went into Cousin Eleanor's room. She was sitting at her dressing table, putting rouge on her lips. Cousin Marie was in there, too, sitting on the edge of the bed. Cousin Eleanor tied our sashes—she had to do mine twice before she got it right—and then gave me a little spank and said, "Now! You'll be the belles of the ball."

They hadn't told us to go out, so we sat down on the edge of the bed too. "Mama, where is Papa?" Hilda asked.

"I have *no* idea, darling," Cousin Eleanor said. "Tom is a law unto himself." She said that to Cousin Marie. I saw her looking at her in the mirror.

Cousin Marie had bright black eyes. She didn't need to use any rouge, her face was so pink. She had a dimple in one cheek. She said, "It's a *world* unto itself. Bob's been telling me about it ever since we were married, but I didn't believe him, till I came and saw for myself. . . . These little girls, now, how are they related?"

"In about eight different ways," Cousin Eleanor said.

Cousin Marie gave a kind of little yip. "It's just like an English novel," she said.

"They are mostly Scottish people," Cousin Eleanor said, "descended from Edward the Confessor and Philippe le Bel of France . . ."

"And the grandfather of George Washington!" Cousin Marie said, and rolled back on the bed in her good dress and giggled. "Isn't Bob priceless? But it *is* just like a book."

"I never was a great reader," Cousin Eleanor said. "I'm an outdoor girl."

She stood up. I never will forget the dress she had on that night. It was black but thin and it had a rose-colored bow right on the hip. She sort of dusted the bow off, though there wasn't a thing on it, and looked around the room as if she never had been there before. "I was, too," she said. "I was city champion for three years."

"Well, my dear, you could have a golf course here," Cousin Marie said. "Heaven knows there's all the room in creation."

"And draw off to swing, and a mule comes along and eats your golf ball up!" Cousin Eleanor said, "No, thank you, I'm through with all that."

They went down to supper. On the stairs Cousin Marie put her arm around Cousin Eleanor's waist, and I heard her say, "Wine for dinner. We don't need it." But Cousin Eleanor kept her face straight ahead. "There's no use for us to deny ourselves just because Tom can't control himself," she said.

Cousin Tom was already at the table when we got into the dining room. He had on a clean white suit. His eyes were bloodshot, and you could still see that vein beating in his temple. He sat at the head of the table, and Cousin Eleanor and Cousin Marie sat on each side of him. Cousin Sidney Grassdale and his daughter, Molly, were there. Cousin Sidney sat next to Cousin Marie, and Molly sat next to Cousin Eleanor. They had to do it that way on account of the overseer, Mr. Turner. He sat at the foot of the table, and Hilda and I sat on each side of him.

We usually played a game when we were at the table. It was keeping something going through a whole meal, without the grown folks knowing what it was. Nobody knew we did it except Aunt Rachel, and sometimes when she was passing things she would give us a dig in the ribs, to keep us quiet.

That night we were playing Petrified Woman. With everything we said we put in something from the fat man's song; like Hilda would say, "You want some butter?" and I would come back with "No, thank you, calkypyrate bone."

Cousin Marie was asking who the lady with the white hair in the blue flowered dress was.

"That is Cousin Olivia Bradshaw," Cousin Eleanor said.

"She has a pretty daughter," Cousin Robert D. Owen said.

"*Mater pulcher, filia pulchrior,*" Cousin Sidney Grassdale said.

"And they live at Summer Hill?" Cousin Marie asked.

Cousin Tom laid his fork down. "I never could stand those Summer Hill folks," he said. "Pretentious."

"But the daughter has a great deal of charm," Cousin Marie said.

"Sweet Sixteen a Hundred Years Ago," Hilda said. "Give me the salt."

"And Sweet Sixteen Today," I said. "It'll thin your blood."

Cousin Tom must have heard us. He raised his head. His bloodshot eyes stared around the table. He shut his eyes. I knew that he was trying to remember.

"I saw a woman today that had real charm," he said.

Cousin Eleanor heard his voice and turned around. She looked him straight in the face and smiled, slowly. "In what did her charm consist, Tom?"

"She was petrified," Cousin Tom said.

I looked at her and then I wished I hadn't. She had blue eyes. I always thought that they were like violets. She had a way of opening them wide whenever she looked at you.

"Some women are just petrified in spots," Cousin Tom said. "She was petrified all over."

It was like the violets were freezing, there in her eyes. We all saw it. Molly Grassdale said something, and Cousin Eleanor's lips smiled and she half bent toward her and then her head gave a little shake and she straightened up so that she faced him. She was still smiling.

"In that case, how did she exert her charm?"

I thought, "Her eyes, they will freeze him, too." But he seemed to like for her to look at him like that. He was smiling, too.

"She just lay there and looked sweet," he said. "I like a woman to look sweet. . . . Hell, they ain't got anything else to do!"

Cousin Sidney's nose was working up and down, like a squirrel I had once, named Adji-Daumo. He said, "Harry Crenfew seems to be very much in love with Lucy Bradshaw."

"*I'm* in love!" Cousin Tom shouted. "I'm in love with a petrified woman."

She was still looking at him. I never saw anything as cold as her eyes.

"What is her name, Tom?"

"Stell-a!" he shouted. "The One and Only Stell-a!" He pushed his chair back and stood up, still shouting. "I'm going down to Arthur's Cave and take her away from that fellow."

He must have got his foot tangled up in Cousin Marie's dress, for she shrieked and stood up, too, and he went down on the floor, with his wineglass in his hand. Somebody noticed us after a minute and sent us out of the room. He was still lying there when we left, his arms flung out and blood on his forehead from the broken glass. . . . I never did even see him get up off the floor.

We moved away that year and so we never went to another family reunion. And I never went to the Fork again. It burned down that fall. They said that Cousin Tom set it on fire, roaming around at night, with a lighted lamp in his hand. That was after he and Cousin Eleanor got divorced. I heard that they both got married again but I never knew who it was they married. I hardly ever think of them anymore. If I do, they are still there in that house. The mockingbird has just stopped singing. Cousin Eleanor, in her long white dress, is walking over to the window, where, on moonlight nights, we used to sit, to watch the water glint on the rocks . . . But Cousin Tom is still lying there on the floor. . . .

28. Zora Neale Hurston

(1901?–1960)

Born in Eatonville, Florida, Zora Neale Hurston was only nine years old when her mother died. Her older brother took Hurston out of school when she was thirteen to care for his children, but three years later she left his family and began working as a maid. Fortunately, Hurston's employer was sympathetic to her desire for further education and helped her get accepted to the high school of Morgan College in Baltimore. After graduating, Hurston entered Howard University, which she attended from 1921 to 1924. At Howard, Hurston began studying anthropology and writing. She published her first story, "John Redding Goes to Sea," in 1924. In 1925 she received a scholarship to Barnard College, Columbia University, and after graduating from there, received a foundation fellowship to help her continue her anthropological studies.

During these years Hurston worked as a secretary for Fanny Hurst in order to support herself. In the 1920s, she also began collecting folklore, both in New York and in Florida, and she was active in the Harlem Renaissance. Much of her short fiction was published during these years. "The Eatonville Anthology," first published in *Messenger* in 1926, contains anecdotal stories that Hurston gathered in her anthropological work in Florida; she later incorporated several of those stories into her novel *Their Eyes Were Watching God* (1937). "The Eatonville Anthology" is included in *I Love Myself When I Am Laughing . . . And Then Again When I Am Looking Mean and Impressive: A Zora Neale Hurston Reader* (1979). In the early 1930s, Hurston collaborated with Langston Hughes on *Mule Bones: A Comedy of Negro Life in Three Acts* (1931) and published her first work of long fiction, *Jonah's Gourd Vine* (1934), which was so successful that she was immediately asked to write stories and articles for several magazines.

In 1935 her first book of folklore, *Mules and Men,* was published; it included more of the stories she had collected in Florida. A Guggenheim Fellowship followed, allowing Hurston to research folklore, songs, and stories from Jamaica and Haiti; from her studies done from 1936 to 1938 she completed *Tell My Horse* (1938), which was republished in 1939 under the title *Voodoo Gods; an Inquiry into Native Myths and*

Magic in Jamaica and Haiti. Hurston's interest in anthropology added distinctive features to her fiction: regional dialects, folk tales, and local customs permeate her work.

In 1937 Hurston published her most highly acclaimed novel, *Their Eyes Were Watching God,* a novel that June Jordan claimed in 1974 was "the most successful, convincing, and exemplary novel of Blacklove that we have." This novel, like many of her stories, demonstrates Hurston's interest in the power her rural, black, southern heritage had in shaping her life and art. Because her created world comprises solely black characters, much like the Eatonville of her childhood, Hurston rarely focuses on race relations or racism but rather on relationships within the black community.

When she returned to Florida in 1942, after spending a year as a writer for Paramount Pictures in Hollywood, Hurston lived on a houseboat and continued writing. Her autobiography, *Dust Tracks on a Road,* had just been published, but it brought Hurston mostly harsh criticism from the black community, which accused her of writing for a white audience. Apart from the publication of an occasional article, Hurston virtually disappeared for the rest of the decade. She was "discovered" working as a maid in Rivo Alto, Florida, when her employer found one of her stories in a magazine. In financial trouble for the rest of her life, Hurston later supported herself working as a reporter for the *Pittsburgh Courier* while trying to complete a never-published novel. She worked at several odd jobs until her death in 1960, at Saint Lucie County Welfare Home in Florida.

The Eatonville Anthology

I. The Pleading Woman

Mrs. Tony Roberts is the pleading woman. She just loves to ask for things. Her husband gives her all he can take and scrape, which is considerably more than most wives get for their housekeeping, but she goes from door to door begging for things.

She starts at the store. "Mist' Clarke," she sing-songs in a high keening voice, "gimme lil' piece uh meat tuh boil a pot uh greens wid. Lawd knows me an' mah chillen is so hongry! Hits uh SHAME! Tony don't fee-ee-eee-ed me!"

Mr. Clarke knows that she has money and that her larder is well stocked, for Tony Roberts is the best provider on his list. But her keening annoys him and he rises heavily. The pleader at his elbow shows all the joy of a starving man being seated at a feast.

"Thass right Mist' Clarke. De Lawd loveth de cheerful giver. Gimme jes' a lil' piece 'bout dis big (indicating the width of her hand) an' de Lawd'll bless yuh."

She follows this angel-on-earth to his meat tub and superintends the cutting, crying out in pain when he refuses to move the knife over just a teeny bit mo'.

Finally, meat in hand, she departs, remarking on the meanness of some people who give a piece of salt meat only two-fingers wide when they were plainly asked for a hand-wide piece. Clarke puts it down to Tony's account and resumes his reading.

With the slab of salt pork as a foundation, she visits various homes until she has collected all she wants for the day. At the Piersons for instance: "Sister Pierson, ple-ee-ease gimme uh hand'ful uh collard greens fuh me an' mah po' chillen! 'Deed, me an' mah chillen is so hongry. Tony doan' fee-ee-eed me!"

Mrs. Pierson picks a bunch of greens for her, but she springs away from them as if they were poison. "Lawd a mussy, Mis' Pierson, you ain't gonna gimme dat lil' eye-full uh greens fuh me an' mah chillen, is you? Don't be so graspin'; Gawd won't bless yuh. Gimme uh han'full mo'. Lawd, some folks is got everything, an' theys jes' as gripin' an stingy!"

Mrs. Pierson raises the ante, and the pleading woman moves on to the next place, and on and on. The next day, it commences all over.

II. Turpentine Love

Jim Merchant is always in good humor—even with his wife. He says he fell in love with her at first sight. That was some years ago. She has had all her teeth pulled out, but they still get along splendidly.

He says the first time he called on her he found out that she was subject to fits. This didn't cool his love, however. She had several in his presence.

One Sunday, while he was there, she had one, and her mother tried to give her a dose of turpentine to stop it. Accidentally, she spilled it in her eye and it cured her. She never had another fit, so they got married and have kept each other in good humor ever since.

III

Becky Moore has eleven children of assorted colors and sizes. She has never been married, but that is not her fault. She has never stopped any of the fathers of her children from proposing, so if she has no father for her children it's not her fault. The men round about are entirely to blame.

The other mothers of the town are afraid that it is catching. They won't let their children play with hers.

IV. Tippy

Sykes Jones' family all shoot craps. The most interesting member of the family—also fond of bones, but another kind—is Tippy, the Jones' dog.

He is so thin, that it amazes one that he lives at all. He sneaks into village kitchens if the housewives are careless about the doors and steals meats, even off the stoves. He also sucks eggs.

For these offenses he has been sentenced to death dozens of times, and the sentences executed upon him, only they didn't work. He has been fed bluestone, strychnine, nux vomica, even an entire Peruna bottle beaten up. It didn't fatten him, but it didn't kill him. So Eatonville has resigned itself to the plague of Tippy, reflecting that it has erred in certain matters and is being chastened.

In spite of all the attempts upon his life, Tippy is still willing to be friendly with anyone who will let him.

V. The Way of a Man With a Train

Old Man Anderson lived seven or eight miles out in the country from Eatonville. Over by Lake Apopka. He raised feed-corn and cassava and went to market with it two or three times a year. He bought all of his victuals wholesale so he wouldn't have to come to town for several months more.

He was different from citybred folks. He had never seen a train. Everybody laughed at him for even the smallest child in Eatonville had either been to Maitland or Orlando and watched a train go by. On Sunday afternoons all of the young people of the village would go over to Maitland, a mile away, to see Number 35 whizz southward on its way to Tampa and wave at the passengers. So we looked down on him a little. Even we children felt superior in the presence of a person so lacking in wordly knowledge.

The grown-ups kept telling him he ought to go see a train. He always said he didn't have time to wait so long. Only two trains a day passed through Maitland. But patronage and ridicule finally had its effect and Old Man Anderson drove in one morning early. Number 78 went north to Jacksonville at 10:20. He drove his light wagon over in the woods beside the railroad below Maitland, and sat down to wait. He began to fear that his horse would get frightened and run away with the wagon. So he took him out and led him deeper into the grove and tied him securely. Then he returned to his wagon and waited some more. Then he remembered that some of the train-wise villagers had said the engine belched fire and smoke. He had better move his wagon out of danger. It might catch fire. He climbed down from the seat and placed himself between the shafts to draw it away. Just then 78 came thundering over the trestle spouting smoke, and suddenly began blowing for Maitland. Old Man Anderson became so frightened he ran away with the wagon through the woods and tore it up worse than the horse ever could have done. He doesn't know yet what a train looks like, and says he doesn't care.

VI. Coon Taylor

Coon Taylor never did any real stealing. Of course, if he saw a chicken or a watermelon he'd take it. The people used to get mad but they never could catch him. He took so many melons from Joe Clarke that he set up in the melon patch one night with his shotgun loaded with rock-salt. He was going to fix Coon. But he was tired. It is hard work being a mayor, postmaster, storekeeper and everything. He dropped asleep sitting on a stump in the middle of the patch. So he didn't see Coon when he came. Coon didn't see him either, that is, not at first. He knew the stump was there, however. He had opened many of Clarke's juicy Florida Favorite on it. He selected his fruit, walked over to the stump and burst the melon on it. That is, he thought it was the stump until it fell over with a yell. Then he knew it was no stump and departed hastily from those parts. He had cleared the fence when Clarke came to, as it were. So the charge of rock-salt was wasted on the desert air.

During the sugar-cane season, he found he couldn't resist Clarke's soft green cane, but Clarke did not go to sleep this time. So after he had cut six or eight stalks by the moonlight, Clarke rose up out of the cane strippings with his shotgun and made Coon sit right down and chew up the last one of them on the spot. And the next day he made Coon leave his town for three months.

VII. Village Fiction

Joe Lindsay is said by Lum Boger to be the largest manufacturer of prevarications in Eatonville; Brazzle (late owner of the world's leanest and meanest mule) contends that his business is the largest in the state and his wife holds that he is the biggest liar in the world.

Exhibit A—He claims that while he was in Orlando one day he saw a doctor cut open a woman, remove everything—liver, lights and heart included—clean each of them separately; the doctor then washed out the empty woman, dried her out neatly with a towel and replaced the organs so expertly that she was up and about her work in a couple of weeks.

VIII.

Sewell is a man who lives all to himself. He moves a great deal. So often, that 'Lige Moseley says his chickens are so used to moving that every time he comes out into his backyard the chickens lie down and cross their legs, ready to be tied up again.

He is baldheaded; but he says he doesn't mind that, because he wants as little as possible between him and God.

IX.

Mrs. Clarke is Joe Clarke's wife. She is a soft-looking middle-aged woman, whose bust and stomach are always holding a get-together.

She waits on the store sometimes and cries every time he yells at her which he does every time she makes a mistake, which is quite often. She calls her husband "Jody." They say he used to beat her in the store when he was a young man, but he is not so impatient now. He can wait until he goes home.

She shouts in Church every Sunday and shakes the hand of fellowship with everybody in the Church with her eyes closed, but somehow always misses her husband.

X.

Mrs. McDuffy goes to Church every Sunday and always shouts and tells her "determination." Her husband always sits in the back row and beats her as soon as they get home. He says there's no sense in her shouting, as big a devil as she is. She just does it to slur him. Elijah Moseley asked her why she didn't stop shouting, seeing she always got a beating about it. She says she can't "squinch the sperrit." Then Elijah asked Mr. McDuffy to stop beating her, seeing that she was going to shout anyway. He answered that she just did it for spite and that his fist was just as hard as her head. He could last just as long as she. So the village let the matter rest.

XI. Double-Shuffle

Back in the good old days before the World War, things were very simple in Eatonville. People didn't fox-trot. When the town wanted to put on its Sunday clothes and wash behind the ears, it put on a "breakdown." The daring younger set would two-step and waltz, but the good church members and the elders stuck to the grand march. By rural canons dancing is wicked, but one is not held to have danced until the feet have been crossed. Feet don't get crossed when one grand marches.

At elaborate affairs the organ from the Methodist church was moved up to the hall and Lizzimore, the blind man, presided. When informal gatherings were held, he merely played his guitar assisted by any volunteer with mouth organs or accordions.

Among white people the march is as mild as if it had been passed on by Volstead. But it still has a kick in Eatonville. Everybody happy, shining eyes, gleaming teeth. Feet dragged 'shhlap, shhlap! to beat out the time. No orchestra needed. Round and round! Back again, parse-me-la! shlap! shlap! Strut! Strut! Seaboard! Shlap! Shlap! Tiddy bumm! Mr. Clarke in the lead with Mrs. Moseley.

It's too much for some of the young folks. Double shuffling commences. Buck and wing. Lizzimore about to break his guitar. Accordion doing contortions. People fall back against the walls, and let the soloist have it, shouting as they clap the old, old double-shuffle songs.

> *"Me an' mah honey got two mo' days*
> *Two mo' days tuh do de buck"*

Sweating bodies, laughing mouths, grotesque faces, feet drumming fiercely. Deacons clapping as hard as the rest.

> *"Great big nigger, black as tar*
> *trying tuh git tuh hebben on uh 'lectric car."*

> *"Some love cabbage, some love kale*
> *But I love a gal wid a short skirt tail."*

> *"Long tall angel—steppin' down,*
> *Long white robe an' starry crown."*

> *"Ah would not marry uh black gal (bumm bumm!)*
> *Tell yuh de reason why*
> *Every time she comb her hair*
> *She make de goo-goo eye."*

> *"Would not marry a yaller gal (bumm bumm!)*
> *Tell yuh de reason why*
> *Her neck so long an' stringy*
> *Ahm 'fraid she'd never die."*

"Would not marry uh preacher
Tell yuh de reason why
Every time he comes tuh town
He makes de chicken fly."

When the buck dance was over, the boys would give the floor to the girls and they would parse-me-la with a sly eye out of the corner to see if anybody was looking who might "have them up in church" on conference night. Then there would be more dancing. Then Mr. Clarke would call for everybody's best attention and announce that *'freshments was served! Every gent'man would please take his lady by the arm and scorch her right up to de table fur a treat!*

Then the men would stick their arms out with a flourish and ask their ladies: "You lak chicken? Well, then, take a wing." And the ladies would take the proffered "wings" and parade up to the long table and be served. Of course most of them had brought baskets in which were heaps of jointed and fried chicken, two or three kinds of pies, cakes, potato pone and chicken purlo. The hall would separate into happy groups about the baskets until time for more dancing.

But the boys and girls got scattered about during the war, and now they dance the fox-trot by a brand new piano. They do waltz and two-step still, but no one now considers it good form to lock his chin over his partner's shoulder and stick out behind. One night just for fun and to humor the old folks, they danced, that is, they grand marched, but everyone picked up their feet. *Bah*!!

XII. The Head of the Nail

Daisy Taylor was the town vamp. Not that she was pretty. But sirens were all but non-existent in the town. Perhaps she was forced to it by circumstances. She was quite dark, with little bushy patches of hair squatting over her head. These were held down by shingle-nails often. No one knows whether she did this for artistic effect or for lack of hairpins, but there they were shining in the little patches of hair when she got all dressed for the afternoon and came up to Clarke's store to see if there was any mail for her.

It was seldom that anyone wrote to Daisy, but she knew that the men the town would be assembled there by five o'clock, and some one could usually be induced to buy her some soda water or peanuts.

Daisy flirted with married men. There were only two single men in town. Lum Boger, who was engaged to the assistant schoolteacher, and Hiram Lester, who had been off to school at Tuskegee and wouldn't look at a person like Daisy. In addition to other drawbacks, she was pigeon-toed and her petticoat was always showing so perhaps he was justified. There was nothing else to do except flirt with married men.

This went on for a long time. First one wife and then another complained of her, or drove her from the preserves by threat.

But the affair with Crooms was the most prolonged and serious. He was even known to have bought her a pair of shoes.

Mrs. Laura Crooms was a meek little woman who took all of her troubles crying, and talked a great deal of leaving things in the hands of God.

The affair came to a head one night in orange picking time. Crooms was over at Oneido picking oranges. Many fruit pickers move from one town to the other during the season.

The *town* was collected at the store-postoffice as is customary on Saturday nights. The *town* has had its bath and with its week's pay in pocket fares forth to be merry. The men tell stories and treat the ladies to soda water, peanuts and peppermint candy.

Daisy was trying to get treats, but the porch was cold to her that night. "Ah don't keer if you don't treat me. What's a dirty lil nickel?" She flung this at Walter Thomas. "The everloving Mister Crooms will gimme anything atall Ah wants."

"You better shet up yo' mouf talking 'bout Albert Crooms. Heah his wife comes right now."

Daisy went akimbo. "Who? Me! Ah don't keer whut Laura Crooms think. If she ain't a heavy hip-ted Mama enough to keep him, she don't need to come crying to me."

She stood making goo-goo eyes as Mrs. Crooms walked upon the porch. Daisy laughed loud, made several references to Albert Crooms, and when she saw the mail-bag come in from Maitland she said, "Ah better go in an' see if Ah ain't got a letter from Oneido."

The more Daisy played the game of getting Mrs. Crooms' goat, the better she liked it. She ran in and out of the store laughing until she could scarcely stand. Some of the people present began to talk to Mrs. Crooms—to egg her on to halt Daisy's boasting, but she was for leaving it all in the hands of God. Walter Thomas kept on after Mrs. Crooms until she stiffened and resolved to fight. Daisy was inside when she came to this resolve and never dreamed anything of the kind could happen. She had gotten hold of an envelope and came laughing and shouting. "Oh, Ah can't stand to see Oneido lose!"

There was a box of ax-handles on display on the porch, propped up against the door jamb. As Daisy stepped upon the porch, Mrs. Crooms leaned the heavy end of one of those handles heavily upon her head. She staggered from the porch to the ground and the timid Laura, fearful of a counter-attack, struck again and Daisy toppled into the town ditch. There was not enough water in there to do more than muss her up. Every time she tried to rise, down would come that ax-handle again. Laura was fighting a scared fight. With Daisy thoroughly licked, she retired to the store porch and left her fallen enemy in the ditch. But Elijah Moseley, who was some distance down the street when the trouble began, arrived as the victor was withdrawing. He rushed up and picked Daisy out of the mud and began feeling her head.

"Is she hurt much?" Joe Clarke asked from the doorway.

"I don't know," Elijah answered. "I was just looking to see if Laura had been lucky enough to hit one of those nails on the head and drive it in."

Before a week was up, Daisy moved to Orlando. There in a wider sphere, perhaps, her talents as a vamp were appreciated.

XIII. Pants and Cal'line

Sister Cal'line Potts was a silent woman. Did all of her laughing down inside, but did the thing that kept the town in an uproar of laughter. It was the general opinion of her village that Cal'line would do anything she had a mind to. And she had a mind to do several things.

Mitchell Potts, her husband, had a weakness for women. No one ever believed that she was jealous. She did things to the women, surely. But most any townsman would have said that she did them because she liked the novel situation and the queer things she could bring out of it.

Once he took with Delphine—called Mis' Pheeny by the town. She lived on the outskirts on the edge of the piney woods. The town winked and talked. People don't make secrets of such things in villages. Cal'line went about her business with her thin black lips pursed tight as ever, and her shiney black eyes unchanged.

"Dat devil of a Cal'line's got somethin' up her sleeve!" The town smiled in anticipation.

"Delphine is too big a cigar for her to smoke. She ain't crazy," said some as the weeks went on and nothing happened. Even Pheeny herself would give an extra flirt to her over-starched petticoats as she rustled into church past her of Sundays.

Mitch Potts said furthermore, that he was tired of Cal'line's foolishness. She had to stay where he put her. His African soup-bone (arm) was too strong to let a woman run over him. 'Nough was 'nough. And he did some fancy cussing, and he was the fanciest cusser in the county.

So the town waited and the longer it waited, the odds changed slowly from the wife to the husband.

One Saturday, Mitch knocked off work at two o'clock and went over to Maitland. He came back with a rectangular box under his arm and kept straight on out to the barn to put it away. He ducked around the corner of the house, but even so, his wife glimpsed the package. Very much like a shoe box. So!

He put on the kettle and took a bath. She stood in her bare feet at the ironing board and kept on ironing. He dressed. It was about five o'clock but still very light. He fiddled around outside. She kept on with her ironing. As soon as the sun got red, he sauntered out to the barn, got the parcel and walked away down the road, past the store and out into the piney woods. As soon as he left the house, Cal'line slipped on her shoes without taking time to don stockings, put on one of her husband's old Stetsons, worn and floppy, slung the axe over her shoulder and followed in his wake. He was hailed cheerily as he passed the sitters on the store porch and answered smiling sheepishly and passed on. Two minutes later passed his wife, silently, unsmilingly, and set the porch to giggling and betting.

An hour passed perhaps. It was dark. Clarke had long ago lighted the swinging kerosene lamp inside.

XIV.

Once 'way back yonder before the stars fell all the animals used to talk just like people. In them days dogs and rabbits was the best of friends even tho both of them was stuck on the same gal—which was Miss Nancy Coon. She had the sweetest smile and the prettiest striped and bushy tail to be found anywhere.

They both run their legs nigh off trying to win her for themselves— fetching nice ripe persimmons and such. But she never give one or the other no satisfaction.

Finally one night Mr. Dog popped the question right out "Miss Coon," he says, "Ma'am, also Ma'am, which would you ruther be—a lark flyin' or a dove a settin'?"

Course Miss Nancy she blushed and laughed a little and hid her face behind her bushy tail for a spell. Then she said sorter shy like, "I does love yo' sweet voice, brother dawg—but—I ain't jes' exactly set my mind yit."

Her and Mr. Dog set on a spell, when up comes hopping Mr. Rabbit wid his tail fresh washed and his whiskers shining. He got right down to business and asked Miss Coon to marry him, too.

"Oh Miss Nancy," he says, "Ma'am, also Ma'am, if you'd see me settin' straddle of a mud-cat leadin' a minnow, what would you think?

Ma'am, also Ma'am?" Which is a out and out proposal as everybody knows.

"Youse awful nice, Brother Rabbit and a beautiful dancer, but you cannot sing like Brother Dog. Both you uns come back next week to gimme time for to decide."

They both left arm-in-arm. Finally Mr. Rabbit says to Mr. Dog. "Taint no use in me going back—she ain't gwinter have me. So I mought as well give up. She loves singing, and I ain't got nothing but a squeak."

"Oh, don't talk that a way," says Mr. Dog, tho' he is glad Mr. Rabbit can't sing none.

"Thass all right, Brer Dog. But if I had a sweet voice like you got, I'd have it worked on and make it sweeter."

"How! How! How!" Mr. Dog cried, jumping up and down.

"Leamme fix it for you, like I do for Sister Lark and Sister Mockingbird."

"When? Where?" asked Mr. Dog, all excited. He was figuring that if he could sing just a little better Miss Coon would be bound to have him.

"Just you meet me t'morrer in de huckleberry patch," says the rabbit and off they both goes to bed.

The dog is there on time next day and after a while the rabbit comes loping up.

"Mawnin', Brer Dawg," he say kinder chippy like. "Ready to git yo' voice sweetened?"

"Sholy, sholy, Brer Rabbit. Let's we all hurry about it. I wants tuh serenade Miss Nancy from the piney woods tuh night."

"Well, den, open yo' mouf and poke out yo' tongue," says the rabbit.

No sooner did Mr. Dog poke out his tongue than Mr. Rabbit split it with a knife and ran for all he was worth to a hollow stump and hid hisself.

The dog has been mad at the rabbit ever since.

Anybody who don't believe it happened, just look at the dog's tongue and he can see for himself where the rabbit slit it right up the middle.

Stepped on a tin, mah story ends.

24. Carson McCullers

(1917–1967)

Born Lula Carson Smith, Carson McCullers grew up in Columbus, Georgia, and demonstrated her artistic ability first in music, showing promise as an excellent pianist by the time she was ten years old. But when McCullers was fifteen, she was stricken with rheumatic fever and gave up her music for the less strenuous art of writing. She had always enjoyed reading and writing, imitating nineteenth- and twentieth-century novelists and playwrights as a young girl, particularly enjoying the works of Eugene O'Neill. Her extensive reading was reflected in some now-lost early works, *The Fire of Life,* essentially a debate between Christ and Nietzsche, and *A Reed of Pan,* a play about a musician madly obsessed with jazz.

By the time she graduated from high school, McCullers was ready to devote herself to writing. Though she went to New York to study at the Juilliard School of Music, McCullers also took courses in writing at Columbia University. She published her first story when she was just nineteen. "Wunderkind," which portrays the failure of a musical wonderchild, appeared in *Story* magazine in 1936. Late in that same year, McCullers again fell ill with rheumatic fever, which forced her to return to Columbus. When she married Reeves McCullers in 1937, she was still in ill health but continued writing nevertheless. By the time she was twenty-three McCullers had completed her first book; *The Heart Is a Lonely Hunter* (1940) was an outstanding success that brought her vast critical attention and thrust her into the literary world. During the summer of 1940, McCullers worked on revising her second novel at the Bread Loaf Writers' Conference. The experience of establishing herself among writers of the day was exciting but traumatic for the young woman, and within the next year she had separated from and then divorced her husband.

An artists' cooperative in Brooklyn, one inhabited at times by W. H. Auden, Richard Wright, and Paul and Jane Bowles, provided McCullers her next home. The next few years proved to be McCullers's most productive ones; "A Tree. A Rock. A Cloud." won an O. Henry Award in 1942, and McCullers was awarded several fellowships, including a Guggenheim (1942) and one from the American Academy of Arts and

Letters (1943). "The Ballad of the Sad Cafe" was included in *Best American Stories* in 1944. A good example of McCullers's interest in the grotesque and of her compassion for her characters, the story itself has many of the characteristics of a ballad: the narrator is a balladeer of sorts, and the story is rooted in folk tradition. Two years after the publication of "Ballad of the Sad Cafe," McCullers finished *The Member of the Wedding,* possibly her greatest and best known work.

This period of success could not be sustained, however, for although McCullers remarried Reeves in 1945, she suffered a paralyzing stroke in 1947, and the following year left her husband and suffered from suicidal depression. Her literary accomplishment reached its height in 1950 when *Member of the Wedding,* which she had adapted for the stage, opened in New York. McCullers also was elected to the National Institute of Arts and Letters in 1952. Shortly afterward, she moved to Paris with Reeves, with whom she had been reunited in 1949. But she was to leave him once again, and this time he committed suicide, late in 1953. McCullers continued to write but produced little of exceptional literary value. One of her finest later stories is "The Haunted Boy," first published in *Mademoiselle* in November 1955; it was first collected in *The Ballad of the Sad Cafe: The Novels and Stories of Carson McCullers* (1955). Her health was failing rapidly, and in the late 1950s and early 1960s she suffered a heart attack, cancer, and pneumonia. Until her death from a series of strokes in 1967, McCullers continued to write and lecture as much as she was able.

The Haunted Boy

Hugh looked for his mother at the corner, but she was not in the yard. Sometimes she would be out fooling with the border of spring flowers—the candytuft, the sweet William, the lobelias (she had taught him the names)—but today the green front lawn with the borders of many-colored flowers was empty under the frail sunshine of the mid-April afternoon. Hugh raced up the sidewalk, and John followed him. They finished the front steps with two bounds, and the door slammed after them.

"Mamma!" Hugh called.

It was then, in the unanswering silence as they stood in the empty, wax-floored hall, that Hugh felt there was something wrong. There was no fire in the grate of the sitting room, and since he was used to the flicker of firelight during the cold months, the room on this first warm day seemed strangely naked and cheerless. Hugh shivered. He was glad John was there. The sun shone on a red piece in the flowered rug. Red-bright, red-dark, red-dead—Hugh sickened with a sudden chill remembrance of "the other time." The red darkened to a dizzy black.

"What's the matter, Brown?" John asked. "You look so white."

Hugh shook himself and put his hand to his forehead. "Nothing. Let's go back to the kitchen."

"I can't stay but just a minute," John said. "I'm obligated to sell those tickets. I have to eat and run."

The kitchen, with the fresh checked towels and clean pans, was now the best room in the house. And on the enameled table there was a lemon pie that she had made. Assured by the everyday kitchen and the pie, Hugh stepped back into the hall and raised his face again to call upstairs.

"Mother! Oh, Mamma!"

Again there was no answer.

"My mother made this pie," he said. Quickly, he found a knife and cut into the pie—to dispel the gathering sense of dread.

"Think you ought to cut it, Brown?"

"Sure thing, Laney."

They called each other by their last names this spring, unless they happened to forget. To Hugh it seemed sporty and grown and somehow grand. Hugh liked John better than any other boy at school. John was two years older than Hugh, and compared to him the other boys seemed like a silly crowd of punks. John was the best student in the sophomore class, brainy but not the least bit a teacher's pet, and he was the best athlete too. Hugh was a freshman and didn't have so many friends that first year of high school—he had somehow cut himself off, because he was so afraid.

"Mamma always has me something nice for after school." Hugh put a big piece of pie on a saucer for John—for Laney.

"This pie is certainly super."

"The crust is made of crunched-up graham crackers instead of regular pie dough," Hugh said, "because pie dough is a lot of trouble. We think this graham-cracker pastry is just as good. Naturally, my mother can make regular pie dough if she wants to."

Hugh could not keep still; he walked up and down the kitchen, eating the pie wedge he carried on the palm of his hand. His brown hair was mussed with nervous rakings, and his gentle gold-brown eyes were haunted with pained perplexity. John, who remained seated at the table, sensed Hugh's uneasiness and wrapped one gangling leg around the other.

"I'm really obligated to sell those Glee Club tickets."

"Don't go. You have the whole afternoon." He was afraid of the empty house. He needed John, he needed someone; most of all he needed to hear his mother's voice and know she was in the house with him. "Maybe Mamma is taking a bath," he said. "I'll holler again."

The answer to his third call too was silence.

"I guess your mother must have gone to the movie or gone shopping or something."

"No," Hugh said. "She would have left a note. She always does when she's gone when I come home from school."

"We haven't looked for a note," John said. "Maybe she left it under the door mat or somewhere in the living room."

Hugh was inconsolable. "No. She would have left it right under this pie. She knows I always run first to the kitchen."

"Maybe she had a phone call or thought of something she suddenly wanted to do."

"She *might* have," he said. "I remember she said to Daddy that one of these days she was going to buy herself some new clothes." This flash of hope did not survive its expression. He pushed his hair back and started from the room. "I guess I'd better go upstairs. I ought to go upstairs while you are here."

He stood with his arm around the newel post; the smell of varnished stairs, the sight of the closed white bathroom door at the top revived again "the other time." He clung to the newel post, and his feet would not move to climb the stairs. The red turned again to whirling, sick dark. Hugh sat down. *Stick your head between your legs,* he ordered, remembering Scout first aid.

"Hugh," John called. "Hugh!"

The dizziness clearing, Hugh accepted a fresh chagrin—Laney was calling him by his ordinary first name; he thought he was a sissy about his mother, unworthy of being called by his last name in the grand, sporty way they used before. The dizziness cleared when he returned to the kitchen.

"Brown," said John, and the chagrin disappeared. "Does this establishment have anything pertaining to a cow? A white, fluid liquid. In French they call it *lait.* Here we call it plain old milk."

The stupidity of shock lightened. "Oh, Laney, I am a dope! Please excuse me. I clean forgot." Hugh fetched the milk from the refrigerator and found two glasses. "I didn't think. My mind was on something else."

"I know," John said. After a moment he asked in a calm voice, looking steadily at Hugh's eyes: "Why are you so worried about your mother? Is she sick, Hugh?"

Hugh knew now that the first name was not a slight; it was because John was talking too serious to be sporty. He liked John better than any friend he had ever had. He felt more natural sitting across the kitchen table from John, somehow safer. As he looked into John's gray, peaceful eyes, the balm of affection soothed the dread.

John asked again, still steadily: "Hugh, is your mother sick?"

Hugh could have answered no other boy. He had talked with one about his mother, except his father, and even those intimacies had been rare, oblique. They could approach the subject only when they were occupied with something else, doing carpentry work or the two times they hunted in the woods together—or when they were cooking supper or washing dishes.

"She's not exactly sick," he said, "but Daddy and I have been worried about her. At least, we used to be worried for a while."

John asked: "Is it a kind of heart trouble?"

Hugh's voice was strained. "Did you hear about that fight I had with that slob Clem Roberts? I scraped his slob face on the gravel walk and nearly killed him sure enough. He's still got scars or at least he did have a bandage on for two days. I had to stay in school every afternoon for a week. But I nearly killed him. I would have if Mr. Paxton hadn't come along and dragged me off."

"I heard about it."

"You know why I wanted to kill him?"

For a moment John's eyes flickered away.

Hugh tensed himself; his raw boy hands clutched the table edge; he took a deep, hoarse breath. "That slob was telling everybody that my mother was in Milledgeville. He was spreading it around that my mother was crazy."

"The dirty bastard."

Hugh said in a clear, defeated voice, "My mother *was* in Milledgeville. But that doesn't mean that she was crazy," he added quickly. "In that big State hospital, there are buildings for people who are crazy, and there are other buildings, for people who are just sick. Mamma was sick for a while. Daddy and me discussed it and decided that the hospital in Milledgeville was the place where there were the best doctors and she would get the best care. But she was the furtherest from crazy than anybody in the world. You know Mamma, John." He said again, "I ought to go upstairs."

John said: "I have always thought that your mother is one of the nicest ladies in this town."

"You see, Mamma had a peculiar thing happen, and afterward she was blue."

Confession, the first deep-rooted words, opened the festered secrecy of the boy's heart, and he continued more rapidly, urgent and finding unforeseen relief.

"Last year my mother thought she was going to have a little baby. She talked it over with Daddy and me," he said proudly. "We wanted a girl. I was going to choose the name. We were so tickled. I hunted up all my old toys—my electric train and the tracks . . . I was going to name her Crystal—how does the name strike you for a girl? It reminds me of something bright and dainty."

"Was the little baby born dead?"

Even with John, Hugh's ears turned hot; his cold hands touched them. "No, it was what they call a tumor. That's what happened to my mother. They had to operate at the hospital here." He was embarrassed and his voice was very low. "Then she had something called change of life." The words were terrible to Hugh. "And afterward she was blue. Daddy said it was a shock to her nervous system. It's something that happens to ladies; she was just blue and run-down."

Although there was no red, no red in the kitchen anywhere, Hugh was approaching "the other time."

"One day, she just sort of gave up—one day last fall." Hugh's eyes were wide open and glaring: again he climbed the stairs and opened the bathroom door—he put his hand to his eyes to shut out the memory. "She tried to—hurt herself. I found her when I came in from school."

John reached out and carefully stroked Hugh's sweatered arm.

"Don't worry. A lot of people have to go to hospitals because they are run-down and blue. Could happen to anybody."

"We had to put her in the hospital—the best hospital." The recollection of those long, long months was stained with a dull loneliness, as cruel in its lasting unappeasement as "the other time"—how long had it lasted? In the hospital Mamma could walk around and she always had on shoes.

John said carefully: "This pie is certainly super."

"My mother is a super cook. She cooks things like meat pie and salmon loaf—as well as steaks and hot dogs."

"I hate to eat and run," John said.

Hugh was so frightened of being left alone that he felt the alarm in his own loud heart.

"Don't go," he urged. "Let't talk for a little while."

"Talk about what?"

Hugh could not tell him. Not even John Laney. He could tell no one of the empty house and the horror of the time before. "Do you ever cry?" he asked John. "I don't."

"I do sometimes," John admitted.

"I wish I had known you better when Mother was away. Daddy and me used to go hunting nearly every Saturday. We *lived* on quail and dove. I bet you would have liked that." He added in a lower tone, "On Sunday we went to the hospital."

John said: "It's a kind of delicate proposition selling those tickets. A lot of people don't enjoy the High School Glee Club operettas. Unless they know someone in it personally, they'd rather stay home with a good TV show. A lot of people buy tickets on the basis of being public-spirited."

"We're going to get a television set real soon."

"I couldn't exist without television," John said.

Hugh's voice was apologetic. "Daddy wants to clean up the hospital bills first because as everybody knows sickness is a very expensive proposition. Then we'll get TV."

John lifted his milk glass. "Skoal," he said. "That's a Swedish word you say before you drink. A good-luck word."

"You know so many foreign words and languages."

"Not so many," John said truthfully. "Just 'kaput' and 'adios' and 'skoal' and stuff we learn in French class. That's not much."

"That's *beaucoup,*" said Hugh, and he felt witty and pleased with himself.

Suddenly the stored tension burst into physical activity. Hugh grabbed the basketball out on the porch and rushed into the back yard. He dribbled the ball several times and aimed at the goal his father had put up on his last birthday. When he missed he bounced the ball to John, who had come after him. It was good to be outdoors and the relief of natural play brought Hugh the first line of a poem. "My heart is like a basketball." Usually when a poem came to him he would lie sprawled on the living room floor, studying to hunt rhymes, his tongue working on the side of his mouth. His mother would call him Shelley-Poe when she stepped over him, and sometimes she would put her foot lightly on his behind. His mother always liked his poems; today the second line came quickly, like magic. He said it out loud to John: "'My heart is like a basketball, bouncing with glee down the hall.' How do you like that for the start of a poem?"

"Sounds kind of crazy to me," John said. Then he corrected himself hastily. "I mean it sounds—odd. Odd, I meant."

Hugh realized why John changed the word, and the elation of play and poems left him instantly. He caught the ball and stood with it cradled in his arms. The afternoon was golden and the wisteria vine on the porch was in full, unshattered bloom. The wisteria was like lavender waterfalls. The fresh breeze smelled of sun-warmed flowers. The sunlit sky was blue and cloudless. It was the first warm day of spring.

"I have to shove off," John said.

"No!" Hugh's voice was desperate. "Don't you want another piece of pie? I never heard of anybody eating just one piece of pie."

He steered John into the house and this time he called only out of habit because he always called on coming in. "Mother!" He was cold after the bright, sunny outdoors. He was cold not only because of the weather but because he was so scared.

"My mother has been home a month and every afternoon she's always here when I come home from school. Always, always."

They stood in the kitchen looking at the lemon pie. And to Hugh the cut pie looked somehow—odd. As they stood motionless in the kitchen the silence was creepy and odd too.

"Doesn't this house seem quiet to you?"

"It's because you don't have television. We put on our TV at seven o'clock and it stays on all day and night until we go to bed. Whether anybody's in the living room or not. There're plays and skits and gags going on continually."

"We have a radio, of course, and a vic."

"But that's not the company of a good TV. You won't know when your mother is in the house or not when you get TV."

Hugh didn't answer. Their footsteps sounded hollow in the hall. He felt sick as he stood on the first step with his arm around the newel post. "If you could come upstairs for a minute—"

John's voice was suddenly impatient and loud. "How many times have I told you I'm obligated to sell those tickets. You have to be public-spirited about things like Glee Clubs."

"Just for a second—I have something important to show you upstairs."

John did not ask what it was and Hugh sought desperately to name something important enough to get John upstairs. He said finally: "I'm assembling a hi-fi machine. You have to know a lot about electronics— my father is helping me."

But even when he spoke he knew John did not for a second believe the lie. Who would buy a hi-fi when they didn't have television? He hated John, as you hate people you have to need so badly. He had to say something more and he straightened his shoulders.

"I just want you to know how much I value your friendship. During these past months I had somehow cut myself off from people."

"That's O.K., Brown. You oughtn't to be so sensitive because your mother was—where she was."

John had his hand on the door and Hugh was trembling. "I thought if you could come up for just a minute—"

John looked at him with anxious, puzzled eyes. Then he asked slowly: "Is there something you are scared of upstairs?"

Hugh wanted to tell him everything. But he could not tell what his mother had done that September afternoon. It was too terrible and— odd. It was like something a *patient* would do, and not like his mother at all. Although his eyes were wild with terror and his body trembled he said: "I'm not scared."

"Well, so long. I'm sorry I have to go—but to be obligated is to be obligated."

John closed the front door, and he was alone in the empty house. Nothing could save him now. Even if a whole crowd of boys were listening to TV in the living room, laughing at funny gags and jokes, it would still not help him. He had to go upstairs and find her. He sought courage from the last thing John had said, and repeated the words aloud: "To be obligated is to be obligated." But the words did not give him any of John's thoughtlessness and courage; they were creepy and strange in the silence.

He turned slowly to go upstairs. His heart was not like a basketball but like a fast, jazz drum, beating faster and faster as he climbed the stairs. His feet dragged as though he waded through knee-deep water and he held on to the banisters. The house looked odd, crazy. As he looked down at the ground-floor table with the vase of fresh spring flowers that too looked somehow peculiar. There was a mirror on the second floor and his own face startled him, so crazy did it seem to him. The initial of his high school sweater was backward and wrong in the reflection and his mouth was open like an asylum idiot. He shut his mouth and he looked better. Still the objects he saw—the table downstairs, the sofa upstairs—looked somehow cracked or jarred because of the dread in him, although they were the familiar things of everyday. He fastened his eyes on the closed door at the right of the stairs and the fast, jazz drum beat faster.

He opened the bathroom door and for a moment the dread that had haunted him all that afternoon made him see again the room as he had seen it "the other time." His mother lay on the floor and there was blood everywhere. His mother lay there dead and there was blood everywhere, on her slashed wrist, and a pool of blood had trickled to the bathtub and lay dammed there. Hugh touched the doorframe and steadied himself. Then the room settled and he realized this was not "the other time." The April sunlight brightened the clean white tiles. There was only bathroom brightness and the sunny window. He went to the bedroom and saw the empty bed with the rose-colored spread. The lady things were on the dresser. The room was as it always looked and nothing had happened . . . nothing had happened and he flung himself on the quilted rose bed and cried from relief and a strained, bleak tiredness that had lasted so long. The sobs jerked his whole body and quieted his jazz, fast heart.

Hugh had not cried all those months. He had not cried at "the other time," when he found his mother alone in that empty house with blood everywhere. He had not cried but he made a Scout mistake. He had first lifted his mother's heavy, bloody body before he tried to bandage her. He had not cried when he called his father. He had not cried those few days when they were deciding what to do. He hadn't even cried when the doctor suggested Milledgeville, or when he and his father took her to the hospital in the car—although his father cried on the way home. He had not cried at the meals they made—steak every night for a whole month so that they felt steak was running out of their eyes, their ears; then they had switched to hot dogs, and ate them until hot dogs ran out of their ears, their eyes. They got in ruts of food and were messy about the kitchen, so that it was never nice except the Saturday the cleaning woman came. He did not cry those lonesome afternoons after he had the fight with Clem Roberts and felt the other boys were thinking queer things of his mother. He stayed at home in the messy kitchen, eating fig newtons or chocolate bars. Or he went to see a neighbor's television— Miss Richards, an old maid who saw old-maid shows. He had not cried when his father drank too much so that it took his appetite and Hugh had to eat alone. He had not even cried on those long, waiting Sundays when they went to Milledgeville and he twice saw a lady on a porch without any shoes on and talking to herself. A lady who was a patient and who struck at him with a horror he could not name. He did not cry when at first his mother would say: *Don't punish me by making me stay here. Let me go home.* He had not cried at the terrible words that haunted him—"change of life"—"crazy"—"Milledgeville"—he could not cry all during those long months strained with dullness and want and dread.

He still sobbed on the rose bedspread which was soft and cool against his wet cheeks. He was sobbing so loud that he did not hear the front door open, did not even hear his mother call or the footsteps on the stairs. He still sobbed when his mother touched him and burrowed his face hard in the spread. He even stiffened his legs and kicked his feet.

"Why, Loveyboy," his mother said, calling him a long-ago child name. "What's happened?"

He sobbed even louder, although his mother tried to turn his face to her. He wanted her to worry. He did not turn around until she had finally left the bed, and then he looked at her. She had on a different dress—blue silk it looked like in the pale spring light.

"Darling, what's happened?"

The terror of the afternoon was over, but he could not tell it to his mother. He could not tell her what he had feared, or explain the horror of things that were never there at all—but had once been there.

"Why did you do it?"

"The first warm day I just suddenly decided to buy myself some new clothes."

But he was not talking about clothes; he was thinking about "the other time" and the grudge that had started when he saw the blood and horror and felt *why did she do this to me*. He thought of the grudge against the mother he loved the most in the world. All those last, sad months the anger had bounced against the love with guilt between.

"I bought two dresses and two petticoats. How do you like them?"

"I hate them!" Hugh said angrily. "Your slip is showing."

She turned around twice and the petticoat showed terribly. "It's supposed to show, goofy. It's the style."

"I still don't like it."

"I ate a sandwich at the tearoom with two cups of cocoa and then went to Mendel's. There were so many pretty things I couldn't seem to get away. I bought these two dresses and look, Hugh! The shoes!"

His mother went to the bed and switched on the light so he could see. The shoes were flat-heeled and *blue*—with diamond sparkles on the toes. He did not know how to criticize. "They look more like evening shoes than things you wear on the street."

"I have never owned any colored shoes before. I couldn't resist them."

His mother sort of danced over toward the window, making the petticoat twirl under the new dress. Hugh had stopped crying now, but he was still angry.

"I don't like it because it makes you look like you're trying to seem young, and I bet you are forty years old."

His mother stopped dancing and stood still at the window. Her face was suddenly quiet and sad. "I'll be forty-three years old in June."

He had hurt her and suddenly the anger vanished and there was only love. "Mamma, I shouldn't have said that."

"I realized when I was shopping that I hadn't been in a store for more than a year. Imagine!"

Hugh could not stand the sad quietness and the mother he loved so much. He could not stand his love or his mother's prettiness. He wiped the tears on the sleeve of his sweater and got up from the bed. "I have never seen you so pretty, or a dress and slip so pretty." He crouched down before his mother and touched the bright shoes. "The shoes are really super."

"I thought the minute I laid eyes on them that you would like them." She pulled Hugh up and kissed him on the cheek. "Now I've got lipstick on you."

Hugh quoted a witty remark he had heard before as he scrubbed off the lipstick. "It only shows I'm popular."

"Hugh, why were you crying when I came in? Did something at school upset you?"

"It was only that when I came in and found you gone and no note or anything—"

"I forgot all about a note."

"And all afternoon I felt—John Laney came in but he had to go sell Glee Club tickets. All afternoon I felt—"

"What? What was the matter?"

But he could not tell the mother he loved about the terror and the cause. He said at last: "All afternoon I felt—odd."

Afterward when his father came home he called Hugh to come out into the back yard with him. His father had a worried look—as though he spied a valuable tool Hugh had left outside. But there was no tool and the basketball was put back in its place on the back porch.

"Son," his father said, "there's something I want to tell you."

"Yes, sir?"

"Your mother said that you had been crying this afternoon." His father did not wait for him to explain. "I just want us to have a close understanding with each other. Is there anything about school—or girls—or something that puzzles you? Why were you crying?"

Hugh looked back at the afternoon and already it was far away, distant as a peculiar view seen at the wrong end of a telescope.

"I don't know," he said. "I guess maybe I was somehow nervous."

His father put his arm around his shoulder. "Nobody can be nervous before they are sixteen years old. You have a long way to go."

"I know."

"I have never seen your mother look so well. She looks so gay and pretty, better than she's looked in years. Don't you realize that?"

"The slip—the petticoat is supposed to show. It's a new style."

"Soon it will be summer," his father said. "And we'll go on picnics— the three of us." The words brought an instant vision of glare on the yellow creek and the summer-leaved, adventurous woods. His father added: "I came out here to tell you something else."

"Yes, sir?"

"I just want you to know that I realize how fine you were all that bad time. How fine, how damn fine."

His father was using a swear word as if he were talking to a grown man. His father was not a person to hand out compliments—always he was strict with report cards and tools left around. His father never praised him or used grown words or anything. Hugh felt his face grow hot and he touched it with his cold hands.

"I just wanted to tell you that, Son." He shook Hugh by the shoulder. "You'll be taller than your old man in a year or so." Quickly his father went into the house, leaving Hugh to the sweet and unaccustomed aftermath of praise.

Hugh stood in the darkening yard after the sunset colors faded in the west and the wisteria was dark purple. The kitchen light was on and he saw his mother fixing dinner. He knew that something was finished; the terror was far from him now, also the anger that had bounced with love, the dread and guilt. Although he felt he would never cry again—or at least not until he was sixteen—in the brightness of his tears glistened the safe, lighted kitchen, now that he was no longer a haunted boy, now that he was glad somehow, and not afraid.

25. Flannery O'Connor

(1925–1964)

Flannery O'Connor's childhood was a quiet one in Savannah, Georgia, where she grew up as an only child, reading, writing, and raising chickens. When she was thirteen, her father fell seriously ill and had to give up his work; the family moved to Milledgeville and lived in the house where O'Connor's mother grew up with her fifteen brothers and sisters. O'Connor's father died in 1941, when she was sixteen. After graduating from high school, O'Connor went to Georgia State College for Women where she studied sociology and was a regular contributor to the college literary magazine. She graduated in 1945 and went to the Iowa Writer's Workshop to pursue her literary career. The following year her short story "The Geranium" was published in *Accent* magazine and she won the Rinehart-Iowa prize for an early version of *Wise Blood*.

After receiving her M.F.A. in 1947, O'Connor went to Yaddo, a retreat for writers in New York, where she met Robert Lowell and several other fine writers. She left there in 1948, intending to settle in New York City, but instead went to live with Robert and Sally Fitzgerald in Connecticut; there she finished her first novel, *Wise Blood*. The novel was not published until 1952, however, because her editor at Holt, Rinehart found it too eccentric, so O'Connor was forced to find another publisher. While it is an eccentric novel in a peculiarly southern way, *Wise Blood* is characteristic of O'Connor's writing, demonstrating her use of the southern gothic, her ear for southern speech, and her pervasive concern for the spiritual condition of the country.

At the end of 1950 O'Connor fell extremely ill with lupus, the disease that had killed her father, and she was sick for a year before the disease was under control. Forced to return home, O'Connor went to live with her mother on a dairy farm in Milledgeville where she began raising her peacocks, a symbol that had already come to be associated with her writing. There she continued her writing, also lecturing and working with young writers as she was able. The publication of her *A Good Man Is Hard to Find and Other Stories* (1955) substantially increased O'Connor's critical reputation; "The Life You Save May Be Your Own," first published in *Kenyon Review* (Spring 1953), is from this collection.

The story is typical O'Connor: it is a tale of the grotesque, focusing on deception, violation, and the dubious nature of identity. After the publication of *A Good Man Is Hard to Find and Other Stories,* O'Connor was recognized as a southern writer—all her works except one short story are set in the South—and one who produced extremely original and highly-crafted work.

By the mid-1950s, O'Connor's condition had worsened considerably, but she continued to write. A grant from the Ford Foundation allowed her to finish her second novel, *The Violent Bear It Away,* which was published in 1960. Like Hazel Motes in *Wise Blood,* the protagonist of this novel, Frances Marion Tarwater, struggles against the pull of "the Divine" and is ultimately defeated. Both novels reflect O'Connor's strong Catholic faith, reminiscent of her claim that one should never write a novel about anything but one's gravest concern, and hers was "the conflict between an attraction for the Holy and the disbelief in it that we breathe in with the air of the times." In 1963 O'Connor's health rapidly declined, and she died in August of 1964. O'Connor's letters and prose writing have also been published in *The Habit of Being* (1979) and *Mystery and Manners: Occasional Prose* (1969).

The Life You Save May Be Your Own

The old woman and her daughter were sitting on their porch when Mr. Shiftlet came up their road for the first time. The old woman slid to the edge of her chair and leaned forward, shading her eyes from the piercing sunset with her hand. The daughter could not see far in front of her and continued to play with her fingers. Although the old woman lived in this desolate spot with only her daughter and she had never seen Mr. Shiftlet before, she could tell, even from a distance, that he was a tramp and no one to be afraid of. His left coat sleeve was folded up to show there was only half an arm in it and his gaunt figure listed slightly to the side as if the breeze were pushing him. He had on a black town suit and a brown felt hat that was turned up in the front and down in the back and he carried a tin tool box by a handle. He came on, at an amble, up her road, his face turned toward the sun which appeared to be balancing itself on the peak of a small mountain.

The old woman didn't change her position until he was almost into her yard; then she rose with one hand fisted on her hip. The daughter, a large girl in a short blue organdy dress, saw him all at once and jumped up and began to stamp and point and make excited speechless sounds.

Mr. Shiftlet stopped just inside the yard and set his box on the ground and tipped his hat at her as if she were not in the least afflicted; then he turned toward the old woman and swung the hat all the way off. He had long black slick hair that hung flat from a part in the middle to beyond the tips of his ears on either side. His face descended in forehead for more than half its length and ended suddenly with his features just balanced over a jutting steel-trap jaw. He seemed to be a young man but he had a look of composed dissatisfaction as if he understood life thoroughly.

"Good evening," the old woman said. She was about the size of a cedar fence post and she had a man's gray hat pulled down low over her head.

The tramp stood looking at her and didn't answer. He turned his back and faced the sunset. He swung both his whole and his short arm up slowly so that they indicated an expanse of sky and his figure formed a crooked cross. The old woman watched him with her arms folded across her chest as if she were the owner of the sun, and the daughter watched, her head thrust forward and her fat helpless hands hanging at the wrists. She had long pink-gold hair and eyes as blue as a peacock's neck.

He held the pose for almost fifty seconds and then he picked up his box and came on to the porch and dropped down on the bottom step. "Lady," he said in a firm nasal voice, "I'd give a fortune to live where I could see me a sun do that every evening."

"Does it every evening," the old woman said and sat back down. The daughter sat down too and watched him with a cautious sly look as if he were a bird that had come up very close. He leaned to one side, rooting in his pants pocket, and in a second he brought out a package of chewing gum and offered her a piece. She took it and unpeeled it and began to chew without taking her eyes off him. He offered the old woman a piece but she only raised her upper lip to indicate she had no teeth.

Mr. Shiftlet's pale sharp glance had already passed over everything in the yard—the pump near the corner of the house and the big fig tree that three or four chickens were preparing to roost in—and had moved to a shed where he saw the square rusted back of an automobile. "You ladies drive?" he asked.

"That car ain't run in fifteen year," the old woman said. "The day my husband died, it quit running."

"Nothing is like it used to be, lady," he said. "The world is almost rotten."

"That's right," the old woman said. "You from around here?"

"Name Tom T. Shiftlet," he murmured, looking at the tires.

"I'm pleased to meet you," the old woman said. "Name Lucynell Crater and daughter Lucynell Crater. What you doing around here, Mr. Shiftlet?"

He judged the car to be about a 1928 or '29 Ford. "Lady," he said, and turned and gave her his full attention, "lemme tell you something. There's one of these doctors in Atlanta that's taken a knife and cut the human heart—the human heart," he repeated, leaning forward, "out of a man's chest and held it in his hand," and he held his hand out, palm up, as if it were slightly weighted with the human heart, "and studied it like it was a day-old chicken, and lady," he said, allowing a long significant pause in which his head slid forward and his clay-colored eyes brightened, "he don't know no more about it than you or me."

"That's right," the old woman said.

"Why, if he was to take that knife and cut into every corner of it, he still wouldn't know no more than you or me. What you want to bet?"

"Nothing," the old woman said wisely. "Where you come from, Mr. Shiftlet?"

He didn't answer. He reached into his pocket and brought out a sack of tobacco and a package of cigarette papers and rolled himself a cigarette, expertly with one hand, and attached it in a hanging position to his upper lip. Then he took a box of wooden matches from his pocket and struck one on his shoe. He held the burning match as if he were studying the mystery of flame while it traveled dangerously toward his skin. The daughter began to make loud noises and to point to his hand and shake her finger at him, but when the flame was just before touching him, he leaned down with his hand cupped over it as if he were going to set fire to his nose and lit the cigarette.

He flipped away the dead match and blew a stream of gray into the evening. A sly look came over his face. "Lady," he said, "nowadays, people'll do anything anyways. I can tell you my name is Tom T. Shiftlet and I come from Tarwater, Tennessee, but you never have seen me before: how you know I ain't lying? How you know my name ain't Aaron Sparks, lady, and I come from Singleberry, Georgia, or how you know it's not George Speeds and I come from Lucy, Alabama, or how you know I ain't Thompson Bright from Toolafalls, Mississippi?"

"I don't know nothing about you," the old woman muttered, irked.

"Lady," he said, "people don't care how they lie. Maybe the best I can tell you is, I'm a man; but listen lady," he said and paused and made his tone more ominous still, "what is a man?"

The old woman began to gum a seed. "What you carry in that tin box, Mr. Shiftlet?" she asked.

"Tools," he said, put back. "I'm a carpenter."

"Well, if you come out here to work, I'll be able to feed you and give you a place to sleep but I can't pay. I'll tell you that before you begin," she said.

There was no answer at once and no particular expression on his face. He leaned back against the two-by-four that helped support the porch roof. "Lady," he said slowly, "there's some men that some things mean more to them than money." The old woman rocked without comment and the daughter watched the trigger that moved up and down in his neck. He told the old woman then that all most people were interested in was money, but he asked what a man was made for. He asked her if a man was made for money, or what. He asked her what she thought she was made for but she didn't answer, she only sat rocking and wondered if a one-armed man could put a new roof on her garden house. He asked a lot of questions that she didn't answer. He told her that he was twenty-eight years old and had lived a varied life. He had been a gospel singer, a foreman on the railroad, an assistant in an undertaking parlor, and he had come over the radio for three months with Uncle Roy and his Red Creek Wranglers. He said he had fought and bled in the Arm Service of his country and visited every foreign land and that everywhere he had seen people that didn't care if they did a thing one way or another. He said he hadn't been raised thataway.

A fat yellow moon appeared in the branches of the fig tree as if it were going to roost there with the chickens. He said that a man had to escape to the country to see the world whole and that he wished he lived in a desolate place like this where he could see the sun go down every evening like God made it to do.

"Are you married or are you single?" the old woman asked.

There was a long silence. "Lady," he asked finally, "where would you find you an innocent woman today? I wouldn't have any of this trash I could just pick up."

The daughter was leaning very far down, hanging her head almost between her knees, watching him through a triangular door she had made in her overturned hair; and she suddenly fell in a heap on the floor and began to whimper. Mr. Shiftlet straightened her out and helped her get back in the chair.

"Is she your baby girl?" he asked.

"My only," the old woman said, "and she's the sweetest girl in the world. I wouldn't give her up for nothing on earth. She's smart too. She can sweep the floor, cook, wash, feed the chickens, and hoe. I wouldn't give her up for a casket of jewels."

"No," he said kindly, "don't ever let any man take her away from you."

"Any man come after her," the old woman said, "I'll have to stay around the place."

Mr. Shiftlet's eye in the darkness was focused on a part of the automobile bumper that glittered in the distance. "Lady," he said, jerking his short arm up as if he could point with it to her house and yard and pump, "there ain't a broken thing on this plantation that I couldn't fix for you, one-arm jackleg or not. I'm a man," he said with a sullen dignity, "even if I ain't a whole one. I got," he said, tapping his knuckles on the floor to emphasize the immensity of what he was going to say, "a moral intelligence!" and his face pierced out of the darkness into a shaft of doorlight and he stared at her as if he were astonished himself at this impossible truth.

The old woman was not impressed with the phrase. "I told you you could hang around and work for food," she said, "if you don't mind sleeping in that car yonder."

"Why listen, Lady," he said with a grin of delight, "the monks of old slept in their coffins!"

"They wasn't as advanced as we are," the old woman said.

The next morning he began on the roof of the garden house while Lucynell, the daughter, sat on a rock and watched him work. He had not been around a week before the change he had made in the place was apparent. He had patched the front and back steps, built a new hog pen, restored a fence, and taught Lucynell, who was completely deaf and had never said a word in her life, to say the word "bird." The big rosy-faced girl followed him everywhere, saying "Burrttddt ddbirrrttdt," and clapping her hands. The old woman watched from a distance, secretly pleased. She was ravenous for a son-in-law.

Mr. Shiftlet slept on the hard narrow back seat of the car with his feet out the side window. He had his razor and a can of water on a crate that served him as a bedside table and he put up a piece of mirror against the back glass and kept his coat neatly on a hanger that he hung over one of the windows.

In the evenings he sat on the steps and talked while the old woman and Lucynell rocked violently in their chairs on either side of him. The old woman's three mountains were black against the dark blue sky and were visited off and on by various planets and by the moon after it had left the chickens. Mr. Shiftlet pointed out that the reason he had improved this plantation was because he had taken a personal interest in it. He said he was even going to make the automobile run.

He had raised the hood and studied the mechanism and he said he could tell that the car had been built in the days when cars were really built. You take now, he said, one man puts in one bolt and another man puts in another bolt and another man puts in another bolt so that it's a man for a bolt. That's why you have to pay so much for a car: you're paying all those men. Now if you didn't have to pay but one man, you could get you a cheaper car and one that had had a personal interest taken in it, and it would be a better car. The old woman agreed with him that this was so.

Mr. Shiftlet said that the trouble with the world was that nobody cared, or stopped and took any trouble. He said he never would have been able to teach Lucynell to say a word if he hadn't cared and stopped long enough.

"Teach her to say something else," the old woman said.

"What you want her to say next?" Mr. Shiftlet asked.

The old woman's smile was broad and toothless and suggestive. "Teach her to say 'sugarpie,'" she said.

Mr. Shiftlet already knew what was on her mind.

The next day he began to tinker with the automobile and that evening he told her that if she would buy a fan belt, he would be able to make the car run.

The old woman said she would give him the money. "You see that girl yonder?" she asked, pointing to Lucynell who was sitting on the floor a foot away, watching him, her eyes blue even in the dark. "If it was ever a man wanted to take her away, I would say, 'No man on earth is going to take that sweet girl of mine away from me!' but if he was to say, 'Lady, I don't want to take her away, I want her right here,' I would say, 'Mister, I don't blame you none. I wouldn't pass up a chance to live in a permanent place and get the sweetest girl in the world myself. You ain't no fool,' I would say."

"How old is she?" Mr. Shiftlet asked casually.

"Fifteen, sixteen," the old woman said. The girl was nearly thirty but because of her innocence it was impossible to guess.

"It would be a good idea to paint it too," Mr. Shiftlet remarked. "You don't want it to rust out."

"We'll see about that later," the old woman said.

The next day he walked into town and returned with the parts he needed and a can of gasoline. Late in the afternoon, terrible noises issued from the shed and the old woman rushed out of the house, thinking Lucynell was somewhere having a fit. Lucynell was sitting on a chicken crate, stamping her feet and screaming, "Burrddttt! bddurrddtttt!" but her fuss was drowned out by the car. With a volley of blasts it emerged from the shed, moving in a fierce and stately way. Mr.

Shiftlet was in the driver's seat, sitting very erect. He had an expression of serious modesty on his face as if he had just raised the dead.

That night, rocking on the porch, the old woman began her business at once. "You want you an innocent woman, don't you?" she asked sympathetically. "You don't want none of this trash."

"No'm, I don't," Mr. Shiftlet said.

"One that can't talk," she continued, "can't sass you back or use foul language. That's the kind for you to have. Right there," and she pointed to Lucynell sitting cross-legged in her chair, holding both feet in her hands.

"That's right," he admitted. "She wouldn't give me any trouble."

"Saturday," the old woman said, "you and her and me can drive into town and get married."

Mr. Shiftlet eased his position on the steps.

"I can't get married right now," he said. "Everything you want to do takes money and I ain't got any."

"What you need with money?" she asked.

"It takes money," he said. "Some people'll do anything anyhow these days, but the way I think, I wouldn't marry no woman that I couldn't take on a trip like she was somebody. I mean take her to a hotel and treat her. I wouldn't marry the Duchesser Windsor," he said firmly, "unless I could take her to a hotel and give her something good to eat.

"I was raised thataway and there ain't a thing I can do about it. My old mother taught me how to do."

"Lucynell don't even know what a hotel is," the old woman muttered. "Listen here, Mr. Shiftlet," she said, sliding forward in her chair, "you'd be getting a permanent house and a deep well and the most innocent girl in the world. You don't need no money. Lemme tell you something: there ain't any place in the world for a poor disabled friendless drifting man."

The ugly words settled in Mr. Shiftlet's head like a group of buzzards in the top of a tree. He didn't answer at once. He rolled himself a cigarette and lit it and then he said in an even voice, "Lady, a man is divided into two parts, body and spirit."

The old woman clamped her gums together.

"A body and a spirit," he repeated. "The body, lady, is like a house: it don't go anywhere; but the spirit, lady, is like a automobile: always on the move, always . . ."

"Listen, Mr. Shiftlet," she said, "my well never goes dry and my house is always warm in the winter and there's no mortgage on a thing about this place. You can go to the courthouse and see for yourself. And yonder under that shed is a fine automobile." She laid the bait carefully. "You can have it painted by Saturday. I'll pay for the paint."

In the darkness, Mr. Shiftlet's smile stretched like a weary snake waking up by a fire. After a second he recalled himself and said, "I'm only saying a man's spirit means more to him than anything else. I would have to take my wife off for the week end without no regards at all for cost. I got to follow where my spirit says to go."

"I'll give you fifteen dollars for a week-end trip," the old woman said in a crabbed voice. "That's the best I can do."

"That wouldn't hardly pay for more than the gas and the hotel," he said. "It wouldn't feed her."

"Seventeen-fifty," the old woman said. "That's all I got so it isn't any use you trying to milk me. You can take a lunch."

Mr. Shiftlet was deeply hurt by the word "milk." He didn't doubt that she had more money sewed up in her mattress but he had already told her he was not interested in her money. "I'll make that do," he said and rose and walked off without treating with her further.

On Saturday the three of them drove into town in the car that the paint had barely dried on and Mr. Shiftlet and Lucynell were married in the Ordinary's office while the old woman witnessed. As they came out of the courthouse, Mr. Shiftlet began twisting his neck in his collar. He looked morose and bitter as if he had been insulted while someone held him. "That didn't satisfy me none," he said. "That was just something a woman in an office did, nothing but paper work and blood tests. What do they know about my blood? If they was to take my heart and cut it out," he said, "they wouldn't know a thing about me. It didn't satisfy me at all."

"It satisfied the law," the old woman said sharply.

"The law," Mr. Shiftlet said and spit. "It's the law that don't satisfy me."

He had painted the car dark green with a yellow band around it just under the windows. The three of them climbed in the front seat and the old woman said, "Don't Lucynell look pretty? Looks like a baby doll." Lucynell was dressed up in a white dress that her mother had uprooted from a trunk and there was a Panama hat on her head with a bunch of red wooden cherries on the brim. Every now and then her placid expression was changed by a sly isolated little thought like a shoot of green in the desert. "You got a prize!" the old woman said.

Mr. Shiftlet didn't even look at her.

They drove back to the house to let the old woman off and pick up the lunch. When they were ready to leave, she stood staring in the window of the car, with her fingers clenched around the glass. Tears began to seep sideways out of her eyes and run along the dirty creases in her face. "I ain't ever been parted with her for two days before," she said.

Mr. Shiftlet started the motor.

"And I wouldn't let no man have her but you because I seen you would do right. Good-by, Sugarbaby," she said, clutching at the sleeve of the white dress. Lucynell looked straight at her and didn't seem to see her there at all. Mr. Shiftlet eased the car forward so that she had to move her hands.

The early afternoon was clear and open and surrounded by pale blue sky. Although the car would go only thirty miles an hour, Mr. Shiftlet imagined a terrific climb and dip and swerve that went entirely to his head so that he forgot his morning bitterness. He had always wanted an automobile but he had never been able to afford one before. He drove very fast because he wanted to make Mobile by nightfall.

Occasionally he stopped his thoughts long enough to look at Lucynell in the seat beside him. She had eaten the lunch as soon as they were out of the yard and now she was pulling the cherries off the hat one by one and throwing them out the window. He became depressed in spite of the car. He had driven about a hundred miles when he decided that she must be hungry again and at the next small town they came to, he stopped in front of an aluminum-painted eating place called The Hot Spot and took her in and ordered her a plate of ham and grits. The ride had made her sleepy and as soon as she got up on the stool, she rested her head on the counter and shut her eyes. There was no one in The Hot Spot but Mr. Shiftlet and the boy behind the counter, a pale youth with a greasy rag hung over his shoulder. Before he could dish up the food, she was snoring gently.

"Give it to her when she wakes up," Mr. Shiftlet said. "I'll pay for it now."

The boy bent over her and stared at the long pink-gold hair and the half-shut sleeping eyes. Then he looked up and stared at Mr. Shiftlet. "She looks like an angel of Gawd," he murmured.

"Hitch-hiker," Mr. Shiftlet explained. "I can't wait. I got to make Tuscaloosa."

The boy bent over again and very carefully touched his finger to a strand of the golden hair and Mr. Shiftlet left.

He was more depressed than ever as he drove on by himself. The late afternoon had grown hot and sultry and the country had flattened out. Deep in the sky a storm was preparing very slowly and without thunder as if it meant to drain every drop of air from the earth before it broke.

There were times when Mr. Shiftlet preferred not to be alone. He felt too that a man with a car had a responsibility to others and he kept his eye out for a hitch-hiker. Occasionally he saw a sign that warned: "Drive carefully. The life you save may be your own."

The narrow road dropped off on either side into dry fields and here and there a shack or a filling station stood in a clearing. The sun began to set directly in front of the automobile. It was a reddening ball that through his windshield was slightly flat on the bottom and top. He saw a boy in overalls and a gray hat standing on the edge of the road and he slowed the car down and stopped in front of him. The boy didn't have his hand raised to thumb the ride, he was only standing there, but he had a small cardboard suitcase and his hat was set on his head in a way to indicate that he had left somewhere for good. "Son," Mr. Shiftlet said, "I see you want a ride."

The boy didn't say he did or he didn't but he opened the door of the car and got in, and Mr. Shiftlet started driving again. The child held the suitcase on his lap and folded his arms on top of it. He turned his head and looked out the window away from Mr. Shiftlet. Mr. Shiftlet felt oppressed. "Son," he said after a minute, "I got the best old mother in the world so I reckon you only got the second best."

The boy gave him a quick dark glance and then turned his face back out the window.

"It's nothing so sweet," Mr. Shiftlet continued, "as a boy's mother. She taught him his first prayers at her knee, she give him love when no other would, she told him what was right and what wasn't, and she seen that he done the right thing. Son," he said, "I never rued a day in my life like the one I rued when I left that old mother of mine."

The boy shifted in his seat but he didn't look at Mr. Shiftlet. He unfolded his arms and put one hand on the door handle.

"My mother was a angel of Gawd," Mr. Shiftlet said in a very strained voice. "He took her from heaven and giver to me and I left her." His eyes were instantly clouded over with a mist of tears. The car was barely moving.

The boy turned angrily in the seat. "You go to the devil!" he cried. "My old woman is a flea bag and yours is a stinking pole cat!" and with that he flung the door open and jumped out with his suitcase into the ditch.

Mr. Shiftlet was so shocked that for about a hundred feet he drove along slowly with the door still open. A cloud, the exact color of the boy's hat and shaped like a turnip, had descended over the sun, and another, worse looking, crouched behind the car. Mr. Shiftlet felt that the rottenness of the world was about to engulf him. He raised his arm and let it fall again to his breast. "Oh Lord!" he prayed. "Break forth and wash the slime from this earth!"

The turnip continued slowly to descend. After a few minutes there was a guffawing peal of thunder from behind and fantastic raindrops, like tin-can tops, crashed over the rear of Mr. Shiftlet's car. Very quickly he stepped on the gas and with his stump sticking out the window he raced the galloping shower into Mobile.

26. Eudora Welty

(1909–)

As a young girl born and raised in Jackson, Mississippi, Eudora Welty was interested in both writing and art. While attending Mississippi State College for Women, she helped establish a literary magazine and began experimenting with writing. After completing her B.A. at the University of Wisconsin in 1929, she studied in the school of business at Columbia University but returned home when her father died in 1931. Back in Mississippi, she worked for newspapers and for a local radio station. While doing publicity work for the WPA, Welty traveled all over the state, taking pictures wherever she went. In 1936 these photographs were displayed at a gallery in New York City, and they were recently collected and published as *Photographs* (1989).

Though Welty had always been interested in writing, she was not able to devote herself to it until returning home to Mississippi. Her first published story, "Death of a Travelling Salesman" (1936), was recognized as an excellent piece of literature; in 1941 "A Worn Path" won second place in the O. Henry Awards, and she published her first collection of stories, *A Curtain of Green and Other Stories*. The collection contains some of her finest stories, including "Why I Live at the P.O." Welty quickly established herself as a writer of merit, and in the following year she received a Guggenheim Fellowship and a first prize in the O. Henry awards for her first novel, *The Robber Bridegroom*. She was the first to win three O. Henry Awards. Her third was in 1943 for "Livvie is Back" (*Atlantic Monthly* [November 1943]); it was later retitled "Livvie" and is part of the collection *The Wide Net and Other Stories* (1943).

After Welty worked for the *New York Times Book Review* in 1944, she spent the next several years writing, lecturing, and giving readings, as well as receiving numerous awards. Her next works of fiction, *The Golden Apples* (1949) and *The Bride of Innisfallen* (1955), were not as popular, though they contain several fine pieces. *Delta Wedding* (1946) is one of her best-loved novels, and *The Ponder Heart* (1954) was so successful as a masterpiece of southern humor that it was adapted for the stage and performed on Broadway. In 1952 Welty was elected to the National Institute of Arts and Letters, and in that same decade she was awarded honorary degrees from the University of Wisconsin and Smith College.

Welty did very little writing for the next fifteen years, but then came back with several additional works of varying form. *The Optimist's Daughter* (1972), her most recent novel, won the Pulitzer Prize in 1973. *One Time, One Place* (1971) is a collection of photographs she took during the thirties, and her essays and book reviews are compiled in *The Eye of the Story* (1978). *One Writer's Beginnings* (1984) is a short autobiographical work covering the early years of her life and writing career. Most recently, her book reviews have been collected in *A Writer's Eye* (1994).

In 1986 the Jackson Public Library was renamed in honor of Welty. She continues to live in Jackson, occasionally lecturing and reading her work. Welty will always be known for her finely crafted details, her mastery of southern dialogue, and her ironic sense of humor.

Livvie

Solomon carried Livvie twenty-one miles away from her home when he married her. He carried her away up on the Old Natchez Trace into the deep country to live in his house. She was sixteen—an only girl, then. Once people said he thought nobody would ever come along there. He told her himself that it had been a long time, and a day she did not know about, since that road was a traveled road with *people* coming and going. He was good to her, but he kept her in the house. She had not thought that she could not get back. Where she came from, people said an old man did not want anybody in the world to ever find his wife, for fear they would steal her back from him. Solomon asked her before he took her, "Would she be happy?"—very dignified, for he was a colored man that owned his land and had it written down in the courthouse; and she said, "Yes, sir," since he was an old man and she was young and just listened and answered. He asked her, if she was choosing winter, would she pine for spring, and she said, "No indeed." Whatever she said, always, was because he was an old man . . . while nine years went by. All the time, he got old, and he got so old he gave out. At last he slept the whole day in bed, and she was young still.

It was a nice house, inside and outside both. In the first place, it had three rooms. The front room was papered in holly paper, with green palmettos from the swamp spaced at careful intervals over the walls. There was fresh newspaper cut with fancy borders on the mantel-shelf, on which were propped photographs of old or very young men printed in faint yellow—Solomon's people. Solomon had a houseful of furniture.

There was a double settee, a tall scrolled rocker and an organ in the front room, all around a three-legged table with a pink marble top, on which was set a lamp with three gold feet, besides a jelly glass with pretty hen feathers in it. Behind the front room, the other room had the bright iron bed with the polished knobs like a throne, in which Solomon slept all day. There were snow-white curtains of wiry lace at the window, and a lace bed-spread belonged on the bed. But what old Solomon slept so sound under was a big feather-stitched piece-quilt in the pattern "Trip Around the World," which had twenty-one different colors, four hundred and forty pieces, and a thousand yards of thread, and that was what Solomon's mother made in her life and old age. There was a table holding the Bible, and a trunk with a key. On the wall were two calendars, and a diploma from somewhere in Solomon's family, and under that Livvie's one possession was nailed, a picture of the little white baby of the family she worked for, back in Natchez before she was married. Going through that room and on to the kitchen, there was a big wood stove and a big round table always with a wet top and with the knives and forks in one jelly glass and the spoons in another, and a cut-glass vinegar bottle between, and going out from those, many shallow dishes of pickled peaches, fig preserves, watermelon pickles and blackberry jam always sitting there. The churn sat in the sun, the doors of the safe were always both shut, and there were four baited mouse-traps in the kitchen, one in every corner.

The outside of Solomon's house looked nice. It was not painted, but across the porch was an even balance. On each side there was one easy chair with high springs, looking out, and a fern basket hanging over it from the ceiling, and a dishpan of zinnia seedlings growing at its foot on the floor. By the door was a plow-wheel, just a pretty iron circle, nailed up on one wall and a square mirror on the other, a turquoise-blue comb stuck up in the frame, with the wash stand beneath it. On the door was a wooden knob with a pearl in the end, and Solomon's black hat hung on that, if he was in the house.

Out front was a clean dirt yard with every vestige of grass patiently uprooted and the ground scarred in deep whorls from the strike of Livvie's broom. Rose bushes with tiny blood-red roses blooming every month grew in threes on either side of the steps. On one side was a peach tree, on the other a pomegranate. Then coming around up the path from the deep cut of the Natchez Trace below was a line of bare crape-myrtle trees with every branch of them ending in a colored bottle, green or blue. There was no word that fell from Solomon's lips to say what they were for, but Livvie knew that there could be a spell put in trees, and she was familiar from the time she was born with the way bottle trees kept evil spirits from coming into the house—by luring them inside the colored bottles, where they cannot get out again. Solomon had made the bottle trees with his own hands over the nine years, in labor amounting to about a tree a year, and without a sign that he had any uneasiness in his heart, for he took as much pride in his precautions against spirits coming in the house as he took in the house, and sometimes in the sun the bottle trees looked prettier than the house did.

It was a nice house. It was in a place where the days would go by and surprise anyone that they were over. The lamplight and the firelight would shine out the door after dark, over the still and breathing country, lighting the roses and the bottle trees, and all was quiet there.

But there was nobody, nobody at all, not even a white person. And if there had been anybody, Solomon would not have let Livvie look at them, just as he would not let her look at a field hand, or a field hand look at her. There was no house near, except for the cabins of the tenants that were forbidden to her, and there was no house as far as she had been, stealing away down the still, deep Trace. She felt as if she waded a river when she went, for the dead leaves on the ground reached as high as her knees, and when she was all scratched and bleeding she said it was not like a road that went anywhere. One day, climbing up the high bank, she had found a graveyard without a church, with ribbon-grass growing about the foot of an angel (she had climbed up because she thought she saw angel wings), and in the sun, trees shining like burning flames through the great caterpillar nets which enclosed them. Scarey thistles stood looking like the prophets in the Bible in Solomon's house. Indian paint brushes grew over her head, and the mourning dove made the only sound in the world. Oh for a stirring of the leaves, and a breaking of the nets! But not by a ghost, prayed Livvie, jumping down the bank. After Solomon took to his bed, she never went out, except one more time.

Livvie knew she made a nice girl to wait on anybody. She fixed things to eat on a tray like a surprise. She could keep from singing when she ironed, and to sit by a bed and fan away the flies, she could be so still she could not hear herself breathe. She could clean up the house and never drop a thing, and wash the dishes without a sound, and she would step outside to churn, for churning sounded too sad to her, like sobbing, and if it made her home-sick and not Solomon, she did not think of that.

But Solomon scarcely opened his eyes to see her, and scarcely tasted his food. He was not sick or paralyzed or in any pain that he mentioned, but he was surely wearing out in the body, and no matter what nice hot thing Livvie would bring him to taste, he would only look at it now, as if he were past seeing how he could add anything more to himself. Before she could beg him, he would go fast asleep. She could not surprise him any more, if he would not taste, and she was afraid that he was never in the world going to taste another thing she brought him—and so how could he last?

But one morning it was breakfast time and she cooked his eggs and grits, carried them in on a tray, and called his name. He was sound asleep. He lay in a dignified way with his watch beside him, on his back in the middle of the bed. One hand drew the quilt up high, though it was the first day of spring. Through the white lace curtains a little puffy wind was blowing as if it came from round cheeks. All night the frogs had sung out in the swamp, like a commotion in the room, and he had not stirred, though she lay wide awake and saying "Shh, frogs!" for fear he would mind them.

He looked as if he would like to sleep a little longer, and so she put back the tray and waited a little. When she tiptoed and stayed so quiet, she surrounded herself with a little reverie, and sometimes it seemed to her when she was so stealthy that the quiet she kept was for a sleeping baby, and that she had a baby and was its mother. When she stood at Solomon's bed and looked down at him, she would be thinking, "He sleeps so well," and she would hate to wake him up. And in some other way, too, she was afraid to wake him up because even in his sleep he seemed to be such a strict man.

Of course, nailed to the wall over the bed—only she would forget who it was—there was a picture of him when he was young. Then he had a fan of hair over his forehead like a king's crown. Now his hair lay down on his head, the spring had gone out of it. Solomon had a lightish face, with eyebrows scattered but rugged, the way privet grows, strong eyes, with second sight, a strict mouth, and a little gold smile. This was the way he looked in his clothes, but in bed in the daytime he looked like a different and smaller man, even when he was wide awake, and holding the Bible. He looked like somebody kin to himself. And then sometimes when he lay in sleep and she stood fanning the flies away, and the light came in, his face was like new, so smooth and clear that it was like a glass of jelly held to the window, and she could almost look through his forehead and see what he thought.

She fanned him and at length he opened his eyes and spoke her name, but he would not taste the nice eggs she had kept warm under a pan.

Back in the kitchen she ate heartily, his breakfast and hers, and looked out the open door at what went on. The whole day, and the whole night before, she had felt the stir of spring close to her. It was as present in the house as a young man would be. The moon was in the last quarter and outside they were turning the sod and planting peas and beans. Up and down the red fields, over which smoke from the brush-burning hung showing like a little skirt of sky, a white horse and a white mule pulled the plow. At intervals hoarse shouts came through the air and roused her as if she dozed neglectfully in the shade, and they were telling her, "Jump up!" She could see how over each ribbon of field were moving men and girls, on foot and mounted on mules, with hats set on their heads and bright with tall hoes and forks as if they carried streamers on them and were going to some place on a journey—and how as if at a signal now and then they would all start at once shouting, hollering, cajoling, calling and answering back, running, being leaped on and breaking away, flinging to earth with a shout and lying motionless in the trance of twelve o'clock. The old women came out of the cabins and brought them the food they had ready for them, and then all worked together, spread evenly out. The little children came too, like a bouncing stream overflowing the fields, and set upon the men, the women, the dogs, the rushing birds, and the wave-like rows of earth, their little voices almost too high to be heard. In the middle distance like some white and gold towers were the haystacks, with black cows coming around to eat their edges. High above everything, the wheel of fields, house, and cabins, and the deep road surrounding like a moat to keep them in, was the turning sky, blue with long, far-flung white mare's-tail clouds, serene and still as high flames. And sound asleep while all this went around him that was his, Solomon was like a little still spot in the middle.

Even in the house the earth was sweet to breathe. Solomon had never let Livvie go any farther than the chicken house and the well. But what if she would walk now into the heart of the fields and take a hoe and work until she fell stretched out and drenched with her efforts, like other girls, and laid her cheek against the laid-open earth, and shamed the old man with her humbleness and delight? To shame him! A cruel wish could come in uninvited and so fast while she looked out the back door. She washed the dishes and scrubbed the table. She could hear the cries of the little lambs. Her mother, that she had not seen since her wedding day, had said one time, "I rather a man be anything, than a woman be mean."

So all morning she kept tasting the chicken broth on the stove, and when it was right she poured off a nice cup-ful. She carried it in to Solomon, and there he lay having a dream. Now what did he dream about? For she saw him sigh gently as if not to disturb some whole thing he held round in his mind, like a fresh egg. So even an old man dreamed about something pretty. Did he dream of her, while his eyes were shut and sunken, and his small hand with the wedding ring curled close in sleep around the quilt? He might be dreaming of what time it was, for even through his sleep he kept track of it like a clock, and knew how much of it went by, and waked up knowing where the hands were even before he consulted the silver watch that he never let go. He would sleep with the watch in his palm, and even holding it to his cheek like a child that loves a plaything. Or he might dream of journeys and travels on a steamboat to Natchez. Yet she thought he dreamed of her; but even while she scrutinized him, the rods of the foot of the bed seemed to rise up like a rail fence between them, and she could see that people never could be sure of anything as long as one of them was asleep and the other awake. To look at him dreaming of her when he might be going to die frightened her a little, as if he might carry her with him that way, and she wanted to run out of the room. She took hold of the bed and held on, and Solomon opened his eyes and called her name, but he did not want anything. He would not taste the good broth.

Just a little after that, as she was taking up the ashes in the front room for the last time in the year, she heard a sound. It was somebody coming. She pulled the curtains together and looked through the slit.

Coming up the path under the bottle trees was a white lady. At first she looked young, but then she looked old. Marvelous to see, a little car stood steaming like a kettle out in the field-track—it had come without a road.

Livvie stood listening to the long, repeated knockings at the door, and after a while she opened it just a little. The lady came in through the crack, though she was more than middle-sized and wore a big hat.

"My name is Miss Baby Marie," she said.

Livvie gazed respectfully at the lady and at the little suitcase she was holding close to her by the handle until the proper moment. The lady's eyes were running over the room, from palmetto to palmetto, but she was saying, "I live at home . . . out from Natchez . . . and get out and show these pretty cosmetic things to the white people and the colored people both . . . all around . . . years and years. . . . Both shades of powder and rouge. . . . It's the kind of work a girl can do and not go clear 'way from home . . ." And the harder she looked, the more she talked. Suddenly she turned up her nose and said, "It is not Christian or sanitary to put feathers in a vase," and then she took a gold key out of the front of her dress and began unlocking the locks on her suitcase. Her face drew the light, the way it was covered with intense white and red, with a little patty-cake of white between the wrinkles by her upper lip. Little red tassels of hair bobbed under the rusty wires of her picture-hat, as with an air of triumph and secrecy she now drew open her little suitcase and brought out bottle after bottle and jar after jar, which she put down on the table, the mantel-piece, the settee, and the organ.

"Did you ever see so many cosmetics in your life?" cried Miss Baby Marie.

"No'm," Livvie tried to say, but the cat had her tongue.

"Have you ever applied cosmetics?" asked Miss Baby Marie next.

"No'm," Livvie tried to say.

"Then look!" she said, and pulling out the last thing of all, "Try this!" she said. And in her hand was unclenched a golden lipstick which popped open like magic. A fragrance came out of it like incense, and Livvie cried out suddenly, "Chinaberry flowers!"

Her hand took the lipstick, and in an instant she was carried away in the air through the spring, and looking down with a half-drowsy smile from a purple cloud she saw from above a chinaberry tree, dark and smooth and neatly leaved, neat as a guinea hen in the dooryard, and there was her home that she had left. On one side of the tree was her mama holding up her heavy apron, and she could see it was loaded with ripe figs, and on the other side was her papa holding a fish-pole over the pond, and she could see it transparently, the little clear fishes swimming up to the brim.

"Oh, no, not chinaberry flowers—secret ingredients," said Miss Baby Marie. "My cosmetics have secret ingredients—not chinaberry flowers."

"It's purple," Livvie breathed, and Miss Baby Marie said, "Use it freely. Rub it on."

Livvie tiptoed out to the wash stand on the front porch and before the mirror put the paint on her mouth. In the wavery surface her face danced before her like a flame. Miss Baby Marie followed her out, took a look at what she had done, and said, "That's it."

Livvie tried to say "Thank you" without moving her parted lips where the paint lay so new.

By now Miss Baby Marie stood behind Livvie and looked in the mirror over her shoulder, twisting up the tassels of her hair. "The lipstick I can let you have for only two dollars," she said, close to her neck.

"Lady, but I don't have no money, never did have," said Livvie.

"Oh, but you don't pay the first time. I make another trip, that's the way I do. I come back again—later."

"Oh," said Livvie, pretending she understood everything so as to please the lady.

"But if you don't take it now, this may be the last time I'll call at your house," said Miss Baby Marie sharply. "It's far away from anywhere, I'll tell you that. You don't live close to anywhere."

"Yes'm. My husband, he keep the *money*," said Livvie, trembling.

"He is strict as he can be. He don't know *you* walk in here—Miss Baby Marie!"

"Where is he?"

"Right now, he in yonder sound asleep, an old man. I wouldn't ever ask him for anything."

Miss Baby Marie took back the lipstick and packed it up. She gathered up the jars for both black and white and got them all inside the suitcase, with the same little fuss of triumph with which she had brought them out. She started away.

"Goodbye," she said, making herself look grand from the back, but at the last minute she turned around in the door. Her old hat wobbled as she whispered, "Let me see your husband."

Livvie obediently went on tiptoe and opened the door to the other room. Miss Baby Marie came behind her and rose on her toes and looked in.

"My, what a little tiny old, old man!" she whispered, clasping her hands and shaking her head over them. "What a beautiful quilt! What a tiny old, old man!"

"He can sleep like that all day," whispered Livvie proudly.

They looked at him awhile so fast asleep, and then all at once they looked at each other. Somehow that was as if they had a secret, for he had never stirred. Livvie then politely, but all at once, closed the door.

"Well! I'd certainly like to leave you with a lipstick!" said Miss Baby Marie vivaciously. She smiled in the door.

"Lady, but I told you I don't have no money, and never did have."

"And never will?" In the air and all around, like a bright halo around the white lady's nodding head, it was a true spring day.

"Would you take eggs, lady?" asked Livvie softly.

"No, I have plenty of eggs—plenty," said Miss Baby Marie.

"I still don't have no money," said Livvie, and Miss Baby Marie took her suitcase and went on somewhere else.

Livvie stood watching her go, and all the time she felt her heart beating in her left side. She touched the place with her hand. It seemed as if her heart beat and her whole face flamed from the pulsing color of her lips. She went to sit by Solomon and when he opened his eyes he could not see a change in her. "He's fixin' to die," she said inside. That was the secret. That was when she went out of the house for a little breath of air.

She went down the path and down the Natchez Trace a way, and she did not know how far she had gone, but it was not far, when she saw a sight. It was a man, looking like a vision—she standing on one side of the Old Natchez Trace and he standing on the other.

As soon as this man caught sight of her, he began to look himself over. Starting at the bottom with his pointed shoes, he began to look up, lifting his peg-top pants the higher to see fully his bright socks. His coat long and wide and leaf-green he opened like doors to see his high-up tawny pants and his pants he smoothed downward from the points of his collar, and he wore a luminous baby-pink satin shirt. At the end, he reached gently above his wide platter-shaped round hat, the color of a plum, and one finger touched at the feather, emerald green, blowing in the spring winds.

No matter how she looked, she could never look so fine as he did, and she was not sorry for that, she was pleased.

He took three jumps, one down and two up, and was by her side.

"My name is Cash," he said.

He had a guinea pig in his pocket. They began to walk along. She stared on and on at him, as if he were doing some daring spectacular thing instead of just walking beside her. It was not simply the city way he was dressed that made her look at him and see hope in its insolence looking back. It was not only the way he moved along kicking the flowers as if he could break through everything in the way and destroy anything in the world, that made her eyes grow bright. It might be, if he had not appeared the way he did appear that day she would never have looked so closely at him, but the time people come makes a difference.

They walked through the still leaves of the Natchez Trace, the light and the shade falling through trees about them, the white irises shining like candles on the banks and the new ferns shining like green stars up in the oak branches. They came out at Solomon's house, bottle trees and all. Livvie stopped and hung her head.

Cash began whistling a little tune. She did not know what it was, but she had heard it before from a distance, and she had a revelation. Cash was a field hand. He was a transformed field hand. Cash belonged to Solomon. But he had stepped out of his overalls into this. There in front of Solomon's house he laughed. He had a round head, a round face, all of him was young, and he flung his head up, rolled it against the mare's-tail sky in his round hat, and he could laugh just to see Solomon's house sitting there. Livvie looked at it, and there was Solomon's black hat hanging on the peg on the front door, the blackest thing in the world.

"I been to Natchez," Cash said, wagging his head around against the sky. "*I* taken a trip, *I* ready for Easter!"

How was it possible to look so fine before the harvest? Cash must have stolen the money, stolen it from Solomon. He stood in the path and lifted his spread hand high and brought it down again and again in his laughter. He kicked up his heels. A little chill went through her. It was as if Cash was bringing that strong hand down to beat a drum or to rain blows upon a man, such an abandon and menace were in his laugh. Frowning, she went closer to him and his swinging arm drew her in at once and the fright was crushed from her body, as a little match-flame might be smothered out by what it lighted. She gathered the folds of his coat behind him and fastened her red lips to his mouth, and she was dazzled by herself then, the way he had been dazzled at himself to begin with.

In that instant she felt something that could not be told—that Solomon's death was at hand, that he was the same to her as if he were dead now. She cried out, and uttering little cries turned and ran for the house.

At once Cash was coming, following after, he was running behind her. He came close, and half-way up the path he laughed and passed her. He even picked up a stone and sailed it into the bottle trees. She put her hands over her head, and sounds clattered through the bottle trees like cries of outrage. Cash stamped and plunged zigzag up the front steps and in at the door.

When she got there, he had stuck his hands in his pockets and was turning slowly about in the front room. The little guinea pig peeped out. Around Cash, the pinned-up palmettos looked as if a lazy green monkey had walked up and down and around the walls leaving green prints of his hands and feet.

She got through the room and his hands were still in his pockets, and she fell upon the closed door to the other room and pushed it open. She ran to Solomon's bed, calling "Solomon! Solomon!" The little shape of the old man never moved at all, wrapped under the quilt as if it were winter still.

"Solomon!" She pulled the quilt away, but there was another one under that, and she fell on her knees beside him. He made no sound except a sigh, and then she could hear in the silence the light springy steps of Cash walking and walking in the front room, the ticking of Solomon's silver watch, which came from the bed. Old Solomon was far away in his sleep, his face looked small, relentless, and devout, as if he were walking somewhere where she could imagine snow falling.

Then there was a noise like a hoof pawing the floor, and the door gave a creak, and Cash appeared beside her. When she looked up, Cash's face was so black it was bright, and so bright and bare of pity that it looked sweet to her. She stood up and held up her head. Cash was so powerful that his presence gave her strength even when she did not need any.

Under their eyes Solomon slept. People's faces tell of things and places not known to the one who looks at them while they sleep, and while Solomon slept under the eyes of Livvie and Cash his face told them like a mythical story that all his life he had built, little scrap by little scrap, respect. A beetle could not have been more laborious or more ingenious in the task of its destiny. When Solomon was young, as he was in his picture overhead, it was the infinite thing with him, and he could see no end to the respect he would contrive and keep in a house. He had built a lonely house, the way he would make a cage, but it grew to be the same with him as a great monumental pyramid and sometimes in his absorption of getting it erected he was like the builder-slaves of Egypt who forget or never knew the origin and meaning of the thing to which they gave all the strength of their bodies and used up all their days. Livvie and Cash could see that as a man might rest from a life-labor he lay in his bed, and they could hear how, wrapped in his quilt, he sighed to himself comfortably in sleep, while in his dreams he might have been an ant, a beetle, a bird, an Egyptian, assembling and carrying on his back and building with his hands, or he might have been an old man of India or a swaddled baby, about to smile and brush all away.

Then without warning old Solomon's eyes flew wide open under the hedge-like brows. He was wide awake.

And instantly Cash raised his quick arm. A radiant sweat stood on his temples. But he did not bring his arm down—it stayed in the air, as if something might have taken hold.

It was not Livvie—she did not move. As if something said "Wait," she stood waiting. Even while her eyes burned under motionless lids, her lips parted in a stiff grimace, and with her arms stiff at her sides she stood above the prone old man and the panting young one, erect and apart.

Movement when it came came in Solomon's face. It was an old and strict face, a frail face, but behind it, like a covered light, came an animation that could play hide and seek, that would dart and escape, had always escaped. The mystery flickered in him, and invited from his eyes. It was that very mystery that Cash with his quick arm would have to strike, and that Livvie could not weep for. But Cash only stood holding his arm in the air, when the gentlest flick of his great strength, almost a puff of his breath, would have been enough, if he had known how to give it, to send the old man over the obstruction that kept him away from death.

If it could not be that the tiny illumination in the fragile and ancient face caused a crisis, a mystery in the room that would not permit a blow to fall, at least it was certain that Cash, throbbing in his Easter clothes, felt a pang of shame that the vigor of a man would come to such an end that he could not be struck without warning. He took down his hand and stepped back behind Livvie, like a round-eyed schoolboy on whose unsuspecting head the dunce cap has been set.

"Young ones can't wait," said Solomon.

Livvie shuddered violently, and then in a gush of tears she stooped for a glass of water and handed it to him, but he did not see her.

"So here come the young man Livvie wait for. Was no prevention. No prevention. Now I lay eyes on young man and it come to be somebody I know all the time, and been knowing since he were born in a cotton patch, and watched grow up year to year, Cash McCord, growed to size, growed up to come in my house in the end—ragged and barefoot."

Solomon gave a cough of distaste. Then he shut his eyes vigorously, and his lips began to move like a chanter's.

"When Livvie married, her husband were already somebody. He had paid great cost for his land. He spread sycamore leaves over the ground from wagon to door, day he brought her home, so her foot would not have to touch ground. He carried her through his door. Then he growed old and could not lift her, and she were still young."

Livvie's sobs followed his words like a soft melody repeating each thing as he stated it. His lips moved for a little without sound, or she cried too fervently, and unheard he might have been telling his whole life, and then he said, "God forgive Solomon for sins great and small. God forgive Solomon for carrying away too young girl for wife and keeping her away from her people and from all the young people would clamor for her back."

Then he lifted up his right hand toward Livvie where she stood by the bed and offered her his silver watch. He dangled it before her eyes, and she hushed crying; her tears stopped. For a moment the watch could be heard ticking as it always did, precisely in his proud hand. She lifted it away. Then he took hold of the quilt; then he was dead.

Livvie left Solomon dead and went out of the room. Stealthily, nearly without noise, Cash went beside her. He was like a shadow, but his shiny shoes moved over the floor in spangles, and the green downy feather shone like a light in his hat. As they reached the front room, he seized her deftly as a long black cat and dragged her hanging by the waist round and round him, while he turned in a circle, his face bent down to hers. The first moment, she kept one arm and its hand stiff and still, the one that held Solomon's watch. Then the fingers softly let go, all of her was limp, and the watch fell somewhere on the floor. It ticked away in the still room, and all at once there began outside the full song of a bird.

They moved around and around the room and into the brightness of the open door, then he stopped and shook her once. She rested in silence in his trembling arms, unprotesting as a bird on a nest. Outside the redbirds were flying and criss-crossing, the sun was in all the bottles on the prisoned trees, and the young peach was shining in the middle of them with the bursting light of spring.

The

Contemporary

South

(1961 to the Present)

The literature of southern women of the past thirty years has faced a decided shift in focus from that of the modern writers. The urban, modernized South is now a given, and in many ways the South portrayed by these writers looks very much like the rest of the United States. Although the women who write in and about the South today carry on the tradition of their predecessors in their creations of theme and character, literary scholars have begun to question the validity of sustaining a distinctly southern literature in an increasingly homogenized United States. Concern for the past, for community, and for the dignity of human beings creates themes that are so universal that the South lacks definite claim to them; and southern characters could easily be relocated in the North or West without seeming out of place. What more than an accent still characterizes the southerner as unique from the rest of the United States? Is there, in fact, still a southern literature? The serious reader or scholar cannot avoid these questions inevitably raised by a study of the literature of the contemporary South.

One critic describes the South in Bobbie Ann Mason's works as a region "vacuumed clean of history and tradition," for the culture depicted is completely enmeshed in contemporary American life (Kakutani C20). This description is a valid one, for Mason's characters, to take *In Country* (1985) as an example, are most obviously shaped by rock music, soap operas and sitcoms, and the Vietnam War. Similarly lacking an affinity with southern culture, Ellen Gilchrist's "The Expansion of the Universe" is set in small-town Illinois and presents moving *to* the South as a primary conflict. Gilchrist's protagonist has grown up moving every three or four years and so has no distinct place that defines her past. In this story, the religious values, the social graces, the loyalty to family and community that we associate with the South are all called into question. And the fact that the new home in Kentucky is only a few hours drive from Illinois reinforces the uncertainty of the South as an explicitly distinct place. In both of these works, however, the southern past is still alive, for it is the loss of tradition and the need to adjust to a changed region that creates anxiety and fear in so many of Mason's characters, and the need for the stability that a region offers troubles Gilchrist's protagonist; by its absence, the past exerts its influence.

Perhaps as a response to the anxiety found in so much of contemporary southern literature, one stabilizing image permeates works by women, and that is the "home"—both the physical structure and the family tied to it. Beth Henley's *Crimes of the Heart* (1981), for example, demonstrates the function of the home as a place for the family to reunite and gain strength before returning to the world outside. In Lee

Smith's short story "Cakewalk," Florrie's home represents the continuity of family in a time when families are becoming more and more fragmented and when the commercial world threatens to squeeze the house itself out of existence. The South endures, also, through the extension of southern traditions beyond the region. When Elizabeth Spencer uses Italy as the setting for her best-known work, *The Light in the Piazza* (1960), the southern manners of the Johnson women are accentuated by contrast to Spencer's rather nebulous Italian characters; much like Henry James's Americans in Europe, the southern women carry the essence of their homeplace with them. Finally, the South remains distinct in part because of the continuity of the writers themselves. We see the political and literary roots of Alice Walker's fiction and poetry in the writing of Zora Neale Hurston and the sociological roots of Gail Godwin's concern for the southern woman in the explorations of women's lives by Eudora Welty and Carson McCullers. Looking back to their literary predecessors as they establish themselves as writers, southern women inevitably continue the southern tradition.

Although many southern writers have chosen to separate themselves from the region, in a 1975 article in *Ms.* magazine Gail Godwin (who has also left the South) advocates remaining in the South and fighting for change; she claims that the stereotypical southern belle continues to flourish largely because of the lack of influence by those very women who abandoned their home states. But in discouraging women from leaving the South, Godwin is not suggesting, as the mother does in her *A Mother and Two Daughters* (1982), that women learn to "blend into the landscape." Keenly aware of women's ability to change stereotypical attitudes of the South, Godwin suggests maintaining only that internal landscape that is truly beneficial. In effect, she calls for holding onto the good of the southern tradition while discarding any values that work to separate classes of people by gender or race. The most recent southern work, then, has the potential to fulfill best of all Eudora Welty's claim that "the art that speaks most clearly, explicitly, directly and passionately from its place of origin will remain the longest understood" (1978, 132)—regardless of the precise location depicted in that art.

But with the departure of southern writers to other parts of the country, the new generation of southern writers more and more admits to a loss of southernness. One of the youngest southern writers, Leigh Allison Wilson, was born in Tennessee in the late 1950s and now teaches in upstate New York; though critics find in her writing "a sort of Southern rural vision" in the tradition of Flannery O'Connor, Wilson claims that most characteristics people call southern—namely the art of storytelling, the recognition of distinctly unique characters, and the concern for human dignity—are part of human nature in general (Hood 45). Likewise, Shirley Ann Grau claimed in a recent interview that she "would like to get rid of the label 'Southern' entirely," though she continues to live in and write about the region (Griffin 70). Certainly we cannot expect contemporary writers, often experiencing life from places and points of view far removed from their region, always to write about the South or to retain some mysterious or undefined traits that keep them permanently tied to the place. Our notion of "southernness," then, may require redefinition if southern literature is to remain distinct.

In the preface to a recent edition of *New Stories from the South,* Shannon Ravenel claims that the following elements, whether individually or "in concert," account for the "magic" of recent southern literature: "A strong narrative voice. A pervasive sense of humor even in the face of tragedy. Deep involvement in place, in family bonds, and in local tradition. A sense of impending loss. Celebration of eccentricity. Themes of racial guilt and of human endurance" (viii-ix). In much of the literature written by southern women in the past thirty years, we find another distinct characteristic that is loosely related to these elements, but that transcends them, as well—a characteristic that is best described as "creation of community." Recognizing the tragedies of the past, particularly of racial conflict, many southern women writers seek to move beyond them by replacing racial guilt with a coming together of blacks and whites. Recognizing the inadequacies of family bonds and local traditions—particularly those that assume the archaic myth of the southern woman—they seek to create communities of women bound by common concerns, desires, even "eccentricities." And finally, recognizing the immense value of sustaining the narrative voice of the South, they seek to support one another as writers; the strength of this literary community may explain the second renaissance the South is now experiencing.

Looking to their literary past to find examples of healthy race relations, contemporary women writers find little upon which to draw. Ellen Glasgow, in her novel *Barren Ground,* presents an unusually strong relationship between a white woman and her black servant, and Harriet Arnow, in *The Dollmaker,* creates a black woman and a white woman drawn together by their love of children and feminine creativity. But in general, white women writers have not expressed much promise for "the durability of black-white friendship in a racist world" (N. Porter 251). Even those who lived through the civil rights movement, such as Lee Smith and Bobbie Ann Mason, rarely wrestle with racial themes in their fiction. More recently, Gail Godwin (in *A Mother and Two Daughters*) and Doris Betts (in "Beasts of the Southern Wild") have explored the possibilities for positive interracial relationships; however, Godwin, following in the tradition of Arnow, admits to the precarious nature of such relations, and Betts, while boldly depicting a sexual liaison between a white woman and a black man, locates the relationship within her protagonist's imagination.

In the midst of these rather ambivalent expressions of hope lies Alice Walker's *Meridian* (1976), which, in addition to being an eminent novel of the civil rights movement and a stunning exploration of a black woman's racial and sexual self-discoveries, is indispensable because it envisions healthy relationships between races. Although Meridian Hill and Lynne Rabinowitz are drawn together because of their commitment to civil rights, their friendship develops as they attempt to transcend stereotypes and recognize themselves and each other as human beings. By the end of the novel the women do become sisters in many ways, and they do so "with racial and sexual stereotypes confronted and demolished so that love does credibly prevail" (Schultz 78). The political and spiritual range of Alice Walker demonstrates a promising direction for the literature and the culture of the new South. And Walker's vision reaches far beyond the South, as well, for she asserts that the creativity of black women, and its right to be expressed, is a formidable measure of the social health of our entire country.

"If I am serious about friendships with women of color, I will keep working to transform the conditions of our lives. I will assume my share of the danger of living in a racist world," poet and essayist Mab Segrest writes, lamenting recent race relations in the South (1985, 176). Tracing the problems she faces as a lesbian to the same southern impulses that perpetuate racism, Segrest seeks to establish a sense of community among women to combat both racism and sexism in the South; her collection of essays, *My Mama's Dead Squirrel: Lesbian Essays on Southern Culture* (1985), attests to her commitment to both causes. In a South that cannot let loose of a feminine ideal, Segrest shows, women like herself are made grotesque, cut off from the parts of themselves that society cannot endure. The grotesque "limits the creative imagination by causing divisions within the self so that the individual is cut off from her deepest parts, from those oracles and visions that could tell of a different reality, of the possibility of wholeness" (29). In her essay "Southern Women Writing," then, Segrest defines a "women's literature of wholeness" that refuses the grotesque and grows out of "a community of Southern women searching together in the delicate connections between solitude and friendship for our visions of ourselves and what our world could be" (41).

As a writer, Segrest has found such communities, primarily through her association with *Feminary* and *Southern Exposure,* two journals devoted to women's and lesbian issues. Indeed, communities of women writers in the South have flourished in this century. In their literature, but also through journals, letters, interviews, and biographies, southern women continuously reveal their sense of connectedness, which extends through time and across racial boundaries. Institutions such as the North Carolina Writers' Network encourage such interaction by pro- viding assistance to writers seeking to support other writers. In her recent collection of works by and about southern women writers, *Friendship and Sympathy: Communities of Southern Women Writers* (1992), Rosemary Magee explains, "the spoken and written words of these writers . . . reveal that they have supported one another, together developed approaches to literature, and with each other pondered what it means to be part of a distinctively southern tradition as women" (xxvi). Such communities keep southern literature alive.

Finally, in her essay entitled "Why There Are No Southern Writers," Daphne Athas claims that the southernness of contemporary writers is found in their style—what lies within and beneath the language they choose to include—rather than in the topics they choose to write about. Southernness is *"under* the prose . . . rather than *in* it," she explains (763). This style is not, however, merely the "southern music" she heard in the voices of the southerners who lived in Chapel Hill when her family first moved to the community in the late 1930s; instead, according to Athas, the style of the contemporary woman writer of the South is "subtly aristocratic" in its tone, retaining a posture that reflects both the unassuming pride and the kindliness associated with the dignified southerner. Certainly the many, richly-varied speaking voices of the South have retained their distinct sound, and perhaps the voices of southern writing have as well. But Athas's claim opens wide the study of southern literature as critics attempt to characterize the unity and dis- tinction of its language, perhaps suggesting a movement away from studies of southern issues and themes in literature to a more linguistic approach to the language of the South.

In spite of, and perhaps because of, this concern about the stability of southern writing, in addition to an increasing popularity of conferences and symposiums on southern writers and the recent formation of the Fellowship of Southern Writers at Chattanooga, it appears that southern literature is not only still alive but still thriving. When literary scholars ask the question, "Is there still a southern literature?" the question can still be answered with a determined "yes," even though this youngest generation of southern writers may be the last to claim a distinct tie to the region, perhaps the last to remember a distinctly "southern landscape" that is now rapidly becoming a part of the larger American past. Indeed, the rich collection of writing by contemporary southerners— Ellen Gilchrist, Alice Walker, Leigh Allison Wilson, Bailey White, Eve Shelnutt, to name a few—evidences a second literary renaissance emerging in the South today, one largely embodied and shaped by its women.

27. Margaret Walker

(1915–)

The daughter of a Methodist minister and a teacher of music, Margaret Walker was born in Birmingham, Alabama, and received an excellent early education from Gilbert Academy, graduating in 1930. She began writing poetry when just twelve years old. Hoping to find better conditions for black people in the North, she entered Northwestern University, only to discover that racial problems were not confined to the South. However, she remained there and graduated from Northwestern in 1935.

After receiving her M.A. at the University of Iowa in 1940, Walker became the first African-American to win the Yale Younger Poets Award, given for her first collection, *For My People* (1942). Walker explains that it took her fifteen years to become a poet, years in which she was "learning [her] craft, finding [her] voice, seeking discipline," and the result was definite success. *For My People* is divided into three sections: the first poems are mostly prose poems or poems in free verse; the second group of poems are blues and folk ballads written in black dialect; the last poems are sonnets which maintain a formal style while discussing personal issues. The title poem of the collection and one often identified as Walker's signature poem, "For My People" is composed of stanza-paragraphs, an innovation that Walker introduced to black poetry.

In the early 1940s Walker worked for the Writer's Project in Chicago and was supervised by Richard Wright. She also became well acquainted with other southern writers, such as Carson McCullers and Katherine Anne Porter, while spending time at Yaddo, the literary retreat. She married in 1943 and began teaching English in the 1940s, first at West Virginia State College Institute and then at Livingstone College. In 1949 she joined the English department faculty at Jackson State College in Mississippi. She has served as the director of the Institute for the Study of History, Life, and Culture of Black People at Jackson State since 1968. In 1965 she completed her Ph.D. at the University of Iowa and the following year received a Houghton Mifflin Literary Fellowship.

Her collections of poetry include *For My People, Prophets for a New Day* (1970), and *October Journey* (1973). Her latest volume, *This Is My*

Century: New and Collected Poems (1989) represents her broad range; "The African Village" and "Birmingham, 1963" are from this collection. "For Malcolm X" (which first appeared in *Prophets for a New Day*) and "Birmingham, 1963" are poems about the modern-day southern battleground for civil rights. Walker has also written one novel, *Jubilee* (1965), an historical account of the Civil War told from the perspective of a slave. Her other works equally reflect her diverse interests and talents, specifically, *A Poetic Equation: Conversations Between Nikki Giovanni and Margaret Walker* (1974) and her critical analysis, *The Daemonic Genius of Richard Wright* (1982). Most recently, Walker has published a collection of essays, *How I Wrote* Jubilee (1990).

For Malcolm X

All you violated ones with gentle hearts;
You violent dreamers whose cries shout heartbreak;
Whose voices echo clamors of our cool capers,
And whose black faces have hollowed pits for eyes.
All you gambling sons and hooked children and bowery bums
Hating white devils and black bourgeoisie,
Thumbing your noses at your burning red suns,
Gather round this coffin and mourn your dying swan.

Snow-white moslem head-dress around a dead black face!
Beautiful were your sand-papering words against our skins!
Our blood and water pour from your flowing wounds.
You have cut open our breasts and dug scalpels in our brains.
When and Where will another come to take your holy place?
Old man mumbling in his dotage, or crying child, unborn?

Birmingham, 1963

Out of my heart's long yearning
        from the fullness and futility
        of an overbearing patience and a suffering long waiting;
Out of the deepest long denial
        of sacrifice and slowly germinating complaint;
Through the streets of Birmingham
        the ghosts of bitter memories
        are waking and walking close with pain.
Hate is beseiged and beseeched in the streets

of Birmingham. O my God, the naked pain
in the streets and jails and alleys
and the overlooking hills of Birmingham.

The African Village

In our beginnings our Blackness was not thought so beautiful
but out of bitterness we wrought an ancient past
here in this separate place
and made our village here.
We brought our gifts to altars of your lives
with singing, dancing, giving,
and moved stumbling stones into the market place.

Dark faces of our living generations
hear voices of our loving dead go echoing
down corridors of centuries.
For those who suffered, bled and died
Let this be monument:
the passing throngs parade before our eyes again.
Our children playing here
our neighbors passing by;
the daily swift encounters hear
and whispering in alleys,
dark corners of our lives
resuscitate.

In this short street a class of Africans create
A jungle world, a desert and a plain,
A mountain road, rain forests, and valleys
green and sweet.
We touch the earth and sky and flowers bloom
around our quivering feet.
Sunshine and rain
beat on these stones and bricks,
and wooden windowpanes.
Green grass grows scantily
and skirts the blackened pools on
muddy streets.

Thundershowers, snow, and sunlight
stream through an open doorway—
Syrian butcher in his bloody apron;
Green grocer with his sidewalk wares,
And hucksters riding wagons down this road
With a cry
for everyone to come and buy.
This is a place of yesteryears,
forgotten street of dreams.
The stardust shines
into the crevices of dingy lives
and gleams across our listlessness.
Oh! hear the song
Go whistling down the empty years
and let the afterglow
of all my hoped tomorrows
Fall on my lonely shadow.

I'll hawk your dreams,
your broken stars of glass
I'll paint your visions
on a rainbow road
that shines across dark starry skies.

(1932–)

Born in Statesville, North Carolina, Doris Betts was on her way to becoming a professional writer by the time she reached the Women's College of the University of North Carolina at Greensboro. While also on the staff of the *Statesville Daily Record,* Betts entered school intending to become a journalist. However, she ended up majoring in English and in 1953 received the *Mademoiselle* College Fiction Award for "Mr. Shawn and Father Scott." That same summer, Betts and her husband, whom she had married in 1952, had their first child. Just one year later, after Betts had transferred to the University of North Carolina at Chapel Hill, her first collection of short stories, *The Gentle Insurrection* (1954), was published and immediately won the G. P. Putnam–University of North Carolina Fiction Award.

Betts continued to work as a journalist, however, for the *Chapel Hill Weekly and New-Leader* and later for the *North Carolina Democrat.* In 1966 she began teaching creative writing in the English Department at Chapel Hill, later serving as director of freshman and sophomore English and as the assistant dean of the honors program. She has been a visiting lecturer to several colleges and universities and on staff at several writing conferences, and her writing has been encouraged by awards such as the Guggenheim fellowship in fiction, which she received in 1958.

Betts's fiction and reviews have been widely anthologized. Her primary concern in her writing is achieving an honest and open understanding among all sorts of people, and how such an understanding affects each individual. The novel *Tall Houses in Winter* (1957), for example, tells the story of a man who becomes reacquainted with the South when he returns home, possibly to die. *The River to Pickle Beach* (1972), set on the North Carolina beach, reveals how damaging fear and hatred can be, especially when directed against the defenseless, such as the mentally disabled woman who comes there for a holiday.

Betts's most recent collection of short stories, *Beasts of the Southern Wild and Other Stories* (1973), has brought her much favorable attention. With this book she became a National Book Award finalist in 1974. In a *New York Times Book Review* article, Michael Mewshaw summarized the greatness of the collection by pointing out that though it contains many of the characteristics of southern gothic, "the writing escapes categorization and remains very much an index of one woman's intriguing mind." Betts typically deals with racial prejudice as well, possibly best demonstrated in the story "Beasts of the Southern Wild," which turns stereotypical thinking about race inside out; this story first appeared in *Carolina Quarterly* (Spring 1973). Although a master of the short story, Betts felt that, with the completion of the novel *Heading West* (1981), she was ready to focus primarily on the novel form. Recently she published a work of nonfiction, *Halfway Home and a Long Way to Go: The Report of the 1986 Commission on the Future of the South* (1988). Her latest work, *Souls Raised from the Dead* (1994), is a novel that is set in North Carolina but demonstrates her ability to work outside of a typical southern tradition in writing. Betts continues to teach English at Chapel Hill today.

Beasts of the Southern Wild

. . . I have been in this prison a long time, years, since the Revolution. They have made me an animal. They drive us in and out our cells like cattle to stalls. Our elbows and knees are jagged and our legs and armpits swarm with hair.

We are all women, all white, bleached whiter now and sickly as blind moles. All our jailers, of course, are black.

So much has been done to us that we are bored with everything, and when they march me and six others to the Choosing Room, we make jokes about it and bark with laughter. I am too old to be chosen—thirty when I came. And now? Two hundred. It is not clear to me what has happened to my husband and my sons. Like a caged chicken on a truck, I have forgotten the cock and the fledglings.

We file into the Choosing Room and from dim instinct stand straighter on the concrete floors and lift our sharp chins. The Chooser sits on an iron stool. Negro, of course, in his forties, rich, his hair like a halo that burned down to twisted cinders. Jim Brown used to look like him; there's a touch of Sidney Poitier—but he has thin lips. I insist on that: thin lips.

They line us up and he paces out of sight to examine our ankles and haunches. He will choose Wilma, no doubt, who still has some shape to her and whose hair is yellow.

The Chooser steps back to his seat and picks up our stacked files and asks the guard a few soft questions while a brown finger is pointed at first this one of us and then that. This procedure is unusual. The dossiers are always there, containing every detail of our past lives. Usually they are consulted only after the field has been narrowed and two finalists checked for general health, sound teeth.

He speaks to the guard, who looks surprised, then beckons to me. The others, grumbling, are herded out and I am left standing in front of the Chooser. He is very tall. I say to his throat, "Why me?" He taps my dossier against some invisible surface in the air and goes out to sign my contract.

"You're lucky," says the guard through his thick lips.

I am beginning to be afraid. That's strange. I've been beaten now, been raped, other things. These are routine. But something will change now and I fear any changes. I ask who the man is who will take me to his house for whatever use he wants, and the guard says, "Sam Porter." He takes me out a side door and puts me in the back seat of a long car and tells me to be quiet and not move around. And I wait for Sam Porter like a mongrel bitch he has bought from the pound.

When the alarm clock rang, she dragged herself upright and hung on to the bookcase. She loved to sleep—a few more seconds prone and she'd be gone again, with the whole family late for work and school. She balanced on one foot and kicked Rob lightly in the calf. "Up, Rob. Rob? Up!"

Fry bacon, cook oatmeal, scramble eggs, make coffee. There was a tiny box, transistorized, under her mastoid bone. All day long it gave her orders, and betweentimes it hummed like a tuning fork deep in her ear. Set table. Bring in milk and newspaper. Spoons, forks. Sugar bowl, cream.

She yelled, "Breakfast!"

Nobody came and the shower was still running. Down the hall both boys quarreled over who got to keep the pencil with the eraser. When the shower stopped, she yelled again, "Breakfast!" (I'm Rob's transistor box.)

Her husband and sons came in and ate. Grease, toast, crumbs, wet rings on the table. Egg yolk running on one plate, a liquefied eye. If thine eye offend thee, pluck it out.

"Don't forget my money," Michael said, and Robbie, "Me, too."

"How much you need?" She counted out lunch money, a subscription to *Weekly Reader*. Rob said he'd leave the clothes at the cleaners, patted her, and went off to the upholstery shop. She drove the boys to school, then across town to the larger one where she taught English, Grade 12, which she liked, and Girls' Hygiene, which she despised. It was November, and the girls endured nutrition charts only because they could look ahead to a chapter on human reproduction the class should reach before Christmas.

Today's lesson was on the Seven Basic Foods, and one smartmouth, as usual, had done her essay on eating all of one type each day, then balancing the diet in weekly blocks. The girl droned her system aloud to the class. "So on Wednesday we indulge in the health-giving green and yellow vegetables group, which may be prepared in astonishing variety, from appetizing salads to delicious soups to assorted nourishing casseroles."

None of the students would use a short word when three long ones would do. They loved hyperbole. Carol Walsh wanted to say, "There's no variety, none at all," but this was not part of their education. She was very sleepy. When she looked with half-closed eyes out the schoolroom window, the landscape billowed like a silk tapestry and its folds blew back in her face like colored veils.

In the hall later, a student asked, "Miz Walsh? What kind of essay you want on Coleridge? His life and all?"

"No, no. His poetry."

"I can't find much on his poetry." The boy was bug-eyed and gasping, helpless as a fish. Couldn't find some library book to tell him in order what each line of the poems *meant*.

She said, "Just think about the poems, George. Experience them. Use your imagination." Flap your wings, little fish. She went into English class depressed. There was nothing to see out this window but a wall of concrete blocks and, blurred, it looked like a dirty sponge.

"Before we move to today's classwork, I'm getting questions about your Coleridge essay. I'm not interested in a record of the man's biography. I don't even want a paper on what kind of poet he might have been without an opium addiction." A flicker of interest in the back row. "I want you to react to the poems, emotionally. To do what Coleridge did, put your emphasis on imagination and sensibility, not just reason." She saw the film drop over thirty-five gazes, like the extra eyelids of thirty-five reptiles. "Mood, feeling," she said. The class was integrated, and boredom did the same thing to a black face as to a white.

The Potter girl raised her hand. "I've done a special project on Coleridge and I wondered if that would count instead?"

Count, count. They came to her straight from math and waited for the logarithms of poetry. Measure me, Miz Walsh. Am I sufficient?

She said, "See me after class, Ann. Now, everybody, turn in your text to the seven poems you read by Thomas Lovell Beddoes." They whispered and craned in their desks, although the section had been assigned for homework. Dryly she said, "Page 309. First of all, against the definition we've been using for the past section, is Beddoes a romantic poet?"

Evelina dropped one choked laugh like a porpoise under water. Romantic, for her, had only one definition.

"Ralph?"

Ralph dragged one shoe on the floor and stared at the scrape it left. "Sort of in between." His heel rasped harder when she asked why. "He was born later? There's a lot of nature in his poems, though." He studied her face for clues. "But not as much as Wordsworth?"

His girl friend raised her hand quickly to save him and blurted, "I like the one that goes, 'If there were dreams to sell, / What would you buy?'" In the back, one of the boys made soft, mock-vomit noises in his throat.

After class Ann Potter carried to the front of the room and unrolled on the desk a poster of a huge tree painted in watercolor. Its roots were buried in the soil of Classicism and Neo-classicism; "18th Century," it said in a black parenthesis. Dryden, Swift, and Pope had been written in amongst the root tangle. James Thomson vertically on the rising trunk. Then there were thick limbs branching off assigned to Keats, Shelley, Byron . . .

When Ann smiled, she showed two even rows of her orthodontist's teeth. "This sort of says it all, doesn't it, Miz Walsh!"

"You could probably be a very successful public schoolteacher."

"It's got dates and everything."

"Everything." Blake's *Songs of Innocence* branched off to one side, where Byron would not be scraped in a high wind. "Tintern Abbey." There was a whole twig allotted to "Kubla Khan."

"I thought you might count this equal to a term paper, Miz Walsh. I mean, I had to look things up. I spent just days on it."

"Ann, why not write the paper anyway? Then this can be extra credit if you need it." She'd need it. There was nothing in her skull but filtered air, stored in a meticulous honeycomb.

"My talents lie more in art, I think. I had to mix and mix to get just that shade of green, since England's a green country. I read that someplace. The Emerald Isle and all. I read a lot."

"It's a very attractive tree."

For last period, Carol Walsh gave a writing assignment; they could keep their textbooks open. Compare Beddoes and Southey. She sat at her desk making bets with herself about how many first sentences would state when each man was born. I'm good at dates, Miz Walsh. That Poe *looks* crazy. Well, Blake had this vision of a tiger, burning bright. He was this visionary. And he wrote this prayer about it.

That night she graded health tests until she herself could hardly remember what part of the digestive tract ran into what other part and whether the small or the large intestine came first. She chewed up an apple as she worked, half expecting its residue to drop, digested, out her left ear. Who knew what a forbidden fruit might take it in its—in *her* head to do?

"You're going to bed this early?" Rob glanced up from the magazine he was skimming during TV commercials.

"Not to sleep. Just to rest my eyes. Leave the TV on. I might decide to watch that movie." She got into bed and immediately curled up facing the wall. She was drowsy but curious, not ready for sleep; and there was nothing on television to compare with the pictures she could make herself. The apple had left her teeth feeling tender, and she had munched out the pulp from every dark seed, cyanide and all. Once she'd read of a man who loved apple seeds and saved up a cupful for a feast and it killed him.

She smiled when the story started.

. . . The car is moving. Its chauffeur is white, a free white who could buy off his contract. Sam Porter has said nothing. He does not even look at me but out the window. For years I have seen no city streets and I long to get off the floor and look, too; but he might strike me with that cane. A black cane, very slim, with a knob of jasper. The tops of buildings glimpsed do not look new. It's hard to rebuild after revolutions.

We stop at last. I follow him through a narrow gate, bordered with a clipped yew hedge. A town house, narrow and high, like the ones they used to build in Charleston. This one is blue. A white man is raking in the tulip beds—spring, then. I had forgotten. Sam Porter walks straight through the foyer and up the stairs and shows me a bedroom. "Clean up and dress." He opens a closet with many dresses, walks through a bathroom and out a door on the far side. So. Our rooms adjoin. Mine seems luxurious.

I do not look at myself until I am deep in the soapy water. My body is a ruin. No breasts at all. I can rake one fingernail down my ribs as if along a picket fence. The flesh which remains on my legs is strung there, loose, like a curtain swag. I am crying. I soak my head but lice do not drown; and finally I find a shampoo he has left for me which makes them float on the water and speckle the ring around the tub. I scrub it and wash myself again.

The dresses are made of soft material, folded crêpes and draped jerseys, and I do not look so thin in the red one, although it turns my face white as a china plate. He may prefer that. I wonder if there is a Mrs. Porter; I hope not. They have grown delicate since the war and faint easily and some of the prison women have been poisoned by them. I pin my wet hair and redden my lips, so thin now I no longer have a mouth, only a hole in my jaw. He knocks on the door. "We'll eat. Downstairs." His voice is very deep. I have lived so long with the voices of women that his sound makes a bass vibration on my skin.

Practicing the feel of shoes again, I go down alone to find him. The table is large, linen-covered. I am set at his right. There's soup and wine. It's hard not to dribble. The white housekeeper changes our plates for fish and a new wine. She looks at me with pity. She must be sixty-five. Where is my mother keeping house? At what tables do my sisters sit tonight?

"Carol Walsh," he says suddenly, looking down as if he can read me off his tablecloth.

The wine has changed me. "Sam Porter," I say in the same tone, to surprise him. He lifts his face and his forehead glistens from heat on its underside. His eyes are larger than mine, wetter, even the tiny veins seem brown.

"What do you expect of me?" I ask, but he shakes his head and begins eating the pale fish meat. I put it in my mouth and it disappears. Only the sweet taste but no bulk, and I am hungry, hungry.

After dinner he waves one hand and I follow him to a sitting room with bookshelves and dark walls. "Your file indicates you are literate, a former English teacher." He has no trouble taking down a book from a very high shelf. "Read to me. Your choice."

I choose Yeats. I choose "Innisfree" and "Sleuth Wood." To him I read aloud: "Be secret and exult / Because of all things known / That is most difficult." He sits in his big chair listening, a cold blue ring on his finger. I turn two pages and read, "Sailing to Byzantium."

When that is done, Sam Porter says, "What poem did you skip? And why?"

I have hurried past the page which has "Leda and the Swan." The lines are in my head but I cannot read them here: " . . . the staggering girl, her thighs caressed / By the dark webs . . . "

I say aloud, "I'll go back and read it, then," but the poem I substitute is "Coole Park," and he knows; he knows. He smiles in his chair and offers me brandy, which turns my sweat gold. He says, "You look well."

"Not yet. I look old and fresh from prison."

He rises, very tall, and does not look at me. "Shall we go up?"

I follow on the stairs, watching his thighs when he lifts each leg, how the muscles catch. He passes through my room and I follow; but he stops at the door to his and shakes his frizzed head. "When you come to me," he says, "it will not be with your shoulders squared."

He closes the door while I am still saying "Thank you." I cannot even tell if what I feel is gratitude or disappointment.

They drove Sunday afternoon to look at a new house in the town's latest subdivision. "Wipe your feet, boys," said Carol. The foyer was tiled with marbleized vinyl, and in the wallpaper mural a bird—half Japanese and half Virginian—flew over bonsai magnolias.

"If the interest rates weren't so damn high," Rob said, muffled in a closet. "That's one more thing George Wallace would have done. Cut down that interest."

"It's got a fireplace. Boys, stay off those steps. They don't have a railing yet."

"Bedrooms are mighty little. Not much way to add on, either. Maybe the basement can be converted."

There were already plastic logs in the fireplace and a jet for a gas flame. Their furniture, all of it old and recovered by Rob's upholsterers, seemed too wide to go through the doorways. He called to her from the kitchen, "Built-in appliances!" She could see the first plaster crack above the corner of the kitchen door. Rob had gone down into the basement and yelled for them to stay out, too many nails and lumber piles. "Lots of room, though," called his hollow voice. "I could have myself a little shop. Build a rumpus room?"

Carol stood in the kitchen turning faucets on and off—though there were no water lines to the house yet—and clicking the wall switches that gave no light. I could get old here, in this house. Stand by this same sink when I'm forty and fifty and sixty. Die in that airtight bedroom with its cedar closets when I'm eighty-two. By the time they roll me out the front walk, the boxwoods will be high.

"Drink of water?"

"Not working, Robbie. See?"

"Well, Michael peed in the toilet!"

"It'll evaporate," she said. They were handsome boys, and Robbie was bright. Michael had been slower to talk and slower to read; nothing bothered him. Robbie was born angry and had stayed angry most of his life. Toys broke for him; brothers tattled; bicycles threw boys on gravel. Balls flew past his waiting glove. Robbie could think up a beautiful picture and the crayons ruined it. She'd say to him, "Thinking's what matters," and doubt if that were true.

"We move in this house, I want a room by myself," he announced now, and punched at the hanging light fixture. "Michael's a baby. Michael wets in the bed."

In the doorway Michael stretched his face with all fingers and stuck out his dripping tongue and roared for the fun of it.

"Michael gets in my things all the time. He marked up my zoo book. He tore the giraffe."

Rob's head rose out of the stairwell. "No harm in asking the price and what kind of mortgage deal we could get. You agree, Carol? It's got a big back yard. We could build a fence."

"Could we get a dog?" Michael yelled.

Robbie pinched his arm. "I want my own dog. I want a big dog with teeth. I'll keep him in my room to bite you if you come in messing things up."

Carol made both boys be quiet, and in the car agreed the house was far better than the one they rented now. Rob smiled and swung the wheel easily, as if the car were an extension of his body, something he wore about him like familiar harness.

"I like that smell of raw wood and paint," he said. "Yesterday we had a nigger couch to cover, a fold-out couch, and it smelled so bad Pete moved it in the back lot and tore it down out there. Beats me why they smell different. It's in the sweat, I guess."

Robbie was listening hard from the back seat, and she was afraid tomorrow he would be sniffing around his school's only Negro teacher. "There's no difference," she said, putting her elbow deep in Rob's side.

"You college people kill me."

They drove in silence while she set up in her mind two columns: His thoughts and Hers. He was thinking how tired he was of a know-it-all wife, who'd have been an old maid if Rob Walsh hadn't come along, a prize, a real catch. With half-interest in his daddy's business just waiting for them. Gave Carol everything, and still she stayed snooty. Didn't drink, didn't gamble, didn't chase women—but by God he might! He might yet! He was two years younger. He was better-looking. He didn't have to keep on with this Snow Queen here, with Miss Icebox. Old Frosty Brain, Frozen Ass. Who needed it?

And Her thoughts, accusing. Who do I think I am? What options did I ever have? Was I beautiful, popular, a genius? Once when we quarreled, Rob said to me, "Hell, you've been in menopause since you were twenty." I'll never forgive him for that. For being mediocre, maybe; but never for saying that.

Turning in to their driveway, Rob said in a sullen voice, "You college people can't be bothered believing your noses. All you believe is books." He got out of the car and went into the house and left them sitting there.

Robbie said to his brother, "I warned you not to pee in that toilet."

After supper of leftover roast, Carol read the boys another chapter from *Winnie the Pooh*. When she had heard their flippant prayers and turned out the light, she stood in the hall and smiled as they whispered from bed to bed. I can love them till my ribs ache, but it still seems like an afterthought. She dreaded to go downstairs and watch the cowboys fight each other on a little screen, one in the white hat, one in the black.

While she was ironing Rob a clean work shirt for tomorrow, she wondered if there were some way she could ask Sam Porter about an odor without offending him. She decided against it.

. . . I have been here two weeks and Sam has never laid a hand on me. Yet I am treated like a favorite concubine. I dine at his table; he dresses me as though the sight of me gave him pleasure. The housekeeper mourns over what she imagines of our nights together. Every evening, I read to him— one night he asked for Othello just to laugh at my startled face. One other evening, he had friends over and made me play hostess from a corner chair. He encouraged me to join in the talk, which was of new writers unknown to me. One of the men—a runt with a chimpanzee's face—looked me over as if I might be proffered to him along with the cigars. Plainly, he could do better on his own. He made one harem joke, a coarse one, and jerked his thumb toward me and up. Sam Porter tapped him atop his spine. "Not in my house," he said. I was looking away, grinding my teeth. To me he said, "Sit straight. There's nothing in your contract which says . . . Some things you need not endure."

"He isn't worth my anger." Sam laughed, but the others worried and took him off in the front hall to offer advice.

Tonight as we sit down with our brandy, he says to me, "You were happy in the old days? As a woman?"

"Sometimes."

"My color and hair. Perhaps they disgust you?"

"No. Although in prison we were often . . . forced. I cannot forget those times."

"And you never had pleasure? From a black?"

"No. None. What shall I read tonight?"

"From yourself, perhaps? Or the women prisoners?"

"Not much," I say quickly, and, "Should we read some of the new things your friends like?"

"What subject did you choose for your Master's thesis?"

By now I know Sam Porter is no quick-rich, quick-cultured black. He is Provost at New Africa University, which I attended under its old name. And my dusty thesis must be stored there, in the prewar stacks. If he wished to know my subject, then he already knows it. I answer truthfully anyway, "John Donne."

He hands me a book of collected writings, from the library at school. "Perhaps the early work?" I reach for it and my fingers graze his. His hand is warmer than mine—unscientific, I know; but I can feel old sunlight pooled in his flesh and my hand feels wintry by his.

I am sorry to have the book again. The blue veins on my hands are high as the runs of moles; when I held Donne last, I had no vein at all and my skin was soft. I was twenty-three then, and not in menopause, No! I felt isolated from all things and swollen with myself as a tree hangs ripe with unplucked fruit. I was ugly, if the young are ever ugly; and sat alone in the caves and tunnels of the library, at a desk heaped high with Donne's mandrake root. Sam Porter says, "When you tire of staring at the cover, perhaps you will read?"

"The Sunne Rising." I look to a different page and, perversely, read aloud, "I can love both faire and brown / Her whom abundance melts and her whom want betraies."

Sam is watching me; I feel it though I do not look up. Sometimes his eye lens seems wide as a big cat's, and it magnifies the light and throws it in perforations onto me. I swallow, read, "Her who loves lonenesse best, and her who maskes and plaies." My voice is thin through my dry mouth. I ask Donne's question, "Will it not serve your turn to do as did your mothers? / Or have you all vices spent, and now would finde out others? / Or doth a fear, that men are true, torment you?"

When the poem is done, there is silence. He drinks his brandy; I drink mine; is it as warm going down inside him as in me? His glass clicks on the table. "You sit awhile. The brandy's there, and the book. I'm tired tonight."

I sit numb in my chair. He passes, then, with one swoop, bends down and touches my mouth with his, and his lips are not thin—not thin at all. He walks out quickly and I sit with the book and the snifter tight in my hands, for there is a smell; yes, it is sweetish, like wilted carnation fermenting on an August grave. Even a mouthful of brandy does not wash out his scent. My lungs are rich with it. And I do not go upstairs for a long time, until Sam Porter is asleep in the other room.

All evening she had been marking the participles which hung loose in the Coleridge essays like rags; and all evening Rob kept interrupting her work. He talked of the new house and what their monthly payments would be if they took a ten-year mortgage, or twenty. Or thirty—like a judge considering a sentence.

"I'm leaving that up to you," she said, trying to figure out on which page Ann Potter had changed Kubla Khan to Genghis Khan in her paper, "The Tree of Romanticism."

Rob said if she'd give less written work she wouldn't have to waste so much time marking papers. One of the themes—George's—appeared to be copied from an encyclopedia. Symptoms of opiate intoxication. There followed a list of Coleridge's poems. "These," George wrote, "show clearly the effects of the drug on his mind." She turned the page but there wasn't a word more.

Rob said, "If the federal government would just quit raising the minimum wage. How can I tell how much I'll earn in a year or two years, the way they eat into profits more and more? You know how much I got to pay a guy just to put chairs on a truck and drive them across town?"

"Umm." Ralph's paper was "Nature in Wordsworth and Coleridge" and how Wordsworth had more of it and wrote prettier.

"The harder I work, the more I send to Washington to keep some shiftless s.o.b. drawing welfare," Rob said, and rattled his newspaper. "And next year they raise my taxes to build back the big cities the bums are burning down. So everybody can draw welfare in new buildings, for Christ's sake. My daddy would turn over in his grave."

There's life, she thought, in the old boy yet. She read an essay on an albatross, a harmless bird feeding on fish and squid, and no need for anybody to fear it.

Rob was asleep when she marked the last red letter grades and slipped between the sheets like an otter going under the surface without a ripple. She lay wide-eyed in the dark. The streetlight shone through the window blinds, and threw stripes across their bed and her face. After a while she slid one hand under the covers and closed her eyes.

. . . *Sam is sick. The doctor who came was the chimpanzee man and he pinched in the air at me—but I moved. There is something of me to pinch now, after Sam's food and his wines and my long, lazy days in his handsome house. The doctor says he has flu, not serious; and for two days I have been giving him capsules and citrus juices. The housekeeper sees I am worried and has lost all her pity. She turns her face from me when I draw near, as if my gaze would leave a permanent stain.*

Last night I sat by his bed and read to him:

> "Are Sunne, Moone, or Starres by law forbidden
> To smile where they list, or lend away their light?
> Are birds divorc'd, or are they chidden
> If they leave their mate, or lie abroad at night?"

He fell asleep from his fever and I read alone and sometimes laid my hand on his blazing forehead. Against his color, my hand had more shape and weight than it has ever had.

Tonight he is much better and sips hot lemonade and listens with half his attention to old favorites. "Come live with me and be my love."

He asks once, "You don't sing, do you?"

"No."

He falls asleep. I tiptoe into my own room. Perhaps in the Choosing Room there is someone new, who sings. I pace on my carpet, John Donne's poems open on my dressing table like a snare. He hooks me with his frayed old line, "For thee, thou needst no such deceit / For thou thy selfe are thine own bait." I close the book; I spring his trap; I leap away.

In the mirror I see who I really am . . . my hair grown long and brown, my eyes brown, my skin toasted by the sun on Sam Porter's noonday roof. I will never be pretty, but this is the closest I have ever come, and I pinch my own cheeks and look at myself sideways. I have grown round again from eating at his table, and my breasts are distended with his brandy. I put on the red robe and walk softly into the next room. Sam sleeps, turned away from me, with one dark hand half open on the pillow as if something should alight in it.

I return to my room and brush out my hair. My body has a foreign fragrance—perhaps from these bottles and creams. Perhaps I absorb it from the air.

I pass through to the next room and drop my robe on the floor. I turn off the lamp and he is darker than the room. I slide in against his back, the whole length of him hot from fever. I reach around to hold him in my right hand. He is soft as flowers. He makes some sound and stirs; then he lies still and I feel wakefulness rise in him and his skin prickles. He turns; his arms are out. I am taken into his warm darkness and lie in the lion's mouth.

The bed shook and she opened her eyes and stared at the luminous face of the clock. Rob said, "You asleep?" She lay very still, breathing deep and careful, pressing her right hand tight between her thighs as if to hold back an outcry. The air was thick with Old Spice shaving lotion—a bad sign. A hand struck her hip like a flyswatter. "Carol? You can't be asleep." The ghostly face of the clock showed 1 A.M. "Honey?"

She jerked her hand free just in time for his. "Ah," he said with satisfaction against her shoulder blades. He curled around her from behind. "Picked a good time, huh?" She moved obediently so it would be quickly done, and he rolled away from her and slept with one arm over hers like a weighted chain.

. . . Sam bends over the bed where I have been crying and now lie weary, past crying. "Who was it, Carol? Tell me who it was?"

I roll my head away from him and he kisses one damp temple, then the other. He whispers, "This isn't prison anymore, hear me, Carol? No more endurance is required. Understand that. You are home, here; and that was rape. Whoever it was, I'll punish him."

I am a single bruise. "No." I run my hand under his shirt. "I didn't encourage him, Sam, I didn't. He broke in here—I was alone. I called for you. I never wanted him."

"If you do," says Sam, "I'll tear up your contract and let you go."

"No." I look in his eyes. "He was never my desire. An intruder. A thief. He forced himself on me. I swear it."

"Tell me one thing." He lies by me and his heat comes through the blanket. "Was he a white man?"

"Yes. He was white."

Gently he holds me, says, "I can have him killed, then. You know that. Did you know him?"

"I know his name. That's all we know, each other's names."

His hair is black and jumbled. "If you tell me his name, I can have him killed. But I won't ask you to do that. You must choose. You'll not be blamed if you choose silence." His hands are so pale on one side, so dark on the other.

"Rob Walsh," I whisper. "Rob Walsh."

"We'll hunt him down," he says, and gets up and goes downstairs.

He does not come back for hours and I wake near dawn to see him stripping off the black suit, the black mask, the black cloak. I sit up in bed. "It's done," he says, sounding tired, maybe sick. He comes naked and curly to me and falls away on the far side. "There's no love left in me tonight."

But I am there, my hands busy, and I can devour him; he will yield to me. The room is dark and he is so dark, and all I can see is the running back and forth of my busy hands, like pale spiders who have lived underground too long.

29. Sonia Sanchez

(1934–)

Sonia Driver Sanchez was born in Birmingham, Alabama, in 1934, and named Wilsonia Benita. Because her mother died when Sanchez was only a year old, Sanchez was raised by various relatives for the next nine years. Her grandmother, as well as the African Methodist Episcopal Church and African-American community, were strong influences in her early life. Sanchez has described that community influence as "a long line of Black people holding each other up against silence." When Sanchez was five years old, her grandmother died; soon after, Sanchez developed a stuttering problem that she struggled with for the next twelve years. She was passed from relative to relative until she moved to Harlem in 1944 to live with her father and his third wife. She lived with them until she graduated from Hunter College in 1955.

Sanchez continued her education at New York University in 1958. There she organized a writers' workshop that involved Amiri Baraka and Larry Neal and began writing under the tutelage of Louise Bogan. It was during this time in New York that she married her first husband, Albert Sanchez, a Puerto Rican American. They had one child and divorced four years later. In 1967 she started teaching at San Francisco State College, and it was there that she began work on the poems collected in *Homecoming* (1969). Strikingly influenced by black speech and music, the experimental poems use black cultural heroes as a way to speak of women as artists and as individuals. The same year that *Homecoming* was published, Sanchez married the poet Ethridge Knight, whom she had met through Gwendolyn Brooks and Dudley Randall. Although their marriage was short-lived, she had two children with Knight.

In her *We a BadddDDD People* (1970), Sanchez continued experimenting with form, particularly with radical spelling, emphatic use of capitalization and slashes, and a singing or chanting voice. Both "We a BadddDDD People" and "Blk/Rhetoric" are from this collection. While attacking the racial problems of her country, the poems celebrate the black community, much like Margaret Walker's *For My People* (1942). Sanchez has won several awards for her work, including the PEN Writing Award in 1969, the American Book Award in 1985 for

Homegirls and Handgrenades (1984), and the Peace and Freedom Award from the Women's International League for Peace and Freedom (1989). Two of the poems included here are from *Homegirls and Handgrenades.* "A Letter to Dr. Martin Luther King" exposes the evils that too often coincide with democracy—racism, apartheid, and imperialism—while also asserting black power and hope for regeneration. The poem ends with a re-creation of the chanting of black women at the death of Stephen Biko: "Ke wa rona," meaning "he is ours." Similar to "From a Black Feminist Conference," the "letter" pays homage to black leaders, but this time in Sanchez's own version of the homeric catalog of heroes.

Sanchez has lectured at more than five hundred colleges and universities, including Rutgers, Amherst, and Spelman, and she is presently poet-in-residence at Temple University and holds the Laura Carnell Chair in English. Recognized as a political activist and an international lecturer on black culture, Sanchez challenges people of all races to change the world. She has been a contributing editor to *Black Scholar* and the *Journal of African Studies.* Her recent books include *I've Been a Woman: New and Selected Poems* (1978), *Under a Soprano Sky* (1987), and *Wounded in the House of a Friend* (forthcoming).

we a badddDDD people
(for gwendolyn brooks
a fo real bad one)

i mean.
        we bees real
bad.
      we gots bad songs
sung on every station
we gots some bad   N A T U R A L S
on our heads
        and brothers gots
some bad loud (fo real)
    dashiki threads
        on them.
                i mean when
we dance   u know we be doooen it
                    when we walk
                    we be doooen it

        when we rap
        we be doooen it
          and

when we love.   well.   yeh.   u be knowen
bout that too.   (uh - huh!)

                                        we got some BAADDD

thots and actions
                    like off those white mothafuckers
                    and rip it off if it ain't nailed
                    down and surround those wite/
                    knee / grow / pigs & don't let them
                    live to come back again into
                    our neighborhoods (we ain't
                    no museum for wite
                    queer/minds/dicks/to
                                        fuck us up)
and we be gitten into a
SPIRITUAL thing.
                         like discipline
of the mind.
soul. body.   no drinken cept to celebrate
our victories / births.
                    no smoken.   no shooten
needles into our blk / veins
                              full of potential blk/
gold cuz our
              high must come from
                    thinking working
                    planning fighting loving
                    our blk / selves
                              into nationhood.
i mean.
    when we spread ourselves thin over our
    land and see our young / warriors /
    sistuhs moven / runnen on blk /
    hills of freedom.
                    we'll boo ga loo
in love.
    aaa-ee-ooo-wah / wah
    aaa-ee-ooo-wah / wah
    aaa-ee-ooo-wah / wah
    aaa-ee-ooo-wah / wah
    git em with yo bad self. don. rat now.
    go on & do it. dudley. rat now. yeah.
      run it on down. gwen. rat now. yeah. yeah.

aaa-e-ooooooo. wah / wah.
aaa-e-ooooooo. wah / wah.
we a BAAAADDD people
                    & every day
                    we be gitting
                    BAAAADDER

blk/rhetoric
(for Killebrew, Keeby, Icewater, Baker, Gary Adams and Omar Shabazz)

who's gonna make all
that beautiful blk/rhetoric
mean something.
                    like
i mean
            who's gonna take
the words
            blk / is / beautiful
and make more of it
than blk / capitalism.
                    u dig?
            i mean
                    like who's gonna
take all the young / long / haired
natural / brothers and sisters
and let them
            grow till
                    all that is
impt is them
            selves
                    moving in straight /
revolutionary / lines
                    toward the enemy
(and we know who that is)
                    like. man.
who's gonna give our young
blk / people new heroes
        (instead of catch / phrases)
        (instead of cad / ill / acs)
        (instead of pimps)

(instead of wite / whores)
(instead of drugs)
(instead of new dances)
(instead of chit / ter / lings)
(instead of a 35¢ bottle of ripple)
(instead of quick / fucks in the hall / way
of wite / america's mind)
like.   this.   is an S O S
me. calling.......
                calling.......
                            some / one
pleasereplysoon.

From a Black Feminist Conference, Reflections on Margaret Walker: Poet

chicago/october 1977/saturday afternoon/margaret walker walks her red clay mississippi walk into a room of feminists. a strong gust of a woman. raining warm honeysuckle kisses and smiles. and i fold myself into her and hear a primordial black song sailing down the guinea coast.

her face. ordained with lines. confesses poems. halleluyas. choruses. she turns leans her crane like neck on the edge of the world, emphasizing us. in this hotel/village/room. heavy with women. our names become known to us.

there is an echo about her. of black people rhyming. of a woman celebrating herself and a people. words ripen on her mouth like pomegranates. this pecan/color/woman. short limbed with lightning. and i swallow her whole as she pulls herself up from youth, shaking off those early chicago years where she and wright and others turned a chicago desert into a well spring of words.

eyes. brillant/southern eyes torpedoing the room with sun. eyes/dressed like a woman. seeing thru riddles. offering asylum from ghosts.

she stands over centuries as she talks. hands on waist. a feminine memory washed up from another shore. she opens her coat. a light colored blouse dances against dark breasts. her words carved from ancestral widows rain children and the room contracts with color.

her voice turns the afternoon brown. this black woman poet. removing false veils, baptizes us with syllables. woman words. entering and leaving at will:

> *Let a new earth rise. Let another world be born. Let a bloody peace be written in the sky. Let a second generation full of courage issue forth; let a people loving freedom come to growth. Let a beauty full of healing and a strength of final clenching be the pulsing in our spirits and our blood. Let the martial songs be written, let the dirges disappear. Let a race of men now rise and take control.**

walking back to my room, i listen to the afternoon. play it again and again. scatter myself over evening walls and passageways wet with her footprints. in my room i collect papers. breasts. and listen to our mothers hummmmming

A Letter to Dr. Martin Luther King

Dear Martin,

Great God, what a morning, Martin!

The sun is rolling in from faraway places. I watch it reaching out, circling these bare trees like some reverent lover. I have been standing still listening to the morning, and I hear your voice crouched near hills, rising from the mountain tops, breaking the circle of dawn.

You would have been 54 today.

As I point my face toward a new decade, Martin, I want you to know that the country still crowds the spirit. I want you to know that we still hear your footsteps setting out on a road cemented with black bones. I want you to know that the stuttering of guns could not stop your light from crashing against cathedrals chanting piety while hustling the world.

Great God, what a country, Martin!

The decade after your death docked like a spaceship on a new planet. Voyagers all we were. We were the aliens walking up the '70s, a holocaust people on the move looking out from dark eyes. A thirsty generation, circling the peaks of our country for more than a Pepsi taste. We were youngbloods, spinning hip syllables while saluting death in a country neutral with pain.

And our children saw the mirage of plenty spilling from capitalistic sands.

* "For My People" by Margaret Walker

And they ran toward the desert.

And the gods of sand made them immune to words that strengthen the breast.

And they became scavengers walking on the earth.

And you can see them playing. Hide-and-go-seek robbers. Native sons. Running on their knees. Reinventing slavery on asphalt. Peeling their umbilical cords for a gold chain.

And you can see them on Times Square, in N.Y.C., Martin, selling their 11-, 12-year-old, 13-, 14-year-old bodies to suburban forefathers.

And you can see them on Market Street in Philadelphia bobbing up bellywise, young fishes for old sharks.

And no cocks are crowing on those mean streets.

Great God, what a morning it'll be someday, Martin!

That decade fell like a stone on our eyes. Our movements. Rhythms. Loves. Books. Delivered us from the night, drove out the fears keeping some of us hoarse. New births knocking at the womb kept us walking.

We crossed the cities while a backlash of judges tried to turn us into moles with blackrobed words of reverse racism. But we knew. And our knowing as like a sister's embrace. We crossed the land where famine was fed in public. Where black stomachs exploded on the world's dais while men embalmed their eyes and tongues in gold. But we knew. And our knowing squatted from memory.

Sitting on our past, we watch the new decade dawning. These are strange days, Martin, when the color of freedom becomes disco fever; when soap operas populate our Zulu braids; as the world turns to the conservative right and general hospitals are closing in Black neighborhoods and the young and the restless are drugged by early morning reefer butts. And houses tremble.

These are dangerous days, Martin, when cowboy-riding presidents corral Blacks (and others) in a common crown of thorns; when nuclear-toting generals recite an alphabet of blood; when multinational corporations assassinate ancient cultures while inaugurating new civilizations. Comeout comeout wherever you are. Black country. Waiting to be born . . .

But, Martin, on this, your 54th birthday—with all the reversals—we have learned that black is the beginning of everything.

it was black in the universe before the sun;
it was black in the mind before we opened our eyes;
it was black in the womb of our mother;
black is the beginning,
and if we are the beginning we will be forever.

Martin. I have learned too that fear is not a Black man or woman. Fear cannot disturb the length of those who struggle against material gains for self-aggrandizement. Fear cannot disturb the good of people who have moved to a meeting place where the pulse pounds out freedom and justice for the universe.

Now is the changing of the tides, Martin. You forecast it where leaves dance on the wings of man. Martin. Listen. On this your 54th year, listen and you will hear the earth delivering up curfews to the missionaries and assassins. Listen. And you will hear the tribal songs:

Sonia

Sanchez

&

325

Ayeeee	*Ayooooo*	*Ayeee*
Ayeeee	*Ayooooo*	*Ayeee*
Malcolm . . .		*Ke wa rona**
Robeson . . .		*Ke wa rona*
Lumumba . . .		*Ke wa rona*
Fannie Lou . . .		*Ke wa rona*
Garvey . . .		*Ke wa rona*
Johnbrown . . .		*Ke wa rona*
Tubman . . .		*Ke wa rona*
Mandela . . .		*Ke wa rona*
(free Mandela,		
free Mandela)		
Assata . . .		*Ke wa rona*

As we go with you to the sun,
as we walk in the dawn, turn our eyes
Eastward and let the prophecy come true
and let the prophecy come true.
    Great God, Martin, what a morning it will be!

* he is ours

30. Alice Walker

(1944–)

"No one could wish for a more advantageous heritage than that bequeathed to the black writer in the South," Alice Walker writes. Born to sharecroppers in Eatonton, Georgia, Walker has paid homage to this heritage as an acclaimed writer of fiction and poetry and as a civil rights activist. Walker began writing when she was eight years old by recording the stories her parents told her. About the same time, she was wounded in one eye by a BB gun, which resulted in permanent blindness in that eye. Nevertheless, she became valedictorian of her high school and won a scholarship to Spelman College. She later transferred to Sarah Lawrence College in Bronxville, New York, where she began writing. Shortly after graduation in 1965, she began receiving awards for her writing, as well as an invitation to the Bread Loaf Writers' Conference.

Walker wrote her first book, *Once: Poems* (1968), just after returning home from a summer in Africa; the collection, published when she was twenty-four years old, describes her experiences in Africa and her views on civil rights but also includes more personal poems about the love and depression of a young woman.

In 1967 Walker married a Jewish attorney, and the two moved to Jackson, Mississippi, where they became the first interracial couple in the city. During the next several years as a writer-in-residence at Jackson State and then at Tougaloo College, Walker began working on her first novel, *The Third Life of Grange Copeland,* which was published in 1970. She then moved to Massachusetts and spent the next few years lecturing at schools there before settling in New York City as a contributing editor for *Ms.* magazine.

In 1973 Walker gathered her stories for publication as a single volume, *In Love and Trouble: Stories of Black Women,* and the book immediately won an award from the American Institute of Arts and Letters. Much of Walker's work was drawn directly or indirectly from her experience, reflected particularly in her next collection of poetry, *Revolutionary Petunias and Other Poems* (1973), which describes a childhood in Georgia, and in her next novel, *Meridian* (1976), which focuses on the civil rights movement during the 1960s.

Walker's work has received increasing recognition through the years;

in 1977 she won a Guggenheim Award, and her best-known and universally praised novel, *The Color Purple* (1982), won both the American Book Award and the Pulitzer Prize in 1983. Walker credits Zora Neale Hurston with substantially influencing her writing, and in 1979 she edited a collection of Hurston's works, *I Love Myself When I Am Laughing* (1979). This work also reflects Walker's interest in the lives and writings of women, but that interest is more explicitly revealed in her collection of essays *In Search of Our Mothers' Gardens: Womanist Prose* (1983). "The Black Writer and the Southern Experience," first published in *New South* (Fall 1970), is included in this collection.

Walker has continued to produce works of all types, including two books of poetry, *Horses Make a Landscape Look More Beautiful* (1984) and *Her Blue Body Everything We Know: Earthling Poems (1965–1990)* (1991); a collection of nonfiction prose entitled *Living By the Word: Selected Writings 1973–1987* (1988); and two novels, *The Temple of My Familiar* (1989) and *Possessing the Secret of Joy* (1992). Most recently, she has published *Warrior Marks* (1993), later a film documentary.

The Black Writer and the Southern Experience

My mother tells of an incident that happened to her in the thirties during the Depression. She and my father lived in a small Georgia town and had half a dozen children. They were sharecroppers, and food, especially flour, was almost impossible to obtain. To get flour, which was distributed by the Red Cross, one had to submit vouchers signed by a local official. On the day my mother was to go into town for flour she received a large box of clothes from one of my aunts who was living in the North. The clothes were in good condition, though well worn, and my mother needed a dress, so she immediately put on one of those from the box and wore it into town. When she reached the distribution center and presented her voucher she was confronted by a white woman who looked her up and down with marked anger and envy.

"What'd you come up here for?" the woman asked.

"For some flour," said my mother, presenting her voucher.

"Humph," said the woman, looking at her more closely and with unconcealed fury. "Anybody dressed up as good as you don't need to come here *begging* for food."

"I ain't begging," said my mother; "the government is giving away flour to those that need it, and I need it. I wouldn't be here if I didn't. And these clothes I'm wearing was given to me." But the woman had already turned to the next person in line, saying over her shoulder to the white man who was behind the counter with her, "The *gall* of niggers coming in here dressed better than me!" This thought seemed to make her angrier still, and my mother, pulling three of her small children behind her and crying from humiliation, walked sadly back into the street.

"What did you and Daddy do for flour that winter?" I asked my mother.

"Well," she said, "Aunt Mandy Aikens lived down the road from us and she got plenty of flour. We had a good stand of corn so we had plenty of meal. Aunt Mandy would swap me a bucket of flour for a bucket of meal. We got by all right."

Then she added thoughtfully, "And that old woman that turned me off so short got down so bad in the end that she was walking on *two* sticks." And I knew she was thinking, though she never said it: Here I am today, my eight children healthy and grown and three of them in college and me with hardly a sick day for years. Ain't Jesus wonderful?

In this small story is revealed the condition and strength of a people. Outcasts to be used and humiliated by the larger society, the Southern black sharecropper and poor farmer clung to his own kind and to a religion that had been given to pacify him as a slave but which he soon transformed into an antidote against bitterness. Depending on one another, because they had nothing and no one else, the sharecroppers often managed to come through "all right." And when I listen to my mother tell and retell this story I find that the white woman's vindictiveness is less important than Aunt Mandy's resourceful generosity or my mother's ready stand of corn. For their lives were not about that pitiful example of Southern womanhood, but about themselves.

What the black Southern writer inherits as a natural right is a sense of *community*. Something simple but surprisingly hard, especially these days, to come by. My mother, who is a walking history of our community, tells me that when each of her children was born the midwife accepted as payment such home-grown or homemade items as a pig, a quilt, jars of canned fruits and vegetables. But there was never any question that the midwife would come when she was needed, whatever the eventual payment for her services. I consider this each time I hear of a hospital that refuses to admit a woman in labor unless she can hand over a substantial sum of money, cash.

Nor am I nostalgic, as a French philosopher once wrote, for lost poverty. I am nostalgic for the solidarity and sharing a modest existence can sometimes bring. We knew, I suppose, that we were poor. Somebody knew; perhaps the landowner who grudgingly paid my father three hundred dollars a year for twelve months' labor. But we never considered ourselves to be poor, unless, of course, we were deliberately humiliated.

And because we never believed we were poor, and therefore worthless, we could depend on one another without shame. And always there were the Burial Societies, the Sick-and-Shut-in Societies, that sprang up out of spontaneous need. And no one seemed terribly upset that black sharecroppers were ignored by white insurance companies. It went without saying, in my mother's day, that birth and death required assistance from the community, and that the magnitude of these events was lost on outsiders.

As a college student I came to reject the Christianity of my parents, and it took me years to realize that though they had been force-fed a white man's palliative, in the form of religion, they had made it into something at once simple and noble. True, even today, they can never successfully picture a God who is not white, and that is a major cruelty, but their lives testify to a greater comprehension of the teachings of Jesus than the lives of people who sincerely believe a God *must* have a color and that there can be such a phenomenon as a "white" church.

The richness of the black writer's experience in the South can be remarkable, though some people might not think so. Once, while in college, I told a white middle-aged Northerner that I hoped to be a poet. In the nicest possible language, which still made me as mad as I've ever been, he suggested that a "farmer's daughter" might not be the stuff of which poets are made. On one level, of course, he had a point. A shack with only a dozen or so books is an unlikely place to discover a young Keats. But it is narrow thinking, indeed, to believe that a Keats is the only kind of poet one would want to grow up to be. One wants to write poetry that is understood by one's people, not by the Queen of England. Of course, should she be able to profit by it too, so much the better, but since that is not likely, catering to her tastes would be a waste of time.

For the black Southern writer, coming straight out of the country, as Wright did—Natchez and Jackson are still not as citified as they like to think they are—there is the world of comparisons; between town and country, between the ugly and crowding and griminess of the cities and the spacious cleanliness (which actually seems impossible to dirty) of the country. A country person finds the city confining, like a too tight dress. And always, in one's memory, there remain all the rituals of one's growing up: the warmth and vividness of Sunday worship (never mind that you never quite believed) in a little church hidden from the road, and houses set so far back into the woods that at night it is impossible for strangers to find them. The daily dramas that evolve in such a private world are pure gold. But this view of a strictly private and hidden existence, with its triumphs, failures, grotesqueries, is not nearly as valuable to the socially conscious black Southern writer as his double vision is. For not only is he in a position to see his own world, and its close community ("Homecomings" on First Sundays, barbecues to raise money to send to Africa—one of the smaller ironies—the simplicity and eerie calm of a black funeral, where the beloved one is buried way in the middle of a wood with nothing to mark the spot but perhaps a wooden cross already coming apart), but also he is capable of knowing, with remarkably silent accuracy, the people who make up the larger world that surrounds and suppresses his own.

It is a credit to a writer like Ernest J. Gaines, a black who writes mainly about the people he grew up with in rural Louisiana, that he can write about whites and blacks exactly as he sees them and *knows* them, instead of writing of one group as a vast malignant lump and of the other as a conglomerate of perfect virtues.

In large measure, black Southern writers owe their clarity of vision to parents who refused to diminish themselves as human beings by succumbing to racism. Our parents seemed to know that an extreme negative emotion held against other human beings for reasons they do not control can be blinding. Blindness about other human beings, especially for a writer, is equivalent to death. Because of this blindness, which is, above all, racial, the works of many Southern writers have died. Much that we read today is fast expiring.

My own slight attachment to William Faulkner was rudely broken by realizing, after reading statements made in *Faulkner in the University*, that he believed whites superior morally to blacks; that whites had a duty (which at their convenience they would assume) to "bring blacks along" politically, since blacks, in Faulkner's opinion, were "not ready" yet to function properly in a democratic society. He also thought that a black man's intelligence is directly related to the amount of white blood he has.

For the black person coming of age in the sixties, where Martin Luther King stands against the murderers of Goodman, Chaney, and Schwerner, there appears no basis for such assumptions. Nor was there any in Garvey's day, or in Du Bois's or in Douglass's or in Nat Turner's. Nor at any other period in our history, from the very founding of the country; for it was hardly incumbent upon slaves to be slaves and saints too. Unlike Tolstoy, Faulkner was not prepared to struggle to change the structure of the society he was born in. One might concede that in his fiction he did seek to examine the reasons for its decay, but unfortunately, as I have learned while trying to teach Faulkner to black students, it is not possible, from so short a range, to separate the man from his works.

One reads Faulkner knowing that his "colored" people had to come through "Mr. William's" back door, and one feels uneasy, and finally enraged that Faulkner did not burn the whole house down. When the provincial mind starts out *and continues* on a narrow and unprotesting course, "genius" itself must run on a track.

Flannery O'Connor at least had the conviction that "reality" is at best superficial and that the puzzle of humanity is less easy to solve than that of race. But Miss O'Connor was not so much of Georgia, as in it. The majority of Southern writers have been too confined by prevailing social customs to probe deeply into mysteries that the Citizens Councils insist must never be revealed.

Perhaps my Northern brothers will not believe me when I say there is a great deal of positive material I can draw from my "underprivileged" background. But they have never lived, as I have, at the end of a long road in a house that was faced by the edge of the world on one side and nobody for miles on the other. They have never experienced the magnificent quiet of a summer day when the heat is intense and one is so very thirsty, as one moves across the dusty cotton fields, that one learns forever that water is the essence of all life. In the cities it cannot be so clear to one that he is a creature of the earth, feeling the soil between the toes, smelling the dust thrown up by the rain, loving the earth so much that one longs to taste it and sometimes does.

Nor do I intend to romanticize the Southern black country life. I can recall that I hated it, generally. The hard work in the fields, the shabby houses, the evil greedy men who worked my father to death and almost broke the courage of that strong woman, my mother. No, I am simply saying that Southern black writers, like most writers, have a heritage of love and hate, but that they also have enormous richness and beauty to draw from. And, having been placed, as Camus says, "halfway between misery and the sun," they, too, know that "though all is not well under the sun, history is not everything."

No one could wish for a more advantageous heritage than that bequeathed to the black writer in the South: a compassion for the earth, a trust in humanity beyond our knowledge of evil, and an abiding love of justice. We inherit a great responsibility as well, for we must give voice to centuries not only of silent bitterness and hate but also of neighborly kindness and sustaining love.

(1940–)

Bobbie Ann Mason claimed in a recent interview that "in that certain way," she is a southern writer. Born in Mayfield, Kentucky, Mason grew up on a fifty-four-acre dairy farm. Her childhood was rather isolated as she was from a rural working-class family and attended a small country school. She began writing at age eleven, most interested in imitating mystery stories written for children. Later, at the University of Kentucky where she received her degree in journalism, Mason wrote for the school paper. After graduating in 1962, Mason moved to New York in order to write for *Movie Stars, Movie Life,* and *TV Star Parade.*

Mason found moving to the North a distressing cultural shock. Along with her separation from the South, Mason also faced living in a city for the first time. She soon quit her job in order to enter graduate school, first at the State University of New York in Binghamton where she received her M.A., and then at the University of Connecticut where she completed her Ph.D. in English in 1972. She then went to work for Mansfield State College in Pennsylvania where her husband taught and where she taught English for seven years. Though known primarily as a writer of fiction, Mason started her writing career with two works of literary criticism. *Nabokov's Garden: A Nature Guide to Ada* (1974) and *The Girl Sleuth: A Feminist Guide to the Bobbsey Twins, Nancy Drew, and Their Sisters* (1975) demonstrate her range of interests and ability.

Mason did not begin writing fiction again until late in the seventies, and her first story was published in 1980. Her first collection of short stories, *Shiloh and Other Stories* (1982), received nominations for both the National Book Critic's Circle Award and the American Book Award and won the Ernest Hemingway Foundation Award in 1983. "Shiloh," Mason's most popular story, was first published in the *New Yorker* (October 20, 1980); it is important for its depiction of the contemporary South and its reminiscence about what has passed. Among the many features of popular culture in the story are characters like Norma Jean, who plays an electric organ, frosts her hair, and lifts weights. Mason's success as a writer of fiction has resulted in a Guggenheim Fellowship, which she was awarded in 1984.

Unique in its portrayal of working-class people as well as of popular culture, Mason's fiction is generally set in rural Kentucky, and her stories focus on the South's adjustment to social change. Also, Mason does not write about the past as traditional southern writers are known to do, for the past rarely interests Mason's characters. Instead, they spend their time discussing television characters or rock music. *In Country* (1985), a novel depicting the effect of the Vietnam war on the lives of the working class, has received considerable recognition for its deep understanding of contemporary southern life.

In 1988 Mason's short novel, *Spence + Lila,* and *Love Life: Stories,* were published, and several new stories have since appeared in such periodicals as *Mother Jones,* the *New Yorker,* and *Paris Review.* Her most recent novel is *Feather Crowns* (1993), and she continues to live and write in Kentucky.

Shiloh

Leroy Moffitt's wife, Norma Jean, is working on her pectorals. She lifts three-pound dumbbells to warm up, then progresses to a twenty-pound barbell. Standing with her legs apart, she reminds Leroy of Wonder Woman.

"I'd give anything if I could just get these muscles to where they're real hard," say Norma Jean. "Feel this arm. It's not as hard as the other one."

"That's 'cause you're right-handed," says Leroy, dodging as she swings the barbell in an arc.

"Do you think so?"

"Sure."

Leroy is a truckdriver. He injured his leg in a highway accident four months ago, and his physical therapy, which involves weights and a pulley, prompted Norma Jean to try building herself up. Now she is at-tending a body-building class. Leroy has been collecting temporary dis-ability since his tractor-trailer jackknifed in Missouri, badly twisting his left leg in its socket. He has a steel pin in his hip. He will probably not be able to drive his rig again. It sits in the backyard, like a gigantic bird that has flown home to roost. Leroy has been home in Kentucky for three months, and his leg is almost healed, but the accident frightened him and he does not want to drive any more long hauls. He is not sure what to do next. In the meantime, he makes things from craft kits. He started by building a miniature log cabin from notched Popsicle sticks. He varnished it and placed it on the TV set, where it remains. It re-minds him of a rustic Nativity scene. Then he tried string art (sailing ships on black velvet), a macramé owl kit, a snap-together B-17 Flying

Fortress, and a lamp made out of a model truck, with a light fixture screwed on the top of the cab. At first the kits were diversions, something to kill time, but now he is thinking about building a full-scale log house from a kit. It would be considerably cheaper than building a regular house, and besides, Leroy has grown to appreciate how things are put together. He has begun to realize that in all the years he was on the road he never took time to examine anything. He was always flying past scenery.

"They won't let you build a log cabin in any of the new subdivisions," Norma Jean tells him.

"They will if I tell them it's for you," he says, teasing her. Ever since they were married, he has promised Norma Jean he would build her a new home one day. They have always rented, and the house they live in is small and nondescript. It doesn't even feel like a home, Leroy realizes now.

Norma Jean works at the Rexall drugstore, and she has acquired an amazing amount of information about cosmetics. When she explains to Leroy the three stages of complexion care, involving creams, toners, and moisturizers, he thinks happily of other petroleum products—axle grease, diesel fuel. This is a connection between him and Norma Jean. Since he has been home, he has felt unusually tender about his wife and guilty over his long absences. But he can't tell what she feels about him. Norma Jean has never complained about his traveling; she has never made hurt remarks, like calling his truck a "widow-maker." He is reasonably certain she has been faithful to him, but he wishes she would celebrate his permanent homecoming more happily. Norma Jean is often startled to find Leroy at home, and he thinks she seems a little disappointed about it. Perhaps he reminds her too much of the early days of their marriage, before he went on the road. They had a child who died as an infant, years ago. They never speak about their memories of Randy, which have almost faded, but now that Leroy is home all the time, they sometimes feel awkward around each other, and Leroy wonders if one of them should mention the child. He has the feeling that they are waking up out of a dream together—that they must create a new marriage, start afresh. They are lucky they are still married. Leroy has read that for most people losing a child destroys the marriage—or else he heard this on *Donahue*. He can't always remember where he learns things anymore.

At Christmas, Leroy bought an electric organ for Norma Jean. She used to play the piano when she was in high school. "It don't leave you," she told him once. "It's like riding a bicycle."

The new instrument had so many keys and buttons that she was bewildered by it at first. She touched the keys tentatively, pushed some buttons, then pecked out "Chopsticks." It came out in an amplified fox-trot rhythm, with marimba sounds.

"It's an orchestra!" she cried.

The organ had a pecan-look finish and eighteen preset chords, with optional flute, violin, trumpet, clarinet, and banjo accompaniments. Norma Jean mastered the organ almost immediately. At first she played Christmas songs. Then she bought *The Sixties Songbook* and learned every tune in it, adding variations to each with the rows of brightly colored buttons.

"I didn't like these old songs back then," she said. "But I have this crazy feeling I missed something."

"You didn't miss a thing," said Leroy.

Leroy likes to lie on the couch and smoke a joint and listen to Norma Jean play "Can't Take My Eyes Off You" and "I'll Be Back." He is back again. After fifteen years on the road, he is finally settling down with the woman he loves. She is still pretty. Her skin is flawless. Her frosted curls resemble pencil trimmings.

Now that Leroy has come home to stay, he notices how much the town has changed. Subdivisions are spreading across western Kentucky like an oil slick. The sign at the edge of town says "Pop: 11,500"—only seven hundred more than it said twenty years before. Leroy can't figure out who is living in all the new houses. The farmers who used to gather around the courthouse square on Saturday afternoons to play checkers and spit tobacco juice have gone. It has been years since Leroy has thought about the farmers, and they have disappeared without his noticing.

Leroy meets a kid named Stevie Hamilton in the parking lot at the new shopping center. While they pretend to be strangers meeting over a stalled car, Stevie tosses an ounce of marijuana under the front seat of Leroy's car. Stevie is wearing orange jogging shoes and a T-shirt that says CHATTAHOOCHEE SUPER-RAT. His father is a prominent doctor who lives in one of the expensive subdivisions in a new white-columned brick house that looks like a funeral parlor. In the phone book under his name there is a separate number, with the listing "Teenagers."

"Where do you get this stuff?" asks Leroy. "From your pappy?"

"That's for me to know and you to find out," Stevie says. He is slit-eyed and skinny.

"What else you got?"

"What you interested in?"

"Nothing special. Just wondered."

Leroy used to take speed on the road. Now he has to go slowly. He needs to be mellow. He leans back against the car and says, "I'm aiming to build me a log house, soon as I get time. My wife, though, I don't think she likes the idea."

"Well, let me know when you want me again," Stevie says. He has a cigarette in his cupped palm, as though sheltering it from the wind. He takes a long drag, then stomps it on the asphalt and slouches away.

Stevie's father was two years ahead of Leroy in high school. Leroy is thirty-four. He married Norma Jean when they were both eighteen, and their child Randy was born a few months later, but he died at the age of four months and three days. He would be about Stevie's age now. Norma Jean and Leroy were at the drive-in, watching a double feature (*Dr. Strangelove* and *Lover Come Back*), and the baby was sleeping in the back seat. When the first movie ended, the baby was dead. It was the sudden infant death syndrome. Leroy remembers handing Randy to a nurse at the emergency room, as though he were offering her a large doll as a present. A dead baby feels like a sack of flour. "It just happens sometimes," said the doctor, in what Leroy always recalls as a nonchalant tone. Leroy can hardly remember the child anymore, but he still sees vividly a scene from *Dr. Strangelove* in which the President of the United States was talking in a folksy voice on the hot line to the Soviet premier about the bomber accidentally headed toward Russia. He was in the War Room, and the world map was lit up. Leroy remembers Norma Jean standing catatonically beside him in the hospital and himself thinking: Who is this strange girl? He had forgotten who she was. Now scientists are saying that crib death is caused by a virus. Nobody knows anything, Leroy thinks. The answers are always changing.

When Leroy gets home from the shopping center, Norma Jean's mother, Mabel Beasley, is there. Until this year, Leroy has not realized how much time she spends with Norma Jean. When she visits, she inspects the closets and then the plants, informing Norma Jean when a plant is droopy or yellow. Mabel calls the plants "flowers," although there are never any blooms. She always notices if Norma Jean's laundry is piling up. Mabel is a short, overweight woman whose tight, brown-dyed curls look more like a wig than the actual wig she sometimes wears. Today she has brought Norma Jean an off-white dust ruffle she made for the bed; Mabel works in a custom-upholstery shop.

"This is the tenth one I made this year," Mabel says. "I got started and couldn't stop."

"It's real pretty," says Norma Jean.

"Now we can hide things under the bed," says Leroy, who gets along with his mother-in-law primarily by joking with her. Mabel has never really forgiven him for disgracing her by getting Norma Jean pregnant. When the baby died, she said that fate was mocking her.

"What's that thing?" Mabel says to Leroy in a loud voice, pointing to a tangle of yarn on a piece of canvas.

Leroy holds it up for Mabel to see. "It's my needlepoint," he explains. "This is a *Star Trek* pillow cover."

"That's what a woman would do," says Mabel. "Great day in the morning!"

"All the big football players on TV do it," he says.

"Why, Leroy, you're always trying to fool me. I don't believe you for one minute. You don't know what to do with yourself—that's the whole trouble. Sewing!"

"I'm aiming to build us a log house," says Leroy. "Soon as my plans come."

"Like *heck* you are," says Norma Jean. She takes Leroy's needlepoint and shoves it into a drawer. "You have to find a job first. Nobody can afford to build now anyway."

Mabel straightens her girdle and says, "I still think before you get tied down y'all ought to take a little run to Shiloh."

"One of these days, Mama," Norma Jean says impatiently.

Mabel is talking about Shiloh, Tennessee. For the past few years, she has been urging Leroy and Norma Jean to visit the Civil War battleground there. Mabel went there on her honeymoon—the only real trip she ever took. Her husband died of a perforated ulcer when Norma Jean was ten, but Mabel, who was accepted into the United Daughters of the Confederacy in 1975, is still preoccupied with going back to Shiloh.

"I've been to kingdom come and back in that truck out yonder," Leroy says to Mabel, "but we never yet set foot in that battleground. Ain't that something? How did I miss it?"

"It's not even that far," Mabel says.

After Mabel leaves, Norma Jean reads to Leroy from a list she has made. "Things you could do," she announces. "You could get a job as a guard at Union Carbide, where they'd let you set on a stool. You could get on at the lumberyard. You could do a little carpenter work, if you want to build so bad. You could—"

"I can't do something where I'd have to stand up all day."

"You ought to try standing up all day behind a cosmetics counter. It's amazing that I have strong feet, coming from two parents that never had strong feet at all." At the moment Norma Jean is holding on to the kitchen counter, raising her knees one at a time as she talks. She is wearing two-pound ankle weights.

"Don't worry," says Leroy. "I'll do something."

"You could truck calves to slaughter for somebody. You wouldn't have to drive any big old truck for that."

"I'm going to build you this house," says Leroy. "I want to make you a real home."

"I don't want to live in any log cabin."

"It's not a cabin. It's a house."

"I don't care. It looks like a cabin."

"You and me together could lift those logs. It's just like lifting weights."

Norma Jean doesn't answer. Under her breath, she is counting. Now she is marching through the kitchen. She is doing goose steps.

Before his accident, when Leroy came home he used to stay in the house with Norma Jean, watching TV in bed and playing cards. She would cook fried chicken, picnic ham, chocolate pie—all his favorites. Now he is home alone much of the time. In the mornings, Norma Jean disappears, leaving a cooling place in the bed. She eats a cereal called Body Buddies, and she leaves the bowl on the table, with soggy tan balls floating in a milk puddle. He sees things about Norma Jean that he never realized before. When she chops onions, she stares off into a corner, as if she can't bear to look. She puts on her house slippers almost precisely at nine o'clock every evening and nudges her jogging shoes under the couch. She saves bread heels for the birds. Leroy watches the birds at the feeder. He notices the peculiar way goldfinches fly past the window. They close their wings, then fall, then spread their wings to catch and lift themselves. He wonders if they close their eyes when they fall. Norma Jean closes her eyes when they are in bed. She wants the lights turned out. Even then, he is sure she closes her eyes. He goes for long drives around town. He tends to drive a car rather carelessly. Power steering and an automatic shift make a car feel so small and inconsequential that his body is hardly involved in the driving process. His injured leg stretches out comfortably. Once or twice he has almost hit something, but even the prospect of an accident seems minor in a car. He cruises the new subdivisions, feeling like a criminal rehearsing for a robbery. Norma Jean is probably right about a log house being inappropriate here in the new subdivisions. All the houses look grand and complicated. They depress him.

One day when Leroy comes home from a drive he finds Norma Jean in tears. She is in the kitchen making a potato and mushroom-soup casserole, with grated-cheese topping. She is crying because her mother caught her smoking.

"I didn't hear her coming. I was standing here puffing away pretty as you please," Norma Jean says, wiping her eyes.

"I knew it would happen sooner or later," says Leroy, putting his arm around her.

"She don't know the meaning of the word 'knock,'" says Norma Jean. "It's a wonder she hadn't caught me years ago."

"Think of it this way," Leroy says. "What if she caught me with a joint?"

"You better not let her!" Norma Jean shrieks. "I'm warning you, Leroy Moffitt!"

"I'm just kidding. Here, play me a tune. That'll help you relax."

Norma Jean puts the casserole in the oven and sets the timer. Then she plays a ragtime tune, with horns and banjo, as Leroy lights up a joint and lies on the couch, laughing to himself about Mabel's catching him at it. He thinks of Stevie Hamilton—a doctor's son pushing grass. Everything is funny. The whole town seems crazy and small. He is reminded of Virgil Mathis, a boastful policeman Leroy used to shoot pool with. Virgil recently led a drug bust in a back room at a bowling alley, where he seized ten thousand dollars' worth of marijuana. The newspaper had a picture of him holding up the bags of grass and grinning widely. Right now, Leroy can imagine Virgil breaking down the door and arresting him with a lungful of smoke. Virgil would probably have been alerted to the scene because of all the racket Norma Jean is making. Now she sounds like a hard-rock band. Norma Jean is terrific. When she switches to a Latin-rhythm version of "Sunshine Superman," Leroy hums along. Norma Jean's foot goes up and down, up and down.

"Well, what do you think?" Leroy says, when Norma Jean pauses to search through her music.

"What do I think about what?"

His mind had gone blank. Then he says, "I'll sell my rig and build us a house." That wasn't what he wanted to say. He wanted to know what she thought—what she *really* thought—about them.

"Don't start in on that again," says Norma Jean. She begins playing "Who'll Be the Next in Line?"

Leroy used to tell hitchhikers his whole life story—about his travels, his hometown, the baby. He would end with a question: "Well, what do you think?" It was just a rhetorical question. In time, he had the feeling that he'd been telling the same story over and over to the same hitchhikers. He quit talking to hitchhikers when he realized how his voice sounded—whining and self-pitying, like some teenage-tragedy song. Now Leroy has the sudden impulse to tell Norma Jean about himself, as if he had just met her. They have known each other so long they have forgotten a lot about each other. They could become reacquainted. But when the oven timer goes off and she runs to the kitchen, he forgets why he wants to do this.

The next day, Mabel drops by. It is Saturday and Norma Jean is cleaning. Leroy is studying the plans of his log house, which have finally come in the mail. He has them spread out on the table—big sheets of stiff blue paper, with diagrams and numbers printed in white. While Norma Jean runs the vacuum, Mabel drinks coffee. She sets her coffee cup on a blueprint.

"I'm just waiting for time to pass," she says to Leroy, drumming her fingers on the table.

As soon as Norma Jean switches off the vacuum, Mabel says in a loud voice, "Did you hear about the datsun dog that killed the baby?"

Norma Jean says, "The word is 'dachshund.'"

"They put the dog on trial. It chewed the baby's legs off. The mother was in the next room all the time." She raises her voice. "They thought it was neglect."

Norma Jean is holding her ears. Leroy manages to open the refrigerator and get some Diet Pepsi to offer Mabel. Mabel still has some coffee and she waves away the Pepsi.

"Datsuns are like that," Mabel says. "They're jealous dogs. They'll tear a place to pieces if you don't keep an eye on them."

"You better watch out what you're saying, Mabel," says Leroy.

"Well, facts is facts."

Leroy looks out the window at his rig. It is like a huge piece of furniture gathering dust in the backyard. Pretty soon it will be an antique. He hears the vacuum cleaner. Norma Jean seems to be cleaning the living room rug again.

Later, she says to Leroy, "She just said that about the baby because she caught me smoking. She's trying to pay me back."

"What are you talking about?" Leroy says, nervously shuffling blueprints.

"You know good and well," Norma Jean says. She is sitting in a kitchen chair with her feet up and her arms wrapped around her knees. She looks small and helpless. She says, "The very idea, her bringing up a subject like that! Saying it was neglect."

"She didn't mean that," Leroy says.

"She might not have *thought* she meant it. She always says things like that. You don't know how she goes on."

"But she didn't really mean it. She was just talking."

Leroy opens a king-sized bottle of beer and pours it in two glasses, dividing it carefully. He hands a glass to Norma Jean and she takes it from him mechanically. For a long time, they sit by the kitchen window watching the birds at the feeder.

Something is happening. Norma Jean is going to night school. She has graduated from her six-week body-building course and now she is taking an adult-education course in composition at Paducah Community College. She spends her evenings outlining paragraphs.

"First you have a topic sentence," she explains to Leroy. "Then you divide it up. Your secondary topic has to be connected to your primary topic."

To Leroy, this sounds intimidating. "I never was any good in English," he says.

"It makes a lot of sense."

"What are you doing this for, anyhow?"

She shrugs. "It's something to do." She stands up and lifts her dumbbells a few times.

"Driving a rig, nobody cared about my English."

"I'm not criticizing your English."

Norma Jean used to say, "If I lose ten minutes' sleep, I just drag all day." Now she stays up late, writing compositions. She got a B on her first paper—a how-to theme on soup-based casseroles. Recently Norma Jean has been cooking unusual foods—tacos, lasagna, Bombay chicken. She doesn't play the organ anymore, though her second paper was called "Why Music Is Important to Me." She sits at the kitchen table, concentrating on her outlines, while Leroy plays with his log house plans, practicing with a set of Lincoln Logs. The thought of getting a truckload of notched, numbered logs scares him, and he wants to be prepared. As he and Norma Jean work together at the kitchen table, Leroy has the hopeful thought that they are sharing something, but he knows he is a fool to think this. Norma Jean is miles away. He knows he is going to lose her. Like Mabel, he is just waiting for time to pass.

One day, Mabel is there before Norma Jean gets home from work, and Leroy finds himself confiding in her. Mabel, he realizes, must know Norma Jean better than he does.

"I don't know what's got into that girl," Mabel says. "She used to go to bed with the chickens. Now you say she's up all hours. Plus her a-smoking. I like to died."

"I want to make her this beautiful home," Leroy says, indicating the Lincoln Logs. "I think she even wants it. Maybe she was happier with me gone."

"She don't know what to make of you, coming home like this."

"Is that it?"

Mabel takes the roof off his Lincoln Log cabin. "You couldn't get *me* in a log cabin," she says. "I was raised in one. It's no picnic, let me tell you."

"They're different now," says Leroy.

"I tell you what," Mabel says, smiling oddly at Leroy.

"What?"

"Take her down to Shiloh. Y'all need to get out together, stir a little. Her brain's all balled up over them books." Leroy can see traces of Norma Jean's features in her mother's face. Mabel's worn face has the texture of crinkled cotton, but suddenly she looks pretty. It occurs to Leroy that Mabel has been hinting all along that she wants them to take her with them to Shiloh.

"Let's all go to Shiloh," he says. "You and me and her. Come Sunday."

Mabel throws up her hand in protest. "Oh, no, not me. Young folks want to be by themselves."

When Norma Jean comes in with the groceries, Leroy says excitedly, "Your mama here's been dying to go to Shiloh for thirty-five years. It's about time we went, don't you think?"

"I'm not going to butt in on anybody's second honeymoon," Mabel says.

"Who's going on a honeymoon, for Christ's sake?" Norma Jean says loudly.

"I never raised no daughter of mine to talk that-a-way," Mabel says.

"You ain't seen nothing yet," says Norma Jean. She starts putting away boxes and cans, slamming cabinet doors.

"There's a log cabin at Shiloh," Mabel says. "It was there during the battle. There's bullet holes in it."

"When are you going to *shut up* about Shiloh, Mama?" asks Norma Jean.

"I always thought Shiloh was the prettiest place, so full of history," Mabel goes on. "I just hoped y'all could see it once before I die, so you could tell me about it." Later, she whispers to Leroy, "You do what I said. A little change is what she needs."

"Your name means 'the king,'" Norma Jean says to Leroy that evening. He is trying to get her to go to Shiloh, and she is reading a book about another century.

"Well, I reckon I ought to be right proud."

"I guess so."

"Am I still king around here?"

Norma Jean flexes her biceps and feels them for hardness. "I'm not fooling around with anybody, if that's what you mean," she says.

"Would you tell me if you were?"

"I don't know."

"What does *your* name mean?"

"It was Marilyn Monroe's real name."

"No kidding!"

"Norma comes from the Normans. They were invaders," she says. She closes her book and looks hard at Leroy. "I'll go to Shiloh with you if you'll stop staring at me."

On Sunday, Norma Jean packs a picnic and they go to Shiloh. To Leroy's relief, Mabel says she does not want to come with them. Norma Jean drives, and Leroy, sitting beside her, feels like some boring hitch-hiker she has picked up. He tries some conversation, but she answers him in monosyllables. At Shiloh, she drives aimlessly through the park, past bluffs and trails and steep ravines. Shiloh is an immense place, and Leroy cannot see it as a battleground. It is not what he expected. He thought it would look like a golf course. Monuments are everywhere, showing through the thick clusters of trees. Norma Jean passes the log cabin Mabel mentioned. It is surrounded by tourists looking for bullet holes.

"That's not the kind of log house I've got in mind," says Leroy apologetically.

"I know *that*."

"This is a pretty place. Your mama was right."

"It's O.K." says Norma Jean. "Well, we've seen it. I hope she's satisfied."

They burst out laughing together.

At the park museum, a movie on Shiloh is shown every half hour, but they decide that they don't want to see it. They buy a souvenir Confederate flag for Mabel, and then they find a picnic spot near the cemetery. Norma Jean has brought a picnic cooler, with pimiento sandwiches, soft drinks, and Yodels. Leroy eats a sandwich and then smokes a joint, hiding it behind the picnic cooler. Norma Jean has quit smoking altogether. She is picking cake crumbs from the cellophane wrapper, like a fussy bird. Leroy says, "So the boys in gray ended up in Corinth. The Union soldiers zapped 'em finally. April 7, 1862."

They both know that he doesn't know any history. He is just talking about some of the historical plaques they have read. He feels awkward, like a boy on a date with an older girl. They are still just making conversation.

"Corinth is where Mama eloped to," says Norma Jean. They sit in silence and stare at the cemetery for the Union dead and, beyond, at a tall cluster of trees. Campers are parked nearby, bumper to bumper, and small children in bright clothing are cavorting and squealing. Norma Jean wads up the cake wrapper and squeezes it tightly in her hand. Without looking at Leroy, she says, "I want to leave you."

Leroy takes a bottle of Coke out of the cooler and flips off the cap. He holds the bottle poised near his mouth but cannot remember to take a drink. Finally he says, "No, you don't."

"Yes, I do."

"I won't let you."

"You can't stop me."

"Don't do me that way."

Leroy knows Norma Jean will have her own way. "Didn't I promise to be home from now on?" he says.

"In some ways, a woman prefers a man who wanders," says Norma Jean. "That sounds crazy, I know."

"You're not crazy."

Leroy remembers to drink from his Coke. Then he says, "Yes, you *are* crazy. You and me could start all over again. Right back at the beginning."

"We *have* started all over again," says Norma Jean. "And this is how it turned out."

"What did I do wrong?"

"Nothing."

"Is this one of those women's lib things?" Leroy asks.

"Don't be funny."

The cemetery, a green slope dotted with white markers, looks like a subdivision site. Leroy is trying to comprehend that his marriage is breaking up, but for some reason he is wondering about white slabs in a graveyard.

"Everything was fine till Mama caught me smoking," says Norma Jean, standing up. "That set something off."

"What are you talking about?"

"She won't leave me alone—*you* won't leave me alone." Norma Jean seems to be crying, but she is looking away from him. "I feel eighteen again. I can't face that all over again." She starts walking away. "No, it *wasn't* fine. I don't know what I'm saying. Forget it."

Leroy takes a lungful of smoke and closes his eyes as Norma Jean's words sink in. He tries to focus on the fact that thirty-five hundred soldiers died on the grounds around him. He can only think of that war as a board game with plastic soldiers. Leroy almost smiles, as he compares the Confederates' daring attack on the Union camps and Virgil Mathis's raid on the bowling alley. General Grant, drunk and furious, shoved the southerners back to Corinth, where Mabel and Jet Beasley were married years later, when Mabel was still thin and good-looking. The next day, Mabel and Jet visited the battleground, and then Norma Jean was born, and then she married Leroy and they had a baby, which they lost, and now Leroy and Norma Jean are here at the same battleground. Leroy knows he is leaving out a lot. He is leaving out the insides of history. History was always just names and dates to him. It occurs to him that building a house out of logs is similarly empty—too simple. And the real inner workings of a marriage, like most of history, have escaped him. Now he sees that building a log house is the dumbest idea he could have had. It was clumsy of him to think Norma Jean would want a log house. It was a crazy idea. He'll have to think of something else, quickly. He will wad the blueprints into tight balls and fling them into the lake. Then he'll get moving again. He opens his eyes. Norma Jean has moved away and is walking through the cemetery, following a serpentine brick path. Leroy gets up to follow his wife, but his good leg is asleep and his bad leg still hurts him. Norma Jean is far away, walking rapidly toward the bluff by the river, and he tries to hobble toward her. Some children run past him, screaming noisily. Norma Jean has reached the bluff, and she is looking out over the Tennessee River. Now she turns toward Leroy and waves her arms. Is she beckoning to him? She seems to be doing an exercise for her chest muscles. The sky is unusually pale—the color of the dust ruffle Mabel made for their bed.

(1949–)

Mab Segrest was born and raised in Tuskegee, Alabama, and her experiences as a child and adolescent during the civil rights movement have strongly influenced her work and writing. She moved to Durham, North Carolina, in 1971 to attend graduate school at Duke University, where she received a Ph.D. in English in 1979. She taught English at Campbell University in Buies Creek, North Carolina, for seven years.

Segrest came out as a lesbian in 1976 and worked on the editorial collective of *Feminary: A Lesbian-Feminist Journal of the South* until 1983. Many of the essays in *My Mama's Dead Squirrel* (1985) were originally written for *Feminary.* As part of this collection, "Southern Women Writing: Toward a Literature of Wholeness" is an exemplary study of southern literature because it challenges not only the southern canon but long-held interpretations of key works and writers as well. As Adrienne Rich explains, it is through writers like Segrest who "reveal, suggest, refocus, and explore" that we come to understand the South, women's history, and the essence of America.

In 1985, Segrest was hired as coordinator for North Carolinians Against Racist and Religious Violence and organized against Klan and neo-Nazi activity until 1990. Her most recent book, *Memoir of a Race Traitor* (1994) seeks to document and make sense of that experience. She is currently coediting an anthology, *The Third Wave: Feminist Essays on Racism* (forthcoming).

Segrest serves on the board of the Center for Democratic Renewal, for which she authored (with Leonard Zeskind) *Quarantines and Death: The Far Right's Homophobic Agenda* (1989). She is also coordinator for the United States Urban-Rural Mission of the World Council of Churches. She lives in Durham with her partner of seventeen years and their eight-year-old daughter.

Southern Women Writing:
Toward a Literature of Wholeness
For Catherine Nicholson

I have started this essay on women's writing in the South innumerable times. Drafts litter my room. Friends grow impatient. Each weekend I face my typewriter in despair. But I'm starting again. I can't give it up. It feels too important for me to explain to myself how my most intense experiences of identity—growing up white in a small Southern town, loving women, reading and believing in Southern literature, beginning to understand the revolutionary implications of feminism—fit together; and for me to announce from this sorting through what seems absolutely clear: that the future of Southern literature depends on the female imagination, on female creative energy that is already spinning a new Southern writing. For it is Southern feminist writers, Black women and white, who have a new vision, who are rediscovering their obscured traditions, seeking new forms and language.

I tried to make this essay expository, analytical, and critical. But it must be primarily personal, intuitive. My understanding of the South and its literature rises too intensely from a lifetime of personal struggle with both over what I am trying to explain to myself—how my Southernness and my love for women relate. Shifting to a personal voice clarified many of the connections that I had sought between feelings and ideas.

I am almost thirty. I grew up in a small Alabama town, where my family on both sides had lived for four generations. I felt from an early age that something there was dreadfully wrong. I knew in my guts that my strongest feelings, for women and girls, put me somehow on the outside, set me apart. Although I did not know what *lesbian* was, I felt myself a closet freak.

As racial conflict increased in Alabama in the 1960s, I also knew deep inside me that what I heard people saying about Black people had somehow to do with me. This knowledge crystallizes around one image: I am thirteen, lying on my stomach beneath some bushes across from the public high school that was to have been integrated that morning. It is ringed with two hundred Alabama Highway Patrol troopers at two-yard intervals, their hips slung with pistols. Inside that terrible circle are twelve Black children, the only students allowed in. There is a stir in the crowd as two of the Black kids walk across the breezeway where I usually play. I have a tremendous flash of empathy, of identification, with their vulnerability and their aloneness inside that circle of force. Their separation is mine. And I know from now on that everything people have told me is "right" has to be reexamined. I am on my own.

Naturally (or unnaturally, perhaps) introspective, I turned to books for some vision of a larger world. I was increasingly drawn to novels about the South. I read *The Sound and the Fury* in my junior year in high school, advised by an article in World Book Encyclopedia that it was "great literature." In college, as an English major, I was drawn intensely into the world of Faulkner, adding women writers—Flannery O'Connor and Carson McCullers—as well. I was reading for explanation and insight. I found instead a world of freaks, of violence, of excess—of everything that literary critics called *Southern Gothic*. What I found did not lead me beyond my Alabama world but back into it.

Southern Gothic Writing: The Literature of the Grotesque

William Faulkner had a huge effect on me for years. Often I would think, "He is writing my life." When I went home from college on weekends, I saw my old world through his eyes. If paint peeled or a porch sagged on my parents' house, I would sigh, "Ah, Compson, O, Sartoris." He seemed to be dealing with race more than any other Southern writer I knew, so I thought his politics were profound. Other female English-major friends—a pride of women in college with whom I was variously in love—shared my obsession. With one friend, in fact, I made a pilgrimage to Oxford, Mississippi, to drink wine under moon and stars sitting on Faulkner's grave. I was, looking back, demented; metaphysically vulnerable, at least. I knew that reality must be redefined, and I swallowed Faulkner's version, hook, line, and sinker.

So when Faulkner wrote about women, I internalized that, too. In Freshman English we read *Light in August* and Faulkner's spinster, Joanna Burden, drew my special attention. In her forties, she lived by herself in her father's house on the outskirts of town—a Yankee, a woman whose work for Black causes alienated her from the community. She was a woman who thought and acted. As critics explained, "one of Faulkner's masculinized women . . . Joanna lives a self-immolating existence, symbolized by the submergence of her femininity. Her stern devotion to her crusade makes her manlike."[1] You get the picture. This self-immolation—which now sounds suspiciously like self-development to me—set Joanna up for conquest. It came at the hands of the tortured protagonist, Joe Christmas, who came to rape her and, when she liked it, stayed. Joanna, after all those "frustrate and irrevocable years," was mad for heterosexuality. She passed through "every avatar of a woman in love"—including "fits of rage," "an unexpected and infallible instinct for intrigue," and (of course) nymphomania:

> Now and then she appointed trysts beneath certain shrubs . . . where he would find her naked, or with clothing half torn to ribbons upon her, in the wild throes of nymphomania, her body gleaming in the slow shifting.[2]

Joanna's character is "balanced" in the novel by that of Lena Grove, "one of Faulkner's goddess figures"—eternally pregnant, mindless, stupidly loyal to the bum who knocked her up and ran. "Sheeplike."[3] Archetypically Female. By dividing Joanna and Lena into character foils, Faulkner—terrified by female power and female sexuality—divided women into breeders and non-breeders, with ominous warnings of what happens to women who use their energy for anything other than bearing children. Female power, female strangeness, man's intolerable dependence on women to knit him into life, were whittled down to size.

"A Rose for Emily" showed marked parallels. Emily Grierson—"vanquishing" males, an "idol" to the town—seemingly lived for forty years alone. Only at the macabre end of the story do we find that Emily had not been alone, but sleeping with the rotting corpse of the lover she killed forty years before because he was going to leave her. The implication, which remains unspoken by the Southern-gentlemanly narrator, hangs heavy in the atmosphere of the story: Emily hoarded and kept virginal by her father, starved for sex and easy prey for the primitive, the "dark, ready man" with a whip. If necessary she will kill him to make him stay. The choices for me as a woman without natural allegiances to men were not good: nymphomania, necrophilia, or the barrenness of a manless life.[4]

Then came Carson McCullers' "Ballad of the Sad Cafe," a poignant, beautifully controlled tale of human strangeness and isolation; its protagonist the unnatural, powerful, six-foot-two witch-doctoring spinster (now I know other words: *Amazon, dyke*) Amelia; its theme, that love is never mutual—"there are the lover and the beloved, but these two come from different countries."

As the cover to my Bantam edition overexplains McCullers' ballad, it is the story of a "grotesque human triangle in a primitive Southern town." This triangle consisted of the Amazon Amelia, her beloved (a dwarf named Cousin Lyman); and her exhusband of ten days, Marvin Macy, whom she had banished on her wedding night when she discovered what all was involved in marriage. Amelia, you see, "cared nothing for the love of men" until Lyman came along. The two of them created between them in their vitalizing strangeness a cafe where townspeople could gather and find relief from the monotony and isolation of their lives in the mill town. Then Marvin came back and broke up the "ill-matched and pitiful conjunction," gaining his revenge when Lyman fell madly in love with him. The two men busted up Amelia's cafe and left her in lonely and heartbroken humiliation: "Her face lengthened, and the great muscles of her body shrank until she was as thin as old maids are thin when they go crazy." Her herbal medicine, formerly a life-giving force in the community, went bad; and her eyes crossed "as though they sought each other out to exchange a little glance of grief and lonely recognition." She boarded herself up in her sad cafe, in the sadder, now completely desolate town.[5]

Reading this story, I was left with an overwhelming sense of human loneliness and the warping of sensitive spirits. I found McCullers' theme of the impossibility of mutual love (Marvin did not love the dwarf, merely used him to gain revenge on Amelia, whom he had loved unrequitedly) especially telling, since my experience loving women at that time could not be openly acknowledged and returned.

Another example is Flannery O'Connor's "Good Country People," a bitter, funny story whose strange humor fascinated me for years. Its female protagonist is Joy Hopewell, thirty-two, unmarried, physically deformed by a hunting accident that blew off her leg when she was twelve, leaving her life devoid of "any normal good times." "Mrs. Hopewell said that every year she grew less and less like other people and more like herself—bloated, rude, and squint-eyed." Joy changed her name to Hulga and got a Ph.D. Barely covering her misery with condescension for the country people she lived among, she was easy prey for Manly Pointer, a fast-talking Bible salesman who sweet-talked Hulga into a barn loft and out of her wooden leg ("it's what makes you different"), only to leave her humiliated, one-legged, and immobile in the barn loft as he hightailed it out across the Georgia fields with her artificial leg in his Bible case. Although Manly Pointer is despicable, the main deformity is Hulga's. And O'Connor's picture of her is terrible and pitiless, one that calls forth in the reader's laughter her/his complicity in Hulga's humiliation.[6]

As one of my friends from these undergraduate days remarked recently, in what seemed to me a brilliant bit of insight: "Reading this stuff, we thought if we could just grow up warped enough, we'd be works of art." This is known as *Southern decadence,* and it has done a lot of people in.

The Patriarchal State of Normalcy and the Southern Freak

I have tried these past weeks, in the process of this writing, to explain how I conspired in this entrapment, why the grotesque held such appeal for me. I think it is because freaks in Southern Gothic literature reflect a process basic to the small-town Southern life I knew. This community life was confined by the narrow boundaries of what it felt was permitted or speakable. The sharply drawn perimeters of normalcy created its opposite, the grotesque. If some people must be normal, then some must be different from normal, or freaks. In reality, everyone is a freak because no human can cram her/himself into the narrow space that is the state of normalcy. But all have to pretend that they fit, and those closet freaks choose the most vulnerable among them to punish for their own secret alienation, to bear the burden of strangeness. O'Connor has deep insight into this discrepancy between the narrowness of people's models for experience—encapsulated in Mrs. Hopewell's cliches about "ladies" and "good country people"—and the chaos and mystery of existence that continues to erupt through the cliches.

The town freak (or eccentric, the *eccentric* being in one's own family, the *freak* in someone else's) is often sacrosanct, protected because her/his insanity is recognized as necessary to preserve collective sanity (as in "Ballad of the Sad Cafe," when the town withers into a wasteland when Amelia's vitalizing differentness is destroyed). I have heard from friends studying family therapy that this scapegoating process occurs in families as well as communities, when one member is often chosen to bear the burden of sickness, allowing other members to be well. And if this scapegoating process cuts the freak off from the community, it builds into the community a death wish. People are cut off from each other and from the strange in themselves. As Adrienne Rich explains, "The unspoken . . . becomes the unspeakable."[7] Wholeness of self of community becomes impossible. Deformity, partiality, grotesqueness perpetuate themselves.

These community demands for normalcy are particularly strong around matters of female sexuality—hence the prevalence of the female grotesque in these fictions and hence my own early sense of "lesbian separation" (to coin a phrase).

Which brings me to the major question: Why do people do this to each other and themselves? Why these narrow boundaries in the first place? I wish I knew the whole answer. I know that it is NOT merely a Southern problem, although we white Southerners—as American Family Freaks, racist and immoral—have acted out our pathology at times with great zest.

To begin to answer: I know that this destructive process in the South is intimately related to racism. It is the legacy of slavery to a people who could not afford to do the right thing so that they could not afford to listen to their consciences, and consequently cut themselves off from the better parts of themselves. Before I can enslave someone, I must first see him/her as less than human, unlike me. Other. Lillian Smith, activist and author, offers profound insight into white racist psychology, with imagery like mine of walls and boundaries:

Our emotions are blunted where Negroes are concerned. It is as though we had segregated an area in our minds, marked it 'colored' and refused our feelings entrance to it.... But when we reserve this humanity of ours, this precious quality of love, of tenderness, and of imaginative identification, for only people of our skin color (or of our family, our own class, or friends) we have split our lives in a way shockingly akin to those sick people whom we call schizophrenics. And we develop—as we whites have developed toward Negroes—a personality picture strongly like theirs of blunted emotions, delusions of persecution, feelings of 'aloneness,' extreme irritability when efforts are made to change our white ways.... We develop a desire to shut ourselves off not only from the Negro by segregation, but also from all science, all influences that are disturbing to the picture we have made of ourselves and of our 'persecutors.' [8]

This walling off of parts of the self—the segregated heart—creates the grotesque.

I have for years understood racism to be despicable in the South. I am coming to understand that Southern patriarchy is at least as insidious. Both patriarchy and racism depend on creating a category of Other—or freak, not "normal like me." In Southern racism, it is the Black person; in patriarchy, the female. And I believe that sexism, rather than racism or classism, is the first oppression and provides the model for the others. In the Biblical tradition, the grotesque IS the female. Woman is both physically and spiritually deformed. Andrea Dworkin in *Woman Hating* quotes the medieval church's *Malleus Maleficarum:*

And it should be noted that there was a defect in the formation of the first woman, since she was formed from a bent rib, that is, rib of the breast, which is bent as it were in a contrary direction to man. And since through this defect she is an imperfect animal, she always deceives. [9]

This is the essence of patriarchal religion, which is to say, Greco-Christian thought, which is to say, Western Civilization. The South—the Bible Belt—offers an intense microcosm of patriarchal process. I suspect that the rigidness that binds Southern society is the same rigidness required to limit female sexuality to marriage so that men can assure themselves of paternity and thus a place in the natural cycle. The South-as-Patriarchy offers a fertile terrain for feminist analysis.

Southern literature and culture, for one thing, show the necessity of the idea of *original sin* to patriarchal religion—to the perpetration of the grotesque. Original sin is a handy explanation for the alienation and misery that result from so narrow a definition of the norm. The world is fallen and cannot be changed by change in temporal power structures or by a reexamination of mythology. The guilt people feel is natural, not due to unnatural social structures that could be overthrown. As Flannery O'Connor, devout Catholic, explains in *Mystery and Manners:*[10] "All this may not be ideal, but the Southerner has enough sense not to ask for the ideal but only for the possible, the workable." The workable did not work well for O'Connor, nor has it in the South for any but those NOT doing the working, those pulling the strings. Folks who know that they have originally sinned, regardless of how they might act, tend to stay in their places; and this perpetuates the status quo.

Guilt also perpetuates existing power structures by becoming a substitute for action. Faulkner's politics—for all his caterwauling about doom and gloom and Southern burdens and curses—stink:

> It (race in the South) will cause a great deal more trouble and anguish. And I, myself, I wouldn't undertake to guess how many years it will be before the Negro has equality in my country, anything approaching equality. But I am convinced that the Negro is the one that will have to do it, not by getting enough white people on his side to pass laws and bayonets, but to make himself—to improve himself to where the white men in Mississippi say, will say, 'Please, join me.' There is too much talk of right and not enough talk of responsibility.[11]

Let Lillian Smith deal with William:

> I know the dread of change; I know all the rationalizations by which the white man eases his guilt and conserves his feeling of superiority: how he concentrates not on his own problem of white superiority, not on his own obsession with skin color, but instead on the Negro, hoping that somehow the Negro can be changed to fit the pattern more harmoniously, as though the white man and his pattern could never be changed.[12]

This entire concept of original sin with its necessary guilt rests squarely on female grotesqueness—woman did the tempting; woman is at fault. And when women are grotesque, humanity is grotesque, since both women and men are "of woman born."

The grotesque, then, serves deliberate political ends. It fastens the creative imagination on images of deformity and despair. Backed by patriarchial myth, it persuades us that this is reality, i.e. not to be questioned or changed. People in power stay in power: it's god-ordained. The grotesque limits the creative imagination by causing divisions within the self so that the individual is cut off from her deepest parts, from those oracles and visions that could tell of a different reality, of the possibility of wholeness. Those imaginations which do not conform are destroyed (millions of witches were killed), erased or ignored (Lillian Smith, Zora Neale Hurston, Kate Chopin), or caused to self-destruct ("Don't kill me, boss. I'm killing myself").

Feminism and the Unloaded Canon

Feminism is the antithesis to the grotesque. It threatens it the most. Southern literary tradition gives evidence to this—it is female and feminist writers who are most rigorously excluded from the canon (which is to say, the canon is unloaded, defused). Even the Black Marxist critique of Black writers Richard Wright and Ralph Ellison made it in. This exclusion of feminists makes sense when we consider the strong tradition that original sin underwrites all serious Southern literature. Walker Percy, one of the foremost accepted Southern novelists writing today, was asked why there are "so many good Southern writers." He replied: "Because we lost the war." As Flannery O'Connor explained: "He didn't mean simply that a lost war makes good subject matter. What he was saying was that we have had our fall."[13] Women who refuse to stay in their place—who refuse to be grotesque, to stay fallen—upset the whole shebang. For there have always been Southern women who knew that they did not want to join the white men in Mississippi for anything; who have known that WE did not lose the war.

I am just beginning to realize, then, how carefully that Southern literary tradition I absorbed was controlled. The grotesque was all I found, so I assumed that that was all there was. I am just beginning to read Southern women writers whom I did not know then existed, writers such as Lillian Smith and Zora Neale Hurston. Reading Michelle Cliff's recent edition of Lillian Smith's writing, I remember reading of Smith's death in *Life* magazine in 1964. I am amazed how many of her insights into race in the South I have had to rediscover. I ask myself why, and she answers:

> When writers about race are discussed, I am never mentioned; when women writers are mentioned, I am not among them. ... This is a curious amnesia. ... I can still laugh it off most of the time; but now and then I truly wonder. Whom among the mighty have I so greatly offended?[14]

Next to Smith's writings by my bed is Zora Neale Hurston's autobiography, *Dust Tracks on a Road.* Hurston writes of growing up Black and female, but passages of her story move me as my own. This especially:

> But no matter whether my probings made me happier or sadder, I kept on probing to know. For instance, I had a stifled longing. I used to climb to the top of one of the huge chinaberry trees which guarded our front gate, and look out over the world. The most interesting thing I saw was the horizon. Every way I turned, it was there, and the same direction away. Our house, then, was in the center of the world. It grew upon me that I ought to walk out to the horizon and see what the end of the world was like. The daring of the thing held me back for a while, but the thing became so urgent that I showed it to my friend, Carrie Roberts, and asked her to go with me. She agreed.... I could hardly sleep that night from the excitement of the thing. I had been yearning for so many months to find out about the end of things. I had no doubts about the beginnings. They were somewhere in the five acres that was home to me. Most likely in Mama's room. Now I was going to see the end, and then I would be satisfied.... I was on the way to her house by a round-about way when I met her. She was coming to tell me that she couldn't go. It looked so far that maybe we wouldn't get back by sundown, and then we would both get a whipping.... No matter how hard I begged, she wouldn't go. The thing was too bold and brazen to her way of thinking. We had a fight, then. I had to hit Carrie to keep my heart from stifling me. Then I was sorry I had struck my friend, and went on home and hid under the house with my heartbreak. But I did not give up on the idea of my journey. I was merely lonesome for someone brave enough to undertake it with me.[15]

These women, and doubtless many others, were withheld from me; and I fed instead on the bitterness and despair of Faulkner, O'Connor, and McCullers.

Spinsters: The Old Maid as Battle Ax

The question of the censorship of feminist values and writing in mainstream Southern literature and criticism has become clearest to me when I realized the issues involved in portraying the spinster as grotesque. It was important for me to read Mary Daly's restored definition of *spinster* in *Gyn/Ecology,* not the pejorative definition of an old maid, a woman who has failed to marry, but:

> *a woman whose occupation is to spin participates in the whirling movement of creation. She who has chosen her Self, who defines her Self, by choice, neither in relation to children, nor to men, who is Self-identified, who is a Spinster, a whirling dervish, spinning a new time-space.*[16]

When I also realized that many of the women writers in the South in this century have been spinsters in both senses—all spinning stories out of themselves, most unmarried or living beyond primary allegiances with men—spinster stories became even more important. Spinster protagonists are often versions of self-portraiture, and the difference feminism makes to women writing is strikingly clear. I would also like to look within and beyond the new spinster writing emerging in the South to see if I can glimpse what a Southern women's literature of wholeness would be: what we as women writing might become.

I look back first at those Gothic stories described earlier, with my new feminist eyes. Now Faulkner's blatant woman-hating appalls me. Then I thought, "This is art." Nor did it bother me that the great tragedy of *Light in August* was Joe's castration, not his decapitation of Joanna (the fate of a woman who uses her head?). Nor did I understand then the anger at female power, female affinity with natural cycles that was to Joe and his creator "periodic filth"; or that, with Joe, Faulkner fled "the lightless hot wet primogentive Female" who gives birth with "that wailing cry in a tongue unknown to man."[17] Faulkner, in the microcosm of the South, was a classically patriarchal writer. But as a freshman I didn't know what patriarchy was.

The pattern set by Faulkner appears in the stories of McCullers and O'Connor as well. The similarities in the four stories are striking: spinsters often have threatening, inherent power; they live alone in what usually seems like self-sufficiency; rescuing male lovers come along, and they leap in frustrated desire into their arms; the lovers jilt them leaving the women in humiliated knowledge of their dependency. This happens in *Light in August,* "A Rose for Emily," "Ballad of the Sad Cafe," and "Good Country People." The message is clear: women must be dependent on men. The use of spinster humiliation by women writers shows the dangerous degree to which women writing in a male tradition internalize male values, like swallowing slow poison.

I do not consider it coincidental that both O'Connor and McCullers lived much of their lives in excruciating physical pain, or that both died young. They inhabited a twisted world—just as their characters lived in twisted fictions—without adequate vision of female, or human, wholeness. As a reading between the lines of *The Lonely Hunter: A Biography of Carson McCullers* makes clear, Carson McCullers was a lesbian without a community. Her most passionate attachments were to women, unrequited, and her most concrete relationships were with homosexual men (thus the situation of "Sad Cafe"). To the amusement of her peers, she dressed in pants and smoked a pipe. With this social reinforcement, she acquired the sense that she was grotesque, in the wrong body. She told a friend: "I was born a man." This sense of lesbian-as-freak was rooted in her Southern childhood: "When Carson was younger, some of the girls gathered in little clumps of femininity and threw rocks at her when she walked nearby, snickering loud asides and tossing within hearing distance such labels as 'weird,' 'freakish looking,' and 'queer.'" McCullers lived outside the South during her adulthood but returned periodically, as she put it, to "renew her sense of horror."[18]

Flannery O'Connor is to me even more disturbing. She was an intensely visionary woman writer, and she knew that hers was a world where "something is obviously lacking, where there is the mystery of incompleteness." She was herself a prophetic novelist, calling the world back to itself. Her writing and life teetered on vision; but within the Christian tradition, it was a vision of the horrific. The mystery for O'Connor was not the mystery of life but the mystery of death: the "central mystery" of her church, as she herself explains in an essay, was that "life, for all its horrors, has been found worth dying for." Encased in what Mary Daly calls a "necrophilic S&M society" O'Connor saw only death: "We lost our innocence in the Fall, and our return to it is through the redemption which was brought about by Christ's death and *our slow participation in it.*" [emphasis added] She herself explains, without irony: "My own feeling is that writers who see by the light of their Christian faith will have in these times the sharpest eye for the grotesque, for the perverse, for the unacceptable." She internalizes: "[The] prophet-freak is an image of [the writer her] self."[19]

Hulga's life in "Good Country People" parallels O'Connor's. Both women are physically impaired and live dependent on their mothers. Hulga, like her creator, knows she is going to die. The emotion that fuses the violent and the comic in "Good Country People" is anger. It is the cold anger of self-hatred. It seems more than coincidence that O'Connor's life recapitulated her religious vision. The disease which killed her was lupus, a condition primarily inflicting women, in which the body overproduces antibodies and attacks itself. Flannery O'Connor strikes me as a visionary woman in patriarchal tradition—a witch who burned herself.

Both McCullers and O'Connor were casualties of the war of female mind with female body. It is a battle in which there are no victors, only victims.

The New Spinster and the Labrys

I would like now to turn to the feminist literature emerging in the South. The strongest fictions in this new literature are, not surprisingly, stories about spinsters, self-identified women spinning a new time and space. These feminist fictions reflect two qualities that traditional spinster tales ignore and, consequently, negate. The first quality is the integrity of female solitude, that turning inward in a room of one's own, a process that puts each woman in touch with her inner self, her void:

> The void is the creatrix, the matrix. It is not mere hollowness and anarchy. But in women it has been identified with lovelessness, barrenness, sterility. We have been urged to fill our 'emptiness' with children. We are not supposed to go down into the darkness of the core.[20]

Female solitude in male-dominated fictions was merely the old maid's frustrated longing for male attention (Amelia's cross-eyed and lonely introspection after Cousin Lyman absconds); a room of one's own for these Southern spinsters, the boarded up and sad cafe, the barn loft in which Hulga sits one-legged, "churning," and alone. The other terrible absence in male-dominated fictions is the absence of female community, or even its possibility. In all the stories I described, the spinster was alone, set apart from both men and married women. The small-town communities within the fictions showed complete lack of support for female self-identification. Without either respect for female solitude or the presence of female community, of course spinsters were seen as freaks.

Feminist fictions clearly value the creative integrity of a woman's solitude and the absolute necessity for the sanity and health of women's community. These values are beginning to show clearly in Southern women's writing. The white foremother of this consciousness is Kate Chopin, whose turn-of-the-century novel, *The Awakening*,[21] has been rediscovered by feminist critics in the past ten years. It tells the story of a New Orleans matron's journey from the boredom and bondage of marriage toward the freedom of the new spinsterhood—a quest that ends for Edna Pontillier in suicide, since she has no supportive community within which she can awaken. But Chopin includes in the universe of her characters an unmarried musician, Madame Reisz, who pays a price for her integrity with an isolation that Edna cannot bring herself to endure.

Lillian Smith bequeaths an ambivalent feminist heritage to the new Southern spinster. As her editor Michelle Cliff points out, Smith's thinking on race fits into a clarifying tradition that was not available to her as a feminist thinker. Cliff highlights Smith's feminist contributions: her observations "about misogyny, about the power and powerlessness of women, and about the invention of male mythology regarding women," as well as about the silences women have conspired in "because to tell the truth would be to shatter the male myths about the nature of women."

But Smith's lack of feminist tradition shows in her failure to gauge the extent to which patriarchal values devalue the female. This failure leads her to internalize—or rather, to fail to exorcize—certain misogynist concepts:

> In war as in peace, in civilization's destruction as well as in its creation, Cherchez La Femme is of eternal relevance. Man's humiliation at her hand has been monstrous and her tyranny a dread thing to endure....

> For not only has she failed in her role as mother but she has used it as an excuse for her empty mind.... It is no wonder that a great man like Sigmund Freud, who taught the world almost all it knows about the child's emotions, spoke of woman a little contemptuously as 'culturally stunted.'[22]

Nor did Smith live in a time or place that validated her lesbianism. In light of her historical context, her insights and her courage to express them are amazing. Both Smith and Chopin provide a feminist heritage for the latest generation of white Southern writers.

Women novelists in the seventies have begun to expand this vision. Alice Walker's *Meridian* is the most important book to come out of the South in years. It is the story of a young Black woman's awakening during the civil rights struggles in the South and her growth toward an intensely spiritual womanhood. I found it moving and important to read a Black woman's account of the turbulent years I grew up in; and I heard in Alice Walker's writing an important voice, previously suppressed in Southern writing.

Meridian places high value both on female relationships and female solitude. When women are divided—by race, class, the guilt between mother and daughter over the daughter's "shattering the mother's emerging self," differences among Black friends on political issues—the book grieves. It also offers analysis of the way oppressed people turn their anger on each other and themselves. Alice Walker presents an American society deeply rent and shows the pain that comes when such divisions separate even people who love one another.

Its spinster, Meridian, moves as her name implies to the "highest point of her power and splendor." She awakens from her marriage and leaves her children to recover her self. She moves beyond sex after an abortion. She is a woman on the edge of change—in her work in the civil rights movement of the sixties; in her return to the South to keep working in the seventies after the revolutionary fervor of the sixties had passed. She is a woman in touch with her visionary powers, first felt in the pit of an Indian burial mound as a kind of trance that "expand[ed] the consciousness of being alive." She is a woman looking for new forms, new transformations. She thinks: "The only new thing now . . . would be the refusal of Christ to accept crucifixion. . . . All saints should walk away. Do their bit, then—just walk away." Meridian does this at the end: she walks out of the book to heal herself of those diseases inflicted by the world she fought to transform. She leaves her friends behind with no choice but to assume her transforming role. She gives them her knowledge:

> There is water in the world for us
> brought by our friends
> though the rock of mother and god
> vanishes into sand
> and we, cast out alone
> to heal
> and re-create
> ourselves.[23]

Meridian, bearing the terror of her past, walks out of the book to spin a new time and space.

Eudora Welty's *The Optimist's Daughter*[24] is not overtly feminist but does show a stronger woman protagonist (a young widow returning to her home town at the death of her father to engage her own past) and a valuing of women's friendships (in Laura's mother's friends, old ladies who take care of each other and Laura, while her generation—"the bridesmaids"—provide hollow support). The novel also deals seriously and poignantly with the mother-daughter relationship. These values are new in Welty's fiction (earlier work, like "Why I Live at the P.O." and *The Ponder Heart* depend for much of their humor on making spinsters the butt of the joke). The writing indicates that although she is not involved in feminist causes, Welty has benefitted from feminism.

It is true that some of the most exuberant women writing in the South today are lesbians, and some of the best lesbian fiction is by Southern-identified women. *Sister Gin,* for instance, is June Arnold's wonderful story of the post-menopausal almost-uppercrust of Wilmington, North Carolina. *Sister Gin*'s women are emphatically not grotesque. In fact, the traditionally grotesque experience of menopause and aging become metaphors for the process of radical growth of the female self. Mamie Carter, seventy-seven-year-old spinster extraordinaire, explains: "The ultimate contempt for a woman is contempt for old age." And Su, menopausal gin drinker, learns from Mamie the courage to be open to the chaos of change:

> I can reach out to age itself, lust after a final different dry silken life and so much grace and elegance from all that knowledge of days. . . . There is no more beautiful word in the language than withered.

The essence of these old women is the spinning mind: "The old mind is the complete novelist. . . . The truly free is she who can be old at any age."

These spinster selves in *Sister Gin* form a nurturing community of Southern white women talking and listening to each other—or trying to know when to be silent. As Su discovers talking to a Northern feminist on the phone: "We Southern women have to speak for each other. We've been practicing that for years now. Thanks, Barbara. I just found out where I belong." *Sister Gin* also offers a model for women's community that wonderful bridge-club-cum-vigilante group of Furies, the Shirley Temple Emeritae, who dress in black robes and emerge at night to avenge the latest rapes, leaving their male victims tied naked to boards in front of various public monuments and official homes.[25]

Female anger is directed where it belongs. No feminine passivity here. If Emily Grierson had had Mamie Carter for a neighbor, things might have turned out differently in Jefferson, Mississippi. In *Sister Gin,* the old battle-ax arms herself; her spiritual weapon the labrys, both its edges keen.

Bertha Harris' critical emphasis on the lesbian as monster shows her Southern upbringing. The grotesque is the monstrous: "Monsters are, and have always been invented to express what ordinary people cannot: feeling." Her analysis of the source of the grotesque agrees with mine:

> Law . . . shows what is *out of law; and makes the divine, which is wor-*
> *shipped; and makes the criminal, which is brutalized—and adored,*
> *and for the same reasons the 'divine' is worshipped: because of its*
> *difference.*[26]

I am uncomfortable, however, with the degree to which she wants us as lesbian writers to embrace the patriarchally created role of monster— even to be "unassimilable, awesome, dangerous, outrageous, different." I am not sure *what* I want to be, but I know I don't care to be a monster. I've already been that. Nor do I think that the alternative to monstrous lesbian writing is what Harris calls the literature of the "winkieburger." The solution lies more in imagining and visioning ourselves out of patri-archally prescribed roles that depend for their power on oppression of the Other.

Toward a Women's Literature of Wholeness

A Southern women's literature of wholeness, then, is beginning to emerge in Southern women's novels. It is a literature that will rise:

- out of our refusal to turn anger inward;
- out of our refusal to accept political analysis that substitutes guilt for action and that divides Black women from white and Northern women from Southern;
- out of our profound respect for female solitude and self-hood;
- out of our refusal to see either female body or female spirit as grotesque;
- out of our continuing tentative searching toward a creative energy, both personal and collective, that will not—like fuses and circuits and nuclear reactors—overload or burn out, but that will—like the sea as she responds to the moon's tug—ebb and flow in ever-replenishing cycles;
- out of a community of Southern women searching together in the delicate connections between solitude and friendship for our visions of ourselves and what our world could be.

We are women who are finding each other for that journey to the end of the world, women who no longer need to be lonesome for women-friends brave enough to travel it with us.

Notes

1. Edward Volpe, *A Reader's Guide to William Faulkner* (New York: Farrar, Straus and Giroux, 1971), p. 170.
2. William Faulkner, *Light in August* (New York: Modern Library, 1968), pp. 244–45.
3. Volpe, p. 152.
4. William Faulkner, "A Rose for Emily" in *The Collected Stories of William Faulkner* (New York: Random House, 1977).
5. Carson McCullers, *The Ballad of the Sad Cafe and Other Stories* (New York: Bantam, 1976), pp. 26, 4, 25, 70. See "'Lines I Dare'" [in *My Mama's Dead Squirrel*] for a later discussion of McCullers.
6. [O'Connor's spelling of Pointer's first name is "Manley."—Ed.] Flannery O'Connor, *The Complete Stories of Flannery O'Connor* (New York: Farrar, Straus and Giroux, 1971), pp. 271–272, 276, 288. See Alice Walker, "Beyond the Peacock: The Reconstruction of Flannery O'Connor" in *In Search of Our Mothers' Gardens* (San Diego: Harcourt Brace Jovanovich, 1983) for a more sympathetic reading of O'Connor as "the first great modern writer from the South." Walker says O'Connor "destroyed the last vestiges of sentimentality in white Southern writing; she caused her white women to look ridiculous on pedestals, and she approached her black characters—as a mature artist—with unusual humility and restraint" (pp. 42–59).
7. Adrienne Rich, "The Transformation of Silence into Language and Action," *Sinister Wisdom* 6 (1978): 18.
8. Lillian Smith, *The Winner Names the Age,* ed. Michelle Cliff (New York: Norton, 1978), pp. 35–38.
9. Andrea Dworkin, *Woman Hating* (New York: Dutton, 1971), pp. 131–132.
10. Flannery O'Connor, *Mystery and Manners* (New York: Farrar, Straus and Giroux, 1967), p. 234.
11. Joseph L. Fant and Robert Ashley, eds. *Faulkner at West Point* (New York: Random House, 1969), p. 88.
12. Smith, p. 35.
13. O'Connor, *Mystery and Manners,* pp. 58–59.
14. Smith, p. 218.

15. Zora Neale Hurston, *Dust Tracks on a Road: An Autobiography* (New York: Lippincott, 1942), pp. 36–37.
16. Mary Daly, *Gyn/Ecology* (Boston: Beacon Press, 1978), pp. 3–4.
17. Faulkner, *Light in August,* pp. 107, 378.
18. Virginia Spencer Carr, *The Lonely Hunter: A Biography of Carson McCullers* (Garden City, New York: Doubleday, 1976), pp. 157–59, 27–28.
19. O'Connor, *Mystery and Manners,* 146–48, 33, 118.
20. Adrienne Rich, "Women and Honor: Some Notes on Lying" in *On Lies, Secrets, and Silence: Selected Prose 1966–78* (New York: Norton, 1979), p. 191.
21. Kate Chopin, *The Awakening and Selected Stories of Kate Chopin* (New York: New American Library, 1976).
22. Smith, pp. 169–70, 177, 184.
23. Alice Walker, *Meridian* (New York: Harcourt Brace Jovanovich, 1976), pp. 41, 17, 51, 151, 219.
24. Eudora Welty, *The Optimist's Daughter* (New York: Random House, 1972).
25. June Arnold, *Sister Gin* (Plainfield, Vermont: Daughters, 1975), pp. 133, 189, 169.
26. Bertha Harris, "What We Mean to Say: Notes Toward Defining the Nature of Lesbian Literature," *Heresies* 3 (1977). See "'Lines I Dare'" for a later interpretation of Harris' remark.

33. Ellen Gilchrist

(1935–)

Ellen Gilchrist was born in Vicksburg, Mississippi, and received her degree from Millsaps College in 1967. The following year she received a poetry award from the Mississippi Arts Festival, but she did not actively pursue writing for several years. In the 1970s she also attended the University of Arkansas but did not complete a degree there. Gilchrist's writing career actually began later in her life when, at the age of forty, she became an editor for a New Orleans newspaper.

Although she had been recognized with her first collection of poetry, *The Land Surveyor's Daughter* in 1979, the same year that she received a National Endowment for the Arts grant, Ellen Gilchrist did not become a household name until she began waking up America each morning in the early 1980s by reading her journal on National Public Radio's "Morning Edition." Much like her first collection of short stories, *In the Land of Dreamy Dreams* (1981), these stories emphasized the distinctive southern voice so finely crafted in her works while also revealing much of Ellen Gilchrist's personality.

Gilchrist tends to write about upper-class southern women trapped by unsatisfying social expectations. Many of her works chronicle the lives of characters like Rhoda Manning, the protagonist in "The Expansion of the Universe" as well as several other stories, from their spoiled childhoods through their sexual awakenings to marriage and its failure. The determination and spirit that these women exude have brought on such labels as "feisty, bratty Southern belles," and "redheaded hellions," but most critics praise Gilchrist's characters for their ability to fight against their stifling straitlaced environment.

The eighties proved to be years of immense success for Gilchrist. Among her several awards are two Pushcart Prizes for "Rich" and "Summer, An Elegy," the American Book Award for fiction from the Association of American Publishers in 1984 for *Victory Over Japan*, and a J. William Fulbright Award for literature in 1985. "The Expansion of the Universe" was published in *Drunk with Love: A Book of Stories* (1986). Her poems, short stories, and articles have appeared in *Atlantic, Cosmopolitan,* and *Southern Living,* but she has also proven herself as a playwright, winning a national scriptwriting award from the National Educational Television network for her play *A Season of Dreams,* which is based on the short stories of Eudora Welty. She has produced several additional works in recent years, including *The Anna Papers: A Novel* (1988), *Falling Through Space: The Journals of Ellen Gilchrist* (1988), *Light Can Be Both Wave and Particle: A Book of Stories* (1989), *Net of Jewels: A Novel* (1993), and *Starcarbon: A Meditation on Love* (1994).

The Expansion of the Universe

It was a Saturday afternoon in Harrisburg, Illinois. Rhoda was lying on the bed with catalogs all around her, pretending to be ordering things. It was fall outside the window, Rhoda's favorite time of year. "The fall is so poignant," she was fond of saying. This fall was more poignant than ever because Rhoda had started menstruating on the thirteenth of September. Thirteen, her lucky number. Rhoda had been dying to start menstruating. Everyone she knew had started. Shirley Hancock and Dixie Lee Carouthers and Naomi and everyone who was anyone in the ninth grade had started. It was beginning to look like Rhoda would be the last person in Southern Illinois to menstruate. Now, finally, right in the middle of a Friday night double feature at the picture show, she had started. She had stuffed some toilet paper into her pants and hurried back down the aisle and pulled Letitia and Naomi back to the restroom with her. They huddled together, very excited. Rhoda's arms were on her friends' shoulders. "I started," she said. "It's on my pants. Oh, God, I thought I never would."

"You've got to have a belt," Letitia said. "I'm going home and get you a belt. You stay right here."

"She doesn't need a belt," Naomi said. "All she needs is to pin one to her pants. Where's a quarter?" Someone produced a quarter and they stuck it in the machine and the Kotex came sliding out and Rhoda pinned it inside her pants and they went back into the theater to tell everyone else. *A Date With Judy,* starring Elizabeth Taylor, was playing. Rhoda snuggled down in her accustomed seat, six rows from the front on the left-hand aisle. It was too good to be true. It was wonderful.

It was almost a week later when her mother discovered what had happened. Rhoda tossed the information over her shoulder on her way out the door. "I fell off the roof last week," she said. "Did I tell you that?"

"You did what? What are you talking about?"

"I started menstruating. I got my period. You know, fell off the roof."

"Oh, my God," Ariane said. "What are you talking about, Rhoda? Where were you? What did you do about it? WHY DIDN'T YOU TELL ME?"

"I knew what to do. I was at the picture show. Naomi gave me some Kotex."

"Rhoda. Don't leave. Wait a minute, you have to talk to me about this. Where are you going?" Rhoda's mother dropped the scarf she was knitting and stood beside the chair.

"I'm going to cheerleader practice. I'm late."

"Rhoda, you have to have a belt. You have to use the right things. I want to take you to Doctor Usry. You can't just start menstruating."

"We're going to get some Tampax. Donna Marie and Letitia and I. We're going to learn to wear it." Then she was gone, as Rhoda was always going, leaving her mother standing in the doorway or the middle of a room with her jaw clenched and her nails digging into her palms and everything she had believed all her life in question.

Now it was October and Rhoda was lying on the bed among the catalogs watching the October sun outside the window and getting bored with Saturday afternoon. She decided to get dressed and go downtown to see if Philip Holloman was sitting on his stool at the drugstore. Philip Holloman was a friend of Bob Rosen's and Rhoda was madly in love with Bob Rosen, who was nineteen years old and off at school in Champaign-Urbana.

Bob Rosen was the smartest person Rhoda had ever known. He played a saxophone and laughed at everything and taught her how to dress and about jazz and took her riding in his car and gave her passionate kisses whenever his girlfriend was mad at him. She was mad at him a lot. Her name was Anne and she worked in a dress shop downtown and she was always frowning. Every time Rhoda had ever seen her she was frowning. Because of this Rhoda was certain that sooner or later Bob Rosen would break up with her and get his pin back. In the meantime she would be standing by, she would be his friend or his protégée or anything he wanted her to be. She would memorize the books and records he told her to buy. She would wear the clothes he told her to wear and write for *The Purple Clarion* and be a cheerleader and march with the band and do everything he directed her to do. *So he would love her.* Love me, love me, love me, she chanted to the dark bushes, alone in the yard at night, sending him messages through the stars. Love me, love me, love me, love me.

Rhoda walked down Rollston Street toward the town, concentrating on making Bob Rosen love her. She walked past the ivy-colored walls of the Clayton Place, past the new Oldsmobile Stephanie Hinton got to drive to school, past the hospital and the bakery and the filling station. The Sweet Shop stood on its corner with its pink-and-white gingerbread trim. I could stop off and get a lemon phosphate before I go to the drugstore, Rhoda thought. Or one of those things that Dudley likes with ice cream in the lemonade. There was something strange about the Sweet Shop. Something spooky and unhealthy. Rhoda was more comfortable with the drugstore, where the vices were mixed in with Band-Aids and hot water bottles and magazines and aspirins.

Leta Ainsley was in the Sweet Shop. Leaning up against a counter with her big foreign-looking face turned toward the door. She had been in Japan before she came to Harrisburg. She had strange ideas and hair that grew around her lips. She was the Junior editor of *The Purple Clarion* where Rhoda was making her start as a reporter. She had let Rhoda wear her coat and her horn-rimmed glasses when the photographer came to take a picture of *The Purple Clarion* staff for the yearbook.

"I'm glad you're here," Leta said, drawing Rhoda over to a table by the window. "You wouldn't believe what happened to me. I've got to talk to someone."

"What happened?" Rhoda moved in close, getting a whiff of Leta's Tabu.

"I've been, ahh, in a man's apartment." Leta paused and looked around. She bent near. The hairs above her lip stood out like bristles. Rhoda couldn't take her eyes off them. Leta was so amazing. She wasn't even *clean*. Rhoda raised her eyes from Leta's lips; Leta's black eyes peered at her through the horn-rims. "I've been dryfucking," she said very slowly. "That's what you call it."

"Doing what?" Rhoda said. A shiver went over her body. It was the most startling thing she had ever heard. People in Harrisburg, Illinois were too polite to talk about something as terrible and powerful as sex. They said "doing it" or "making babies," but, except when men were alone without women, no one said the real words out loud.

"Dryfucking," Leta said. "You do it with your clothes on."

"Oh, my God," Rhoda said. "I can't believe it."

"It feels so wonderful," Leta said. "I might go crazy thinking about it. He's going to call me up tomorrow. He's coming to band practice on Tuesday night and see us march. I'll show him to you."

"Good," Rhoda said. "I can't wait to see him."

"What you do," Leta went on, taking a cigarette out of its package without lifting her elbows from the table. "Is get on a bed and do it. You need a bed." Rhoda leaned down on the table until her head was almost touching Leta's hands. The word was racing around her head. The word was unbelievable. The word would drive her mad.

"I have to go up to the drugstore and look for Philip Holloman," she said. "You want to come with me?"

"Not now," Leta said. "I have to think."

"I'll see you tomorrow then," Rhoda said. "I'll turn in my gossip column stuff before class. I've almost got it finished. It's really funny. I pretended Carl Davis was Gene Kelly and was dancing in Shirley Hancock's yard."

"Oh, yeah." Leta sat back. Unfurled herself into the chair. "That sounds great."

"I'll see you then."

"Sure. I'll see you in the morning."

Rhoda proceeded on down the street, past the movie theater and the cleaners and the store where Bob Rosen's unsmiling girlfriend sold clothes to people. Rhoda considered going in and trying on things, but she didn't feel like doing it now. She was too haunted by the conversation with Leta. It was the wildest word there could be in the world. Rhoda wanted to do it. Right that very minute. With anyone. Anyone on the street. Anyone in a store. Anyone at all. She went into the drugstore but no one was there that she knew, just a couple of old men at the counter having Alka-Seltzers. She bought a package of Nabs and walked toward the park eating them, thinking about Leta and band practice and men that took you to apartments and did that to you. The excitement of the word was wearing off. It was beginning to sound like something only poor people would do. It sounded worse and worse the more it pounded in her head. It sounded bad. It made her want to take a bath.

She went home and went up to her room and took off her clothes and stood in front of the full-length mirror inspecting her vagina. She lifted one foot and put it on the doorknob to get a better look. It was terrible to look at. It was too much to bear. She picked up her clothes and threw them under the bed and went into the bathroom and got into the tub. She ran the hot water all the way up to the drain. She lay back listening to the sucking noises of the drain. Dryfucking. She sank down deeper into the water. She ran her hands across her stomach, found her navel, explored its folds with her fingers, going deeper and deeper, spiraling down. It was where she had been hooked on to her mother. Imagine having a baby hooked on to you. Swimming around inside you. It was the worst thing that could happen. She would never marry. She would never have one swimming in her. Never, never, never as long as she lived. No. She would go to Paradise Island and live with Queen Hippolyta. She would walk among the Amazons in her golden girdle. She would give her glass plane away and never return to civilization.

"Rhoda, what are you doing in there?" It was her real mother, the one in Illinois. She was standing in the doorway wearing a suit she'd been making all week. Dubonnet rayon with shoulder pads and a peplum, the height of style. "You're going to shrink."

"No, I'm not. What was it like to have me inside of you? How did it feel?"

"It didn't feel like anything. I've told you that."

"But it was awful when I came, wasn't it?"

"You came too fast. You tore me up coming out. Like everything else you've ever done." Ariane drew herself up on her heels. "You never could wait for anything."

"I'm not going to do it," Rhoda said. "You couldn't pay me to have a baby."

"Well, maybe no one will want you to. Now get out, Rhoda. Your father's bringing company home. I want you dressed for dinner."

"How far in does a navel go?"

"I don't know. Now get out, honey. You can't stay in the tub all day."

Rhoda got out of the tub and wrapped herself in a towel and padded back into her room.

"Hello, Shorty," Dudley said. He was standing in the doorway of his room with a sultry look on his face. His hands were hooked in the pockets of his pants. He filled the doorframe. "Where you been all day?"

"None of your business," she said. "Get out of my way."

"I'm not in your way. We're going to move again, did you know that?"

"What are you talking about?"

"He's buying some mines. If he gets them we have to move to Kentucky. I was at the office today. I saw the maps. He's going to make about a million dollars."

"You don't know what you're talking about."

"You wait and see."

"Shut up. He wouldn't make us move in the middle of high school."

"He might have to."

"You're crazy," she said, and went on into her room and shut it out. She had gone to four grade schools. She was never going to move again. She was going to live right here in this room forever and wait for Bob Rosen to take his pin back and marry her. "He's crazy," she said to herself and pulled her new pink wool dress off the hanger and began to dress for dinner. "He doesn't know what he's talking about."

Monday was a big day at Harrisburg High School. They were taking achievement tests. Rhoda liked to take tests. She would sharpen three pencils and take the papers they handed her and sit down at a desk and cover the papers with answers that were twice as complicated as the questions and then she would turn the tests in before anyone else and go outside and sit in the sun. Rhoda considered achievement test day to be a sort of school holiday. She went out of the study hall and past the administrative offices and out the main door.

She sat in the sun, feeling the October morning on her legs and arms and face, watching the sunlight move around the concrete volumes of the lions that guarded the entrance to Harrisburg Township High School. The Purple Cougars, Harrisburg called its teams. It should be the marble lions, Rhoda thought. I ought to write an editorial about that. He told me to write editorials whenever I formed an opinion. She imagined it, the lead editorial. Not signed, of course, but her mark would be all over it. Her high imagination. He still got the paper up in Champaign-Urbana, since he had been its greatest editor.

She picked up her books and hurried into the school and up the broad wooden stair to the *Purple Clarion* office. She sat down at a table and pulled out a tablet and began to write.

> I was out in the October sun getting tanned around my anklets when it occurred to me that we have been calling our teams the wrong name. Purple Cougars, what does that mean? There aren't any cougars in Harrisburg. No one even knows what one is. When we try to make a homecoming float no one knows what one looks like. Everyone is always running around with encyclopedias in the middle of the night trying to make a papier-mâché cougar.
> WE SHOULD BE THE MARBLE LIONS. Look at what is out in front of the school. JUST GO AND LOOK…

"What you doing, Scoop? I was just looking for you." It was Philip Holloman.

"Oh, God, I've got this great idea for an editorial. Leta said I could write one whenever I got in the mood. You want to hear it?"

"I have a letter for you." He was wearing his blue windbreaker. He looked just like Bob Rosen. They had matching windbreakers, only Bob's was beige. She had been in the arms of Bob Rosen's beige windbreaker and here was Philip's blue one, not two feet away. He was holding out a letter to her. A small white envelope. She knew what it was. At her house there were three of them wrapped in blue silk in the bottom of her underwear drawer.

"Why did he write me here?"

"I don't know. Look at the address. Isn't that a kick? God, I miss him. I miss him every day." She took the letter. *To,* Miss Scoop Cheetah, R.K. Manning, Ltd., *The Purple Clarion,* Harrisburg Township High School, Harrisburg, Illinois.

In the left-hand corner it said: Rosen, Box 413, University of Illinois, Champaign-Urbana, Illinois.

Rhoda took the letter and held it in her hand, getting it wet from her palms, and left her notebook on the table with her editorial half-finished and excused herself, breathing, still breathing, barely breathing, and went out into the hall. Philip watched her from the vantage point of eighteen years old. He liked Rhoda Manning. Everyone that knew her liked her. People that understood her liked her and people that thought she was crazy did too. Rosen was going to direct her career and someday marry her. That was clear. Anybody could see what was going to happen. She was on her way. She was going to set Harrisburg Township High School on its ear. Rosen had decreed it.

Dear Cheetah, [*the letter began. Rhoda had found a quiet place in the abandoned lunchroom.*]

I am going to be home this coming weekend. November 1, 2, and 3. If you will be waiting for me wearing a black sweater and skirt and brown shoes and get that hair cut into a pageboy I'll be over about 6:30 to take you to the ball game in Benton. If you have to wear your cheerleading things (Is there a freshman-sophomore game that night?) you can bring the black skirt and sweater and change at my cousin Shelton's house.

If you show up in that pink dress looking like Shirley Temple you will have to find someone else to violate the Mann Act with. I have been thinking about you more than seems intelligent.

Things aren't going well up here now. I have had to miss a lot of classes and will have to go to Saint Louis on the 4th for some more surgery. Mother is coming from Chicago. Tell Philip. I left it out of his letter.

Did you read that style book I sent you? You *must* study that or no one will ever take your pieces seriously. Leave the feature section to the idiots. We are after news.

Love,
Bob

She went home that afternoon and took the other letters out of their drawer and got up on her bed and read them very slowly, over and over again.

Dear Cheetah,
I made it to Champaign-Urbana in the midst of the worst winter storm in history. They want me. They took me over and showed me the Journalism Department. You wouldn't believe how many typewriters they have. It must be twenty.
Coleman Hawkins is going to play here next week. Stay away from those Nabs. See you soon. In a hurry.
Love,
Bob

Dear Cheetah,
My roommate brought a cake from home and a cute habit of picking his nose when he studies. The classes look like a snap except for Biology which is going to require "thought and memory." This Williard guy teaching it has decided that science will save the world and I am going to sit on the front row and keep him from finding out I'm a History major. If at all possible.
Mother cursed out the Lieutenant Governor of Illinois at a street corner. Where in the hell do you think you're going, she was muttering and I looked at the license plate and it said 2.
Remember what I told you about those tryouts. Team up with Letitia and don't think about anything but the routine. And remember what I told you about talking to Harold about writing the play. You can do it if I did.
Big kisses,
Bob

Dear Cheetah,
I was sick in bed for two days and still can't go to class. I've memorized everything in the room including the nosepicker's daily Bible study guide. Here's his program for the day.

FOR SEPTEMBER 29
DO'S AND DON'TS

Do decide that those in power are there to take care of you. Do listen when they speak for they are there by the will of the Lord for your benefit. Honor the ones the Lord has put over you to help you on the way to your recovery from the sickness and disease of ignorance of the Lord.

Don't be one of those that question the wisdom of older people. Sit at the feet of your parents and teachers. Let love be on our face and shine unto them the light of the Lord.

Don't let vice call out to you. The devil is everywhere. Be on the lookout for his messengers. Do not be fooled by smiles and flattery.

The nosepicker suspects me of being in the legions of the devil. He has asked to be transferred to another room. If the devil *is* on my side that will happen soon. I cough as much as possible and ask him what the Bible is and try to get into as many conversations as possible tidbits about my mother's notoriously filthy mouth. I can't wait till you meet her. She is coming to Harrisburg this summer to stay with grandmother and me.

I'm tired a lot but it's better. Write me. I love your letters and get some good laughs.

What is happening about the play? What did Harold say?

Love,
Bob

Dear Cheetah,

Back in class. Your letter came Monday. That's great about the play. I think you should call it Harrisburg Folly's, not Follies. Or something better. We'll work on it when I'm home Christmas.

Why skits? How many? Too busy to make this good. Hope you can read it. Out the door.

Bob

That was it. The entire collection. Rhoda folded them neatly back into their creases and put them in their envelopes and wrapped them in the silk scarf and put them beside the bed on the table. Then she rolled the pillow under her head. He's coming home, she said to herself as she cuddled down into the comforter and fell asleep. He is coming home.

He's coming over here and get me and take me to Benton to the game. I'm not going to eat a bite until Friday. I will eat one egg a day until he gets here. I'll be so beautiful. He will love me. He'll do it to me. He doesn't even know I started. I might tell him. Yes, I'll tell him. I can tell him anything. I love him. I love him so much I could die.

Then it was Tuesday, then it was Wednesday, then it was an interminable Thursday and Rhoda was starving by the time she dragged herself home from school and went into the kitchen and scrambled her daily egg.

"You are going to eat some supper, young lady," her mother said. "This starvation routine is going to stop."

"I ate at school. Please leave me alone, Mother. I know what I'm doing."

"You look terrible, Rhoda. Your cheeks are gaunt and you aren't sleeping well. I heard you last night. And I know what it's about."

"What's it about? What do you know?"

"It's about that Jewish boy, that Rosen boy you're going to go to Benton with. I don't know about your driving over there with him all alone, Rhoda. Your father's coming home tomorrow night. I don't know what he's going to say."

"Philip Holloman and Letitia's sister, Emily, are driving over with us. I mean, he's the editor of the paper. That ought to be enough chaperones. Emily's going. You call her mother and see." If her mother did call, Rhoda would have to try something else. "Call Emily's mother and see. We're going together. The ex-editor of my newspaper I happen to write for and the editor this year and Letitia's sister. I guess that's enough for anybody. I am so lucky to get to go with them, with some people that have some sense instead of those idiots in my grade."

"Well, if Emily's going."

"She's going."

"Please eat some supper."

"I can't eat supper. I can barely fit in my cheerleader skirt. Did you finish the black one? I have to have it. Is it done yet?"

"It's on the worktable. We'll try it on after dinner. I don't know why they want you to have black. I think it's very unflattering on young girls."

"It's just what they want." Rhoda kissed her mother on the cheek and went back to scrambling her egg. She scrambled it in several pats of butter. At the last minute she added an extra egg. If she didn't eat anything else until tomorrow night it would be all right. Already she could feel her rib cage coming out. She would be so beautiful. So thin. Surely he would love her.

"That's really all you're going to eat?"

"That's all. I ate a huge lunch." She dumped the scrambled eggs onto a plate and went out of the kitchen and through the living room and sat in the alcove of the stairs, with the phone sitting about three feet away. Soon it would be tomorrow. It would ring and his voice would be on the line and he would call her Cheetah and then he would be there and she would be in his arms and life would begin.

Then death will come, she remembered. Then you will die and be inside a coffin in a grave. Forever and ever and ever, world without end, amen. Rhoda shivered. It was true. Death was true. And she was included. She ate the eggs.

℘

Then it was Friday, then Friday night. Then he was there, standing in her living room, with his wide brow and his wide smile and his terrible self-confidence, not the least bit bothered by her mother's lukewarm welcome or that her father didn't come out of the dining room to say hello. Then they were out the door and into his car and it was just as she had dreamed it would be. The quality of his skin when she touched his arm, the texture, was so pure, so white, even in the dark his skin was so white. He was sick and his body was fighting off the sickness and the sickness was in the texture of his skin but something else was there too. Power, will, something like his music was there, something going forward, driving, something that was not going to let him die. She wanted to ask him about the sickness, about Saint Louis, about the operations, but she did not dare. The forward thing, the music, would not allow it. Even Rhoda, as much as she always talked of everything, knew not to talk of that. So she was quiet, and kept her hand on his arm as he drove the car. She waited.

"I'm so goddamn proud of you," he said. "You're doing it. You're going to do it, just like I said you would."

"It's just because of you," she answered. "It's just to make you like me. Oh, hell, now I'm going to cry. I'm pretty sure I'm going to cry." He stopped the car on the side of the road and pulled her into his arms and began to kiss her. There was a part of her rib cage in the back that was still sort of fat but not too fat. If I was standing up I'd be skinny, she decided. It's not fair to kiss sitting down.

"You don't ever wait for anything, do you?" he said. "I had meant to make you wait for this." He handed it to her. Put it in her hand. The metal cut into her palm, the ruby in the center embedded in her palm. "You'll have to wear it on the inside of your bra. We aren't supposed to give them to children."

"I'm not a child. You know I'm not a child."

"Yeah, well Tau chapter of ZBT doesn't know anything except you're a freshman in high school. Don't get me thinking about it."

"Are you giving me this pin or not?"

"I'm giving it to you." He turned her around to face him. "I'm giving it to you because I'm in love with you." He laughed out loud, his wonderful laugh, the laugh he had been laughing the first time she laid eyes on him, when he was leaning up against the concrete block wall of the Coca-Cola bottling plant picking her out to be his protégée. "I'm in love with a girl who is fourteen years old."

"Say it again," she said. "Say you love me."

"After the ball game."

"No, right now. In front of Janet Allen's house. Right here, so I'll always remember where it was."

"I love you. In this Plymouth in front of Janet Allen's house." Then he kissed her some more. There were a lot of long crazy kisses. Then Rhoda pinned the ZBT pin to the inside of her bra and later, every time she jumped up to cheer at the ball game she could feel it scratch against her skin and send her heart rampaging all over the Benton football field and out across the hills and pastures of Little Egypt and down the state of Illinois to the river.

On Sunday he went back to school. Drove off down the street smiling and waving and left her standing on the sidewalk, by the nandina bushes. She walked down Bosworth Street to Cynthia's house and sat on the swing all afternoon telling Cynthia every single thing they had said and done all weekend, every word and nuance and embrace, every bite they ate at the drive-in and what kind of gas he bought and how he cursed the gas tank and the story of his mother cursing out the Lieutenant Governor of Illinois. When Cynthia's mother called her to dinner, Rhoda walked back home, trying to hold the day inside so it would never end.

There was a meatloaf for dinner and macaroni and cheese and green peas and carrots and homemade rolls. All her favorite dishes. After dinner her father called them into the living room and told them the news. They were moving away. He had bought them a white Victorian mansion in a town called Franklin, Kentucky, and in a month they would move there so he could be nearer to the mines. "It's too far to drive," he said. "I can't make these drives with all I have to do."

"We're going to move again?" Rhoda said. "You are going to do this to me?"

"I'm not doing anything to you, Sister," he said. "You're a little silly girl who's still wet behind the ears. I know what's best for all of us and this is what we're going to do. You're going to love it there."

"I'm going to have a play," she said. "I've just written the Senior Play. I have written the Senior Play for the whole school. They're going to put it on. Are you listening to me?" No one else said a word. It was only Rhoda and her father. Her mother was on the green chair with her arms around Dudley. "I won't leave. I don't believe you'd do this to me. You can't do this to me."

He lifted his chin. He stuck his hands in his pockets. Their eyes met. "You do what I tell you to do, Miss Priss. I'm the boss of this family."

"He can't do this to me." Rhoda turned to her mother. "You can't let him do this. You can't let it happen."

"I tried, my darling," her mother said. "I have told him a hundred times."

"I won't go," Rhoda said. "I'll stay here and live with Cynthia." Then she was out the door and running down the street and was gone a long time walking the streets of Harrisburg, Illinois, trying to believe there was something she could do.

Four weeks later the yellow moving van pulled up in front of the house on Rollston Street and the boxes and furniture and appliances were loaded on the van. Rhoda stayed down the street at Mike Ready's house talking and listening to the radio. She didn't feel like seeing her friends or telling them goodbye. She didn't tell anyone goodbye, not Dixie Lee or Shirley or Naomi, not even Letitia or Cynthia Jane. She just sat at Mike Ready's shuffling a deck of cards and talking about the basketball team. Around four o'clock she went home and helped her mother close the windows and sweep the debris on the floor into neat piles. "We can't leave a mess for the next people," her mother said. "I can't stand to move into a dirty house."

"Where's Dudley?" Rhoda asked. "Where's he gone?"

"He went with your father. They've gone on. You're going to drive with me. We need to finish here, Rhoda, and get on our way. It's going to be dark before too long. I want to drive as far as possible in the light."

"How long will it take?"

"About three hours. It isn't that far away. We can come back all the time, Rhoda. You can come back to see your play."

"I don't care about the goddamn play. Don't talk about the play. Let's get going. What else do we have to do?"

Then they were in the car and headed out of town. They drove down the main street, then turned onto Decatur and drove past the store where

Anne Layne was working still, selling clothes to people off of racks, a frown on her face, caught forever in a world she could not imagine leaving for good reasons or bad ones, past the drugstore where Philip Holloman would sit every Saturday of his life on the same stool until it closed the year he was thirty-nine and he had to find a new place to hang out in on Saturdays. Past the icehouse and the filling station and the drive-in and past the brick fence of Bob Rosen's grandmother's house, where his gray Plymouth would come to rest. Past the site of the new consolidated school and the park where Rhoda had necked with Bob Rosen when he was still going steady with Anne Layne and past the sign that said City Limits, Harrisburg, Illinois, Population 12,480. Come Back Soon. You're Welcome.

It grew dark swiftly as it was the middle of December. December the fourteenth. At least it's not my lucky number, Rhoda thought, and fell asleep, her hand touching the edge of her mother's soft green wool skirt, the smell of her mother's expensive perfume all around them in the car. The sound of the wheels on the asphalt road. When she woke they were pulling on to the wide steel bridge that separates Illinois from Kentucky. Rhoda sat up in the seat. It was the Ohio River, dark and vast below her, and the sky was dark and vast above with only a few stars and they were really leaving.

"I don't believe it," she said. "I don't believe he'd do this to me." Then she began to weep. She wept terrible uncontrollable tears all across the bridge, weeping into her hands, and her mother wept with her but she kept her hands on the wheel and her eyes on the road. "There was nothing I could do about it, darling," she said. "I told him over and over but he wouldn't listen. He doesn't care about anything in the world but himself. I don't know what else I could have done. I'm so sorry. I know how you feel. I know what you are going through."

"No, you don't," Rhoda said, turning her rage against her mother. "You don't know. You could have stopped him. You don't know. You lived in the same house every day of your life. Your house is still there. Your mother is still there in that same house. You went to one school. You had the same friends. I don't care about this goddamn Franklin, Kentucky. I hope it burns to the ground. I won't like it. I hate it. I already hate it. Oh, my God. I hate its guts." Her mother took one hand from the wheel and touched her arm.

"Good will come of it, Rhoda. Good comes of everything."

"No, it doesn't," she said. "It does not. That's a lie. Half the stuff you tell me is a lie. You don't know what you're saying. You don't know a goddamn thing. STOP THIS GODDAMN CAR. I HAVE TO GO TO

THE BATHROOM. STOP IT, MOTHER. I MEAN, STOP IT RIGHT
THIS MINUTE. THE MINUTE YOU GET OFF THIS BRIDGE."
Ariane stopped the car and Rhoda strode off across a field and urinated
behind a tree. The warm urine poured out upon the ground and steam
rose from it and that solaced her in some strange way and she pulled up
her pants and walked back across the stubble and got into the car.

"It better be a big house," she said. "It had better be the biggest
house in that goddamn town."

84. *Leigh Allison Wilson*

(1959–)

The youngest of the writers anthologized here, Leigh Allison Wilson is possibly the most concerned with universalizing the southern experience, though her stories are known for their distinctive southern flavor. Born in Rogersville, Tennessee, Wilson attended Williams College, the University of Virginia, and the Iowa Writer's Workshop before settling in Oswego, New York, where she teaches fiction writing at the State University of New York, Oswego.

The publication of her first collection of short stories, *From the Bottom Up* (1983), brought Wilson considerable attention, including the Flannery O'Connor Award for Short Fiction and a James A. Michener fellowship. Wilson has also published a second collection of stories, *Wind: Stories* (1989), and contributed articles and stories to journals and magazines.

Wilson's short stories comprise what Gregory Morris calls "a marvelous metaphorical structure for the Southern way of thought." Morris's comment is especially helpful to an understanding of stories like "The Snipe Hunters," in which hope for the South is represented by the belief, expressed by one character, that "though snipes do not exist, still you must hunt . . . or else you are utterly lost." This attitude echoes the beliefs of Flannery O'Connor, as Wilson's characters—often children-obsessed or near madness—resemble O'Connor's. In "South of the Border," published in *From the Bottom Up,* we meet characters distorted by their inability to work out their conflicting feelings for the South, feeling equally drawn to and repulsed by the region.

Wilson once said that her writing was shaped by all the places she has lived because "we all of us on earth appreciate the familiar and titillating and mysterious details of our homes, wherever they are." While the stories collected in *From the Bottom Up* remain tied to the mountains of eastern Tennessee, Wilson's later stories are often set in the North.

South of the Border

In a car, headed point-blank down an interstate, there is a sanity akin to recurring dreams: you feel as if every moment has been lived and will be lived exactly according to plan. Landscapes and peripheral realities blur and rush headlong backwards through the windows like the soft edges of sleep. And the road ahead and behind you becomes a straight line, framed in the perfect arc of a dashboard.

My sister sits hunkered against the side of the car and fiddles with the radio, careful not to touch my right leg. On a Sunday morning in the midlands of South Carolina all radio stations play either gospel music or black church services. Jane Anne chooses a church service and claps her hands, eyes closed, to the hiccuping rhythm of the preacher, both his voice and her percussion sounding disembodied in the smallness of the Volkswagen. "Take Jesus, oh Lord take Jesus," the preacher says, "take Jesus for New Year's." Clap clap clap goes my sister, clap clap. "Jesus is my friend" clap "Jesus is your friend" clap "Friends, accept Jesus" clap clap. Deep in her bowels she is a fundamentalist, a lover of simple truths and literal facts; her resolution for the coming year is "to see things more clearly." In this she is resolute, commenting often on points of interest as we careen northward through cotton fields and marshy bottomland and stark-colored advertisements.

I have no such resolution. While driving I develop an acute myopia and it is all I can do to concentrate on the pavement that blears and dashes like water underneath the car. Outside the world flashes by as if switched on and off in a two-dimensional slide show, one frame at a time, the whole universe condensed to a television screen.

"Look at that!" Jane Anne cries and points frantically somewhere outside. "Look, look!"

"What was it?"

"You didn't even look," she says. She claps her hand together with a violence that means she wishes one of them was mine. "Didn't even god-damn look at what I saw. You probably had something more important on your mind, I'm sure, probably aren't even interested in that cow I just saw with the human face."

"You just saw a cow with a human face?"

"No," she says, almost happily, "I didn't see a thing," and then she stares sullenly out her window.

Just last night my father and stepmother engaged in a domestic cat-fight over this kind of optical delusion. During a television football game, the Gator Bowl in Florida, they break out in an almost-brawl over forces beyond their control, forces five hundred miles to their south. Clemson, a South Carolina school, and Ohio State are playing and my father perversely roots for Ohio, a state that exists for him only during television football and basketball games. My stepmother was raised in the thick of Clemson patriotism, a twitch at the corner of one eye blossoming into a full-blown spasm, possibly hindering her vision, at every Clemson penalty and first down.

By the end of the game tension is extreme, my stepmother's eye winks rapidly, my father's mien settles like concrete as he stares at a commercial. Clemson is winning, my palms are sweating and slick, my stepmother is exalted, and my father steadily slips into a familiar attitude. Once, eight years ago, he almost hit me when I won a Monopoly game. His is a competitive madness that operates at a slow boil until all is lost, then his expression explodes into a kind of pseudo-apocalyptic blitz. So when a Clemson player intercepts a key Ohio State pass and Woody Hayes, ex-coach of Ohio State, smacks the Clemson player in the face, my father blitzes out, saying "Kill him, kill the bastard, Woody." My stepmother blithers to her feet (they sit in identical easy chairs, separated by a coffee table), winks and gasps, arms akimbo and shivering, shouting now:

"You might as well say 'kill me' that's what you mean!"

Blitz over, my father settles back into concreteness while my step-mother marches, footstep-echoes beating into the walls against one another, into their bedroom. An hour later everyone is sleeping heavily and even the television has sunk into a blank stupor. Today she poked her head in my bedroom doorway, flashing a smile birthed and bred in South Carolina and cultivated like white cotton, and told me goodbye before she left for church. She plays the organ for the Methodist Church of Fort Motte.

Jane Anne points out advertisements for the South of the Border tourist complex still an hour and a half in the future. CONFEDERATE FOOD YANKEE STYLE, BEST IN THIS NECK OF THE WOODS one sign reads. So frequent are these advertisements that they serve as punctuation along the sameness of the interstate and I begin to despise them because I feel my utter dependence on their familiarity. I come South twice a year, once at Christmas, once in the summer, each time more of an amnesiac experience than the visit before. I am fearful that after another few visits I may go home and never be able to leave, my present and future eradicated by the vicious tenacity of the past. But, truly, I am hypnotized home by the staid reality of what I remember—a somnambulatory reality so familiar and so unchanging that it appears to be the only true god in my life.

"I'd be a fool to stick around," Jane Tressel sings from the radio. My sister has found an AM station. Lips taut and round, she sings along with her mouth forming the words as if molded around an ice-cream cone. The way she sings turns the words into nonsensical baby-noise, but this is also a special function of AM radio, this ablution of meaning into a catchy anonymity. Jane Anne carefully reads several beauty magazines, pining over the structured perfection of the models, always running out to buy new beauty products although she is as frugal with her money as a squirrel in autumn. A stranger, she sits so close to her door that no place in the car could be equally far from me and she eyes the side of my face with the wariness of a stray dog. She could be a nervous hitchhiker, except that she controls the radio. This trip is the first time we have been together alone in eight years. She is a stranger, stranger still because for thirteen years we slept in the same bedroom and now she resembles a kewpie doll rather than a younger sister.

With her left hand, when it is not spiraling around the radio tuner, Jane Anne tosses boiled peanuts between her lips. They look like a pile of swelled ticks, gray-skinned and blood-bloated, in the palm of her hand, and she is soberly emptying a paper sack full of them. I have noticed that she eats in a dazed trance, similar to the manner in which she sings to the radio, as if eating were a habitual duty. She was always a dutiful child, and now she weighs one hundred and seventy-five pounds, has a prematurely stooped back, and the corners of her mouth pucker down in a perpetual expression of bad humor. An unhappy kewpie doll.

Fifteen years ago she was a beautiful, dutiful child. Fifteen years ago I would bring her red and purple ribbons, watch her thread them through her hair. It looked like miniature maypoles, and when she tossed a braid I wanted to grab one and swing out. Today she wears a mud-colored scarf tied tightly at the nape of her neck.

"Why don't you ever talk seriously to me?" she asks and I grip the wheel, staring hard at the car in front of me, abruptly aware of the scores of vehicles swarming the interstate ahead and behind me. Each one is a possible fatal accident.

"What do you want to talk about?" I say warily, my thighs beginning to feel cramped in the immobile space-time of the traveling Volkswagen interior. In the event of an accident, all is lost in a Volkswagen.

"What do you want to talk about?" Jane Anne mimics in a voice that, remarkably, is more like my own than my own sounds to me. She is full of surprises, this sister of mine whom I do not know. "I'll tell you one damn thing," she says, really angry this time, her tongue flailing against a stray peanut, "you may be smart, but I have all the common sense in this family." Snorting, she clings to the side of her door.

This is true. She does have the common sense in our family, a fact uttered and re-uttered by my paternal grandmother who likens me to my Uncle George Wilkins. My Uncle George was so smart, she says, that he was almost an idiot. He died with a moonshine-ruined liver and a cancer that ate from his breast right through to his back, and Grandmother said it would have gone on through the bed and into the hospital linoleum if his heart hadn't stopped first.

He was a geologist and forever poking rocks with his cane, head bent forward, arm flicking, cane flicking, eyes pouncing toward the ground to examine and file away every square inch of land that his feet passed over. Once he broke his nose against a haybaler, never saw it, saw only the gray-black pieces of sedimentary rock that flipped over and under the tip of his cane. But he was a smart one, my Uncle George, and twice a year scientists from Washington came down to sober him up and fetch him back to a laboratory where he performed penetrating geological studies. They wanted him to fly up there, but he always said he did his traveling on the ground. Now he's his own specimen, buried under six feet of sand and sedimentary rock in Calhoun County, South Carolina, and he's not going anywhere.

"I'll tell you another damn thing," Jane Anne says and warms up to one of our childhood wrangles, the kind where neither of us is aware of the reason but both of us will stake our lives on a resolution in our favor. It is our father's blood that swells up at these times, bubbles of madness that break at the mouth. "I'll miss your sweet, sweet eyes," Willie Neal croaks from the radio, "I told you when I left, I couldn't live with your lies."

"I'm sick and tired of you making me feel stupid. You act like I'm eleven years old, like I'm still your devoted and moronic pawn. I'm nineteen, damn you, I've read Sartre and Camus." She utilizes her French education in all arguments, since I have studied only Latin and vaguely remember it anyway—French is her code language through which she can curse me to my ignorant face. "I've seen Chicago and New York, I've seen Paris and *you* don't even have a passport."

"A passport isn't exactly a rite of passage, Jane Anne."

"Not," she says, "if you don't even have one." Furious now, she sputters like a cat and is just seconds away from a serious assault. Sometimes when we were younger we'd forget what we were angry about in the middle of the wrangle, and so kept on with it anyway, only louder and with more passion.

"Not," she says, "if you travel with your heart incognito like a goddamn ghost. You've been just a barrel of laughs for two weeks."

"Didn't come down here," I say, grim as a soldier, "in order to entertain my family." There is a white Pontiac endangering my rear bumper.

"Then why, in God's name, did you come at all?" Jane Anne kicks the peanut sack; the Pontiac veers to the left and passes safely, though in a glance I can tell that the man inside it is a lunatic.

"I know one thing and don't you forget it: I am as educated as you are, I am as competently conversive as you are."

This, too, is true. In fact, Jane Anne can shift facilely between Sunday dinner chatter at my grandmother's and mournful sympathetico at my aunt's where my first cousin, Jonathan, is dying of cancer. Both situations strike me dumb.

At my grandmother's Christmas dinner, I deaf-mute my way through the awkward vacuum during which butt-pinching uncles watch football games and bouffant-headed aunts question me as to how many boyfriends I have and my grandmother pounces at odd moments to bark in my ear, "Can't go to school forever!" Normally I wink and grin like a demon, offer condolences for my slovenly personality, giggle madly while my butt is tweaked, and create countless football players who appear and disappear as boyfriends according to my whim. Once I created a rather bookish law student who was poorly received and he disappeared during the course of dessert, an hour later reappearing as a dashing quarterback who was a well-received pre-med. This time, however, I sleepwalk, staring maniacally at each relative until they leave me alone.

"Time to eat!" Grandmother cries, pertly, her presence in its element and as relentless as a Mack truck. Fourteen grown men and women rise as one and throng into the kitchen where dishes of food, festive-colored and bubbling, are lined in perfect rows to be picked over, placed on china plates and retired to the dining room, there to be consumed in dutiful silence. But first comes the continuum in which fourteen grown men and women hang back, hem-haw, pluck at their sleeves or pick their noses, succumb to the cowardliness of not being first in line though for five hours their appetites have been titillated to the peak of a savage desire. For a few seconds we stand like tame vultures and just peer, ravenous, at the untouched food. I believe I will faint from hunger, until I finally find myself at the table, slapping mashed potatoes onto crisply cool china.

"Jane Anne," Grandmother says in her grand commandeering tone, a tone reminiscent of both grade-school teachers and Methodist preachers, "would you please say grace." Jane Anne positively glistens with glee, jubilant while all eyes pin me against the profaned table, potatoes puffed and accusing on my plate.

"For these Thy gifts, Oh Lord let us be thankful," Jane Anne croons, in a strangerly fashion. The surge is on now, compliments and condiments fly across the table, and I sleepwalk through dinner, an attendant to disapproval.

FREE IN-ROOM MOVIES: TWENTY HONEYMOON SUITES

I read on a huge sign. In twenty minutes we will pass through the middle of South of the Border, almost into North Carolina. The peanuts have risen once more into Jane Anne's lap, and she nimbly eats them. "It's my last night in town, I'd be a fool to stick around," the radio says. I do not know the performer although his song is appealing in its drowsy insistence. At South of the Border Jane Anne will meet a boyfriend from her school and I will continue north to my school alone. Both of us are hyper-aware of the advertisements, as if they are motes of sand trickling time away. She wants to get out of my presence as badly as I do hers; we are both morbidly afraid of each other. FREE—ADVICE, AIR, WATER, EVERYTHING ELSE REASONABLE.

"And another thing," she says, wrapping up her side of the dialectic before handing the floor to me, "you have been nothing but rude and ill-mannered this whole vacation, to me, to Daddy, even to Aunt Louise. You lack discrimination, that's what you lack."

"Jonathan . . . how is he?" Jane Anne whispers to my aunt. I perch on the lips of a couch, finger wringing finger, my tongue thick as a marble tombstone.

"Dying," my aunt chokes, "dy—ing."

"How long?" Jane Anne looks absolutely engrossed, a dutiful child.

"Days, weeks, God knows when he'll be free from the pain." Solemnly Jane Anne acknowledges the mercy of God with a slow, dazed nodding of her chin. She is gathering momentum for the predictable eventuality wherein my aunt will begin to sob and she can console with a firm and warm arm across the heaving back. But—surprise—my aunt visibly marshals her circumference and pulls herself together with a pro-longed sigh. My palms are clammy with the dead and the living.

"Sarah Louise is home," my aunt says, giddy with recovered strength, but poised along some precipice of mental breakdown. Sarah Louise is also my first cousin. "She's in the back bedroom getting dressed." Sarah Louise is in the back bedroom getting dressed, Jonathan is in the front bedroom, blinds drawn, dying. For a while we sit in an uncomfortably loud silence until Sarah Louise comes into the living room. Like her mother, Sarah Louise has reddish-brown hair and a pointed face that articulates itself at the breach of the nose. She looks like a rumpled domesticated animal, exhaustion whitening her cheeks in random places like frostbite. She is looking directly into my eyes.

"He wants to see you, Bo."

"Me?"

"He's asking for you."

Jane Anne shivers and recoils, I recoil, a creeping nausea deep inside my throat; I wish to hell I was somewhere, anywhere, somebody someplace else. When I was two, Jonathan christened me into the family by nicknaming me Bo, a name used only by blood relatives and, to them, a name coincidental with my very existence. Only recently has Jane Anne begun to call me Jennifer, her statement of self-determination. Nomenclature is her forte.

I remember Jonathan in two ways: first, the way he looked at eleven, knobby-kneed and skinny as a fence post, my best friend and comrade. Like rabid dogs we chased the cows on his father's farm until they ran idiotically into their pond water and grouped together up to their buttocks in sludge and cattails. The days I spent with him were always warm and cloudless and kinetic with revelry. We played doctor inside the very room where he now lies dying; he was the first man I ever studied. Once my father found us together and beat me with a leather belt until welts crisscrossed by bare legs and back like textile woof. Afterwards, since we lived in different towns, he grew out of revelry and into proms and long-legged cheerleaders. I saw him last two years ago, a young man so handsome he could send pangs of romance down the back of Ayn Rand herself. Blond hair feathered and long around his neck, the face of a beautiful woman made a little rough at the edges, an unaware body oozing casual strength and grace, the man was unbearably pretty. I believe the mythic Christ, aided by centuries of imagination, could never approach the fullness of reality in Jonathan's splendor.

I stand and rub my hands together and they slide against their own moisture. In times of stress I enter into a semicomatose state like an instinct-driven opossum. Automatically my brain begins to decline a Latin noun, a ae ae am a, ae arum is as is. The room is shadowed and unlit, a thickly-queer smell of medicine and urine and *sweet Jesus* the smell of life itself condensed into a pungent and rancid death-room, without light and without hope. I feel an acute hatred for myself, sweat trickling—an endless beading health—under my armpits: da ta ta ta, a ae am a, this is the way the world ends. Across the room the bed seems to rest against the far wall but surely to God he is not in it, there is no indentation under the quilt, there is only a skull resting on the pillow, a yellow hairless sunken skull.

"Bo," he says, a muffled, anonymous sound, drugged, removed, a physical impossibility save in nightmare. Dipping strangely, the lines of the room combat with a nausea, and I realize my mouth is whimpering and salivating. The nausea moves around the throat like unconscious prayer. The sting is for the da ta ta ta, arum is as is.

"Bo," he whispers, "I wanted to tell you . . ."

"Tell me."

"It's not so bad."

"Tell me quick."

He coughs without coughing, resting. Two more minutes and I will go mad and this thought is comforting. Someone is whimpering somewhere.

"Are you still my friend?"

("Fucking Jesus!" Jonathan yells and punches the air with his fist. The cowshed blows up in slow motion, splinters of wood fall like dust on his hair and shoulders. Large pieces of board fly over the fence, landing with dull thuds in the pasture. Down below, huddled up and frightened, Bo studies the delicate white hairs on the back of his right leg.)

"I wanted to tell you goodbye," he says.

(The others said, "Don't tiddle in the pond," but they pay no attention. They are full, with the warm brown water pressing against them, and they pay no attention. Across the water, stabbed by erect cattails, the cows stand knee-deep and black near the pond's edge, tails slapping onto their backs, heads browsing onto the surface then easing back up to stare at pine trees. Bo and Jonathan know that they think of great things, standing there in the water, staring. They tiddle freely and silently into the pond.)

"It's not so bad," he says.

I pretend I haven't heard.

"It leaves."

"Jonathan . . ."

"Goodbye," he says. "I loved you, yes," and then he starts to doze. "Goodbye."

I return to the living room and begin to cry. My aunt and Sarah Louise begin to cry. Jane Anne stares at me with narrow eyes, her mouth puckered in distaste, then she pats and coos and comforts Sarah Louise. Uncontrollably I want to punch her in the nose, kiss her on the mouth, dash outside to the car, and get the hell out of South Carolina. A past is dying out from under my feet and I notice for the first time the blinking red lights on my aunt's Christmas tree. One two three, one two three they waltz, immobile, on the outskirts of the fir needles. I picture my sister wrapped in red lights, clapping her hands—one two three. When we get into the Volkswagen, she says: "You should have controlled yourself, you shouldn't have cried in front of them. We were guests in their house."

Ramona Stewart sings: "The sun's falling from the sky and night ain't far behind." Jane Anne waits for my defensive remarks, contemplating her retort through a wriggling at the lips, the worrying to death of a boiled peanut at the tip of her tongue. "Sun's falling," Ramona goes on, "night ain't far behind."

"Listen, Jane Anne," I say, glancing briefly in her direction, then staring straight ahead, a cheap power play although my hands and eyes are truly busy. She is filing away the information, noting the brevity and attributing it to arrogance.

"Can't we part as friends, can't we please just forget our old roles and part as friends? Please?"

Up ahead a huge sombrero sits atop a five-story tower. We have arrived at our connection, South of the Border. My sister sits in complete silence, one of her half-dutiful trances, and I pull off at the exit and enter the parking lot of a coffee house that is partly Mexican, partly southern, and mostly middle-American slough. Jane Anne's friend slumps manfully against the wheel of a red Datsun hatchback with Wisconsin plates and, suddenly businesslike, Jane Anne is out of the car, suitcase in hand, pocketbook slung in a noose around her neck.

"Goodbye," she says and is gone. I watch while she situates herself in the Datsun, then I pull out of the parking lot, drive up the entrance ramp to the interstate, alone inside the throbbing, hurtling Volkswagen, then insert myself into the welter of anonymous northbound vehicles.

I can go home again, again and again, each episode like a snowflake that sticks to your eyelashes. They melt and mingle with your tears. Take a memory, any memory, and it becomes an inviolable god, a sanity exactly according to plan. But those soft edges—those peripheral realities that blur, those landscapes that shift and rush past—those are the crucibles of emotion, and they flow headlong backwards beneath your feet. I come South only twice a year, once at Christmas, once in the summer. Each time is a possible fatal accident.

Selected Bibliography

Primary Sources

Doris Betts
Tall Houses in Winter. New York: Putnam, 1957.
The Scarlet Thread. New York: Harper, 1964.
The River to Pickle Beach. New York: Harper, 1972.
Beasts of the Southern Wild and Other Stories. New York: Harper, 1973. Reprinted in *Masterworks of the Southern Gothic.* Introduction by Lewis P. Simpson. Atlanta: Peachtree, 1985.
Heading West. New York: Knopf, 1981.
Halfway Home and a Long Way To Go: The Report of the 1986 Commission on the Future of the South. Research Triangle, N.C.: Southern Growth Policies Board, 1988.
Souls Raised from the Dead: A Novel. New York: Knopf, 1994.

Susan Petigru King Bowen
Busy Moments of an Idle Woman. New York: D. Appleton, 1854.
Lily: A Novel. New York: Harper, 1855.
Sylvia's World; and, Crimes Which the Law Does Not Reach. New York: Derby and Jackson, 1859.
Gerald Gray's Wife. Augusta: Stockton, 1864. Reprinted as *Gerald Gray's Wife and Lily: A Novel.* Durham, N.C.: Duke University Press, 1993.

Mary Boykin Chesnut
A Diary from Dixie. Edited by Isabella D. Martin and Myrta L. Avary. New York: D. Appleton, 1906. Reprint, edited by Ben Ames Williams. Boston: Houghton, 1949.
Mary Chesnut's Civil War. Edited by C. Vann Woodward. New Haven: Yale University Press, 1980.
The Private Mary Chesnut: The Unpublished Civil War Diaries. Edited by C. Vann Woodward and Elisabeth Muhlenfeld. New York: Oxford University Press, 1984.

Kate Chopin
At Fault. St. Louis: Nixon-Jones, 1890.
Bayou Folk. Boston: Houghton, 1894.

A Night in Acadie. Chicago: Way and Williams, 1897.

The Awakening. Chicago: Herbert S. Stone, 1899.

The Complete Works of Kate Chopin. Edited by Per Seyersted. Baton Rouge: Louisiana State University Press, 1969.

Alice Dunbar-Nelson

Violets and Other Tales. Boston: Monthly Review, 1895.

The Goodness of St. Rocque, and Other Stories. New York: Dodd, 1899. Reprint, New York: AMS, 1975.

Masterpieces of Negro Eloquence: The Best Speeches Delivered by the Negro from the Days of Slavery to the Present Time. New York: Bookery, 1913.

The Dunbar Speaker and Entertainer. Naperville, Ill.: J. L. Nichols, 1920.

Biography of General Oliver O. Howard. [Wilmington?, 1924?].

Caroling Dusk. Edited by Countee Cullen. New York: Harper and Row, 1927.

Mine Eyes Have Seen. Black Theater, U.S.A.; Forty-Five Plays by Black Americans, 1847–1974. Edited by James V. Hatch. New York: Free, 1974.

An Alice Dunbar-Nelson Reader. Edited by Ora Williams. Washington, D.C.: University Press of America, 1979.

Give Us Each Day: The Diary of Alice Dunbar-Nelson. Introduction and notes by Gloria T. Hull. New York: Norton, 1984.

The Works of Alice Dunbar-Nelson. Edited by Gloria T. Hull. New York: Oxford University Press, 1988.

Ellen Gilchrist

The Land Surveyor's Daughter. Fayetteville, Ark.: Lost Roads, 1979.

In the Land of Dreamy Dreams. Boston: Little, 1981.

The Annunciation. Boston: Little, 1983.

Victory over Japan: A Book of Stories. Boston: Little, 1984.

Drunk with Love: A Book of Stories. Boston: Little, 1986.

Riding Out the Tropical Depression: Selected Poems, 1975–1985. New Orleans: Faust, 1986.

Falling through Space: The Journals of Ellen Gilchrist. Boston: Little, 1988.

The Anna Papers: A Novel. Boston: Little, 1988.

Some Blue Hills at Sundown. New York: Albondocani, 1988.

Light Can Be Both Wave and Particle. Boston: Little, 1989.

The Blue-Eyed Buddhist and Other Stories. Boston: Faber and Faber, 1990.

I Cannot Get You Close Enough. Boston: Little, 1990.

Net of Jewels: A Novel. Boston: Little, 1993.

Starcarbon: A Meditation On Love. Boston: Little, 1994.

Anabasis: A Journey to the Interior. Jackson: University Press of Mississippi, 1994.

Caroline Howard Gilman

Recollections of a Housekeeper. New York: Harper, 1834.
The Poetry of Travelling in the United States. New York: Colman, 1838.
Recollections of a Southern Matron. New York: Harper, 1838.
Tales and Ballads. Boston: J. Munroe, 1839.
Love's Progress. New York: Harper, 1840.
Oracles from the Poets. New York: Wiley and Putnam, 1844.
The Sibyl. New York: Wiley and Putnam, 1848.
Verses of a Life Time. Boston: J. Munroe, 1849.
Oracles for Youth. New York: Putnam, 1852.
Recollections of a New England Bride and of a Southern Matron. New York: Putnam, 1852.
Stories and Poems by Mother and Daughter. Boston: Lee and Shepard, 1872.
"Letters of a Confederate Mother." *Atlantic Monthly* 137 (Apr. 1926): 503–15.

Caroline Gordon

Penhally. New York: Scribner's, 1931.
Aleck Maury, Sportsman. New York: Scribner's, 1934.
The Garden of Adonis. New York: Scribner's, 1937.
None Shall Look Back. New York: Scribner's, 1937.
Green Centuries. New York: Scribner's, 1941.
The Women on the Porch. New York: Scribner's, 1944.
The Forest of the South. New York: Scribner's, 1945.
The House of Fiction: An Anthology of the Short Story with Commentary. With Allen Tate. New York: Scribner's, 1950.
The Strange Children. New York: Scribner's, 1951.
The Malefactors. New York: Harcourt, 1956.
How to Read a Novel. New York: Viking, 1957.
"A Narrow Heart: The Portrait of a Woman." *Transatlantic Review* 3 (1960): 7–19.
A Good Soldier: A Key to the Novels of Ford Madox Ford. Davis: University of California Library, 1963.
Old Red and Other Stories. New York: Scribner's, 1963.
The Glory of Hera. Garden City, N.Y.: Doubleday, 1972.
"A Master Class: From the Correspondence of Caroline Gordon and Flannery O'Connor." Edited by Sally Fitzgerald. *Georgia Review* 33 (1979): 827–46.
The Collected Stories of Caroline Gordon. Introduction by Robert Penn Warren. New York: Farrar, 1981.
The Southern Mandarins: Letters of Caroline Gordon to Sally Wood, 1924–1937. Edited by Sally Wood. Foreword by Andrew Lytle. Baton Rouge: Louisiana State University Press, 1984.

Sarah Grimké

Appeal to the Christian Women of the South. New York: Anti-Slavery Society, 1836.

An Epistle to the Clergy of the Southern States. Bailey Pamphlets No. 3. New York, 1836.

Letters on the Equality of the Sexes and the Condition of Woman, Addressed to Mary S. Parker, President of the Boston Female Anti-Slavery Society. Boston: Isaac Knapp, 1838. Reprint, New York: Source Books, 1970.

American Slavery As It Is. With Angelina Grimké and Theodore Weld. New York: Anti-Slavery Society, 1839.

Dreadful Effects of Irresponsible Power. Leeds Anti-Slavery Series No. 69. London: W. Cash and F. G. Cash, 1853.

The Public Years of Sarah and Angelina Grimké: Selected Writings, 1835–1839. Edited by Larry Ceplair. New York: Columbia University Press, 1989.

Frances E. W. Harper

Forest Leaves. Baltimore: privately printed, 1845.

Poems on Miscellaneous Subjects. Boston: Yerrington, 1854.

Moses: A Story of the Nile. Philadelphia: Merrihew, 1869.

Sketches of Southern Life. Philadelphia: Merrihew, 1872.

Iola Leroy, or Shadows Uplifted. Boston: James H. Earle, 1892.

Idylls of the Bible. Philadelphia: 1901. Reprint, New York: AMS, 1975.

Atlanta Offering. Miami: Mnemosyne, 1969.

Complete Poems of Frances E. W. Harper. Edited by Maryemma Graham. New York: Oxford University Press, 1988.

A Brighter Coming Day: A Frances Ellen Watkins Harper Reader. Edited by Frances Smith Foster. New York: Feminist, 1990.

Zora Neale Hurston

Mule Bone: A Comedy of Negro Life in Three Acts. With Langston Hughes. New York: Harper, 1931.

Jonah's Gourd Vine. Philadelphia: Lippincott, 1934.

Mules and Men. Philadelphia: Lippincott, 1935.

Their Eyes Were Watching God. Philadelphia: Lippincott, 1937.

Tell My Horse. Philadelphia: Lippincott, 1938. Reprinted as *Voodoo Gods; An Inquiry into Native Myths and Magic in Jamaica and Haiti.* Dent, 1939.

Moses, Man of the Mountain. Philadelphia: Lippincott, 1939.

Dust Tracks on a Road. Philadelphia: Lippincott, 1942.

Seraph on the Suwanee. New York: Scribner's, 1948.

I Love Myself When I Am Laughing . . . And Then Again When I Am Looking Mean and Impressive: A Zora Neale Hurston Reader. Edited by Alice Walker. New York: Feminist, 1979.

The Sanctified Church. Edited by Toni Cade Bambara. Berkeley: Turtle Island, 1981.
Spunk: The Selected Stories of Zora Neale Hurston. Berkeley: Turtle Island, 1985.

Harriet Jacobs
Incidents in the Life of a Slave Girl. Boston: privately printed, 1861. Reprint, Cambridge: Harvard University Press, 1987. New York: Oxford University Press, 1988.

Elizabeth Keckley
Behind the Scenes, or Thirty Years a Slave and Four Years in the White House. New York: G. W. Carlton, 1868. Reprint, Schomburg Library of Nineteenth-Century Black Women Writers Series. New York: Oxford University Press, 1989.

Fanny Kemble
Francis the First. London: J. Murray, 1832.
Journal of a Residence in America. Paris: Galignani, 1835.
The Star of Seville. New York: Saunders, 1837.
The Christmas Tree, and Other Tales. London: John W. Parker, 1856.
Poems. Boston: Ticknor and Fields, 1859.
Journal of a Residence on a Georgian Plantation in 1838–1839. New York: Harper, 1863. Reprint, edited by John A. Scott. Athens: University of Georgia Press, 1984.
Record of a Girlhood. London: R. Bentley, 1878.
Notes upon Some of Shakespeare's Plays. London: R. Bentley, 1882.
Record of Later Life. New York: Holt, 1882.
The Adventures of Mr. John Timothy Homespun in Switzerland. London: R. Bentley, 1889.
Far Away and Long Ago. New York: Holt, 1889.
Further Records, 1848–1883. London: R. Bentley, 1890.

Grace King
Monsieur Motte. New York: A. C. Armstrong, 1888.
Jean Baptiste le Moyne, Sieur de Bienville. New York: Dodd, 1892.
Tales of a Time and Place. New York: Harper, 1892.
Balcony Stories. New York: Century, 1893.
New Orleans: The Place and the People. New York and London: Macmillan, 1895.
De Soto and His Men in the Land of Florida. New York: Macmillan, 1898.
The Pleasant Ways of St. Médard. New York: Holt, 1916.
Creole Families of New Orleans. New York: Macmillan, 1921.
La Dame de Sainte Hermine. New York: Macmillan, 1924.
Memories of a Southern Woman of Letters. New York: Macmillan, 1932.

Grace King of New Orleans: A Selection of Her Writings. Edited by
    Robert Bush. Baton Rouge: Louisiana State University Press, 1973.

Bobbie Ann Mason

Nabokov's Garden: A Nature Guide to Ada. Ann Arbor: Ardis, 1974.
The Girl Sleuth: A Feminist Guide to the Bobbsey Twins, Nancy Drew,
    and Their Sisters. New York: Feminist Press, 1975.
Shiloh and Other Stories. New York: Harper, 1982.
In Country. New York: Harper, 1985.
Spence + Lila. New York: Harper, 1988.
Love Life: Stories. New York: Harper, 1988.
Feather Crowns. New York: Harper, 1993.

Carson McCullers

The Heart Is a Lonely Hunter. Boston: Houghton, 1940.
Reflections in a Golden Eye. Boston: Houghton, 1941.
The Member of the Wedding. Boston: Houghton, 1946.
The Member of the Wedding (Play). New York: New Directions, 1951.
Clock Without Hands. Boston: Houghton, 1953.
The Ballad of the Sad Cafe: The Novels and Stories of Carson McCullers.
    Boston: Houghton Mifflin, 1955.
The Square Root of Wonderful. Boston: Houghton, 1958.
Sweet as a Pickle and Clean as a Pig. Boston: Houghton, 1964.
The Mortgaged Heart. Edited by Margarita G. Smith. Boston: Hought-
    on, 1971.

Katherine McDowell

The Radical Club: A Poem. Boston: Times Publishing, 1876.
Like Unto Like; A Novel. New York: Harper, 1878.
Dialect Tales. New York: Harper, 1883.
Suwanee River Tales. Boston: Roberts Brothers, 1884.

Mary Noailles Murfree

In the Tennessee Mountains. Boston: Houghton, 1884.
Where the Battle Was Fought. Boston: James R. Osgood, 1884.
Down the Ravine. Boston: Houghton, 1885.
The Prophet of the Great Smoky Mountains. Boston: Houghton, 1885.
In the Clouds. Boston: Houghton, 1886.
The Story of Keedon Bluffs. Boston: Houghton, 1888.
The Despot of Broomsedge Cove. Boston: Houghton, 1889.
In the "Stranger People's" Country. New York: Harper, 1891.
His Vanished Star. Boston: Houghton, 1894.
The Mystery of Witch-Face Mountain and Other Stories. Boston:
    Houghton, 1895.
The Phantoms of the Foot-Bridge and Other Stories. New York: Harper,
    1895.

The Juggler. Boston: Houghton, 1897.
The Young Mountaineers. Boston: Houghton, 1897.
The Bushwackers and Other Stories. Chicago: Herbert S. Stone, 1899.
The Story of Old Fort Loudon. New York: Macmillan, 1899.
The Champion. Boston: Houghton, 1902.
A Spectre of Power. Boston: Houghton, 1903.
The Frontiersmen. Boston: Houghton, 1904.
The Storm Centre. New York: Macmillan, 1905.
The Amulet. New York: Macmillan, 1906.
The Windfall. New York: Macmillan, 1907.
The Fair Mississippian. Boston: Houghton, 1908.
The Ordeal: A Mountain Romance of Tennessee. Philadelphia: Lippincott, 1912.
The Raid of the Guerilla and Other Stories. Philadelphia: Lippincott, 1912.
The Story of Duciehurst: A Tale of the Mississippi. New York: Macmillan, 1914.

Flannery O'Connor
Wise Blood. New York: Harcourt, 1952.
A Good Man Is Hard to Find and Other Stories. New York: Harcourt, 1955.
The Violent Bear It Away. New York: Farrar, 1960.
Everything That Rises Must Converge. New York: Farrar, 1965.
Mystery and Manners: Occasional Prose. Edited by Sally Fitzgerald and Robert Fitzgerald. New York: Farrar, 1969.
The Complete Stories of Flannery O'Connor. New York: Farrar, 1971.
The Habit of Being: Letters of Flannery O'Connor. Edited by Sally Fitzgerald. New York: Random, 1979.
The Presence of Grace and Other Book Reviews. Edited by Carter W. Martin. Athens: University of Georgia Press, 1983.

Julia Mood Peterkin
Green Thursday: Stories. New York: Knopf, 1924.
Black April. New York: Grosset and Dunlap, 1927.
Scarlet Sister Mary. Indianapolis: Bobbs, 1928.
Boy-Chillen. New York: Samuel French, 1932.
Bright Skin. Indianapolis: Bobbs, 1932.
Roll, Jordan, Roll. New York: R. O. Ballou, 1933.
A Plantation Christmas. Boston: Houghton, 1934.
Collected Short Stories of Julia Peterkin. Edited by Frank Durham. Columbia: University of South Carolina Press, 1970.

Eliza Lucas Pinckney
Recipe Book of Eliza Lucas Pinckney. 1756. Reprint, Charleston: J. Furlong, 1956.

Journal and Letters of Eliza Lucas. Wormsloe, Ga.: George Wymberley-Jones, 1850. Reprint, edited by Harriott Pinckney Holbrook. Spartanburg, S.C.: privately printed, 1967. Reprinted as *The Letterbook of Eliza Lucas Pinckney, 1739–1762.* Edited by Elise Pinckney. Introduction by Walter Muir Whitehill. Chapel Hill: University of North Carolina Press, 1972.

Pinckney Family Papers, 1703–1847. Charleston: South Carolina Historical Society, 1980.

Katherine Anne Porter

Flowering Judas. New York: Harcourt, 1930.
Hacienda; a Story of Mexico. New York: Harrison Co., 1934.
Noon Wine. Detroit: Schuman's, 1937.
Pale Horse, Pale Rider. New York: Modern Library, 1939.
The Leaning Tower and Other Stories. New York: Harcourt, 1944.
The Days Before: Collected Essays and Occasional Writings of Katherine Anne Porter. New York: Harcourt, 1952.
Ship of Fools. Boston: Little, 1962.
The Collected Stories of Katherine Anne Porter. New York: Harcourt, 1965.
The Collected Essays and Occasional Writings of Katherine Anne Porter. New York: Delacorte, 1970.
The Never-Ending Wrong. Boston: Little, 1977.

Margaret Junkin Preston

Silverwood. New York: Derby, 1856.
Beechenbrook; A Rhyme of the War. Richmond: J. W. Randolph, 1865.
Old Song and New. Philadelphia: Lippincott, 1870.
Cartoons. Boston: Roberts Brothers, 1875.
Centennial Poem for Washington and Lee University, Lexington, Virginia, 1775–1885. New York, Putnam's, 1885.
For Love's Sake. New York: Randolph, 1886.
"Personal Reminiscences of Stonewall Jackson." *Century* 32 (Oct. 1886): 927–36.
Colonial Ballads, Sonnets, and Other Verse. Boston: Houghton, 1887.
Chimes for Church-Children. Philadelphia: Presbyterian Board, 1889.
"General Lee after the War." *Century* 38 (June 1889): 271–76.
Aunt Dorothy; An Old Virginia Plantation Story. New York: Randolph, 1890.

Anne Newport Royall

Sketches of History, Life, and Manners in the United States. New Haven: privately printed, 1826.
The Tennessean. New Haven: privately printed, 1827.
The Black Book; or, A Continuation of Travels in the United States. Washington, D.C.: privately printed, 1828–29.

Mrs. Royall's Pennsylvania. Washington, D.C.: privately printed, 1829.
Mrs. Royall's Southern Tour. Washington, D.C.: 1830–31.
Letters from Alabama on Various Subjects. Washington, D.C.: privately printed, 1830. Reprinted as *Letters from Alabama, 1817–1822*. Birmingham: University of Alabama Press, 1969.

Sonia Sanchez

Homecoming; Poems. Introduction by Don L. Lee. Detroit: Broadside, 1969.
Liberation Poem. Detroit: Broadside, 1970.
We a BaddDDD People. Introduction by Dudley Randall. Detroit: Broadside, 1970.
It's a New Day; Poems for Young Brothas and Sistuhs. Detroit: Broadside, 1971.
Ima Talken Bout the Nation of Islam. Astoria, N.Y.: Truth Del., 1972.
Love Poems. New York: Third, 1973.
A Blues Book for Blue Black Magical Women. Detroit: Broadside, 1974.
I've Been a Woman: New and Selected Poems. Sausalito: Black Scholar, 1978.
Crisis and Culture: The Poet as a Creator of Social Values; The Crisis of the Black Community. Harlem: Black Liberation, 1983.
Homegirls and Handgrenades. New York: Thunder's Mouth, 1984.
Generations: Poetry, 1969–1985. London: Karnak House, 1986.
Under a Soprano Sky. New York: Thunder's Mouth, 1987.

Evelyn Scott

Precipitations. New York: Nicholas L. Brown, 1920.
The Narrow House. New York: Boni and Liveright, 1921.
Narcissus. New York: Harcourt, 1922.
Escapade. New York: Seltzer, 1923.
The Golden Door. New York: Seltzer, 1925.
In the Endless Sands: A Christmas Book for Boys and Girls. With Cyril Kay Scott. New York: Holt, 1925.
Ideals: A Book of Farce and Comedy. New York: A. and C. Boni, 1927.
Migrations: An Arabesque in Histories. New York: A. and C. Boni, 1927.
On William Faulkner's "The Sound and the Fury". New York: Cape and Smith, 1929.
The Wave. New York: Cape and Smith, 1929. Reprint, New York: Carroll and Graf, 1985.
Witch Perkins: A Story of the Kentucky Hills. New York: Holt, 1929.
Blue Rum. As Ernest Souza. New York: Cape and Smith, 1930.
The Winter Alone. New York: Cape and Smith, 1930.
A Calendar of Sin: American Melodramas. New York: Cape and Smith, 1932.
Eva Gay: A Romantic Novel. New York: H. Smith and R. Haas, 1933.
Breathe upon These Slain. New York: H. Smith and R. Haas, 1934.

Bread and A Sword. New York: Scribner's, 1937.
Background in Tennessee. New York: R. M. McBride, 1937.
The Shadow of the Hawk. New York: Scribner's, 1941.

Mab Segrest

Living in a House I Do Not Own. Durham: Night Heron, 1982.
My Mama's Dead Squirrel: Lesbian Essays on Southern Culture. Ithaca: Firebrand, 1985.
Quarantines and Death: The Far Right's Homophobic Agenda. With Leonard Zeskind. Atlanta: Center for Democratic Renewal, 1989.
Memoir of a Race Traitor. Boston: South End, 1994.

Alice Walker

Once: Poems. San Diego: Harcourt, 1968.
The Third Life of Grange Copeland. New York: Harcourt, 1970.
In Love and Trouble: Stories of Black Women. New York: Harcourt, 1973.
Revolutionary Petunias and Other Poems. New York: Harcourt, 1973.
Langston Hughes, American Poet. New York: Crowell, 1974.
Meridian. New York: Harcourt, 1976.
Goodnight Willie Lee, I'll See You In the Morning. New York: Dial, 1979.
You Can't Keep A Good Woman Down. New York: Harcourt, 1981.
The Color Purple. New York: Washington Square, 1982.
In Search of Our Mothers' Gardens: Womanist Prose. San Diego: Harcourt, 1983.
Horses Make A Landscape Look More Beautiful. San Diego: Harcourt, 1984.
The Temple of My Familiar. San Diego: Harcourt, 1989.
Possessing the Secret of Joy. New York: Harcourt, 1992.
Warrior Marks: Female Genital Mutilation and the Sexual Blinding of Women. New York: Harcourt, 1993.

Margaret Walker

For My People. New Haven: Yale University Press, 1942.
Jubilee. Boston: Houghton, 1965.
Ballad of the Free. Detroit: Broadside, 1966.
Prophets for a New Day. Detroit: Broadside, 1970.
A Brief Introduction to Southern Literature. Jackson, Miss.: University Press of Mississippi, 1971.
October Journey. Detroit: Broadside, 1973.
A Poetic Equation: Conversations Between Nikki Giovanni and Margaret Walker. Washington, D.C.: Howard University Press, 1974.
The Daemonic Genius of Richard Wright. Washington, D.C.: Howard University Press, 1982.
This Is My Century: New and Collected Poems. Athens: University of Georgia Press, 1989.
How I Wrote Jubilee *and Other Essays on Life and Literature.* New York: City University Feminist Press, 1990.

Eudora Welty

A Curtain of Green and Other Stories. New York: Doubleday, 1941.
The Robber Bridegroom. New York: Doubleday, 1942.
The Wide Net and Other Stories. New York: Harcourt, 1943.
Delta Wedding. New York: Harcourt, 1946.
The Golden Apples. New York: Harcourt, 1949.
Selected Stories. New York: Modern Library, 1953.
The Ponder Heart. New York: Harcourt, 1954.
The Bride of the Innisfallen. New York: Harcourt, 1955.
The Shoe Bird. New York: Harcourt, 1964. Reprint, Jackson: University
    Press of Mississippi, 1993.
Losing Battles. New York: Random, 1970.
One Time, One Place: Mississippi in the Depression; A Snapshot Album.
    New York: Random, 1971.
The Optimist's Daughter. New York: Random, 1972.
The Eye of the Story: Selected Essays and Reviews. New York: Random,
    1978.
The Collected Stories of Eudora Welty. New York: Harcourt, 1980.
Conversations with Eudora Welty. Edited by Peggy Whitman Prenshaw.
    Jackson: University Press of Mississippi, 1984.
One Writer's Beginnings. Cambridge: Harvard University Press, 1984.
Photographs. Jackson: University Press of Mississippi, 1989.
A Writer's Eye: Collected Book Reviews. Jackson: University Press of
    Mississippi, 1994.

Eliza Wilkinson

*Letters of Eliza Wilkinson, During the Invasion and Possession of
    Charleston, S.C., by the British in the Revolutionary War.* New York:
    S. Colman, 1839. Reprint, New York: New York Times, 1969.

Augusta Jane Evans Wilson

Inez: A Tale of the Alamo. New York: Harper, 1855.
Beulah. New York: Derby and Jackson, 1859. Reprint, Baton Rouge:
    Louisiana State University Press, 1992.
Macaria; or, Altars of Sacrifice. Confederate edition, Richmond: West and
    Johnson, 1863. Northern edition, New York: Lippincott, 1864.
    Reprint, Baton Rouge: Louisiana State University Press, 1992.
St. Elmo. New York: G. W. Carleton, 1866.
Vashti; or, Until Death Us Do Part. New York: G. W. Carleton, 1869.
Infelice. New York: G. W. Carleton, 1875.
At the Mercy of Tiberius. New York: G. W. Dillingham, 1887.
A Speckled Bird. New York: G. W. Dillingham, 1902.
Devota. New York: G. W. Dillingham, 1907.

Leigh Allison Wilson

From the Bottom Up: Stories. Athens: University of Georgia Press, 1983.
    Reprint, New York: Penquin, 1983.

Wind: Stories. New York: Morrow, 1989. Reprint, New York: Penguin, 1990.

Secondary Sources

Athas, Daphne. "Why There Are No Southern Writers." *Southern Review* 18 (October 1982): 755–66.

Awkward, Michael. *Inspiriting Influences: Tradition, Revision, and Afro-American Women's Novels.* New York: Columbia University Press, 1989.

Baym, Nina. *Woman's Fiction: A Guide to Novels by and about Women in America, 1820–1870.* Ithaca: Cornell University Press, 1978.

Beatty, Richmond Croom, Floyd C. Watkins, and Thomas Daniel Young, eds. *The Literature of the South.* Chicago: Scott, Foresman, 1952, 1968.

Bell, Bernard W. *The Afro-American Novel and Its Tradition.* Amherst: University of Massachusetts Press, 1987.

Bell, Roseann P., Bettye J. Parker, and Beverly Guy-Sheftall, eds. *Sturdy Black Bridges: Visions of Black Women in Literature.* Garden City, N.Y.: Anchor/Doubleday, 1979.

Bernhard, Virginia, Betty Brandon, Elizabeth Fox-Genovese, and Theda Perdue, eds. *Southern Women: Histories and Identities.* Columbia: University of Missouri Press, 1992.

Betts, Doris. Introduction to *Southern Women Writers: The New Generation.* Edited by Tonette Bond Inge. Tuscaloosa: University of Alabama Press, 1990.

Brantley, Will. *Feminine Sense in Southern Memoir: Smith, Glasgow, Welty, Hellman, Porter and Hurston.* Jackson: University Press of Mississippi, 1993.

Carby, Hazel V. *Reconstructing Womanhood: The Emergence of the Afro-American Woman Novelist.* New York: Oxford University Press, 1987.

Castille, Philip, and William Osborne, eds. *Southern Literature in Transition.* Memphis: Memphis State University Press, 1983.

Clinton, Catherine. *The Plantation Mistress: Women's World in the Old South.* New York: Pantheon, 1982.

Core, George, ed. *Southern Fiction Today: Renascence and Beyond.* Athens: University of Georgia Press, 1969.

Coulter, E. Merton. *The South during Reconstruction, 1865–1877.* Vol. 8 of *The History of the South.* Edited by Wendell Holmes Stephenson and E. Merton Coulter. 10 vols. Baton Rouge: Louisiana State University Press, 1947.

Davidson, James Wood. *The Living Writers of the South.* New York: Carleton, 1869.

Davis, Richard Beale, Hugh Holman, and Louis D. Rubin, eds. *Southern Writing, 1585–1920.* New York: Odyssey, 1970.

Dawson, Sarah Morgan. *The Civil War Diary of Sarah Morgan*. Edited by Charles East. Athens: University of Georgia Press, 1991.

Dew, Thomas R. "Professor Dew on Slavery." In *The Pro-Slavery Argument*. Charleston: Walker, Richards, 1852.

Dillman, Caroline Matheny. *Southern Women*. New York: Hemisphere, 1988.

Dixon, Melvin. *Ride Out of the Wilderness: Geography and Identity in Afro-American Literature*. Urbana: University of Illinois Press, 1987.

Douglas, Ann. *The Feminization of American Culture*. New York: Doubleday, 1988.

Fitzhugh, George. *Sociology for the South*. Richmond: Morris, 1854.

Forrest, Mary (Julia Deane Freeman). *Women of the South Distinguished in Literature*. New York: Derby and Jackson, 1860.

Fox-Genovese, Elizabeth. *Within the Plantation Household: Black and White Women of the Old South*. Chapel Hill: University of North Carolina Press, 1988.

Gates, Henry Louis, Jr. Foreword to *Incidents in the Life of a Slave Girl*, by Harriet Jacobs. New York: Oxford University Press, 1988.

Gibson, Mary Ellis, ed. *Homeplaces: Stories of the South by Women Writers*. Columbia: University of South Carolina Press, 1991.

———. *New Stories by Southern Women*. Columbia: University of South Carolina Press, 1989.

Godwin, Gail. *A Mother and Two Daughters*. New York: Viking, 1982.

Griffin, William. "PW Interviews: Shirley Ann Grau." *Publishers Weekly*, 10 January 1986, 70–71.

Gwin, Minrose. *Black and White Women of the Old South: The Peculiar Sisterhood in American Literature*. Knoxville: University of Tennessee Press, 1985.

———. "Green-Eyed Monsters of the Slavocracy: Jealous Mistresses in the Slave Narratives." *Conjuring: Black Women, Fiction, and Literary Tradition*. Edited by Marjorie Pryse and Hortense J. Spillers, 39–52. Bloomington: Indiana University Press, 1985.

Hague, Parthenia Antoinette. *A Blockaded Family: Life in Southern Alabama during the Civil War*. Introduction by Elizabeth Fox-Genovese. Lincoln: University of Nebraska Press, 1991.

Harper, Frances Watkins. "Colored Women of America." *Englishwomen's Review*, 15 January 1878.

Harrison, Elizabeth Jane. *Female Pastoral: Women Writers Re-Visioning the South*. Knoxville: University of Tennessee Press, 1991.

Hawks, Joanne V., and Shiela L. Skemp, eds. *Sex, Race, and the Role of Women in the South*. Jackson: University Press of Mississippi, 1983.

Hellman, Lillian. *The Little Foxes*. New York: Random House, 1939.

Henley, Beth. *Crimes of the Heart*. Dramatists' Play Service, 1981. First produced, 1979.

Henry, Josephine. "The New Woman of the New South." *Arena* 11 (February 1895): 353–62.

Hentz, Caroline Whiting. *Eoline*. Philadelphia: T. B. Peterson, 1852.

Hobson, Fred. *The Southern Writer in the Postmodern World*. Athens: University of Georgia Press, 1991.

Hood, Mary, et al. "A Stubborn Sense of Place." *Harper's*, August 1986, 35–45.

Hooks, Bell. *"Ain't I a Woman?": Black Women and Feminism*. Boston: South End, 1981.

Hubbell, Jay B. *The South in American Literature, 1607–1900*. Durham: Duke University Press, 1954, 1973.

Inge, Tonnette Bond, ed. *Southern Women Writers: The New Generation*. Tuscaloosa: University of Alabama Press, 1990.

Johnston, Mary. *To Have and To Hold*. Boston: Houghton, 1899.

———. *Hagar*. Boston: Houghton, 1913.

Jones, Anne Goodwyn. *Tomorrow Is Another Day: The Woman Writer in the South, 1859–1936*. Baton Rouge: Louisiana State University Press, 1981.

Jones, Jacqueline. *Labor of Love, Labor of Sorrow: Black Women, Work, and the Family from Slavery to the Present*. New York: Basic, 1985.

Jordan, June. "On Richard Wright and Zora Neale Hurston: Notes Toward a Balancing of Love and Hatred." *Black World*, August 1974, 4–8.

Juncker, Clara. "Behind Confederate Lines: Sarah Morgan Dawson." *Louisiana Women Writers: New Essays and a Comprehensive Bibliography*. Edited by Dorothy H. Brown and Barbara C. Ewell. Baton Rouge: Louisiana State University Press, 1992.

Kakutani, Michiko. Review of *In Country*. *New York Times*. 4 September 1985: C20.

Kazin, Alfred. *Contemporaries*. Boston: Little, Brown, 1962.

King, Richard H. *A Southern Renaissance: The Cultural Awakening of the American South, 1930–1955*. New York: Oxford University Press, 1980.

Kirby, Jack Temple. *Rural Worlds Lost: The American South, 1920–1960*. Baton Rouge: Louisiana State University Press, 1987.

Kolodny, Annette. *The Lay of the Land: Metaphor as Experience and History in American Life and Letters*. Chapel Hill: University of North Carolina Press, 1975.

———. "'Stript, shorne and made deformed': Images on the Southern Landscape." *South Atlantic Quarterly* 75 (winter 1976): 55–73.

MacDonald, Edgar E. "The Ambivalent Heart: Literary Revival in Richmond." In *The History of Southern Literature*, edited by Louis D. Rubin. Baton Rouge: Louisiana State University Press, 1985.

MacKethan, Lucinda H. *Daughters of Time: Creating Woman's Voice in Southern Story*. Athens: University of Georgia Press, 1990.

Magee, Rosemary M. *Friendship and Sympathy: Communities of Southern*

Women Writers. Jackson and London: University Press of Mississippi, 1992.

Manning, Carol S., ed. *The Female Tradition in Southern Literature.* Urbana and Chicago: University of Illinois Press, 1993.

Massey, Mary Elizabeth. *Bonnet Brigades.* New York: Knopf, 1966.

Mewshaw, Michael. Review of *Beasts of the Southern Wild,* by Doris Betts. *New York Times Book Review,* 28 October 1973, 40–41.

O'Connor, Flannery. "The Catholic Writer in the Protestant South." In *Mystery and Manners: Occasional Prose.* Edited by Sally and Robert Fitzgerald. New York: Farrar, 1961.

Porter, Nancy. "Women's Interracial Friendships and Visions of Community in *Meridian, The Salt Eaters, Civil Wars,* and *Dessa Rose.*" In *Tradition and the Talents of Women.* Edited by Florence Howe. Urbana: University of Illinois Press, 1991.

Prenshaw, Peggy Whitman, ed. *Women Writers of the Contemporary South.* Jackson: University Press of Mississippi, 1984.

Pryse, Marjorie, and Hortense J. Spillers. *Conjuring.* Bloomington: Indiana University Press, 1985.

Rable, George C. *Civil Wars: Women and the Crisis of Southern Nationalism.* Urbana: University of Illinois Press, 1989.

Ravenel, Shannon, ed. *New Stories from the South: The Year's Best, 1990.* Chapel Hill: Algonquin, 1990.

Ridgely, J. V. *Nineteenth-Century Southern Literature.* Lexington: University Press of Kentucky, 1980.

Roberson, John R., ed. "Two Virginia Novelists on Woman's Suffrage: An Exchange of Letters between Mary Johnston and Thomas Nelson Page." *Virginia Magazine* 64 (July 1956): 286–90.

Rubin, Louis D. *The American South: Portrait of a Culture.* Baton Rouge: Louisiana State University Press, 1980.

———, ed. *The History of Southern Literature.* Baton Rouge: Louisiana State University Press, 1985.

———, ed. *The Literary South.* New York: Wiley, 1979.

———, and Robert D. Jacobs. *South: Modern Southern Literature in Its Cultural Setting.* Garden City, N.Y.: Doubleday, 1961.

Sala, George A. *My Diary in America in the Midst of War.* I. London: Tinsley, 1865.

Schultz, Elizabeth. "Out of the Woods and into the World: A Study of Interracial Friendships between Women in American Novels." In *Conjuring: Black Women, Fiction, and Literary Tradition.* Edited by Marjorie Pryse and Hortense J. Spillers, 67–85. Bloomington: Indiana University Press, 1985.

Scott, Anne Firor. *Making the Invisible Woman Visible.* Urbana: University of Illinois Press, 1984.

———. "The 'New Woman' in the New South." *South Atlantic Quarterly* 61 (autumn 1962): 473–83.

————. *The Southern Lady: From Pedestal to Politics, 1830–1930.* Chicago: University of Chicago Press, 1970.

————, ed. *Unheard Voices: The First Historians of Southern Women.* Charlottesville: University of Virginia Press, 1993.

Seidel, Kathryn Lee. *The Southern Belle in the American Novel.* Tampa: University of South Florida Press, 1985.

Shepperson, William. *War Songs of the South.* Richmond: West and Johnson, 1862.

Simkins, Francis Butler, and James Welch Patton. *The Women of the Confederacy.* Richmond: Garrett and Massie, 1936.

Simms, William Gilmore. *War Poetry of the South.* New York: Richardson, 1866.

Simpson, Lewis. *The Dispossessed Garden.* Athens: University of Georgia Press, 1975.

Singal, Daniel Joseph. *The War Within: From Victorian to Modernist Thought in the South, 1919–1945.* Chapel Hill: University of North Carolina Press, 1982.

Smith, Lillian. *Killers of the Dream.* Garden City, N.Y.: Anchor, 1963.

Spencer, Elizabeth. *The Light in the Piazza.* New York: McGraw Hill, 1960.

Spruill, Julia Cherry. *Women's Life and Work in the Southern Colonies.* 1938. New York: Norton, 1972.

Sterkx, H. E. *Partners in Rebellion: Alabama Women in the Civil War.* Rutherford: Fairleigh Dickinson University Press, 1970.

Sweeney, Patricia. *Women in Southern Literature: An Index.* New York: Greenwood, 1986.

Tate, Linda. *A Southern Weave of Women: Fiction of the Contemporary South.* Athens: University of Georgia Press, 1994.

Taylor, Helen. *Gender, Race and Region in the Writings of Grace King, Ruth McEnery Stuart, and Kate Chopin.* Baton Rouge: Louisiana State University Press, 1989.

Taylor, William R. *Cavalier and Yankee.* New York: Harper, 1961.

Tillett, Wilbur Fisk. "Southern Womanhood as Affected by the War." *Century,* n.s. 21 (Nov. 1891): 9–16.

Underwood, John Levi. *The Women of the Confederacy.* New York: Neale, 1906.

Welter, Barbara. *Dimity Convictions: The American Woman In the Nineteenth Century.* Columbus: University of Ohio Press, 1976.

Wiley, Bell Irvin. *Confederate Women.* Westport, Conn.: Greenwood, 1975.

————. *The Plain People of the Confederacy.* Baton Rouge: Louisiana State University Press, 1943.

Willis, Susan. *Specifying: Black Women Writing the American Experience.* Madison: University of Wisconsin Press, 1986.

Wilson, Charles Reagan, and Willian Ferris, eds. *Encyclopedia of*

Southern Culture. Chapel Hill: University of North Carolina Press, 1989.

Wood, Ann Douglas. "The Literature of Impoverishment: The Women Local Colorists in America, 1865–1914." *Women's Studies* 1 (1972): 3–45.

Wood, Sally, ed. *The Southern Mandarins: Letters of Caroline Gordon to Sally Wood, 1924–1937.* Baton Rouge: Louisiana State University Press, 1984.

Woodward, C. Vann. *Origins of the New South, 1877–1913.* Vol. 9 of *A History of the South.* Edited by Wendell Holmes Stephenson and E. Merton Coulter. 10 vols. Baton Rouge: Louisiana State University Press, 1951.

Wright, Richard. "Between Laughter and Tears." *New Masses* 25 (October 25, 1937): 22–25.

Wyatt-Brown, Bertram. *Southern Honor: Ethics and Behavior in the Old South.* New York: Oxford University Press, 1982.

Young, Thomas D. *The Past in the Present: A Thematic Study of Modern Southern Fiction.* Baton Rouge: Louisiana State University Press, 1981.